THE WAR OF 1812

AND THE RISE OF THE U.S. NAVY

THE WAR

OF 1812

AND THE RISE OF THE U.S. NAVY

MARK COLLINS JENKINS *AND* DAVID A. TAYLOR

Foreword by Douglas Brinkley

NATIONAL GEOGRAPHIC

WASHINGTON, D.C.

FOR ALL THOSE WHO SERVE, OR HAVE SERVED,
IN THE UNITED STATES MILITARY

CONTENTS

PREFACE

The United States is a maritime nation.

This has been a fact throughout our history and remains very much the case today. The oceans connect us to the world, and they sustain our trade and economy. For the past two hundred years, the world's oceans have also witnessed the presence and the growth of the United States Navy and Marine Corps. On the waves, we have become what we are and will remain: the most formidable expeditionary fighting force the world has ever known.

It is a journey that began in earnest during the War of 1812, the first true global conflict of our still young and expanding nation. Born during the Revolution, the Continental Navy and Marine Corps were drawn down in the 1780s and 90s, only to be reborn at the turn of the eighteenth century through the first six frigates of the fleet, commissioned in response to the threat of Barbary piracy and constructed up and down the East Coast from New Hampshire to Virginia. Only a decade later, during the War of 1812, the young fleet came of age in conflict with Britain, and the seeds of today's modern Navy were sown.

Since those first six frigates, our enduring sea power has proven essential to winning wars abroad, countering threats to our coasts, and furthering the interests of peace and prosperity worldwide. Unique in history, the umbrella of security that our fleet has provided has been used for the benefit of all nations, and has guaranteed freedom of the seas to all.

Over the next three years, the United States Navy and Marine Corps will commemorate this legacy and the bicentennial of the War of 1812.

Much has changed in the past two hundred years. Britain, once our staunch foe, has become our strong friend. Where we once depended upon the wooden walls of our sailing ships, we now sail ships of steel. The smoothbore cannons of 1812 have become the modern naval guns, missiles, and torpedoes of today. Wind power has given way consecutively to coal-fired steam power, then oil and nuclear power, and now the fleet is on the cusp of another change to biofuel and renewable energy. Situational awareness was once limited to the horizon, based on the eyesight of a keen lookout from a ship's tops. This has given way to instantaneous communications to any point on the globe, to submarines sailing the depths, to aircraft soaring the skies and rocketing into outer space, and to sailors on the cyber sea.

But as has been said, "The Navy has both a tradition and a future—and we look with pride and confidence in both directions." One of the first six frigates, USS *Constitution*, is still a commissioned vessel in the United States Navy. She is a tangible link to the War of 1812 and to our early history and anchors one end of the arc of technological change and naval innovation.

The book that follows was produced by the Naval History and Heritage Command as an authoritative history of the naval War of 1812. It is the work of many years and many hands and was written with an eye toward encompassing every detail of American naval operations in one of the most formative conflicts of our early history. However, I encourage you to read the book with an eye toward what has not changed; or as history has taught us, read the work with an eye toward the changeless principles of naval warfare: that "men mean more than guns in the rating of a ship" and "that without a decisive naval force we can do nothing definitive, with it, everything honorable and glorious."

The lessons that the Navy and Marine Corps learned during the War of 1812 continue to shape our history. Our earliest heroes—Decatur, Hull, Perry, Macdonough, Porter, and others—set the standard for leadership, courage, seamanship, and innovation that our modern leaders strive to emulate. Likewise, the performance of our sailors and marines in that war, fighting always against adverse odds and in great peril, established the legacy of greatness that has been met time and again over the subsequent two hundred years, from Vera Cruz to Manila Bay, Belleau Wood, Midway, Khafji, and Marjah.

In commemorating the bicentennial of the War of 1812, we honor every sailor and marine who has ever fought under the Stars and Stripes. The commemoration also reminds us that sailors and marines continue to live up to the legacy of our forefathers and defend both the United States and our freedoms across the world. The battlefields of today extend farther, even into the mountains of Afghanistan. The mission of our Fleet has expanded to encompass security assistance and development in Africa, and humanitarian assistance and disaster relief from Haiti to Pakistan. The basic fact remains that the commitment and dedication of our people is the strong foundation upon which our Fleet depends.

~ THE HONORABLE RAY MABUS
Secretary of the Navy

Opposite: Thomas Birch's rendering of the famed engagement between USS *Constitution* and HMS *Guerrière* on August 19, 1812.

FOREWORD

Nothing fascinated President Theodore Roosevelt more than the naval battles of the War of 1812. Upon graduating from Harvard University in 1880, Roosevelt embarked on a major two-volume history that showcased ship-to-ship actions. He described how Captain Isaac Hull in USS *Constitution* ("Old Ironsides") defeated HMS *Guerrière*, and how Commodore Oliver Hazard Perry's stunning victory in the Battle of Lake Erie saved America from ruin. In writing the masterful *The Naval War of 1812*, Roosevelt relied mostly upon primary source materials, ranging from ship logs, correspondence, official reports, diaries, and newspaper accounts. After absorbing reams of information, Roosevelt concluded that two things contributed to America's victory over Great Britain in 1815: the superiority of armed U.S. vessels and the skillful seamanship of our naval officers. Whether it was Commodore Thomas Macdonough on Lake Champlain turning back a British invasion from Canada or Commodore Daniel Patterson precisely guessing that the Royal Navy thrust would come at New Orleans—not Mobile—the fighting spirit of the U.S. Navy was breathtaking.

Ever since my childhood growing up in Perrysburg, Ohio, a town of eight thousand named for Oliver Hazard Perry, I've been a War of 1812 buff. My personal library includes well over fifty books on the subject. Never before, however, have I encountered a book on that war more intellectually engaging than *The War of 1812 and the Rise of the U.S. Navy*. Authors Mark Collins Jenkins and David A. Taylor, both inspired historians, couldn't have done a better job of weaving together first-person accounts of the War of 1812 into a single volume.

The illustrations that accompany this text are nothing short of spectacular. The amount of painstaking work done by the book's illustrations editors is remarkable. There are privateer recruiting posters, prints depicting famous naval duels, oil portraits, frigate ship models chiseled out of bone by prisoners of war, and myriad artifacts, from tattered battle ensigns to the epaulette that Perry once wore as a master commandant. Every page brings the War of 1812 vividly to life. Someone had to have searched high and low to unearth such priceless treasures from the United States' second war of independence in order to make this timely book.

Master researchers Jenkins and Taylor bring to light a surprising range of fresh historical recollections from the workaday lives of sailors, marines, women, and Navy wives and families, including insights into the painful doldrums of maritime medicine. While Roosevelt's *The Naval War of 1812* is more sweeping regarding naval strategy, Jenkins and Taylor's tapestry of personal reminiscences of the war is sui generis. Clearly, the bicentennial of the war that birthed the U.S. Navy of John Paul Jones holds surprises for even scholars of the era. Jenkins and Taylor have profited by research gathered through the modern-day instruments of underwater archaeology and, yes, even the Internet. *The War of 1812 and the Rise of the U.S. Navy* unearths connections and sequences previously unsuspected even by such heavyweight historians as Donald R. Hickey (*The War of 1812: A Forgotten Conflict*), Jon Latimer (*1812: War with America*), and Alan Taylor (*The Civil War of 1812*).

The authors convince us that even the familiar outlines of the War of 1812 are worth revisiting, given the mythmaking that surrounded that first war to defend our forested shores following the American Revolution. Who knew of the riots and divisions of the time? Or that famous Civil War Admiral David Farragut began his naval career as a young boy with a prize crew during the 1812 conflict? Or that a freedman fought to defend besieged Baltimore, "under the rockets' red glare," only to be forced back into slavery a few years later?

Jenkins and Taylor's narrative of the naval battles at sea, on the Great Lakes, on Lake Champlain, in the Gulf of Mexico, and in other waters, told through firsthand accounts, is a welcome reminder of many original memoirs bound between crumbling covers and silted over by time, as well as a grab bag full of fresh historical discoveries.

~ DOUGLAS BRINKLEY
Perrysburg, Ohio, June 4, 2011

Opposite: Thomas Birch's portrayal of USS *Constitution*'s astounding getaway during the "Great Chase" of July 1812.

PROLOGUE

YARDARM TO YARDARM

"BOTH PARTIES TO THE WAR OF 1812 BEING CONSPICUOUSLY MARITIME IN DISPOSITION AND OCCUPATION, WHILE SEPARATED BY THREE THOUSAND MILES OF OCEAN, THE SEA AND ITS NAVIGABLE APPROACHES BECAME NECESSARILY THE MOST EXTENSIVE SCENE OF OPERATIONS."

~Alfred Thayer Mahan, *Sea Power in Its Relations to the War of 1812*

Evening was only touching the sea when at six o'clock on May 19, 1812, a long-awaited U.S. Navy sloop-of-war finally anchored in Boston Harbor. The U.S. brig *Hornet* had crossed the Atlantic in only twenty-two days, battling storms that shredded her rigging and ripped off her foretopmast, to bring certain dispatches to the president.

Three days later those dispatches were opened in the muddy new capital that had arisen on the banks of the Potomac River. They contained only more bad news. The diplomats that *Hornet* had carried to Britain and France, at war with each other, were not able to convince those governments to relax the restrictions each had placed on the United States.

Word of the bad news spread like wildfire. Citizens and congressmen both thronged the small building next door to the White House that the U.S. State Department shared with the War and Navy Departments, as did the French minister, who soon reported to his government that the "furious declamations of the Federalists, of the commercial interests, and of the numerous friends of England were redoubled; the Republicans, deceived in their hopes,

joined in the outcry, and for three days nothing was heard but a general cry for war against France and England at once . . ."

The war would be with England, though, not with France. It would be with England for all of the reasons that President James Madison, leaving the White House on the morning of June 1, 1812, for the Corinthian-columned but still domeless Capitol, was prepared to lay out item by item before a joint session of Congress.

He had a long list of grievances. "Without going back beyond the renewal in 1803, of the war in which Great Britain is engaged," the small, slender, sixty-one-year-old chief executive began as he stood before the 36 senators and 143 representatives, "the conduct of her government presents a series of acts, hostile to the United States as an independent and neutral nation."

It had been exactly twenty years, with only a brief period of peace in 1802, since Great Britain and most of Europe had gone to war with a France made newly militant by its 1789 revolution. In that time, as George Washington, John Adams, and Thomas Jefferson preceded Madison as its president, the young

Opposite: "A Sailor of USS *Constitution* Toasting a New Recruit in a Saloon." This painting offers a rare depiction of a common sailor (identified as being a member of *Constitution*'s crew by his hatband) found in early nineteenth-century maritime painting.

republic had grown from its original thirteen to seventeen states. Most of them, from the borders with British Canada in the north to those with Spanish Florida in the south, still fronted on the Atlantic, but across the forested spine of the Appalachians lay Kentucky, Tennessee, and most recently, Louisiana. In what was called the "Old Northwest"—including the territories of Indiana, Illinois, and Michigan—Ohio had also achieved statehood.

Most people, however, still lived in the East, and despite such flourishing cities as Boston, New York, Philadelphia, and Baltimore, most of them lived on farms. And most still supported Madison's own Democratic-Republican (or simply "Republican") party, with its praise of rural virtues and its distrust of centralized government. Only New England remained a bastion of the rival Federalist party, more urban and mercantile, and because of deep trading ties more inclined to support the one foreign power the Republicans loathed: Great Britain.

Though the population of the United States was only a third the size of Great Britain's and a fifth the size of France's, American citizens possessed an energy out of all proportion to their numbers. And they soon began exploiting the trading opportunities that opened as the more established maritime nations became ever more embroiled in conflict. As a neutral nation, the United States took on more and more of the world's carrying trade, its merchant fleet tripling in size. Though war would grant the new nation sudden prosperity, war would also take it away.

In October 1805, the Royal Navy had hardly finished destroying its French counterpart in the Battle of Trafalgar when an American merchant vessel steered through the floating wreckage, selling lumber to the victors so that they could patch their holed and splintered ships. The Americans were then ubiquitous at sea. Their merchant fleet ranked second in importance only to that of Great Britain. Nearly ten thousand American sloops, brigs, and deep-drafted square-riggers were carrying casks and crates, barrels and bundles around the globe.

Sugar and molasses in the West Indies, pepper and sandalwood in the East Indies, tea and silk and porcelain in China—there was no market that sharp Yankee traders hadn't penetrated. American flour, salt pork, and salt beef were carried across the stormy Atlantic to feed the warring nations of Europe. Timber and naval stores were loaded in New England. Hogsheads of tobacco rolled down wharves in the Chesapeake Bay. Bales of short-staple cotton were stacked in the holds of ships docked in Charleston and Savannah. Even frontiersmen in the remote Ohio River country participated in the boom. They shipped their grain and hemp down the Mississippi River to exotic New Orleans—the nation's newest acquisition, a part of the enormous Louisiana Purchase of 1803—and from there out to Havana, Guadeloupe, and Barbados.

So fast had been the U.S. maritime growth during those halcyon days that upwards of five thousand new hands were needed annually to man the ships. Wages furthermore had tripled. And that had proven too irresistible for many

a miserable Royal Navy tar. They deserted in droves for better prospects with American vessels. That was a drain an England at war could not endure. She began reclaiming her own.

Impressment—the forcible seizure of sailors from seagoing American merchant ships—was the first grievance against Great Britain that President Madison enumerated before Congress. "British Cruisers," the president declared, had long been "violating the American flag on the great highway of nations." Under the pretext of searching for deserters, they had been seizing American citizens with impunity—thousands of whom, he elaborated, had disappeared into the maw of His Majesty's warships, "exiled to the most distant and deadly climes, to risk their lives in the battles of their oppressors, and to be the melancholy instruments of taking away those of their own brethren." American diplomatic protests had only fallen on deaf ears.

British arrogance on the high seas was one thing, but to these "most insulting pretentions," Madison continued, "they have added the most lawless proceedings in our very harbors and have wantonly spilt American blood within the sanctuary of our territorial jurisdiction"—an unmistakable reference to that dark day five years prior, when in June 1807, just seaward of the Virginia Capes, HMS *Leopard*, hunting for deserters, fired on the U.S. frigate *Chesapeake*, killing three sailors and nearly spurring an outraged nation to declare war.

Although the issue of impressment had clouded America's every relation with Britain, the more far-reaching threat to the republic's sovereignty was economic. In Europe, a brilliant young Corsican general named Napoleon Bonaparte had led French armies from victory to victory, crowning himself emperor of a domain embracing most of the continent. Those in Britain who believed they were in a fight to the finish against a new European tyrant began to eye the burgeoning American merchant fleet with hostility. Neutral shipping was a "fraud," some of them loudly declaimed, being as often as not a cover for supplying Napoleon with food and war *matériel*.

With the will to dictate the terms of maritime trade and the might to enforce her edicts, Great Britain's writ was practically fiat over the sea. Soon she began to strangle American seaborne commerce. After 1805, neutral vessels that had not been strictly abiding by British laws defining "contraband," or those that ignored troublesome maritime regulations governing the re-export trade, were increasingly subject to seizure and confiscation. As a result, Madison said, British cruisers had begun to "hover over and harass our entering and departing Commerce." American ships had been "plundered in every Sea," and some three hundred had been seized.

Worse still had been what Madison called the "sweeping system of Blockades" that Great Britain and France had imposed on each other. Napoleon, unable to invade an island kingdom protected by the Royal Navy's "wooden walls," instead tried undermining the British economy. Though after Trafalgar

he had scant means of enforcing it, in 1806 he declared what he called "perfidious Albion" to be under blockade; neutral nations were not to trade with her. The following year Britain retaliated with a draconian series of royal Orders in Council, blockading the Continent in return. Not only would the British now seize any neutral ship hoping to discharge a cargo in a European port, they also arrogated to themselves the right to search that cargo on the high seas and, moreover, to make that neutral pay a stiff tariff for it in a British port. Napoleon's counterblast—should anyone obey these British strictures, or even submit to a British search, his became de facto a British ship and would be declared a "good and lawful prize"—finally put American sea captains in an untenable position. Between 1807 and 1812, in fact, more than nine hundred U.S. ships were seized by one or the other of the belligerents.

Yet resentment was directed at the British rather than the French. It was the British prime minister who admitted that the Orders in Council implied that "either [the neutral] countries will have no trade, or they must be content to accept it through us." In American eyes, they were a thinly disguised attempt to stifle Great Britain's primary commercial rival—the United States. As a "claim to regulate our external commerce, in all cases whatsoever," Madison explained, the Orders really meant a return to colonial status. American prosperity should not be "sacrificed," he maintained, simply because it interfered "with the monopoly which [Great Britain] covets for her own commerce and navigation."

On the contrary, as no congressman needed reminding, American prosperity had nearly been sacrificed by Madison's predecessor. Hoping to starve the grain-importing belligerents into relaxing their trade restrictions, President Thomas Jefferson had taken the radical step of shutting down all U.S. foreign commerce whatsoever. But the disastrous Embargo Act of 1807 resulted only in the near collapse of the American economy. Within a year, American trade plummeted by some eighty percent. Casks and crates and hogsheads piled up on docks and in warehouses. Ten thousand ships were left idling in port. Smuggling grew to such epidemic proportions that revenue agents up and down the coast began unloading all suspicious holds, unshipping masts, and patrolling decks and wharves.

The catastrophic embargo soon had to be scaled back, first to a prohibition just on trade with Britain and France, and then, once Bonaparte agreed to drop restrictions on U.S. ships (though he continued seizing them), to one only on Great Britain, which remained unyielding. Meanwhile, the U.S. resumed its shipping of grain to British armies in Spain that were at last making inroads on Napoleon.

Even in North America the hand of perfidious Albion was seen to be at work. One of His Majesty's secret agents, Madison announced, had been "employed in intrigues, having for their object, a subversion of our Government, and a dismemberment of our happy union." The administration had emptied its own secret service fund to purchase from this shadowy agent a sheaf of letters purportedly revealing that British authorities in Canada were fomenting secession fever in staunchly Federalist New England, where citizens believed that if war was inevitable, it should be with France, not Great Britain.

In the Old Northwest, meanwhile, a powerful Native American confederacy, led by the great Shawnee warrior Tecumseh, had seven months earlier been checked at the Battle of Tippecanoe, in the Indiana Territory, by its governor, William Henry Harrison. Giving voice to what everyone in Washington believed to be the case, an obscure colonel of Tennessee volunteers named Andrew Jackson had written Harrison that the tribes were "excited to war by the secret agents of Great Britain." Operating out of a string of forts along the Great Lakes, these subversive soldiers and traders had been providing the Native Americans with not only blankets but also guns and powder.

"Such is the spectacle of injuries and indignities, which have been heaped on our Country," Madison concluded as he wrapped up his address. "We behold, in fine, on the side of Great Britain, a state of war against the United States . . ." Since every peaceable means of coercion had been exhausted, and both national honor and national survival were at stake, the president urged Congress that it was now time to declare war in return.

Later that afternoon, secure in the knowledge that the Republican majority in Congress would follow his lead before the month was out, the president and members of his administration gathered in the small building housing the State, War, and Navy Departments. Military planners were already at work, but they gazed not east over the ocean but rather north, toward Canada. Soldiers and militiamen, with their tall shakos and flintlock muskets, would soon be mustering along the southern shores of the Great Lakes, for the conquest of Canada, as Thomas Jefferson put it, surely would be but "a mere matter of marching." That was the only feasible way to attack Great Britain directly—she was practically invulnerable at sea.

A maritime strategy had in fact been considered but was rejected. While swarms of privateers might nip at British convoys, the U.S. Navy would face steep odds. Its five thousand officers and men had proven their valor in small wars against the French and the Barbary pirates. But in the past few years they had been largely reduced to gunboat duty patrolling quiet harbors. *Hornet* was one of the handful of sloops and frigates the service still possessed. Though admirably constructed, many of them were under repair or laid up in ordinary.

Perhaps a few lone vessels or small squadrons might slip to sea, raid British commerce, or ambush a chance man-of-war if it appeared not too formidable an opponent. But many men in the government believed that its ships might be better employed as floating batteries to protect the nation's ports and harbors. After all, could their puny navy, stretched thin on stations ranging from Maine to New Orleans, really be expected to grapple, yardarm to yardarm, with the mightiest fleet on the globe?

CHAPTER ONE

THE LITTLE BELT, SLOOP OF WAR, Cap.ⁿ Bingham nobly supporting the Honor of the British Flag, against the President United States Frigate, Commodore Rogers, May 15.1811.

Pub.ᵈ & Sold Oct.ʳ 25 1811 by Edw.ᵈ Orme, Printseller to his Majesty & Royal Family, Engraver & Publisher, Bond St corner of Brook St London.

This engraving by nineteenth-century artist William Elmes depicts the contentious, middle-of-the-night encounter between Rodgers' frigate, *President*, and Captain Arthur Bingham's sloop-of-war, HMS *Little Belt*.

Overleaf: Painted in 1806 by the thoughtful hand of deaf-mute artist George Ropes, Jr., a shipmaster's son who sought normalcy through his painting, this landscape of Crowninshield's Wharf embodies one of the great themes of the era's maritime art: the prosperity of American shippers, who formed the lifeblood of the economy and forged America's early identity. The Salem-based, seafaring Crowninshield family, which attained wealth and prominence through over-seas trade—and produced the fifth secretary of the Navy—represented the height of such prosperity. Crowninshield & Sons exchanged codfish for rum-yielding West Indies molasses, sparked the sea trade in pepper, and brought the first elephant—from Calcutta—to American soil. Jefferson's embargo, which left scores of New England merchants dis-affected, nearly ruined the family fortune, and the Crowninshields, in an attempt to boost sagging finances, converted their merchantmen into privateers during the War of 1812—ironically, a war fought to uphold the "free trade" that had made them Boston Brahmins.

"OUR LITTLE NAVY"

LIGHTNING STRIKES IN THE ATLANTIC

June–December 1812

"ENGLAND'S NAVAL POWER STOOD
AT A HEIGHT NEVER REACHED BEFORE OR SINCE BY THAT OR ANY OTHER NATION . . .
[I]N EVERY SEA THEIR CRUISERS COULD BE FOUND, OF ALL SIZES,
FROM THE STATELY SHIP-OF-THE-LINE, WITH HER TIERS OF HEAVY CANNON AND HER MANY HUNDREDS
OF MEN, DOWN TO THE LITTLE CUTTER CARRYING BUT A SCORE OF SOULS
AND A COUPLE OF LIGHT GUNS . . . FRENCH AND ITALIAN FRIGATES WERE OFTEN FOUGHT
AND CAPTURED WHERE THEY WERE SKIRTING THEIR OWN COASTS . . .
SO THE ENGLISH MARINE WAS IN CONSTANT EXERCISE, ATTENDED WITH ALMOST INVARIABLE SUCCESS.

SUCH WAS GREAT BRITAIN'S NAVAL POWER
WHEN THE CONGRESS OF THE UNITED STATES DECLARED WAR UPON HER."

~ Theodore Roosevelt, *The Naval War of 1812*

"It is the duty of every American to avoid imprisonment in a British ship of war," wrote a forty-two-year-old New Yorker named Joshua Penny in 1815. "It ought to be the first article of the impressed seaman's creed, that a British vessel of war is a Pandora's box—a nefarious floating dungeon, freighting calamities to every part of this lower world."

Penny had every right to pen those scathing sentences. Though he was a native of Long Island, he had been press-ganged into the Royal Navy when he was scarcely more than a boy. "Those who regard the rights of an American sailor as those of an American citizen, and who can sympathize in the sufferings of their fellow men," he implored, "will listen to my story and overlook its necessary imperfections."

Penny wrote his story and paid for its publication himself because he saw it as emblematic of many similar narratives, most of which would never see print but which taken together helped fuel the momentum that carried the nation into war that summer of 1812.

My parents had nine children, and like most others with a numerous progeny, they were very poor. My mother . . . examined us in rotation, and on asking me, "Well, Joshua, what will you do for a living in this world?" I answered that I intended to go as far as sea and land would carry me.

The infamous cat o' nine tails, a much-loathed disciplinary device used to flog unruly sailors, most notably in the Royal Navy. This nineteenth-century example is made of wood, baize, twine, and rope.

. . . I was anxious to try my fortune at sea. This was done, and I entered on board of a sloop under command of Capt. Webb, and sailed to Guadaloupe. On our return to New York I visited my friends, who were rejoiced at my safe arrival, expecting to find me disgusted with a seafaring life . . . They were disappointed; my fondness for the sea was undiminished.

I solicited for and obtained leave to visit my brother, in Philadelphia, but on my arrival at New York, went from one vessel to another inquiring if a cabin boy was wanted, without ever asking to what port they were bound; when at last I went on board the brig Perseverance, George Lippencott, master. Being very small for my age, he asked me whose child I was, and if I had my parents' liberty to go to sea. I told him that I had been once with their permission, and wished to do the same again. Upon this he shipped me at two and a half dollars per month, which I thought great wages, and must confess that for once I did feel proud . . .

The brig Minerva, of Portsmouth, N.H. captain E. Schofield, was lying at Savannah, bound to Cork [Ireland]. In her I took passage and was within three days sail of our destined port, when the brig was boarded from a French privateer . . . They examined the Minerva's papers, drank freely of porter, and returned carelessly on deck . . . This was the first year of their revolutionary war (1793) with England. They had already manned so many prizes, as they informed us, that we were suffered to proceed without further molestation. In three days more we were in Cork . . . I wished to travel . . . in the county of Tipperary . . . No sooner was I in readiness to commence the journey, than a press gang took me to a 74; the captain of this ship looked at my certificate [from the Minerva's captain], and humanely ordered me to be set again on shore. On the road I was often taken up on suspicion of being a deserter . . .

Among other things, I had discovered that an American in the dominions of his Britannic majesty should be provided with a protection—even then his safety is not ensured . . . I had frequently seen the papers of neutrals torn in pieces by the press gang, and thrown into the fire—declaring their protections good for nothing; that "they could buy them anywhere for a quarter of a dollar." How wretched is that government, which compels men to become murderers of their countrymen, and exerts her power to entrap and enslave those whom she professes to preserve free! . . .

Found by mountaineers in Joshua Penny's hideout on the Cape of Good Hope's Table Mountain, these relics tell the tale of his misadventure. On display are limpet shells believed to have been carried by Penny on a two-day journey down to the western shore and back; two steels for sparking fires; clay smoking pipes; a fragment of pottery from a jar that probably contained preserves; and all that remained of Penny's attire: a belt buckle, a neckerchief ring, a handful of buttons, and a few ragged scraps of clothing. "My clothes, by creeping through the rocks and bushes, were so tattered," Penny wrote, "that I had become almost naked."

Not many days had passed after our arrival, ere [we] were again haunted by press-gangs, and our whole crew impressed. We were put into the Alligator frigate of 28 guns, under the command of Captain Africk. Four of us were Americans; the others chiefly Danes and Swedes. A fever raged in this ship, and out of forty men, there were eleven corpses to be interred on the first morning . . .

I was drafted to the Sphinx, a ship of 20 guns, bound to cruise off St. Helena. An American whaling ship lay near us at St. Helena and four of us who messed together, all Americans, agreed to escape to the whaler; and after bribing the sentinel, plunged into the water. The others succeeded; but not being a good swimmer, I rested on our buoy and got with difficulty into the ship's head by climbing on the cable . . .

A few days after my unsuccessful attempt to reach the American ship . . . all hands were called to get our ship underway, and on calling the foretop-men, the three yankees were missing. The captain then called the purser's steward to ascertain the missing yankees' mess. I was called upon to relate what I knew of their running off . . . He then took a book out of his pocket and said, "You are a yankee, sir, and have been seven years in the navy without ever being flogged, and now I'll flog you if you are God Almighty's first lieutenant!!!"

All hands were now called on deck to witness my punishment . . . My senses left me when I had received three strokes of the cat. I fell (so I was afterwards informed) hanging by the wrists, with my head on one shoulder, until the whole number of stripes had been applied. The surgeon informed the captain of my condition, when the captain said, "He shall take his dozen, dead or alive!" I was cut down, and at the first recollection of myself, they were washing my face with a tub of water.

Like many impressed sailors, Penny eventually returned home, though his journey back was long and fraught with hardships. After deserting HMS *Sceptre* in South Africa, for instance, he was forced to hide out in Table Mountain's sandstone caves, donning animal skins for warmth. When he did finally make it to his native township of East Hampton, Long Island, he not only began life anew but also remained "determined to avail myself of the first opportunity of doing mischief to those who had so long tortured me."

There were many Americans ready to line up alongside him—men who felt it was the manifest destiny of the United States to quell British influence in the Old Northwest; men who worried about purported British mischief-making among Native American tribes between the Ohio River and the Great Lakes, where the dynamic Shawnee warrior Tecumseh hoped to establish a Native American state; and men secretly planning to annex Canada, with its wealth of furs and timber. But, in the end, the banners beneath which they went to war bore the slogan "Free Trade and Sailors' Rights."

"A GREAT TYRANNY"

The Long History of the Press Gang

"The most hateful and terrible word to a seaman's ear is press gang," declared Scottish author Robert Chambers in 1854, recalling the cudgel-wielding bands, led by naval officers, that had prowled the British seaports of his childhood. Sweeping through the warren of docks, alleyways, and taverns, a press gang might seize any able-bodied man it encountered and drag him onto a Royal Navy vessel, where he might disappear for years, if not forever. "But Lord, how some poor women did cry," recorded diarist Samuel Pepys, chief secretary to the Admiralty, after witnessing a press gang tear men from their families in seventeenth-century London. "It is a great tyranny."

It was a longstanding one, too. Forcible impressment was a centuries-old practice driven by frequent if sporadic wars. Although universally condemned, no attempt was seriously undertaken to prohibit it because no other method had been found to man the ships of Britain's gargantuan and growing fleet in times of emergency. By the mid-eighteenth century, the official Impress Service was at least attempting to regulate the activities of press gangs. In theory, they were to target only able-bodied seamen, but as Chambers noted, they "did not stickle much about law" and had made a habit of seizing "not only common laborers, but farmers and constables, not sparing a Justice of the Peace."

Yet when wars broke out, and the Royal Navy required thousands of additional seamen at the drop of a hat, even "protections"—certificates of exemption issued for a wide variety of seafaring occupations—would be temporarily suspended. At such times men might literally head for the hills. Some took drastic measures of evasion, such as feigning insanity or dressing in women's garb. So detested was the custom that some British communities tried fighting back, and local magistrates were known to turn the tables, occasionally carting press gangs off to the clink.

Even more resistance was met overseas. Americans in particular despised impressment. In 1708, during Queen Anne's War (1701-1713), Parliament passed a law forbidding the practice in its North American colonies. To the British it was but a temporary expedient to buoy the vital colonial trade, but to the Americans that exemption was permanent. Parliament tried clarifying the law in 1746, exempting the West Indies but not North America. That only led to

A creamware mug, circa 1800, transfer printed in black with a scene of impressment on Tower Hill—a variation of the 1790 etching "Manning the Navy" by John Barlow.

violent protests. On November 16, 1747, a press gang swept through Boston Harbor. Hours later an enraged mob seized officials and even broke into the State House. The press-ganged men were soon released.

Facing such difficulties ashore both at home and abroad, the Royal Navy found it more productive to impress at sea, a favorite target being merchant ships returning to British ports. An approaching boat bearing an officer and a riled gang of toughs was a dismaying sight for homeward-bound sailors just entering a harbor. During wartime, the Royal Navy impressed sailors far out on the high seas as well. And no wars so demanded extra manpower as did the interminable struggles with revolutionary France (1793-1802) and Napoleon (1803-1815).

When the Napoleonic Wars commenced, the Royal Navy was increased from 25,000 to 45,000 men. By 1810, that figure had swelled to 140,000, a need that neither volunteers nor a national quota system could fill. Besides the growth in numbers, there was also a high turnover rate, sparked by disease and especially desertion. Admiral Lord Nelson estimated that between 1793 and 1801, nearly 40,000 men deserted from the navy's ships, not to escape the lash but more often because of abysmally low, and sometimes nonexistent, pay. Furthermore, impressed men, unwilling sailors to begin with, were the most likely to desert—leading to even more impressments. By 1805, the Impress Service was employing no fewer than twenty-seven navy captains and sixty-eight lieutenants.

Many deserters resurfaced on American merchant ships, lured by more generous pay, better working conditions, and—the easier for passing as American citizens—a common language. U.S. Secretary of the Treasury Albert Gallatin told President Thomas Jefferson that between 1805 and 1807 perhaps half of the 18,000 able seamen in the American merchant fleet were British subjects.

Whether true or not, the Royal Navy believed it to be so. Each time a shorthanded British warship stopped an unarmed American merchantman—and they had plenty to choose from because the United States possessed the largest merchant fleet of any neutral nation—there was a good chance that the boarding party would impress some of the crew, claiming they were British deserters. It mattered not that a sailor waved a notarized document stating that he was indeed a citizen of the United States. Such "protections" might be swept aside at the point of a cutlass. These papers could be fraudulently obtained in any American seaport and could be purchased without difficulty on the black market.

On the contrary, just bearing a Scottish surname, for instance, might be warrant enough for a press gang at sea. The Admiralty, anyway, maintained that once a British subject, always a British subject. And by those lights, when England went to war with France in 1792, the British considered any naturalized U.S. citizen who immigrated to the United States after the signing of the 1783 Treaty of Paris, which recognized the independence of the new republic, still to be a British subject.

British insistence on impressment thus collided with the ingrained American hatred of the practice. The British claimed that national survival was at stake; the life-or-death hornlocking with Napoleon did not allow for niceties; victory demanded such measures. Americans countered that the king was as despicable a tyrant at sea as Napoleon was on land. Seizing its citizens was an inexcusable assault on U.S.

sovereignty, and the State Department eventually compiled a list of 9,991 sailors, impressed between 1796 and 1812, who had somehow managed to contact American diplomats in London seeking help and redress. The headcount of the many others who found no way to appeal is still a matter of guesswork. These unknowns would have been virtually enslaved for the duration of the war with France, and then perhaps compelled to fight against their own countrymen.

That war arrived in the summer of 1812—a war, as the popular slogan put it, fought for "Free Trade and Sailors' Rights." Even many Britons came to admit that had indeed been the case. In 1824, the *Edinburgh Review* neatly summed up the vicious circle that had spiraled down to armed conflict: "Impressment was the cause why our seamen deserted; and their desertion brought on war, to preserve a right to impress them wherever they could be found!"

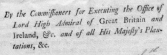

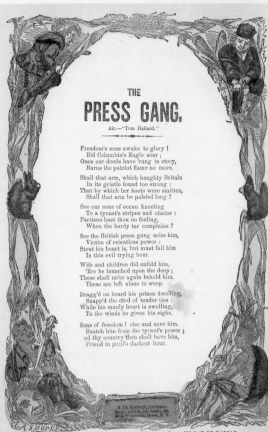

Painted by Orlando S. Lagman, this oil portrait of Commodore John Rodgers depicts him as a youthful officer. "He was a muscular, vigorous man, buoyantly alive, brave and modest, capable of deep feelings and strenuous energy," according to naval historian Charles Oscar Paullin. As this portrait attests, he had "abundant coal-black hair, dark eyes, and dark shaggy eyebrows; a handsome face bronzed by sea winds and sunshine; an open countenance as befitted a sailor; and a look of firmness and resolution with a touch of imperiousness."

With such discontent against the British simmering in ports up and down America's Eastern Seaboard, minor incidents between the two countries had the potential to escalate quickly into armed confrontation. That's what happened in 1807, when HMS *Leopard* fired a broadside at the U.S. frigate *Chesapeake*. This episode had convinced President Thomas Jefferson and those who agreed with him that possession of a standing navy would only increase the chances of such encounters, any one of which might let slip the dogs of war. Naval officers, of course, concluded otherwise. And there was no more senior officer than Commodore John Rodgers, whose squadron was based in New York.

Rodgers, in fact, so heartily agreed with Secretary of the Navy Paul Hamilton's denouncement of *Leopard*'s unprovoked assault, which he called an "inhuman and dastardly attack . . . an outrage which prostrated the flag of our country and has imposed on the American people cause of ceaseless mourning," that the commodore distributed copies of Hamilton's missive among his commanders, dashing off some additional words of his own. "Every man, woman, and child in our country," he wrote in part, "will be disposed to examine into our actions with jealous and scrutinizing eyes, equally ready to applaud those calculated to do honor to our insulted country, as they will be active in consigning our names to disgrace and even the very vessels composing at present our little navy to the ravages of the worms . . . should we not fulfill their expectations."

A born leader who cut a redoubtable figure and had a temperament that toggled between intensely passionate and coolly even-keeled, Rodgers had made up his mind in boyhood to pursue a life at sea, setting out by foot—unbeknownst to his parents—for Baltimore, that bustling port he had only read about in books, some forty miles away from Havre de Grace, his native town at the head of the Chesapeake Bay. Beginning as a humble shipmaster's apprentice, he soon became a shipmaster himself. In 1798, during the Quasi-War with France, he was commissioned a lieutenant in the Navy, serving aboard the U.S. frigate *Constellation*, where as a prize captain he brought a captured French frigate, *L'Insurgente*, safely into a U.S. port. In 1799, he took the helm of *Maryland*. Advancing steadily upward, he performed brilliantly in the First Barbary War (1801-1805), commanding a squadron and making the pasha of Tripoli sign a peace accord before taking charge of the Navy's small, New York-based flotilla.

In 1802, he had met Minerva Denison, twelve years his junior and the daughter of a prosperous West Indies merchant who had begun the construction of Sion Hill, the family estate in Havre de Grace that overlooked the Susquehanna River and the Chesapeake Bay beyond. Minerva, too, had early exposure to the sea, once recalling her "childish glee in running down to the wharf with packages." The brunette beauty was only seventeen when she first laid eyes on Rodgers. Her initial impression was not favorable, though it was perhaps tinged by her mother's disapproval. Mother and daughter had been invited to a dinner at a neighbor's house, where Rodgers was also a guest. Much later in life, she recalled that pivotal encounter.

I remained quietly at Sion Hill following an uneventful life until I met Captain Rodgers . . . One fine morning in June when I was just seventeen, my mother received a note from Mrs. Hughes saying that Captain Rodgers had been invited to dine with them . . . [T]hey desired that my mother would come over in the evening and take tea with them, bringing [me] with her. Accordingly we went. I had previously heard Captain Rodgers spoken of. His reputation was known to the country . . . I had known his mother and sisters and his brother Alexander. I had heard them speak of John, but had never seen him as he was seldom at home, most of his time being spent at sea.

When we arrived at Mount Pleasant we were asked into the parlor where the ladies, who had just returned from the dinner table, were discussing Captain Rodgers. One maiden lady . . . said that she thought he was very rough and abrupt . . . She thought he had a bad countenance, with his black and heavy eyebrows. She said he had talked at dinner of an action in which he had been engaged when the deck was slippery with blood and that she had nearly fainted with horror . . . Soon after that the gentlemen came in from the dinner table. I was sitting at one end of a card table which was placed near the wall. Upon the table sat a large French clock which effectually concealed any one sitting behind it. Captain Rodgers came in with the quiet and determined step, which I learned to know so well, and sat down at the further end of the table from me. While I was sitting at the table I thought that I would take a peep at the gentleman on the other side of the clock. I bent forward to do so, and to my consternation I found a pair of piercing black eyes fixed upon me. I withdrew my gaze hastily. The gentlemen all arose and walked into the garden, while the ladies remained in the drawing room . . .

When my mother and myself were going home, I asked her what she thought of Captain Rodgers, who seemed to be the hero of the day. She replied that she did not like him at all, that his countenance was dreadful, and that those black and heavy eyebrows gave him such a forbidding look that it made her tremble to look at him.

Several days later, Minerva's mother had a change of heart, returning from a visit to town with nothing but praise for Rodgers. "That is a very marvelous change," Minerva quipped. "To what can it be ascribed?" Minerva's mother replied that the young officer had been "exceedingly polite and friendly," helping her as she went about her sundry shopping. What's more, he now seemed to possess such a "bright" appearance that "it made him very fascinating."

Painted sometime in 1814, this portrait of the ethereal Minerva Rodgers is attributed to popular American portraitist John Wesley Jarvis (1780–1840), who had many prominent sitters. "We know that she was a most comely and amiable young woman," Charles Oscar Paullin said of Minerva. "She sang remarkably well, preferring the old ballads, and played the pianoforte with much skill and spirit. Of the English poets, she was partial to Gray, Thomson, and Pope."

It wasn't long before Minerva was formally introduced to the young officer. "After that his visits became frequent," she recalled, "and his attentions to me very conspicuous." Their courtship was cut short when the First Barbary War took Rodgers to the faraway Mediterranean, but his letters from that distant post captured her heart. Though she had asked that he not write to her—perhaps out of distress over his departure—he disobeyed her wishes, choosing instead, in a letter dated December 17, 1802, to profess his love for her.

There is no command you could have charg'd me with so severe as to deny me the priviledge of a correspondence . . . From retrospective recollection I can still figure to my imagination every branch and leaf of the unfeeling little peach tree, in presence of, and under which, your sensible heart, although cruel tongue pass'd the agonizing sentence of denying me the priviledge of a communication by letter. But Minerva, did you possess the power of the wise idol whose name you bear? My love for you is such as would (in this instance) force me to disobey you . . . I am not afraid to face the enemies of my country, even in the shape of furies from Hell, and could you suspect me of being coward enough to submit with pusillanimity to a charge so directly in disunion with my soul? 'Tis often said by the good people of Terra Firma that salt water and long absence cures all pains to which sailors' hearts are subject. With the candor of one of Neptune's pupils, I honestly confess it had always been the case with me, until I had the happiness or unhappiness to be honor'd with your acquaintance . . . I am now on a part of the globe where even the compass itself is false, as all points have revoked their constancy, since I left America, and chang'd their direction upwards of twenty degrees to embrace some nearer object. But Minerva (forgive the familiar appellation) the magnetic power of your charms have to this moment prevented my heart from varying a single second.

In 1806, the couple wed at Sion Hill, but since Rodgers was so often gone—sometimes for months at a time—their letters became the bulwark of their surprisingly egalitarian relationship. Their correspondence not only reflects a mutual and heartfelt devotion but also provides an illuminating glimpse into one family's experience of a war that was, by 1811, rapidly approaching.

It was at Sion Hill, where he was spending his shore leave in the spring of that year, that Rodgers received some disquieting news. On May 1, it seemed, a party from HMS *Guerrière*, a 38-gun frigate, had halted the U.S. brig *Spitfire* off the coast of New Jersey and hauled away her master apprentice, a native of Maine by the name of Jon Diggio. At the directive of Hamilton, Rodgers hastened down to Annapolis, where his handpicked flagship, the U.S. frigate *President*, lay at anchor. Within two hours she was underway, though a quarter of her crew had not made it back after the recall was sounded. Many were picked up in Norfolk, where the frigate had stopped over to lay in supplies before hunting down *Guerrière*, believed to be somewhere off the coast between New York and the Virginia Capes.

On the afternoon of May 16, as *President* stood off from Cape Henry and entered the Atlantic not far from where *Leopard* had accosted *Chesapeake* four years earlier, her maintop lookouts espied a sail approaching on the eastern horizon—a sail that might have belonged to a frigate. She certainly appeared to be a warship, though the distance was too great to make a more precise identification. *Guerrière* was one of the few British warships reported to be roving the area. Believing—or maybe just hoping—that the faraway sail might indeed belong to that troublesome vessel, Rodgers cracked on all canvas and, when the distant ship abruptly turned and ran for the south, began to pursue her, bent on reclaiming Diggio from the clutches of the Royal Navy. Perhaps he was also motivated by a year-old command whose fulfillment had vexingly eluded him: "Be prepared and determined at every hazard to vindicate the injured honor of our navy and revive the drooping spirits of our nation."

By the time *President* closed on the mysterious quarry, however, twilight had descended upon the ocean, obscuring any colors she might have been flying. From his own frigate's quarterdeck, Rodgers raised a well-worn brass speaking trumpet to his lips and thundered out the seafarer's age-old hail: "What ship is that?"

Several moments passed before the same words came booming back to him with pitch-perfect clarity—the other ship's commander, refusing

A watercolor of Sion Hill, the Rodgers family estate in Havre de Grace, Maryland. Minerva Rodgers took great pride in the upkeep of the gable-roofed Georgian homestead, and its handpicked furnishings were reputed to be the most splendorous around. Bitten by envy, the society-minded Mary Boardman Crowninshield, wife of Secretary of the Navy Benjamin W. Crowninshield, once even sent her husband over on a mission to ascertain whether or not the furniture was "handsomer than ours."

the challenge to first divulge his vessel's name, was simply reprising the American commodore's demand. Rodgers again sounded his trumpet. This time, instead of an echo, a shot whizzed by. "What the devil was that?" he asked, swiveling around to question his men; Henry Caldwell, who'd seen the glinting flash of a gun, replied that the other ship must have fired on them. Rodgers ordered retaliation, and the unknown foe was all but blown to smithereens in the ensuing hour. For the remainder of the night, the two ships lay hove-to within cannon shot of each other.

By the stark light of dawn, however, Rodgers saw that it was a small, 20-gun corvette, not a stricken British frigate, wallowing out there in the swell. She was HMS *Little Belt*, it turned out, commanded by Captain Arthur Batt Bingham, who had also been searching for *Guerrière*, hoping to deliver orders from the commander of the Bermuda station. Bingham had nine dead and twenty-three wounded aboard, as he told the lieutenant whom Rodgers had dispatched over the intervening sea by rowboat. Bingham also accused the Americans of opening fire first and peremptorily refused their proffer of aid. With that, *President* summarily resumed her cruise, running up to Cape Cod while *Little Belt* struggled all the way to Halifax, Nova Scotia, headquarters of the Royal Navy's North America squadron. But when Rodgers and his ship returned to New York, they had scarcely dropped anchor before they discovered that they'd become national heroes. Finally, someone had dared to beard the British lion. When Hamilton heard the news of the *Little Belt* incident, he was said to have planted a rapturous kiss on his wife before shouting, "Thank God, the attack upon *Chesapeake* is now equaled!"

Rodgers himself was more subdued, insisting that he hadn't been out for blood. "Neither my passions nor prejudices had any agency in this affair," he wrote before requesting that a court of inquiry be convened. Though he was subsequently acquitted of any misconduct, he braced himself for a storm of controversy. Newspapers on both sides of the Atlantic fired broadsides back and forth across the ocean, questioning the veracity of the contending commanders' accounts—each had adamantly maintained that the other fired first—and impugning their characters whenever the opportunity arose. London's *Morning Courier*, bolstering Bingham's version of events, concluded that American "insolence must be punished!!" Conversely, U.S. papers, with the exception of those run by antiwar Federalists, defamed the British captain—one called him an "impertinent" lush—and heralded Rodgers as a hero, a man of "known reputation and unsullied character," as Baltimore's influential *Niles' Weekly Register* put it, "whose honor is as unimpeachable as his courage is unquestioned."

Two weeks afterward, on June 3, 1811, Rodgers wrote to Minerva, downplaying the *Little Belt* affair and instead chatting about their straitened finances. Although his salary was $3,500 a year, twice as much as a captain's

pay, it was not enough to support a brood that would eventually grow to include eleven children.

> My conduct in my late [episode] with the *Little Belt* gained the approbation of the nation generally, with the exception of a few souls who dare not speak loudly. I have been almost inundated with letters . . . I shall sail about the 8th on another cruise of not more than two or three weeks . . . and on my return shall promise myself the happiness of seeing you . . . I have purchased Frederick a lottery ticket No. 9.9n/4th. Robert's is still in the wheel of fortune . . . I hope they may be more fortunate in pecuniary matters than their father. Keep up your spirits, my wife, for my own peace of mind depends upon yours . . . Kiss Robert and Frederick for me. Your own devoted, J.R.

He had every reason to seek some peace of mind. Despite all the fanfare—the hog roasts and serenades and thoroughfare renamings in his honor—the war clouds over the Atlantic had grown darker and more ominous. Hamilton, while praising Rodgers' conduct in the *Little Belt* incident, nevertheless cautioned the commodore that he—and by extension the Navy itself—was now surely "marked for British vengeance." Indeed, *Guerrière* was said to be prowling the coast, her name now painted in large letters on her topsail alongside the mocking taunt "NOT THE LITTLE BELT." Rodgers could only respond by painting his own ship's name on each of her topsails in letters so large that they "might be seen ten miles off." Though he spent most of the autumn and winter months patrolling the Atlantic shores, he never encountered his would-be nemesis. Even in early April 1812, after *Guerrière* and a sister frigate had harassed U.S. merchant ships off the Delaware Capes and he was ordered to secure the coast, Rodgers failed to glimpse that insulting sail, though he cruised from Sandy Hook to Hatteras and back again.

It was but the calm before the storm. By June 13, Hamilton, scenting an imminent declaration of war in the humid Washington air, was urging his senior commander, "For God's sake, get ready and let us strike a good blow!"

A brass speaking trumpet of the kind that Rodgers would have used to hail passing ships.

FIGHTING FOR FREE TRADE

Opposite: This 1808 political cartoon depicts President Thomas Jefferson addressing a group of disgruntled merchants as he defends the Embargo Act. "Yea, friend, thou may as well tell us to cut off our nose to be revenged of our face," one speech bubble reads.

In June 1813, when Captain James Lawrence ran a flag up the mainmast of the U.S. frigate *Chesapeake* bearing the slogan "Free Trade and Sailors' Rights," he hoped it would hearten his crew for the coming combat with HMS *Shannon*. That rallying cry was also a reminder that the U.S. Navy had been born out of a determination to fight for free trade, and that its entire eighteen-year history had been framed by a conflict of which the approaching battle formed but a small part, a two-decade struggle for empire that, in one historian's words, extended "from London to Ceylon, from Moscow to Mexico City, from Copenhagen to Cape Town, encircling the globe with fire."

After the American Revolution, the few ships of the Continental Navy that had not been captured or destroyed in battle were quickly sold by a debt-burdened new nation. But that had left its growing merchant fleet, protected in colonial days by the Royal Navy, exposed and vulnerable. It wasn't long before the first predator hove into view: a lateen-rigged pirate vessel from Morocco that seized an unarmed American schooner near the Strait of Gibraltar in the summer of 1784.

The Barbary States of North Africa, stretching east from Morocco and encompassing Algiers, Tunis, and Tripoli, had long sustained themselves through a mixture of piracy and extortion. The worst offender, the dey of Algiers, soon had his corsairs attacking American ships at every opportunity, capturing thirteen in all by 1792 and holding 119 captives for ransom. Most languished in foul prisons for years, their nation being too powerless to rescue them. An exasperated President George Washington finally persuaded Congress, on March 27, 1794, to help protect its merchant ships and seamen by agreeing to finance the construction of six frigates, thus creating the U.S. Navy.

In this endeavor, however, the United States did what most European states were accustomed to doing: it bought off the pirates, shamefully agreeing to pay Algiers a tribute approaching twenty percent of the U.S. annual revenue. Nevertheless, a reluctant Congress allowed three of the six frigates—*United States*, *Constitution*, and *Constellation*—to be built and launched by 1797. Both Washington and his successor, John Adams, were already pushing a naval preparedness policy. They soon had additional frigates on the stocks and were even planning to build six 74-gun ships-of-the-line. Both men also kept a weather eye not only on the Mediterranean but also on the colossal conflict storming across Europe, as by 1793 most of the Continent had gone to war with revolutionary France.

France had been the United States' first ally, helping it to win its war for independence, but after 1794, when the Americans reestablished friendly relations with Great Britain, the French turned against their former protégés and began plundering U.S. ships up and down the Eastern Seaboard. Matters quickly deteriorated into mutual hostility. While far away in Europe a young Napoleon Bonaparte led French armies to one victory after another, the United States slipped into an undeclared Quasi-War with France (1798-1800).

The three original frigates had hardly been outfitted when the Adams administration swiftly began to build or purchase others. By July 1798, some thirty ships—including twelve frigates—were underway to protect the nation's merchant fleet. Most sailed for the West Indies—a favorite destination of traders—where the British and French were already battling over their island possessions. Whether convoying merchantmen home from Havana or cruising off Guadeloupe and St. Kitts, the American men-of-war performed surprisingly well, given their hastily assembled origins. They captured dozens of French privateers, and in a memorable ship-to-ship action, the U.S. frigate *Constellation* soundly defeated its French counterpart, *L'Insurgente*, reputedly one of the swiftest warships in the world.

In the autumn of 1800, the squadrons were recalled after diplomats made peace with Napoleon, who was fast becoming the dictator of France. Within months of President Thomas Jefferson's March 1801 inauguration, however, the Navy was reduced to thirteen frigates and a single schooner. Then news arrived that the pasha of Tripoli, jealous of the tribute paid to Algiers, had declared war on the United States.

Diminished though it was, the Navy nonetheless promptly embarked on its first deployment across the Atlantic. During the four years of the First Barbary War (1801-1805), nearly every vessel and every officer in the fleet took some part in the blockade of Tripoli. *Constitution* engaged in several furious bombardments of the harbor and its fortifications. A detachment of U.S. Marines crossed five hundred miles of desert to lead a surprise attack on the pirate stronghold of Derne. And after the U.S. frigate *Philadelphia* was stranded on a reef and captured by corsairs, on the night of February 16, 1804, Lieutenant Stephen Decatur led a party of seventy-five volunteers into Tripoli's well-guarded harbor, where the frigate had been removed and turned into a floating battery, and there set the war trophy spectacularly ablaze. News of the feat traveled far and wide, and the daring Decatur became the epitome of the intrepid young naval officer.

As a result, on June 4, 1805, the pasha made peace on American terms. The U.S. Navy, barely a decade old, had reached out five thousand miles to safeguard its nation's trade, ensuring that its merchant vessels could sail the Mediterranean unmolested.

That would not long be the case. American prosperity depended on foreign trade, sixty-five percent of which was with Europe. That trade was booming by 1803, but 1803 was also the year when the Napoleonic Wars were renewed after a few months' fitful truce. Initially, with many European ships bottled up by a British blockade, commerce sought the protection of neutral American vessels, which swarmed across every ocean on the globe. That prosperity, however, was soon threatened. After October 1805, when Vice Admiral Horatio Nelson smashed the combined French and Spanish fleets with thundering finality at Trafalgar, Britain was incontestably the mistress of the seas. Napoleon, however, was by now undisputed master of the Continent. Each then tried strangling the other through economic warfare, which meant squeezing neutral commerce.

Because Napoleon controlled Holland and Spain, American ships that loaded sugar in Cuba or spices in the Dutch East Indies were, in British eyes, guilty of aiding

The happy Effects of that Grand System of shutting Ports against the English !!

Above: This iconic painting by Dennis Malone Carter (1827–1881) shows Lieutenant Stephen Decatur boldly boarding the Tripolitan gunboat during the bombardment of Tripoli on August 3, 1804.

was designed to squeeze Britain and France into relaxing their constraints on neutral shipping, but since it shut down all U.S. foreign trade whatsoever, restricting the merchant fleet to home waters, the draconian measure did more damage to the American economy than to those across the Atlantic. Annual revenues from foreign commerce plunged from $108 million to $22 million.

Even after that misguided measure was repealed, and American sails again billowed over the seas, President James Madison continued the duel of measure and counter-measure. In 1810, the cunning Napoleon promised to ease his restrictions on American shipping if the United States would cease trading altogether with Britain. Madison accepted the offer, enraging the British, while Napoleon continued to seize American vessels under the flimsiest of pretexts.

While Britain and France were both equally oppressive, the British were the focus of American anger. British warships had virtually blockaded American ports. Their boarding parties were mustering merchant crews and impressing American sailors, and British agents were supposedly stirring up trouble along the Canadian border and among the Native American tribes. It was British insolence on the high seas that in 1807 had led to HMS *Leopard*'s unprovoked attack on the U.S. frigate *Chesapeake*, and American naval officers were spoiling for a chance to avenge the insult.

Convinced it was in a fight to the death—the Napoleonic Wars would kill more than three million people before Napoleon was defeated—Britain believed that any concession to American demands would undermine its war effort, and it didn't tolerate neutrals that threatened to use their navies to defend free trade. In 1801, after Denmark chose to resist British searches and seizures, its fleet was decimated by a Royal Navy squadron in the roadstead outside Copenhagen.

The tiny American fleet faced even longer odds when the United States declared war on Great Britain on June 18, 1812. Though its ships were few, its officers—including John Rodgers, William Bainbridge, Stephen Decatur, Isaac Hull, James Lawrence, Thomas Macdonough, Oliver Hazard Perry, David Porter, and Charles Stewart—had gained valuable experience in both the Quasi-War and the battles against the Barbary pirates. The approaching conflict, however, would prove the pivotal one in the U.S. Navy's fight to uphold the freedom of the seas.

and abetting the enemy. Such vessels began to be seized and condemned by British Admiralty courts. Great Britain further tightened the screws on trade when it issued a series of Orders in Council decreeing that all neutral shipping bound for the Continent first stop in British ports, where cargoes might be examined. Napoleon retaliated by threatening to seize any ship that obeyed such strictures or even submitted to a British search. Pressed by the Royal Navy on one side and Napoleon's privateers on the other,

no sea lane remained safe for commerce. Between 1803 and 1812, nearly 1,700 American vessels were seized in this way.

Jefferson could not respond to such outrages with his navy. He had laid most of it up, scrapping further construction and preferring instead to rely on a fleet of small gunboats to protect the nation's ports and harbors. So he tried turning the tables on the warring powers, whose voracious appetites for imported foodstuffs and raw materials had never slackened. The Embargo Act of 1807

Free Trade and Sailors' Rights.

Artist Edward Moran (1829–1901) painted this effulgent scene of USS *Philadelphia*, previously captured by the Tripolitans, ablaze after she was boarded and set afire by Decatur's party on February 16, 1804.

Left: In this broadside, printed sometime between 1800 and 1812, David Woods rails against the press-ganging of American sailors. With all the power of period oratory, Woods harangues his audience—"Rouse from your lethargy . . . Awake from your slumbers. Can you fold your arms to sleep when the howling tempest is beating upon you?"—and encourages the people to take action against this raging tempest, a political hurricane that had the potential to destroy as many sailors as a storm at sea.

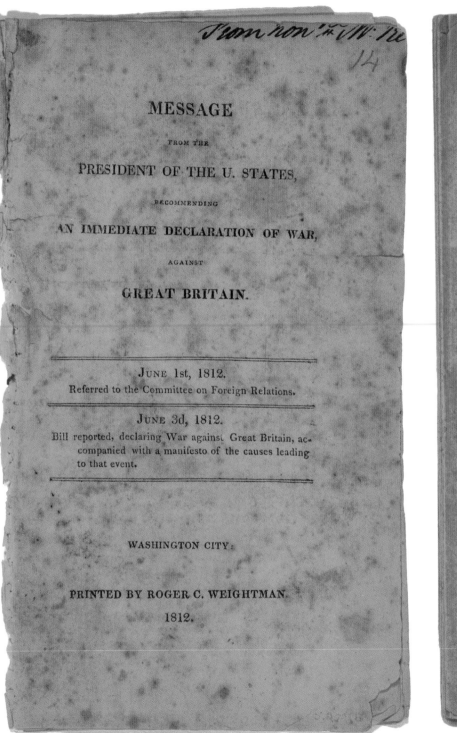

Right: President James Madison's war message, published by Roger Chew Weightman, an American politician and printer whose shops were located only blocks away from the White House. In his speech to Congress, Madison enumerates the injustices committed by Great Britain against the United States, including, among other grievances, the impressment of American sailors, the harassment of merchant vessels, and the blockading of commerce.

Far right: In this pamphlet, John Lowell, farmer, retired lawyer, and staunch Federalist, known among his family as "the Boston rebel" and "the Roxbury farmer," questions the Madison administration's true motives for declaring war on Great Britain. He views the war as a secret understanding between the American government and France designed to further the interests of Napoleon. Lowell also criticizes the government's lack of preparedness for war. In response to these government "errors," Lowell proposes a "legal and constitutional" plan that the citizens of the United States should instead follow. Like Lowell, many New Englanders openly opposed the war, speaking out through broadsides and pamphlets and in some areas continuing to trade directly with the British.

On June 1, 1812, President James Madison sent his war message to Congress. Three days later, in a secret vote, the House of Representatives voted 79 to 49 for war. Nearly two weeks later, the Senate also weighed in, 19 votes to 13 votes, for war. The following day, June 18, 1812, Madison signed the measure. The United States was officially at war with an empire whose court and capital lay three thousand miles across the ocean.

To say that the United States was unprepared for such a conflict is an understatement. Americans on the western frontier may have welcomed its prospects, as it gave hope to many desirous of seeing the United States absorb Canada and other British lands in North America. Others, especially in Federalist New England, were flabbergasted. The nation had narrowly won its independence only thirty years before. How could it even dream of challenging the mightiest navy the world had ever seen? For a decade U.S. policy had been to *not* build its own navy, in the belief that a standing navy would only provoke the warring powers of Britain and France. Many Americans would have agreed with the judgment of the London *Statesman*, which on June 10, 1812, six days before Madison cast down the gauntlet, had confidently asserted, "America certainly cannot pretend to wage war with us; she has no navy to do it with."

Former president John Adams was among them. The national navy that he had tried so hard to establish when he was chief executive in the late 1790s had now become "so Lilliputian," as he wrote to his son, that "Gulliver might bury it in the deep by making water on it."

It did seem to be preposterous folly to take on a navy that boasted well over six hundred warships, including more than two hundred fifty battleships and frigates. The United States, by contrast, had only fifteen serviceable commissioned vessels (with a few others laid up in various states of disrepair) in its entire fleet, with but seven frigates and a handful of brigs and sloops-of-war. Its sixty-two gunboats were unseaworthy and restricted to patrolling rivers and harbors. Britain also possessed numerous flourishing dockyards and naval establishments; its arsenals were among the best in the world. Of the five naval dockyards in the United States, only one, in Washington, was still functioning.

More importantly, the Royal Navy was at the zenith of its glory. It had demolished all of its European rivals, blockading the remnants of those defeated fleets in their Continental harbors. This gave it a tremendous psychological advantage over all of its would-be opponents. Britain was the unquestioned Goliath of the seas. "Our maritime superiority," trumpeted the London *Star*, "is in fact a part of the law of nations."

Yet as Rodgers and his brother officers well knew, the Lilliputians were not without some advantages. However mighty it looked on paper, the far-flung Royal Navy was stretched to its limits. Hundreds of British men-of-war were deployed in the ongoing blockade of Napoleonic Europe. The others were mostly dispersed around the globe, committed to protecting the interests of the growing British Empire. Although eighty of its vessels—including three battleships and twenty-three frigates—were on station in the Western Hemisphere, only twenty-five of them, including that scourge of the coast, *Guerrière*, happened to be off North America's eastern seaboard. That made the initial odds, at least, a little less daunting. Furthermore, the king's ships were chronically undermanned, and the thousands of forcibly impressed crewmen had low morale and performed poorly.

There were other less tangible factors as well. Whatever hawkish congressmen from the West might claim to the contrary, Federalist New England, leery of going to war at all, had it right: the United States was an overwhelmingly maritime nation. Most Americans lived closer to the sea in that era. Each small coastal town from Maine to Georgia had at least some vessels in the maritime trade. In New England, as Theodore Roosevelt wrote, "few of the boys would reach manhood without having made at least one voyage to the Newfoundland Banks after codfish, and in the whaling towns of Long Island it used to be an old saying that no man could marry till he struck his whale." Each year, raw young men went down to the sea in ships and were soon toughened by the rigors of the seafaring life. They learned to train their bare hands and feet to the feel of ropes. As Herman Melville later wrote, "Sailors, even in the bleakest weather, never wear mittens aloft; since aloft, they literally carry their lives in their hands, and want nothing between their grasp of the hemp and the hemp itself."

Should it come to war, these thousands of sailors could easily become a horde of privateers, an invaluable auxiliary force to the Navy proper, preying on the lifeblood of British merchant shipping.

Finally, there was its fleet. Though its frigates were few, they were truly first class, *President*, *United States*, and *Constitution* being larger and more heavily armed than those belonging to the Royal Navy. And the officers who would command them were young and bold and most had proved their valor in the First Barbary War. In fact, no less an authority than Vice Admiral Horatio Nelson himself, having once appraised a U.S. squadron on maneuvers in the Mediterranean, had ominously predicted, "There is in the handling of those transatlantic ships a nucleus of trouble for the navy of Great Britain."

Signed by the dynamic Captain David Porter, this certificate grants Lieutenant John Downes a share in the prizes captured by *Essex* early in the war.

On June 21, 1812, within an hour of learning of the congressional declaration of war, Rodgers put to sea. He was simply too impatient to await orders from Hamilton and too distrustful of a vacillating Congress that had declared war but then refused to grant the Navy more resources and, furthermore, was persuading Hamilton to use his frigates as mere "floating batteries" for the defense of harbors. Rodgers was also too anxious to wait for the 32-gun *Essex* to finish fitting out. Instead, he weighed anchor and stood out from New York Harbor with a squadron now consisting of only two ships: his flagship, the 44-gun frigate *President*, and the sloop *Hornet*. Off New Jersey's Sandy Hook, however, he met Commodore Stephen Decatur's southern squadron, up from Norfolk and not much larger, consisting of the 44-gun frigate *United States*, the 36-gun frigate *Congress*, and the 20-gun brig *Argus*. Together they turned into the Atlantic.

Before war was even declared, Hamilton had been charting the Navy's strategy once the inevitable conflict came to pass: attack British shipping while buying time for the widespread U.S. merchant fleet to beat its way back home. Just how to do this was a question he had put to his two commodores. Rodgers argued for a single strike force, while Decatur maintained that smaller detachments or even single-ship sorties would prove more effective. Hamilton sided with his senior officer, so Decatur joined forces with Rodgers, who retained command.

Within a few weeks the Admiralty in London would learn of the declaration of war, and then it would only be a matter of time before the Royal Navy hustled to blockade U.S. ports. So Rodgers intended to wreak whatever damage he could before the window of opportunity closed. He was also tempted by reports that a large convoy, bound for Britain and worth an obscene amount of money, happened to be sailing up the Gulf Stream from Jamaica and would soon be within striking distance. At dawn two days out, while hunting for this promising fleet, the U.S. ships chanced upon a lone British frigate.

Startled to find five U.S. cruisers bearing down on him, Captain Richard Byron of HMS *Belvidera* sensibly decided to turn tail and make a run for it. Rodgers turned in pursuit—only to have the breeze slacken and die. All that long day, each ship had every sail set, hoping to catch the slightest hint of wind. When *President* finally closed within range of *Belvidera*, Rodgers advanced to the forecastle and personally fired what was quite likely the opening shot of the war, the ball from his bow chaser smashing into *Belvidera*'s rudder. Then more misfortune struck. One of *President*'s main-deck guns, situated directly beneath where Rodgers was standing, burst apart, killing or maiming more than a dozen men and not only hurling the commodore to the forecastle deck but also breaking his leg. Meanwhile, *Belvidera* kept the pursuer at bay with her stern

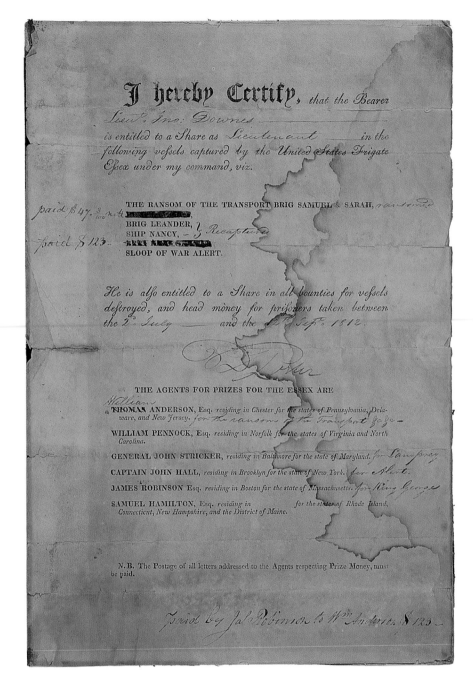

chasers, whose solid shot tore through *President*'s rigging. She also kept her distance, her crew cutting away anchors, heaving boats overboard, and pumping out the water supply to lighten the load. With the fall of night and a freshening breeze, she disappeared altogether. Three days later, she turned up in Halifax, where every British ship in the roadstead was soon buzzing with the tale of American treachery.

It had been an inauspicious beginning, and the rest of Rodgers' cruise was plagued by similar bad luck. Chasing *Belvidera* had distracted him from his quest for the Jamaican convoy; soon the U.S. squadron found only a flotsam of orange rinds and coconut shells marking those vessels' passage. In vain Rodgers pursued that will-o'-the-wisp, combing the ocean for two weeks on a front sometimes sixty miles wide, even venturing as close to Great Britain as the approaches to the English Channel. But thick fogs clung about his ship, and he never even glimpsed those sails. By mid-July a disappointed commodore, hobbling about the quarterdeck, finally broke off the chase. Instead, he steered his little flotilla on a great southward sweep to the Madeira Islands, but even in those waters, which should have been swarming with British warships, French privateers, and richly laden East Indiamen, he saw hardly a sail. He had taken only seven small merchantmen as prizes by the time he had recrossed the Atlantic and made for Boston, easing carefully along the Nova Scotian coast, watchful for any British activity. On August 31, he entered the harbor, having been at sea for seventy days. Once ashore, he caught up on the latest war news.

For one thing, Captain David Porter had finally put *Essex* to sea, slipping out of New York's harbor within two weeks of Rodgers' departure. On a seven-week cruise Porter had exceptional luck, taking no fewer than ten prizes. One moonlit July night near Bermuda he chanced upon a convoy of British troop transports ferrying soldiers from the West Indies to Halifax; he captured one of the vessels after winning a duel with the convoy's escort, HMS *Minerva*, a 32-gun frigate. One sunlit August day in the middle of the Atlantic he encountered HMS *Alert*, an 18-gun sloop. Posing as a merchantman, Porter lured the British warship within range of his guns and then hoisted his true colors before loosening a broadside from his powerful carronades. It took only eight minutes before the shattered *Alert* struck—the first Royal Navy vessel to be captured during the war.

Even more exciting was the presence of the 44-gun U.S. frigate *Constitution* in Boston, which had arrived only two days beforehand. Its battle-splintered masts had a stirring tale to tell.

A model of Commodore John Rodgers' beloved frigate, *President*.

THE AMERICAN FRIGATE

*I*n January 1793, just as the idea of establishing a national navy for the young United States was being debated, a forty-two-year-old Philadelphia shipbuilder who had helped design some of the Continental Navy's warships weighed in with his two cents. "[A]s our navy for a considerable time will be inferior in numbers," Joshua Humphreys wrote to financier Robert Morris, "we are to consider what size ships will be most formidable . . . Frigates, I suppose, will be the first object."

Frigates were an eighteenth-century innovation largely pioneered by the French navy. The name had come to apply to any warship that carried its armament on a single covered gun deck. They quickly proved their versatility—Vice Admiral Horatio Nelson famously called them the "eyes of the fleet"—and soon grew in size, first carrying 28 guns, then 32, then 36, then 38, with the caliber of the guns ascending accordingly until by

the turn of the century British frigates were regularly carrying formidable 18-pounders.

Humphreys, however, envisioned a frigate larger than anything else of its class then afloat. Humphreys knew that if the United States established a navy, it would be many years before that navy could amass fleets of double- and triple-decked ships-of-the-line, with 74 guns or more, that made up the great navies of Europe. So Humphreys suggested building men-of-war that were not quite battleships but were still more powerful than conventional frigates—very long of hull so as to mount 44 guns or more, speedy enough to outrun anything larger, and practically invincible to anything smaller.

As it happened, piracy on unarmed American merchant vessels in the Mediterranean and apprehension about the outbreak of war between Great Britain and France so alarmed President George Washington that he soon pushed the landmark 1794 Naval Act through Congress. This legislation not only established the U.S. Navy but also stipulated the construction of six frigates with which to send it to sea. Although conservative, if not hidebound, shipwrights looked askance at Humphreys' ideas for "super frigates," they were eventually adopted, because his assurances that such vessels could dominate everything afloat under 64 guns, he later wrote, were "paramount to all objections, and annihilated opposition."

Appointed the master constructor of the frigates, Humphreys began, as shipwrights traditionally did, by constructing a half model, with all of the vessel's dimensions portrayed in accurate proportion. Using that model, a loftsman then scaled up the dimensions to full size, first chalking them out on the floor of an enormous "mold loft" and then transferring them onto pieces of thin wood called molds. Still, the frigate existed only as an idea, the secretary of war reporting to Congress in December 1794 that "the wood of which the frames were to be made [still stands] in the forests; the iron for the cannon lies in its natural bed, and the flax and hemp perhaps in their seed."

No raw material, in an age of wooden warships, was more important than oak. More than ninety percent of a warship was made of that hard, versatile substance. Although Humphreys also specified southern yellow pine, red cedar, and the durable white oak for his frigates, his clear choice was southern live oak, perhaps the finest shipbuilding timber then known in the world. But it grew only in a narrow band along the coasts of the southeastern states.

Since thousands of large, mature trees were needed—more than 1,500 oaks went into the building of *Constitution* alone—the felling parties were dispatched to one of the few places they could still be found in some abundance: St. Simon's Island off the coast of Georgia. To a shipbuilder's eye, the gnarled trunks and spreading, almost horizontal limbs of live oaks called to mind the fabled English oaks out of which the "wooden walls" of the Royal Navy had been constructed. But live oak was even stronger and harder than those trees—hard with an ax-blunting, saw-dulling quality that was only one of the lumbermen's challenges. As they carried their molds into the woods, comparing the dimensions sketched out on those with the branching

This late eighteenth-century side axe belonged to Jacob Sibley, no stranger to flying chips and the smell of new-cut wood. A native of Maine, he helped build the first bridge across the Winnipiseogee River at eighteen and not long after hewed a homestead in Hopkinton out of the rugged pines of New Hampshire. During the Revolution, he lent a hand in the building of Portsmouth's Fort Constitution, and in 1795 he headed south to work on another "Constitution," this one under construction at Hartt's shipyard in Boston's North End. Family tradition says that Sibley used this axe to shape that venerable frigate's timbers. The head is original, but the handle has been replaced. The handle is offset, so that when the axe is swung, the cutting edge will come down to the side of the hewer's work, as is shown in Peter Guillet's *Timber Merchant Guide* (right).

Peter Guillet's *Timber Merchant's Guide*, published in 1823 and dedicated to Commodore John Rodgers, contains thirty hand-colored lithographic plates that illustrate how to efficiently make use of different tree types for shipbuilding timber. Plates one and two (left) show what parts of the trees made up what parts of the ship, including the keel piece, upper deck knee, futtock, top timber, and lower stem piece. Plate thirty (below, left) shows the hewing of a ship knee.

This hanging knee, carved from live oak, was part of *Constitution*'s upper deck until the frigate's reconstruction in 1927. The holes in the knee once contained iron "button head" bolts, which secured the knee to the bulkhead of the ship.

This mahogany bevel, dating between 1790 and 1824, belonged to Bunker Hill veteran and crackerjack shipwright George Claghorn, who was tasked with overseeing *Constitution*'s construction. As Hartt's shipyard workers lofted, or scaled up from the builders' plans, the frigate's towering frames and massive beams, Claghorn was there with his bevel, checking the angles of this member or that, making sure that everything was just so. His bevel, and his workman's eye, must have been true, because Old Ironsides is with us still.

A section of larch wood, valued for its durability and rot resistance, as it would appear before builders carved it into a ship knee.

A copper spike that was part of the hull of *Constitution* until she underwent restoration in the 1970s.

This oak nail served as a peg, or dowel, that shipwrights drove into a hole in order to secure the planking to *Constitution*'s frame.

Far left: This payroll, documenting carpenters' names, times of service, and receipts of pay over a one-week repair period in November 1801, is signed by the carpenters and certified by N. Morris and Isaac Hull.

Left: Schedule of lumber and knees bought, 1794. One of the earliest records pertaining to *Constitution*, this document details the amount of lumber bought to begin construction, how much it cost, and where it originated.

Preparation for WAR to defend Commerce.

The Swedish Church Southwark with the building of the FRIGATE PHILADELPHIA.

This hand-colored engraving by Thomas Birch shows the building of USS *Philadelphia* in Joshua Humphreys' shipyard.

wherever the shipyard, once the slips were laid and the stocks in place, work on the frigates followed the same general pattern. The finest live oak timbers were first scarfed together with long copper bolts to make the keel. Dubbers with adzes smoothed the rough-hewn timbers into the knees and futtocks, breast-hooks and sternposts, and other arcane load-bearing structures traditionally comprising a ship's frame. Everything had to join together as snugly as possible. Massive live oak beams rose diagonally from the keelson and reached forward to tie into huge knees. These innovative braces would keep the extra long keel from "hogging," or rising up in the middle when stressed at sea.

Huge curved ribs of live oak arose, spaced less than two inches apart rather than the customary twelve inches. After three layers of tough white oak planking were nailed to both their inside and outside faces, a practically solid oak wall, twenty-two to twenty-five inches thick, was created, comparing favorably with the fourteen-inch walls of other frigates.

Plankers ensured that the extra thick decking planks fit snugly from one end to the other, guaranteeing an unusually stiff deck. The hull was then caulked with oakum—bits of old tarred rope fiber—and sheathed entirely in copper below the waterline to protect it against shipworms—saltwater clams, dubbed "termites of the sea," notorious for boring into submerged wooden structures—and other ravages of the sea. Finally, what had once been a pile of timber stood on the stocks transformed into

a lethally beautiful expression of human artistry, ready to slip down the waxed ways into the water.

Initially known as frigates A-F, the completed vessels were named by Washington after principles enshrined in the U.S. Constitution: *United States* (44 guns), *Constellation* (38 guns), and *Constitution* (44 guns) were all launched in 1797. *Congress* (38 guns) had to wait until 1799 and *President* (44 guns) until 1800. Rigged out and duly commissioned, the vessels proved to be tight and strong and, after cracking on sail, exceedingly fast. The one all-around exception turned out to be *Chesapeake*, launched in December 1799. The smallest and shortest of the group, *Chesapeake* was named by Benjamin Stoddert, the first secretary of the Navy, for the Chesapeake Bay and was described by Commodore Stephen Decatur as sailing "uncommonly dull." She was the only one of the six frigates that Joshua Humphreys explicitly disavowed, perhaps because of a longstanding antipathy toward her builder, Joshua Fox, who had departed from the original Humphreys design.

The ships were also well armed. The 44-gun frigates routinely carried 24-pounder long guns, which had both a longer reach and a more powerful punch than did the 18-pounders routinely carried aboard their British counterparts. In addition, they might mount on their spar decks nearly two dozen 22- or 32-pounder carronades. The extra tons of iron did not make the vessels top-heavy; the weight ultimately rested on those well-braced keels.

As a class, the big "44s" were, as one naval historian put it, the "flower of the sailing period," arriving at a crucial juncture in the new nation's history and answering the question of whether or not the young United States should become a maritime power and fight for freedom of the seas. As warriors, they justified all the faith and care that Joshua Humphreys had put into them. In the summer of 1813, having suddenly lost three frigate duels after being undefeated for a decade, the Admiralty ordered that the Royal Navy "should not attempt to engage, single-handedly, the larger class of American ships." British officers were publicly complaining that they were really defeated by ships-of-the-line in disguise. A quarter century later, however, in 1840, when passions had cooled, one British authority bestowed the era's ultimate naval accolade: "It is but justice in regard to America to mention that England has benefited by her example, and that the large class of frigates now employed in the British service are modeled after those of the United States."

patterns on the trees so as to locate the corresponding "compass timber" for the ships' frames, the foresters battled malaria and unceasing tropical downpours.

Eventually the timber reached the six shipyards—one each in Philadelphia, New York, Boston, Baltimore, Norfolk, and Portsmouth—selected for the work. Shipyards were perhaps the most labor-intensive places in the preindustrial world, swarming with sawyers, framers, joiners, riggers, chandlers, and shipwrights all plying their trades in the midst of an immense ringing cacophony of banging and hammering. While some workers operated cranes and sheerlegs for hoisting masts and logs, others cut finger-sized treenails out of rot-resistant locust for use as timber-framing pegs. Still more labored over ropes and sails. But

On the afternoon of June 22, 1807, the U.S. frigate *Chesapeake* weighed anchor in Hampton Roads, Virginia, and, with the broad pennant of Commodore James Barron rippling from her masthead, set a course for the Mediterranean Sea, where Barron was to assume command of the small U.S. squadron cruising there. Several miles off the coast, *Chesapeake*'s lookouts reported the approach of a British frigate, HMS *Leopard*. British men-of-war were frequently encountered in these waters, as a pair of French warships had holed up in Annapolis, Maryland. But *Leopard* was hunting other quarry. After hailing *Chesapeake*, her officers insisted on searching the U.S. vessel for several Royal Navy deserters they asserted were lurking among *Chesapeake*'s crew.

Barron, of course, refused such a peremptory demand. "I know of no such men," he wrote in response. "I am also instructed never to permit the crew of any ship that I command to be mustered by any other but her own officers; it is my disposition to preserve harmony, and I hope this answer to your dispatch will prove satisfactory." Hardly had this reply been returned, however, when *Leopard* let loose a devastating point-blank broadside. *Chesapeake*, which had women and children on board, was caught completely off guard, her own

guns being lashed down for the Atlantic crossing and her decks strewn with anchor cables, luggage trunks, and other impedimenta. As the gunner tore apart the magazine in a mad scramble to fill up cartridges with powder, his crew waited beside their unprimed guns, helpless, as another broadside wreaked its havoc. "For God's sake, gentlemen, will nobody do his duty?!" Barron shouted. He was astonished. "For God's sake, fire one gun for the honor of the flag, I mean to strike." With the match tub empty, Third Lieutenant William Henry rushed to the galley and with his bare hands grabbed a flaming hot coal, which he used to ignite an 18-pounder. It was the only shot that the U.S. vessel could muster before striking her colors. Three men had been killed and eighteen wounded, including Barron. A British boarding party took away the four crewmen it had said were deserters, and *Leopard* was soon underway, leaving the wounded *Chesapeake* to limp back to Hampton Roads and national outrage. "Never since the Battle of Lexington have I seen this country in such a state of exasperation," President Thomas Jefferson declared.

The United States nearly went to war over the incident. Jefferson managed to avert it, and the British, as good as admitting that they had fired upon a neutral national warship without provocation, offered to pay reparations. Although one of the deserters was hanged from the yardarm and one died in prison, the two survivors were acknowledged to be U.S. citizens after all and duly returned.

More than any other event in the troubled years leading up to 1812, the episode typified the dangerous level that British-American

relations had reached. It also cast a long shadow over the U.S. Navy. Why these expensive frigates, congressional kvetching went, if they were only to be beaten so handily? Naval officers were bent on redeeming the good name of their service, one factor leading to the *Little Belt* affair of 1811. Moreover, a court-martial found Barron, the ranking officer on board *Chesapeake*, guilty of "neglecting, on the probability of an engagement, to clear his ship for action" and suspended him from active service for five years.

A long shadow, indeed—Barron as commodore had barely set foot on *Chesapeake* before she sailed that fateful June day. The ship's actual captain, in charge of preparing her for the voyage, escaped all censure. Barron's belief that he had been made a scapegoat five years before the outbreak of hostilities came full circle five years after their conclusion when he challenged Stephen Decatur, a hostile member of the court-martial and an erstwhile friend, to a duel. On the morning of March 22, 1820, the two foes met in the shade of the alder trees at the Bladensburg dueling ground. "If we meet in another world," Barron told Decatur, "let us hope that we may be better friends." Decatur, among the most celebrated of the war's naval heroes, received a fatal shot and died later that night.

This hand-colored woodcut shows the naval officers of *Chesapeake* surrendering to *Leopard*.

Left: In the nineteenth century, sailors stored their belongings on board ship in chests like this one, which belonged to John A. Bates (hence the initials "J.A.B"), a crewman with *Chesapeake* when she was attacked on the high seas by *Leopard*. Given how cumbersome such trunks were, it's easy to see how they could have gotten in the way.

"THAT FAVORITE FRIGATE"

When war was declared, *Constitution* had just finished having her bottom recoppered at the Washington Navy Yard, so she wasn't able to sail with Rodgers' squadron. In 1810, the commodore had actually been assigned to *Constitution*, but he found her too slow and preferred *President*. The captain of *President* at that time, Isaac Hull, was only too glad to switch commands with Rodgers. For him, *Constitution* had always been "that favorite frigate."

Hull was hardly the image of the dashing sea captain. Short and fat, he possessed neither Rodgers' imperious dark-browed presence nor Decatur's poise and charisma. But he was an exceptionally fine sailor, the son of a long line of Connecticut farmers and seafarers. He had sailed in ships since he was a boy, and by the age of twenty-one he was the master of a merchant vessel. Having in that capacity been captured twice by the French, he lost no time, after war with France broke out in 1798, in securing a commission as a Navy lieutenant. His first berth was with *Constitution*.

In May 1800, Hull had proven his mettle by leading a daring foray into the neutral Spanish harbor at Puerto Plata in the Dominican Republic, seizing the privateer *Sandwich* beneath the very noses of the Spaniards. After leaving *Constitution* in 1802, he captained both the schooner *Enterprise* and the brig *Argus* during the First Barbary War, providing the offshore naval support for the eight Marines who so famously strode the shores of Tripoli during the Derne campaign. In 1806, he was promoted to captain, and by 1809 he had been given *Chesapeake* as the first of his three frigate commands.

In those furious June days of 1812, under orders to proceed to New York, it was with *Constitution* that he was hastily putting to sea. One challenge was the unfortunate need to embark a new and largely inexperienced crew, so it was three weeks before the frigate sailed past the Virginia Capes and out into the open Atlantic. Five days later, on July 17, *Constitution* was off New Jersey when her lookouts spotted five sails ahead on the northern horizon. Hull initially hoped that by some happy chance this was Rodgers' five-ship squadron. As night drew on, however, and his coded lantern signals went unanswered, he cautiously beat the crew to quarters. Then, increasingly worried, he had the helmsman turn the ship around.

Dawn only confirmed his worst fears. Five British warships had closed in on *Constitution*. Though Hull could not know it, the squadron belonged to Admiral Sir Philip Bowes Vere Broke, dispatched south from Halifax after *Belvidera*'s arrival there had brought the tidings of war. In fact, *Belvidera* was one of the five ships revealed by the rising sun, as were *Aeolus* and *Shannon*, Broke's flagship. Farther

Hull's gold pocket watch, crafted by a London watchmaker in 1808. Many officers of the day carried such timepieces.

Painted on ivory sometime between 1807 and 1812, this miniature of Isaac Hull, unlikely hero, is set in a simple gold locket, the back of which holds a plaited tress of Hull's chestnut-brown hair. Like many of his fellow officers, Hull sported the "Brutus crop," a popular men's hairstyle of the day that owed its existence to the French Revolution and supposedly gave the wearer a more "natural" look.

This exquisite tortoiseshell hair comb, made from the carapace of a hawksbill sea turtle, now an endangered species, was a gift from Hull to his wife, Ann. She was only twenty-three when she surrendered her heart to Hull, newly crowned with the laurels of his triumph over HMS *Guerrière*. A classic beauty, Ann was a much-desired woman, and her nuptials to the hero of the moment left a train of disappointed suitors bemoaning their fate. "Miss Ann Hart bestowed her hand . . . on Victory as personified in our little fat captain, Isaac Hull, who is now reposing in the shade of his laurels," one sniveled bitterly. Despite such caustic remarks, the marriage turned out to be a long and happy one. The comb's motif of flowers and fish links the lovers' two worlds—one of the land, the other of the sea.

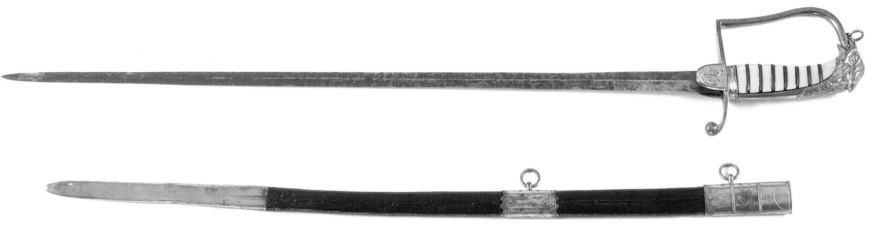

out to sea was *Guerrière*, while on the horizon was an imposing ship-of-the-line, HMS *Africa*.

Broke, too, was looking for Rodgers' squadron; now he had as good as captured *Constitution*. Making matters worse, the wind had fallen, and a sultry calm was hanging oppressively over an oil-smooth sea. Each ship, including the U.S. one, soon had every yard of canvas set, hoping to be the first one to catch the breeze. At least—given the circumstances—*Constitution* was just out of cannon range, as the occasional plumes of spray raised by British solid shot amply testified. Having no other choice, Hull unlimbered the ship's boats and, with men sweating at the oars, tried towing the big frigate out of harm's way. Of course, the British were doing the same thing, only hoping to close the gap instead. Broke soon had all of his squadron's boats towing Shannon. Hull then resorted to kedging his way forward. Soundings showed that only 26 fathoms—about 150 feet—of water lay beneath his keel, shallow enough for his boatmen to carry *Constitution*'s kedge anchors, attached to strong cables, far forward of the vessel, where they sank them. Once the anchors bit into the bottom, crewmen heaving at the capstan wound in the cables, literally pulling their ship forward in the process. The boats then carried the anchors far forward again, and the process was repeated, hour after sweltering

hour. It resulted in a marginal increase in speed. But the British, of course, began kedging, too. *Shannon*, employing a dozen boats, kedging or towing, was gaining.

Occasionally, the lightest of breezes sprang up, and the boats were called in, the sailors clambering to man every sail, every spanker, every royal the ship carried in vain hopes of catching the fugitive wind. Only wet sails could capture such faint stirrings, so a kind of bucket brigade was set up, which was perhaps even more exhausting. Then the wind would die, the boats were again put out, and the kedging resumed. It went like that all day, the slightest breezes pulling the boats in, the flat calms pushing them back out. It went like that all the stifling night as well, hour after endless hour. It even continued most of the next day, the boats going out and coming back in, the buckets going up full and coming down empty. Men reeled with exhaustion. Hull pumped out ten tons of fresh water, hoping to gain an inch in draft. Still, *Shannon* closed. She was only about a half mile shy of being in cannon range, and solid shot still arched occasionally over the becalmed sea, still as glass. *Aeolus* was gaining, too, while *Belvidera* had pulled even with *Constitution*.

A close-up view of Hull's scabbard, which has retained its original throat locket and middle band of gilt brass. The locket bears the inscription "Capt. I. Hull U.S.N." on one side and a trophy of crossed flags, a shield, a drum, a spear, and a trumpet on the other.

Hull's eye glasses, which he probably acquired later in life.

This dramatic painting by Julian Oliver Davidson, a distinguished nineteenth-century American maritime painter who worked mostly with oils, depicts the "Great Chase" of USS *Constitution* in July 1812. During a windless spell, the American frigate escaped from a British squadron in hot pursuit by using anchors and capstans to kedge her way out of being captured.

That afternoon a feeble breeze held for about four hours. Kedging was suspended, but the sails still had to be kept wet. Now *Constitution* began to gain, her recently cleaned and recoppered bottom giving her an edge. *Belvidera* began falling off. Night then brought a brief squall. Taking advantage of the curtains of rain, Hull ordered sails set and, close-hauled to the wind, *Constitution* was soon making eleven knots. Though the breeze petered out again and it was back to wetting the sails, he had caught the British by surprise. *Constitution* was now clearly drawing away. The enemy's sails appeared smaller and smaller. By the following morning they were hull down and soon disappeared altogether. Broke had called off the pursuit.

Hull had displayed masterful seamanship. He had proven more resourceful and had reacted more quickly to each vagary of wind than had his opponent. A greenhorn crew that had been on the ocean for only five days had also shown surprising grit and fortitude. Soon the breezes returned, the men sheeted home the great sails, and *Constitution* stood out to sea, making a wide turning arc for Boston.

"OLD IRONSIDES" EARNS HER NICKNAME

Hull had chosen Boston because New York, with Broke's squadron in the neighborhood, was out of the question, and he needed to replenish the water he had pumped out of *Constitution* during what came to be called the "Great Chase." Arriving on July 26, Hull stayed in Boston for less than a week, putting to sea again before orders from Hamilton—requesting that he turn *Constitution* over to Captain William Bainbridge, head of the Charlestown Navy Yard—could catch up with him.

Knowing that Broke was still at sea, Hull steered northeast for Halifax and the nearby Gulf of St. Lawrence, enticed by the prospect of taking prizes in those shipping lanes, busy with vessels carrying war supplies to British forces on the Great Lakes. In the next two weeks, *Constitution* took and burned two small brigs; she also recaptured a U.S. merchantman from a British prize crew. That's when Hull caught wind that Broke was on his way back from escorting that elusive Jamaican convoy, and one of his frigates had been sighted a few days' sail to the south, apparently making for Halifax. Hull ordered the helm about and set a course to intercept it.

Dawn on August 19 brought cloudy weather, freshening breezes, and the probability of another lonely day at sea. At two o'clock, however, a sail was spotted to the south. An hour later, as *Constitution* closed in, Hull was told that the "chace" appeared to be a frigate. He then cleared the decks for action. The marines took their positions in the fighting tops. The diarist-surgeon, Dr. Amos Evans, carefully arranged his sinister-looking instruments in the cockpit. Most of the crew had never seen action, although Hull had been drilling them in gunnery.

But when the drummer beat to quarters, and each man took his battle station, they still "gave three cheers," as Hull noted in his log.

> [A]t ¼ before 5 PM the Frigate lay her Main Topsail to the Mast, Took in our Top Gallant Sails, stay sails, flyingjib, hauled the Courses up, took the 2d. Reef in the Topsails, and sent down the Royal Yards, and got all snug, and ready for Action and beat to Quarters, at which our Crew gave three Cheers, at 5 PM bore more up bringing the Chace to bear rather off the Starboard Bow, she at that time discovering herself to be our Enemy by hoisting three English Ensigns.

The enemy was none other than HMS *Guerrière*, returning to Halifax for refitting.

Captain James Richard Dacres, lying hove-to in the ocean, was in a position to rake—fire down the length of a vessel for maximum destructiveness—the fast-approaching and obviously hostile ship, now that she was hoisting U.S. colors. Just after five o'clock, the range now lessening to a thousand yards, he loosened his starboard broadside. The shot fell short. *Guerrière* merely wore round, and Dacres fired his port broadside, but only two of those balls struck home. The British gunners not only had to contend with a heaving sea, throwing off their aim, but also faced a ship yawing—swerving back and forth across her course—as she advanced, further minimizing their chances of raking her from stem to stern. *Constitution* held the weather gauge—the wind was aiding her approach—so Dacres turned *Guerrière* around and also ran before the wind, looking for an opportunity to use it to his tactical advantage.

Much was at stake as they ran, two greyhounds of the sea. There was national honor, of course, the Americans still smarting at the memory of the *Chesapeake-Leopard* humiliation and still fuming over the high-handedness of British frigates along their coast. There was the British insistence that victory at sea was their privilege alone. And there was the quest for individual glory, which gave the approaching combat the aspect of a duel. Both ships were running under "fighting sail," topgallants only. Then Hull set his main course and with a burst of speed pulled even with his opponent. "Now, boys, pour it into them!" the captain bellowed from atop the arms chest, jumping up and down with such brio that his snug-fitting breeches split wide open from waistband to knee. Oblivious, he spirited his men on. "By heaven, that ship is ours!"

For the next few minutes it became a running fight, broadside traded for broadside, the British gunners firing with the rise of the waves, tearing and shredding *Constitution*'s rigging, the Americans on the down roll, punching holes in *Guerrière*'s hull. Despite the pall of smoke, the U.S. frigate was clearly a third again as large as her opponent, and her 24-pounders threw a heavier weight of broadside than did the British 18-pounders, whose solid shot seemed to slam into *Constitution*'s thick oak planking only to bounce straight off. "Huzzah!

Her sides are made of iron!" one sailor marveled, in that moment giving rise to an enduring nickname: "Old Ironsides."

In the midst of the din and fog, *Guerrière*'s mizzenmast soon shivered and toppled, significantly slowing her momentum. With all sails set, *Constitution* surged across her bow and let loose a tremendous raking broadside. Hull instantly wore his ship, came around again, and raked *Guerrière* with the other broadside. But he crossed too closely, and the ships suddenly collided, the British frigate's bowsprit tangling itself in *Constitution*'s mizzen rigging. The momentum of the shock sent the ships careening round and round in the pitching sea. Men scrambled to form boarding parties while marines swept each other's decks with musketry. Both *Constitution*'s first lieutenant, Charles Morris, and her marine lieutenant, William Bush, were shot down—"Mr. Morris first jumped on the Taffrail with an intention of boarding her and was instantly wounded in the parieties of the abdomen," Evans recorded in his diary. "Mr. Bush jumped into his place the instant he fell and immediately one musket shot entered his face and passed into his brain." Meanwhile, *Guerrière*'s gun crews ran cannons through the windows of Hull's quarters, the resulting blasts igniting a fire that was quickly doused out. Just when the two ships began pulling free of each other, one great crash after another rent the British warship's timbers: "His Foremast and Mainmast went by the board," Hull reported, "and took with them the Gib-boom, and every other Spar except the Bowsprit."

Kept by Maryland surgeon Amos A. Evans during his time aboard USS *Constitution*, this timeworn journal is one of only two known surviving naval medical journals from the War of 1812, and its pages contain a rare eyewitness account of the American frigate's legendary battle with HMS *Guerrière*. The journal is shown opened to the epigraph. Tellingly, Evans borrows a Latin line from Virgil's *Aeneid*: "Bella, horrida bella!" or "Wars, terrible wars!" He also quotes several lines from "The Task," a blank verse work by melancholic poet and hymnodist William Cowper: "O for a lodge in some vast wilderness, / Some boundless contiguity of shade, / Where rumour of oppression and deceit, / Of unsuccessful or successful war / Might never reach me more!"

The guns fell silent, and the wind began carrying away the smoke. *Guerrière* was now a dismasted hulk, her guns rolling dangerously loose, her decks, according to one midshipman, strewn with "pieces of skulls, brains, legs, arms & blood." She was helplessly wallowing in the trough of the sea. *Constitution*, hauling off to repair her shredded rigging, had all her spars intact and remained every inch the frigate.

In the gathering dusk, Dacres, with no colors left to strike, fired a gun to leeward, tokening surrender.

The bested Briton was escorted over the waves to face the man who had outdone him. Hull met him on the quarterdeck. "Captain Hull, what have you got for men?" Dacres asked, handing over his sword, as custom dictated. Hull's wry response—"Only a parcel of green bush-whackers"—elicited some due praise: "Bush-whackers! They are more like tigers than men. I never saw men fight so."

Twenty-three of Dacres' men had been killed and fifty-six wounded, compared to Hull's fourteen casualties.

In the heavy seas it took all night for *Constitution*'s boats to transfer *Guerrière*'s crew from the now badly listing ship. Among the dozens wounded, ten press-ganged Americans were discovered without a scratch. Graciously, Dacres had sent them below decks, sparing them the indignity of having to take up arms against their own.

Evans, the surgeon, was soon joined by his British counterpart and side by side in *Constitution*'s cramped cockpit, which measured only thirteen feet by eight feet and had less than five feet of headroom, they worked, kneeling over the writhing and groaning men, cauterizing wounds, setting bones, and amputating limbs. Gunner Moses Smith later recalled the gruesome detritus of battle, the hardihood of the wounded, and Hull's endearing compassion.

> Their sufferings were greater than can be described, or even imagined. One poor fellow had his under jaw shot off; and while we were watching him, he bled to death. Others, deprived of arms and legs, lingered in the greatest torture, until death put an end to their pains. There was one of our men—Dick Dunn— who bore the amputation of his leg with a fortitude I shall always bear in mind. "You are a hard set of butchers," was all he said to the surgeons, as his torn and bleeding limb was severed from his body. Others, whom I could name, bore their amputations equally well. Some of these brave defenders of the nation are among my friends; and I sometimes meet them stumping it through life. In the midst of all this suffering, Captain Hull was frequently found tendering the consolations needed in such an hour, and showing his humanity to the best advantage. He even looked more truly noble, bending over the hammock of a wounded tar than when invading and conquering the enemy.

Dawn found the surgeons still at it, while above on the quarterdeck Hull took in the view.

A personal letter from Lieutenant John Contee, only seventeen years old at the time, to Lewis Bush, recounting the first combat death of an American marine officer, the death of Lewis' brother, Lieutenant William Bush, on board USS *Constitution* during her engagement with HMS *Guerrière*. Writing in response to a query from Lewis, Contee, who fought alongside William, first expresses regret over belatedly relaying the news of his comrade's death. Contee's admiration for William, whom he describes in the letter as "gallant," "illustrious," and "beloved," is clear. He also addresses a more mundane aspect of the death of a hero: he promises to return William's personal belongings to the family as soon as possible. Lewis was later presented with William's posthumous silver medal for his service in the battle.

At daylight we found the Enemy's Ship a perfect Wreck, having many Shot holes between wind, and water, and above Six feet of the Plank below the Bends taken out by our round Shot, and her upperwork[s so] shattered to pieces, that I determined to take out the sick and wounded as fast as possible, and set her on fire, as it would be impossible to get her into port.

It was a spectacular demise. Even Evans took time out from his duties in the cockpit to watch it.

About 3 or 4 o'clock having got all the men from the *Guerriere* we set her on fire, and before the officer had time to get on board our ship she blew up, presenting a sight the most incomparably grand and magnificent I have experienced. No painter, no poet or historian could give on canvas or paper any description that could do justice to the scene.

Smith, however, came pretty close.

It was like waiting for the uncapping of a volcano—or the bursting up of a crater. Scarcely a word was spoken on board the *Constitution*, so breathless was the interest felt in the scene. The first intimation we had that the fire was at work was the discharge of the guns. One after another, as the flame advanced, they came booming toward us. Roar followed roar, flash followed flash, until the whole mass was enveloped in clouds of smoke. We could see but little of the direct progress of the work, and therefore we looked more earnestly for the explosion— not knowing how soon it might occur. Presently there was a dead silence; then followed a vibratory, shuddering motion, and streams of light, like streaks of lightning running along the sides; and the grand crash came! The quarter deck, which was immediately over the magazine, lifted in a mass, broke into fragments, and flew in every direction. The hull, parted in the center by the shock, and loaded with such masses of iron and spars, reeled, staggered, plunged forward a few feet, and sank out of sight. It was a grand and awful scene. Nearly every floating thing around her went down with the *Guerrière*. Scarcely a vestige remained to tell the world that such a frigate had ever swept the seas.

Above: Said to have been used on board USS *Constitution* during the War of 1812, this boarding pike is a fine example of the 1797 pattern, or leaf-head, American pike that was produced in large quantities for the Navy.

Left: A page from Amos A. Evans' journal. In frenetic handwriting—having injured his right hand, his writing and operating hand, he was making do with his left one—Evans describes the burning of HMS *Guerrière*. "About 3 or 4 o'clock, having got all the men from the *Guerriere* we set her on fire, and before the officer had time to get on board our Ship with the boat she blew up, presenting a sight the most incomparably grand and magnificent I have experienced," he scribbled. "No painter, no poet or historian could give on canvas or paper any descrip-tion that could do justice to the scene ... In the evening we committed the bodies of Lt. Bush and one of the *Guerriere*'s men who died of his wounds, to the deep ..."

This series of four watercolors, painted by George Ropes, Jr. in 1813, depicts with gem-like clarity one of the most iconic engagements in American naval history: the defeat of HMS *Guerrière* by USS *Constitution* on August 19, 1812. Though strategically inconsequential, the victory boosted the morale of the American public and burnished the reputation of not only *Constitution's* officers but also the Navy as a whole, proving that the fledgling force was every bit the match for the mighty Royal Navy.

"The word [that they had met the *Guerrière*] passed like lightning from man to man; and all who could be spared came flocking up like pigeons from a net bed. From the spar deck to the gun deck, from that to the berth deck, every man was roused and on his feet. All eyes were turned in the direction of the strange sail, and quick as thought studding-sails were out, fore and aft. The noble frigate fairly bounded over the billows, as we gave her a rap full, and spread her broad and tall wings to the gale . . . Hull was now all animation. He saw that the decisive moment had come. With great energy, yet calmness of manner, he passed around among the officers and men, addressing to them words of confidence and encouragement. 'Men!' said he, 'now do your duty. Your officer cannot have entire command over you now. Each man must do all in his power for his country.'"

~ Able Seaman Moses Smith

CONSTITUTION & GUERRIERE

G. Ropes Salem
1813

"We instantly followed the thunder of our cannon with three loud cheers, which rang along the ship like the roar of waters, and floated away rapidly to the ears of the enemy. This was a Yankee style which the British had not adopted. The English officers often spoke of it to ours, after the war was over. They said they were astonished at the spirit of our men in the toil and heat of the battle. Amid the dying and the dead, the crash of timbers, the flying of splinters and falling of spars, the American heart poured out its patriotism with long and loud cheers. The effect was always electrical, throughout all the struggle for our rights."
~ Moses Smith

"There was something melancholy and grand in the sight. Although the frigate was a wreck, floating about a mastless hulk at the sport of the waves, she bore marks of her former greatness. Much of her ornamental work had been untouched; and her long, high, black sides rose in solitary majesty before us, as we bade her farewell. For years she had been the house of thousands of human beings; for years she had withstood the shocks of the wind, the billows and the battle; for years she had borne the insignia of English valour to different and distant climes. But her years were now ended; her course was run; she was about to sink into the deep ocean forever."
~ Moses Smith

"It was like waiting for the uncapping of a volcano— or the bursting up of a crater. Scarcely a word was spoken on board the *Constitution*, so breathless was the interest felt in the scene. The first intimation we had that the fire was at work was the discharge of the guns. One after another, as the flame advanced, they came booming toward us. Roar followed roar, flash followed flash, until the whole mass was enveloped in clouds of smoke. We could see but little of the direct progress of the work, and therefore we looked more earnestly for the explosion— not knowing how soon it might occur. Presently there was a dead silence; then followed a vibratory, shuddering motion, and streams of light, like streaks of lightning running along the sides; and the grand crash came! The quarter deck, which was immediately over the magazine, lifted in a mass, broke into fragments, and flew in every direction. The hull, parted in the center by the shock, and loaded with such masses of iron and spars, reeled, staggered, plunged forward a few feet, and sank out of sight. It was a grand and awful scene. Nearly every floating thing around her went down with the *Guerrière*. Scarcely a vestige remained to tell the world that such a frigate had ever swept the seas."
~ Moses Smith

CONSTITUTION & GUERRIERE

A SECOND FRIGATE STRIKES HER COLORS

When Hull next set foot on land he, like Rodgers, found himself a hero. Soon after *Constitution* appeared in the offing of Boston Harbor on the evening of August 29, men in the usual fleet of small boats and tenders heard firsthand from her sailors the story of triumph and defeat. As the brawny U.S. frigate eased past Long Wharf and headed for the Charlestown Navy Yard, bells were pealing, cannons were firing salutes, and great crowds of people were cheering. Hull and his men were feted from one end of town to the other, and soon from one end of the country to the other. Evans attended one of the celebrations.

September 5.—Wind from N&E—cold rain. Were honoured with a superb dinner at Faneuil Hall by the citizens of Boston to-day. Much order and decorum were preserved on the occasion. Several excellent Patriotic toasts drunk . . . In the Gallery, fronting the President's chair, was a model of the Constitution Frigate with her masts fished and the Colours as they flew during the action . . . A band of musick played in the Gallery, and every toast was honored by several guns from the street.

Perhaps within earshot, Dacres, prisoner of war, sat down with a heavy heart and, on September 7, began writing to his superior in Halifax.

Sir,
I am sorry to inform you of the Capture of His Majesty's late Ship *Guerriere* by the American Frigate *Constitution* after a severe action on the 19th of August in Latitude 40.20 N and Longitude 55.00 West.

His task was made all the more painful because Dacres, born into a naval dynasty, the son of a highly esteemed admiral, knew that no British captain had lost a frigate in single-ship combat for nearly a decade.

With Rodgers' and Decatur's squadrons having safely arrived, the only reason that virtually the entire U.S. Navy could gather in Boston Harbor was the slow response of the Royal Navy to the threat they posed. Sooner rather than later, British warships would be turning up in force, blockading U.S. ports and seeking to avenge the loss of *Guerrière*.

Before that happened, the U.S. cruisers had to finish refitting and get back to sea.

Only this time they would not sail as a single squadron. Hamilton was now siding with Decatur: they would disperse in three squadrons, each composed of a 44-gun frigate, a smaller-sized frigate, and a sloop-of-war. Scattering across the trade routes of the Atlantic, they would raid British commerce, especially East Indiamen returning from Bombay, Canton, Calcutta, and Sumatra, holds overflowing with chintz and chutney, cloves and cinnamon, chests of tea and bales of silk. Or they might seize any opportunity that chance provided—Hamilton gave each of his commodores wide-ranging discretion over the routes he would follow and the prizes he would take. Commodore Rodgers with *President*, accompanied by *Congress* and the sloop *Wasp*, would steer east toward European waters. Commodore Decatur with *United States*, accompanied by *Chesapeake* and the brig *Argus*, would set a course for the Azores. And Commodore Bainbridge with *Constitution*

A portrait of the dashing and dauntless Stephen Decatur, always a glimmer in his eye.

As this illustration by artist Roy Andersen attests, powder monkeys like Samuel Leech were often boys or young teens. Small and nimble, they could swiftly run sacks of powder from the magazine—the copper-lined ammunition hold at the bottom of the ship—to the gun crews, and they were a hard target for sharpshooters.

nation's foremost naval hero during the First Barbary War after leading seventy-five volunteers on a night mission into the corsairs' stronghold, the harbor at Tripoli, fighting a desperate hand-to-hand battle but succeeding in burning the captured frigate *Philadelphia* down to its keel. He was hot-tempered and touchy, quick to take to the dueling ground at any perceived slight to his honor. Though he had hardly returned to Boston from his own cruise before he found himself aboard *Constitution*, congratulating Hull on his victory, the fireball was only the more consumed by his ambition.

He was now hunting for glory with *United States*. Though she was nicknamed the "Old Wagon" for her dubious sailing qualities, Decatur had been associated with her in much the same way that Hull had been with *Constitution*: she was his first frigate. As a youth, he had even helped fell oak for her timbers in New York's Catskill Mountains. After being commissioned as a naval officer during the Quasi-War with France, it was *United States* to which he was initially assigned. Thus, years later, when he was made commander of the Norfolk Navy Yard, he chose her as his flagship. She was as powerful a warship as any in the U.S. fleet. By dawn on Sunday, October 25, *United States* was some five hundred miles south of the Azores and on a line west of the Canary Islands, her course set for the Cape Verdes. The breeze was steady in the southeast when the lookouts, scanning the brightening horizon for the sails of returning East Indiamen, spotted one sail far to the south that, as it turned out, belonged not to a merchant vessel but to a British frigate.

The 38-gun *Macedonian* had departed England several weeks before, escorting a troop ship to Madeira. Since then she had been cruising north and south, hunting for U.S. prizes. It was sheer coincidence, given the immensity of the ocean, that two opposing warships would just happen upon each other. It was more astonishing still that the respective captains were old friends. Captain John Surinam Carden had frequently dined with the Decaturs in Norfolk, and it was said that they had once wagered a beaver hat on the outcome of a battle between their respective frigates.

Yet, closing fast on the ship that had refused to answer his signals and instead hoisted the Stars and Stripes, Carden thought it must be the 32-gun *Essex*, rumored to be in those waters. He would not realize his mistake until it was too late.

Carden drove straight for his adversary. With the breeze on her starboard beam, *Macedonian* held the weather gauge. She was a fast ship anyway, but Decatur misjudged her speed, and *United States*' first broadside plunked harmlessly into the sea. *Macedonian*'s reply was equally futile, but she was closing rapidly.

Any Royal Navy captain would have expected his opponent to be closing as well, anxious to slug it out broadside to broadside. But the U.S. frigate was instead standing away from the oncoming *Macedonian*. Actually, Decatur was cleverly exploiting his leeward—or downwind—position, keeping just out

would take *Essex* and the sloop *Hornet* down to the Cape Verde Islands, the coast of Brazil, and perhaps even around either the Cape of Good Hope or Cape Horn, where they might find good hunting in the Indian or Pacific Ocean.

Rodgers and Decatur were soon underway, sailing out of Boston on October 8, though neither *Chesapeake* nor *Wasp* had finished refitting; they would rendezvous with their respective squadrons at a later time. Four days out to sea, Rodgers and Decatur parted company. A day after that, Decatur even detached *Argus*, ordering her to make a broad sweep toward South America. Each vessel would complete its cruise alone.

At age thirty-three, Decatur was the beau ideal of an American naval officer. Tall and broad-shouldered with a head full of dark curls, he was as compelling as he was handsome. Philadelphia-bred, he came from an old maritime family but worked initially in a shipping office before his unbridled competitiveness soon found him striding a deck instead. Decatur became the of range of Carden's 18-pounders but just within range of his own 24-pounders. Through a series of intricate maneuvers he drew the British cruiser onward, then fired his second broadside. Some British tars, unused to such heavy and earsplitting ordnance, thought that the Americans' magazine had exploded—that is, until the iron balls smashed into their ship at full force, knocking her mizzen topmast down and dismantling some of her guns.

Macedonian plunged recklessly on. Suddenly, Decatur backed his sails, came into the wind, and surged into a raking position on the frigate's quarter, his crewmen firing their guns as fast as they could reload and aim them.

The next fifteen minutes were pure bedlam. One of *Macedonian*'s "powder monkeys"—boys who flew up and down the ladders carrying satchels of black powder from magazine to gun crew—never forgot the sound made by the American solid shot as it streaked overhead. It was "like the tearing of sails," Samuel Leech recalled. In fact, all of the events he witnessed that terrible Sabbath day remained so vivid in his memory that they spilled out through his pen when he wrote his memoirs decades later.

The roaring of cannon could now be heard from all parts of our trembling ship, and, mingling as it did with that of our foes, it made a most hideous noise. By-and-by I heard the shot strike the sides of our ship; the whole scene grew indescribably confused and horrible; it was like some awfully tremendous thunder-storm, whose deafening roar is attended by incessant streaks of lightning, carrying death in every flash, and strewing the ground with the victims of its wrath . . .

I was busily supplying my gun with powder, when I saw blood suddenly fly from the arm of a man stationed at our gun. I saw nothing strike him; the effect alone was visible; in an instant, the third lieutenant tied his handkerchief round the wounded arm, and sent the groaning wretch below to the surgeon.

The cries of the wounded now rang through all parts of the ship. These were carried to the cockpit as fast as they fell, while those more fortunate men, who were killed outright, were immediately thrown overboard. As I was stationed but a short distance from the main hatchway, I could catch a glance at all who were carried below. A glance was all I could indulge in, for the boys belonging to the guns next to mine were wounded in the early part of the action, and I had to spring with all my might to keep three or four guns supplied with cartridges. I saw two of these lads fall nearly together. One of them was struck in the leg by a large shot; he had to suffer amputation above the wound. The other had a grape or canister shot sent through his ancle. A stout Yorkshireman lifted him in his arms, and hurried him to the cockpit. He had his foot cut off, and was thus made lame for life. Two of the boys stationed on the quarter deck were killed. They were both Portuguese. A man, who saw one of them killed, afterwards told me that his powder caught fire and burnt the flesh almost off his face. In this pitiable situation, the agonized boy lifted up both hands, as if imploring relief, when a passing shot instantly cut him in two.

I was an eye-witness to a sight equally revolting. A man named Aldrich had one of his hands cut off by a shot, and almost at the same moment he received another shot, which tore open his bowels in a terrible manner. As he fell, two or three men caught him in their arms, and, as he could not live, threw him overboard.

One of the officers in my division also fell in my sight. He was a noble-hearted fellow, named Nan Kivell. A grape or canister shot struck him near the heart: exclaiming, "Oh! my God!" he fell, and was carried below, where he shortly after died.

Mr. Hope, our first lieutenant, was also slightly wounded by a grummet, or small iron ring, probably torn from a hammock clew by a shot. He went below, shouting to the men to fight on . . .

The battle went on. Our men kept cheering with all their might, I cheered with them, though I confess I scarcely knew for what. Certainly there was nothing very inspiriting in the aspect of things where I was stationed. So terrible had been the work of destruction round us, it was termed the slaughter-house . . . The schoolmaster received a death wound. The brave boatswain, who came from the sick bay to the din of battle, was fastening a stopper on a back-stay which had been shot away, when his head was smashed to pieces by a cannon-ball; another man, going to complete the unfinished task, was also struck down . . . A fellow named John, who, for some petty offence, had been sent on board as a punishment, was carried past me, wounded. I distinctly heard the large blood-drops fall pat, pat, pat, on the deck; his wounds were mortal. Even a poor goat, kept by the officers for her milk, did not escape the general carnage; her hind legs were shot off, and poor Nan was thrown overboard.

Onward *Macedonian* surged through the murderous hail, still vainly trying to close the range. Suddenly, her main topmast teetered, then tumbled into the foretopmast, both of them crashing down together onto the forecastle. A desperate Carden now called for boarders to assemble, hoping to run what was left of his disintegrating ship straight into his enemy's blazing gunports, when the stump of his mizzenmast fell by the boards. *Macedonian* was finished.

Out of the smoke, scarcely a hundred yards away, emerged the towering shape of *United States*. Only now her guns had fallen silent. Crossing his adversary's crushed bow, Decatur drew off several hundred yards to patch up his own ship. Her mizzen topgallant mast had been shot away, her sails were holed, and her rigging was in shreds. Five of her men had been killed, and another seven had been wounded. She was otherwise unscathed. Only a few minutes were needed for emergency refitting before she advanced again, her lofty figure

This powder horn belonged to gunner John Lord and is scrimshawed with various naval motifs, including a likeness of *Constitution*, the frigate aboard which Lord served, and the name of Lord's gun, "Big Will." Though conforming in size to Navy priming horns of the period, this one lacks several features common to government-issued pieces, such as the spring-loaded brass dispenser used to regulate the flow of powder from the horn to the gun's vent—an essential safety feature. The base's form, a bulbous walnut plug, is also quite distinct. These features suggest that Lord privately purchased the horn for his own use. Lord's choice of motifs indicates that, in addition to being functional, the horn was a talisman of sorts. Just as Herman Melville's veteran seamen carried "about their persons bits of 'Old Ironsides,' as Catholics do the wood of the true cross," so too did John Lord avail himself of the famed frigate's seemingly super-natural powers.

A sword gifted to Decatur in tribute to his heroics. It became his favorite piece of armor for special occasions.

Right: This ornate 1805 pattern Royal Navy sword, complete with a lion pommel, is similar to the one Captain John Carden would have surrendered to the victorious Captain Stephen Decatur, who refused to accept it. "Sir, I cannot receive the sword of a man who has so bravely defended his ship," Decatur purportedly said. According to some accounts, though, he did accept the beaver hat that had been the subject of a friendly bet.

once more nearly shaving *Macedonian*'s bow. The surviving British officers awaited the coup de grâce. But the Americans' guns remained quiet. Decatur was demonstrating that there was nothing his opponents could do to prevent him from raking them.

His decks a bloodbath, his hold resounding with the cries of his sixty-eight wounded, his frigate reduced to a "perfect wreck and unmanageable log," Carden, as he would note in his official report, "deemed it prudent, though a painful extremity, to surrender His Majesty's ship."

Standing in the wind on *United States*' quarterdeck, Carden offered his sword to his erstwhile friend. Decatur refused it. Carden confessed that he was now an "undone man." Decatur assured him that he was not, after all, the first Royal Navy captain to lose a frigate to the Americans; *Guerrière* had been taken only a few weeks earlier. It did little good. "I do all I can to console him," Decatur later wrote to his wife.

One reason the commodore had refrained from firing his guns at the close of battle was to spare *Macedonian* further destruction. He meant to take her home as a prize, thus outdoing Hull, who'd had to set his trophy aflame. That meant two weeks of lying hove-to in the open ocean while carpenters mended the battered frigate and jury-rigged new masts. When that work was completed, Decatur cut short his cruise and put the wheel hard over for home. Patched and plastered as she was, *Macedonian*, manned by a prize crew, still easily outsailed the Old Wagon.

Decatur had once more covered himself in glory. His return to the United States, once he had dodged patrolling British warships, was like a triumphal progress, beginning in Newport, Rhode Island—where a similarly

ambitious young officer, Oliver Hazard Perry, was in charge of the naval base—and proceeding through New London, Connecticut, to a grand arrival in New York Harbor. Everywhere throngs of people gathered to see his frigate and her spoil of war. The name Decatur was again on everyone's lips; he was again the toast of the nation. The climactic moment in a glittering Washington Christmas ball came when *Macedonian*'s ensign was unfurled and placed alongside those of *Guerrière* and *Alert*. Soon, President Madison was commending the commodore for the "consummate skill and conspicuous valor by which this trophy has been added to the naval arms of the United States."

Meanwhile, an ocean away, there was even more reason to celebrate.

A WRECK UPON THE WATER

Nearly three weeks after the squadrons of Rodgers and Decatur had weighed anchor, Commodore William Bainbridge with *Constitution* and Master Commandant James Lawrence with *Hornet* finally sailed past the old Boston Light and set a course for the far South Atlantic. It would be a day later still—October 28—before Captain David Porter and the frigate *Essex* slipped out of the Delaware River, hoping to join them.

Only Porter never caught up with the pair. Despite touching at agreed-upon rendezvous points from the Cape Verdes to Brazil's Fernando de Noronha, and despite the coded messages that Bainbridge left behind at such places, identifying where *Constitution* and *Hornet* could next be found, Porter missed them entirely. Should that be the case, his instructions went, he was to operate on his own initiative. A few months later he would do just that.

Many men aboard *Constitution* would have joined him willingly. Old Ironsides' crew had grown to love short, fat Isaac Hull during the few months they had served under him, but after Hull's brother died, he'd requested a leave of absence to attend to family affairs. When Bainbridge first moved into the captain's quarters, bringing with him the long pennant of a commodore, there had been a near mutiny below decks. Where Hull had spared the lash, Bainbridge had the reputation of being a notorious disciplinarian—a reputation made even worse by whispers that he was an unlucky captain to boot.

Born to Tory parents during the Revolution, Bainbridge had grown up a headstrong and combative youth and was a ship's master before he reached twenty. In 1798, however, during the Quasi-War with France, he became the first officer in the U.S. Navy to ever surrender a vessel, the schooner *Retaliation*, to an enemy warship. Five years later, during the First Barbary War, he lost his ship, the magnificent frigate *Philadelphia*, after grounding it on the reefs outside Tripoli. The corsairs took him, his crew, and his ship. For nearly three years Bainbridge languished in a squalid North African prison while Decatur burned *Philadelphia* to cinders and Rodgers negotiated a peace treaty with the pasha.

The long cruise to the South Atlantic didn't win the commodore many new friends among the crew. He held one drumhead court-martial and tamped down another threatened mutiny by crewmen protesting scanty rations. He also drilled the men relentlessly in gunnery.

By mid-December, *Constitution* and *Hornet* were well south of the equator, keeping the green, palm-fringed hills of Brazil close on their starboard quarter. Running low on water and provisions, Bainbridge ordered *Hornet* to stand in for the old Portuguese port of Salvador to replenish supplies. Entering the harbor, Lawrence discovered a British sloop-of-war at anchor there. *Bonne Citoyenne*, captained by Pitt Burnaby Greene, was undergoing repairs after having been damaged on her voyage north from Rio de Janeiro. The spirited Lawrence quickly

An engraving of William Bainbridge, created circa 1863 after a painting by American painter Alonzo Chappel (1828-1887).

DEDICATED BY PERMISSION TO THE RIGHT HONOURABLE THE LORDS COMMISSIONERS OF THE ADMIRALTY.

Plate 1. *Situation of His Majesty's Frigate JAVA, Captain Lambert at 5 Min. past 3 P.M. after an hour's close & severe Action with the American Frigate CONSTITUTION, in which she was so much disabled in her Masts Sails & Rigging, by the Enemys very superior Force & Weight of Metal that in the attempt to Board with every prospect of success her Foremast fell & she was rendered totally unmanageable.*

The first three in a series of four hand-colored aquatints, engraved in 1814 after watercolor paintings by Nicholas Pocock, portraying the battle that unfolded between USS *Constitution* and HMS *Java* on December 29, 1812.

As it turned out, she was HMS *Java*, a 38-gun frigate, seven weeks out of England and carrying the new lieutenant governor of Bombay, along with his sizeable entourage, to India. She also happened to be convoying both a merchant schooner and a captured prize. None of this was known aboard *Constitution*, of course. Those scrutinizing the oncoming vessel through their spyglasses had only to recognize the British colors waving from her masts to know that an enemy warship was bearing down upon them—and fast.

Shortly before noon a deadly dance began in earnest. A light breeze was blowing from the northeast, but the sea was little disturbed when *Constitution*, which had been approaching her enemy from the south, veered off to the southeast to stand away from land and get out of Brazilian territorial waters. *Java* hauled up and veered off, too, tracking the U.S. frigate on a parallel course to the north. She practically skimmed over the sea, such was her speed, so Bainbridge, as Hull and Decatur had done before him, tried using the superior range of his 24-pounders to trounce his opponent from a distance. But *Java*, superbly handled by her captain, Henry Lambert, waited until she was within the range of her own 18-pounders to fire. Her first broadside sundered spars, mangled rigging, and mowed down more than a few crewmen.

Moving faster and faster, *Java* closed the gap until gunners on both ships switched to grapeshot and small arms. A sharpshooter got Bainbridge in the hip, leaving blood seeping through his trousers. Just as *Java* promised to cross *Constitution*'s bow and rake her from stem to stern, a limping commodore ordered his own frigate to abruptly wear about in the smoldering air and run off to the west. *Java* wore as well, maintaining her position on *Constitution*'s weather beam. Again *Java* promised to cross *Constitution*'s bow, and again the U.S. frigate wore about, returning to a southeast course. *Java* mirrored her every move, once more surging into a position from which to rake *Constitution*'s bow. Suddenly, she wore into the wind and crossed *Constitution*'s stern instead, hurtling a broadside down the quarterdeck. Bainbridge was struck again, a stray shard of metal slicing through his thigh, and *Constitution*'s wheel was smashed to atoms. Bainbridge's ship couldn't be steered.

It was a critical moment. Leaning on a midshipman, Bainbridge gambled that *Java* wouldn't have time to capitalize on *Constitution*'s vulnerable state if he acted fast enough. While below decks crewmen feverishly rigged tackles to the tiller, their captain ordered the fore and main courses set and with that gust of speed let the wind carry him almost upon his enemy, who was just coming around through the smoke. Then Bainbridge unleashed his forecastle carronades, and those "smashers" carried away *Java*'s bowsprit, jibboom, and headsails in a cloud of canvas and splinters.

That stopped the British frigate's momentum just as *Constitution* regained her steering. The Americans' long hours at gunnery drill now began paying off: their aim was unerring, and their salvoes of shot ripped through *Java*'s hull and

challenged Greene to a single-ship duel. Though his vessel was about the equal of the U.S. one, and naval convention, in such circumstances, frowned on a refusal, the British captain nevertheless declined to relinquish the safety of a neutral port. The rumored reason, Lawrence soon heard, was that *Bonne Citoyenne* was carrying half a million pounds of government specie—coined money—in her hold.

Not wanting to lose such a valuable prize, Bainbridge had *Hornet* keep an eye on the port while he roamed the coast with *Constitution*. On the morning of December 29, 1812, while still in sight of land, lookouts high in the mastheads spotted two sails on the northern horizon, clearly making for Salvador. Within the hour, one of them turned in the direction of *Constitution*.

swept across her decks. Marine marksmen poured in a barrage of musket balls. Surrounded by dead and dying men, Lambert ordered the helm put aweather, and with the wind behind her *Java* came ploughing into *Constitution*, the jagged stub of her bowsprit slashing through her rival's mizzen shrouds.

As an attempt to board, the gambit failed. The marines kept up their fire, and sure hands heaved *Constitution*'s stern chasers around so that they shot pointblank down *Java*'s forecastle. The British ship's foremast was shot away, and her main topmast went, too. Her ruined bowsprit then slid rearward over *Constitution*'s taffrail, and Old Ironsides pulled free.

Java was now crippled. Her starboard guns were buried beneath the rubble of fallen masts and spars, and shooting through the debris only set the mess ablaze. *Constitution*, meanwhile, hadn't lost all maneuverability. As Bainbridge shouted steering directions down through a small grating, his broadside gunners furiously raked *Java* fore and aft. They "[s]hot away Gafft and Spanker Boom," Bainbridge wrote laconically in his journal. "Shot away his Mizen Mast nearly by the board." By late afternoon—"Having silenced the Fire of the Enemy completely"— he pulled *Constitution* out of battle and stood to windward, securing his own masts, all of which had taken a beating, and repairing his ragged rigging. Twelve men were dead or dying, while twenty-seven more, himself included, were wounded.

Unsure whether or not *Java*—or rather what remained of her—had struck, Bainbridge directed *Constitution* to make a cautious approach. A flag was indeed still bravely fluttering from the stump of *Java*'s mizzenmast.

> Got very close to the Enemy [Bainbridge wrote] in a very effectual Raking Position, athwart his Bows, and was at the very instance of Raking him, when he most prudently Struck his Flag; for had he suffered the Broadside to have Raked him, his additional Loss must have been extremely great, as he laid an unmanageable Wreck upon the Water.

It had all been eerily like *Constitution*'s last fight, and with the same result.

SURGEONS AT SEA

This mahogany medicine chest, fitted with a lock and carrying handle, was owned by surgeon Sir Benjamin Outram (1774–1856) and is said by his descendants to have been used at the Battle of Copenhagen (1801), Vice Admiral Horatio Nelson's "hardest fought" battle.

Among all the stores loaded into an early nineteenth-century warship, the wooden, brassbound medicine chests should have been considered as important as any single item of supply. Yet in 1812, when the U.S. frigate *Constitution* was refitting in Boston, her surgeon found himself reduced to bargaining with a local apothecary for medicines to fill his chest—despite waving an official requisition form. Though their positions had been established by law in 1794, naval surgeons and surgeon's mates ashore were caught in what William Barton, father of the Navy's hospital system and a former surgeon himself aboard the frigates *United States* and *President*, called "a perplexing and distressing situation." They suffered from bureaucratic neglect and were held in low esteem.

At sea, however, the surgeon was rarely idle, and his medicine chest was indispensible, for it held endless antidotes for all the ails that bedeviled life at sea. He had balms and plasters for bruised and sprained limbs, trusses for hernias, nippers to pull diseased teeth. Among his bottles and vials, he had unguents and ointments to ease a variety of ills, including salves and tinctures of mercury to treat the inescapable pox or syphilis—sometimes employing a brass syringe to inject them directly into a sailor's bladder.

He might even have had a remedy for scurvy, which for centuries had been killing more sailors than all other maladies, accidents, and wounds combined. In 1811, the reform-minded Barton sent a bottle of lime juice to Secretary of the Navy Paul Hamilton. He may not have known what a later generation discovered—that scurvy resulted from a deficiency of vitamin C—but citrus fruits had been proven to hold the scourge at bay, and Barton hoped that the U.S. Navy would institute a lime juice ration, as the Royal Navy had done in 1796, drastically reducing the incidence of scurvy on its ships.

Less enlightened methods, however, were still employed to fight infectious diseases. The surgeon might utilize a wicked-looking lancet to bleed those suffering from a range of maladies, including such killers as "ship fever" (typhus), malaria, and yellow fever. The object of bleeding was to readjust the body's internal equilibrium, the balance of its "humors," or vital fluids, a medical doctrine reaching back thousands of years to the ancient Greeks. A more effectual remedy for malaria was Peruvian bark, shavings from the South American cinchona tree, which contained quinine, but the dose was so bitter it was often washed down with wine.

Then there were the ominous knives, saws, cauterizing irons, screw tourniquets, and splints also secreted in the medicine chest or surgeon's kit. Battles may have been infrequent, but they could strew the decks with carnage. One enemy broadside after another might altogether hurl hundreds of solid shot into a warship, ripping men to pieces or tearing through the planking with clouds of lethal flying splinters. The wounded were hustled below to improvised aid stations, usually located in the cockpit or wardroom, stable central regions of a vessel well below the fighting decks. Powder-burned gunners or cutlass-slashed marines might be laid alongside men injured by bullets, splinters, or cannonballs. Without the benefit of any anesthesia (the only effective anodyne, or painkiller, being opium), the surgeon might amputate a shattered limb, cauterize the blood vessels, and wrap the stump before ten minutes had elapsed.

Wood and ivory scales from an 1808 medicine chest.

Above: A paper full of pins, which Swift used to hold things in place during surgery, and an ivory brush designed to sweep away bone dust when trepanning.

Left: Swift's dental key, used, as its name suggests, for extracting teeth.

Swift used this trephine for boring a hole in the skull to relieve pressure on the brain, a procedure known as trephining, or trepanning.

Below: This surgeon's kit belonged to William Swift (1779–1864), who graduated from Harvard Medical School in 1812 and served with the Navy from the time of his graduation until his retirement in 1861. He was serving with USS *Chesapeake* when she was defeated by HMS *Shannon* in a legendarily bloody battle off Boston's coast on June 1, 1813. The items in Swift's kit are typical of the tools of the trade during that era: amputation knives, bone saws, scalpels, and the sharpening stones with which to whet these blades; needles for stitching internal wounds; bullet probes and forceps; catheters and trocars for puncturing drainage holes in the bladder; sponges to sop up blood; and other crude essentials.

Dr. James Inderwick was surgeon aboard the U.S. brig *Argus* when she was captured off the British Isles by HMS *Pelican* after a fierce fight on August 14, 1813. The entries he made in his journal are all the more graphic for their brevity. "Mr. Rich'd Delphy, midshipman. Had both legs nearly shot off at the knees—he survived the action about three hours . . . Geo Gardiner, Seaman—His thigh taken off by a round shot close to his body, he lived about [half] an hour . . . Jn Finlay, Seaman—His head was shot off at the close of the action."

Argus' commander, Captain William Allen, had his "left knee shattered by a cannon shot. Amputation of the thigh was performed about 2 hours after the action—An anodyne was previously administered—An anodyne

at night." He died a few days later. Lieutenant Watson had part of "the Scalp on the upper part of the head torn off by a grape shot—the bone denuded. It was dressed lightly and he returned and took command of the deck." The boatswain received "a severe lacerated wound on the upper part of the thigh, a slight one on the face and a contusion on the right shoulder. Dressed simply with lint and roller Bandage." But the poor boatswain's mate had a "large wound thro the left thigh the bone fractured and splintered,—the back part of the right thigh carried off and nearly the whole of the fleshy nates [buttocks] carried away—Dressed with lint imbued with ol. olivar [medicinal olive oil]—gave him a large anodyne—repeated it at night—Case hopeless." He died the next morning.

Perhaps the most celebrated medical achievement of the war took place three weeks later during the Battle of Lake Erie. Surgeon's mate Usher Parsons was the only medical man not too ill to report for duty when Oliver Hazard Perry's nine ships defeated six British vessels on September 10, 1813. During the worst of the fighting, *Lawrence*, Perry's flagship, was so severely pummeled that most of her guns were wrecked and most of her crew killed or wounded. Sixty-one men were carried below decks to the small room, barely twelve by eighteen feet, where a blood-spattered Parsons was at work. "During the action, I cut off six legs in the cockpit, which were nearly divided by cannon balls," he later wrote. Overwhelmed, he soon had no time for further amputations. "I aimed only

to save life during the action by tying arteries or applying tourniquets to prevent fatal hemorrhage, and sometimes applying splints as a temporary support to shattered limbs." Cannons thundered above him, but since *Lawrence* had a shallow draft, the cockpit being situated at nearly surface level, they blasted at him as well. "Five cannon balls passed

Above: Lecture notebooks, from 1802–1803 and 1806, belonging to USS *Constitution*'s surgeon, Amos A. Evans. When or why Evans, who probably received only the rudiments of a formal education, decided to pursue the medical profession is unknown, but in the fall of 1802, at the tender age of seventeen, he began to attend lectures by pre-eminent Philadelphia physician Dr. Benjamin Rush. The subject of the ninety-nine lectures that Evans attended ranged from advice on siting hospitals to philosophical disquisitions on reproduction and longevity. He clung to every word, and his notebooks contain painstakingly written regurgitations of Rush's own words. Evans mostly took Rush's teachings at face value, adding little commentary of his own. Occasionally, though, the good doctor's musings provoked a rise in the young student: "The Doctor thinks that Latin & Greek languages [are] by no means essentially necessary to the study of medicine!!!" At other times, however, Rush's advice was quite practical: "A legible handwriting is particularly enforced, as serious mischief has been done by prescriptions being indistinctly written."

Below: Swift's amputation tourniquet stopped blood flow to the limb, preventing excessive bleeding.

through the room in which I was attending to the wounded," he recalled. "Midshipman Laub was moving from me with a tourniquet on his arm, when a cannon ball struck him in the breast; and a seaman brought down with both arms fractured was struck by a cannon ball in both legs."

When the fighting ended, Parsons accepted thirty additional wounded sailors from other ships in Perry's squadron. For several days, the young surgeon's mate amputated limbs, dressed wounds, and otherwise tended to nearly a hundred severely injured men, almost entirely alone. Only three of them died.

Due in no small part to such diligence, after the War of 1812, the Navy increased its efforts to create a more professional medical service, instituting qualifying examinations, building permanent hospitals ashore, and in 1842 establishing the Bureau of Medicine and Surgery, with the formidable William Barton as its first chief. A decade later, Dr. Usher Parsons, then one of the country's most renowned physicians, received the reward that meant the most to him. Visiting Cleveland, he encountered a man whose arm he had amputated, and whose life he had saved, some forty years earlier in the heat of the Battle of Lake Erie.

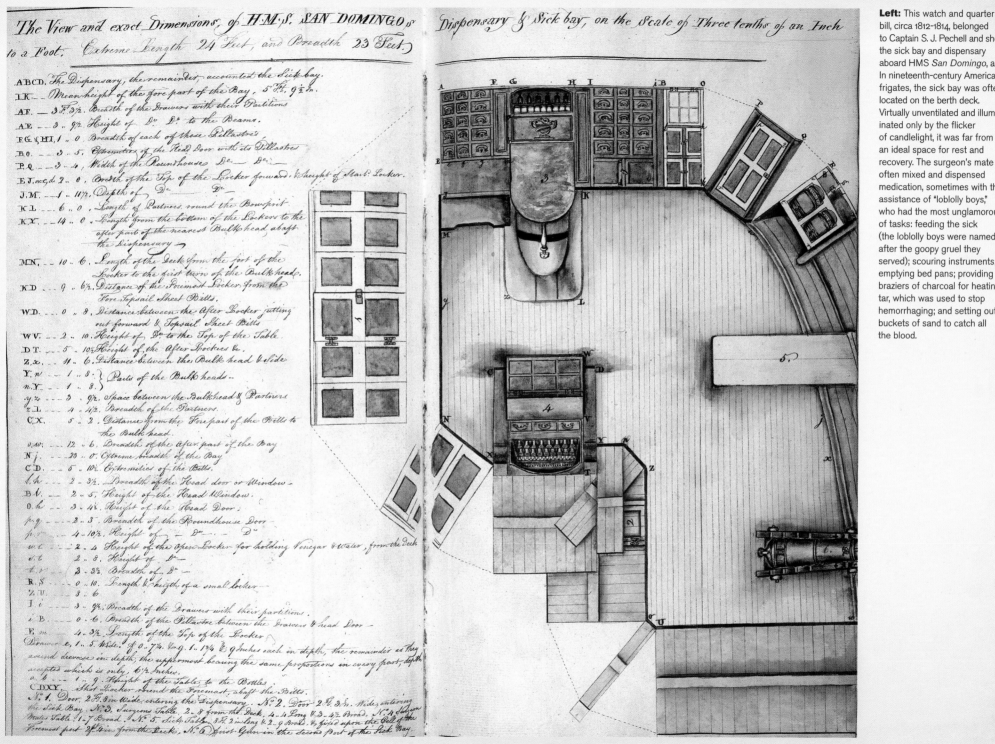

With every boat on *Java* and all but the cutter on *Constitution* reduced to fragments, it took the whole night, in the increasing swell, and much of the next day to transfer, one boatload at a time, more than a hundred wounded men and several hundred prisoners into the U.S. frigate's holds. They left behind them decks slick with the blood of their forty-eight fallen comrades. Lambert, shot in the chest, was in such bad shape he couldn't move.

Meanwhile, the conflict that had seen these men fight to the death in the isolation of a distant sea had been underway for only five months. In the United States, the Navy's plucky and surprisingly successful performance, honored with banquets and bunting and congressional gold medals, was the only bright spot in a war that otherwise looked to be veering toward disaster. The attempt to invade Upper Canada and hold it hostage until London renounced its maritime outrages had proved a dismal failure. Hastily assembled, poorly equipped armies had surrendered at Detroit and been repulsed along the Lake Champlain corridor, the natural invasion route from New York to Montreal. State militias had everywhere turned out to be undependable. Only the Navy had performed beyond all expectations.

Word of the victories of *Constitution* over *Guerrière* and *Essex* over *Alert* had helped to ensure Madison's reelection in November, and when that was followed up by news that *United States* had vanquished *Macedonian*, Congress voted in December to bankroll four 74-gun ships-of-the-line and six additional 44-gun frigates—an extraordinary about-face and a piece of legislation that would lay the basis for the nation's future fleet. While *Constitution* was crossing the equator, Hamilton, Bainbridge's friend, lost his job as secretary of the Navy; the pressures of the war had driven him to embrace the bottle even more than was his usual habit, and when pressured to do so by Madison, he agreed to resign by the end of the year.

Across the Atlantic, there was outright incredulity that the Royal Navy had lost not one but *two* frigates in single-ship encounters with the Americans. That this upset the ordained course of things was demonstrated by the alacrity with which Royal Navy officers, from Halifax to Portsmouth, London to Gibraltar, explained away such exceptional events. *Guerrière*'s timbers were rotten, they declared; she was overdue for refitting, that's why her mizzenmast fell.

A pennant from *Constitution*'s encounter with *Java*.

This dressing case, or "vanity box," belonged to Commodore William Bainbridge and was probably crafted by a Boston cabinetmaker, purportedly out of wood from USS *Constitution* following her engagement with HMS *Java*. The elegant case's interior, lined with rosewood veneers, was fitted with compartments, each originally containing a razor or strop, perfume bottles, scissors, tweezers, combs, and other grooming tools. Unlike the more public commemorative pieces celebrating Bainbridge's victory, this was a personal, private memorial to his success, one that reminded him of his achievements every time he shaved or combed his hair.

Such contests had been uneven, anyway. The U.S. frigates, with their 24-pounders and enormous crews, were really ships-of-the-line in disguise; didn't Carden of *Macedonian* describe *United States* as having been built on the "scantlings of a 74"?

Such protestations aside, in November the Sea Lords of the Admiralty had quietly prohibited any further ship-to-ship duels with U.S. frigates. More quietly still, they had ordered the construction of new British frigates that would mount 24-pounders and be laid along the lines of the U.S. ones.

Other officers looked the truth squarely in the face. "American success upon the water proves we are not invincible," declared one former Sea Lord, Admiral Philip Patton. That bald admission was more than many Englishmen could face with equanimity, so accustomed had they become to the assumed invulnerability of their protecting fleet. "In the name of God, what was done with this immense superiority of force!" bewailed the London *Times* on December 28. "Oh, what a charm is hereby dissolved!"

By the end of 1812, the Navy's little fleet had done the seemingly impossible—shattered the "sea spell," as the London *Times* bewailed, of the world's mightiest navy. Overnight, a few frigates had turned into iconic symbols of national pride. All the rage, naval imagery found its way into the fabric of everyday objects, gracing everything from pincushions to plateware. This tin snuff box, an early souvenir, depicts a starboard broadside view of USS *Constitution*.

Two days after that column was printed, faraway in the South Atlantic, a dying Captain Henry Lambert was being carefully hoisted aboard *Constitution*; he was the last man to be removed from the wreckage of yet a third British frigate.

However galling in the United Kingdom and stirring in the United States they might have been, such American triumphs had little strategic impact on the course of the war. They hardly dented, much less hulled, the massive Royal Navy, and only damaged the pride of its officers. Should the war continue, the weight of British numbers would inevitably be brought to bear. The U.S. Navy was already overstretched, and increasingly it was depending on hundreds of armed privateers to raid British commerce in the waters off Canada and the West Indies. Furthermore, Admiral Sir John Borlase Warren—since September the new commander of the Halifax, Leeward Islands, and Jamaica stations—had already mounted an effective blockade on the nation's southern ports, despite concentrating his limited resources on convoy protection and occasional coastal raiding. The Sea Lords in London had simply refused to send him reinforcements, as that meant stripping ships from the blockade of Napoleon's Europe.

Yet "Boney" was surely on the verge of defeat. On June 22, 1812— mere days after Congress had declared war against Great Britain—Napoleon had overreached himself by invading Russia. By December, when but a few frozen survivors of what had been the six-hundred-thousand-man Grand Armée staggered home barefoot through the snow, the sheer scale of that disaster was beginning to register. With the end of Napoleon imminent, the Sea Lords might very well shift the might of the Royal Navy across the Atlantic, sweeping the U.S. Navy from the seas.

If the British seized control of the Great Lakes, or if a British army marched down the Lake Champlain corridor and took New York, no number of victories on the open ocean would matter much anyway. The war would be lost.

That was the situation on December 31, when the frigates *President* and *Congress*, both badly in need of refitting and refurbishing, slipped into Boston Harbor. Rodgers was finishing yet another disappointing cruise, returning after three months with fewer than ten prizes, only one of which, the Jamaica packet *Swallow*, with its eighty-one boxes of gold and silver—some $200,000— was at all noteworthy. He sat down and penned a final report to the departing secretary of the Navy.

It will appear somewhat extraordinary when I inform you that in our late cruise we have sailed by our log nearly 11'000 Miles, that we chased every thing we saw, yet that we should have seen so few Enemies Vessels and more particularly when we have from time to time been in the track of his whole commerce to every part of the Globe.

In the hope of being afforded an opportunity of adding additional reputation to our little Navy, we did not return until I may say our Provisions were nearly indeed entirely expended.

DEDICATED BY PERMISSION TO THE RIGHT HONOURABLE THE LORDS COMMISSIONERS OF THE ADMIRALTY.
Plate 4.th The JAVA in a Sinking state, set fire to, & Blowing up. The CONSTITUTION at a distance a head, Laying to, unbending Sails, repairing her Rigging &c. in the Evening of 29.th Dec.r 1812.

That same day, five thousand miles to the south, Bainbridge had done his part to augment that reputation. He would now stand in for Salvador, there parole his several hundred shackled prisoners, instruct Lawrence and *Hornet* to keep watching *Bonne Citoyenne*, and then set a course for home. Only he would not be taking a trophy with him. Deeming *Java* too wrecked to attempt such a long passage, he ordered her burned instead. Watching the British frigate go up in flames, the men of *Constitution* had in only five months learned what the proud fleets of Europe had failed to discover—they had learned, in Theodore Roosevelt's words, "a way to do more damage than we received in a naval contest with England." When late that afternoon *Java* finally exploded, it made for a spectacular ending to that little Navy's most remarkable of years—1812.

CHAPTER TWO

Part of an ensign that *Chesapeake* was flying when she met Shannon off the coast of Boston. *Chesapeake* was wearing three ensigns that June day, in case one or more got shot away. Observing this spectacle as the American frigate drew near, a British tar turned to his captain and asked, "Mayn't we have three ensigns, sir, like she has?" The modest Sir Philip Bowes Vere Broke firmly replied, "No, we've always been an unassuming ship." And it was that unassuming ship whose single ensign was left waving. As for *Chesapeake*'s ensigns, one was taken in battle by the British, who wrapped James Lawrence's body in it after he breathed his last during the passage to Halifax. This is all that remains of that flag—a fifteen-star canton with two stripes still attached. The bunting is made of silk and cotton, the stars of linen, and the hoist of silk.

Overlay: South Sea whalers boiling blubber, with a whale alongside. During his Pacific cruise, Captain David Porter made many detailed observations about sperm whaling. "When the whale is killed and brought alongside the ship," he wrote in his journal, "the separating the head from the body, baling the liquid oil or head matter from the case which contains it, and flinching the whale, or separating the blubber or thick fat from the carcass, as well as trying out the oil, cooling, straining, starting it below, coopering the casks, and frequently wetting and examining them, are all laborious operations, and which it is sup-posed everyone who undertakes to conduct the voyage must be acquainted with, before he engages in the business. If the voyage is successful, everything that can be made to contain oil is filled with it, even to the buoys of their anchors, jugs, cans, kids, and buckets."

"EVERY SHIP IN CHACE"

THE WAR AT SEA

1813

"HIS COMMERCE IS OUR TRUE GAME, FOR THERE HE IS INDEED VULNERABLE."

~ Secretary of the Navy William Jones

The enemy sails had first appeared off Savannah and Charleston, where soon not even a coaster, much less a merchant vessel, whatever its flag, was permitted entrance or exit. Like a red tide those sails gradually appeared farther and farther north, off the coast of North Carolina, then off the entrance to the Chesapeake Bay, until by early 1813 they were reaching New York. The long-awaited, much-feared blockade was arriving.

The Sea Lords of the Admiralty had not wanted a war with their former colonies. Their first instinct was to starve them into terminating it—that, and to bottle up their navy in port while chasing down their few vessels still at sea. All that was left was to convoy their own merchant fleet, and that was the Royal Navy's strategy for defeating the Americans in 1813.

Imposing an economic blockade was a complex operation. By international agreement, Britain not only had to declare, as the wording customarily went, "the whole of the said Harbours, Bays, Rivers, Creeks, and Sea Coasts" of a given area "to be in a state of strict and rigorous Blockade," but also had to prove it

could enforce that decree by stationing a naval force "adequate and sufficient" to enforce it. And finally, it had to "caution and forbid" the ships of every other nation from "entering, or attempting to enter, or from coming out, or attempting to come out of any of the Ports, Harbours, Bays, Rivers or Creeks before-mentioned, under any Pretence whatsoever."

Notwithstanding its difficulties, Admiral Sir John Borlase Warren, commander in chief of the North American Station, still managed, as one month slipped into another, to extend that vise-like blockade ever northward. Only New England was at first spared, partially to reward the Federalists' antiwar stance and to keep a thriving contraband trade furnishing British armies, and partially because it was just so difficult to maintain a station there, especially during the winter, when the nor'easters were unendurable. "The blockade of the American coast was kept up with ever increasing rigor," Theodore Roosevelt wrote a century later. "The British frigates hovered like hawks off every seaport . . . On the northern coasts in particular, the intense cold of the furious winter gales

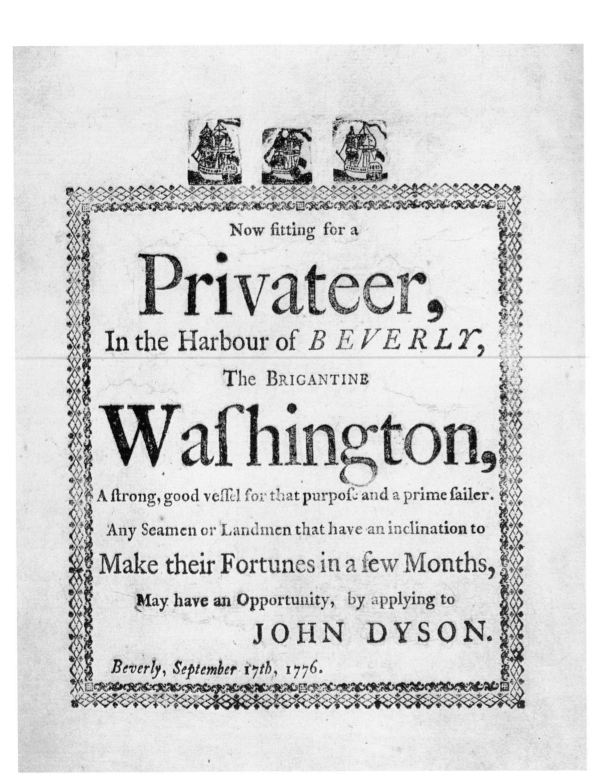

rendered it no easy task to keep the assigned stations; the ropes were turned into stiff and brittle bars, the hulls were coated with ice, and many, both of men and officers, were frost-bitten and crippled."

Everywhere else, though, the blockade had its desired effect. "Commerce is becoming very slack," wrote a Baltimore resident in the spring of 1813, "no arrivals from abroad, and nothing going to sea but sharp vessels." Those sharp—meaning fast—vessels were usually blockade runners or privateers, sleek fore-and-aft rigged craft that could sail into the wind on the dark of the moon and outrun the patrolling squadrons.

"The people in the Eastern States are laboring almost night and day to fit out privateers," one newspaper noted on July 1, 1812. As the British had suspected, the owners of every pilot boat or coasting vessel that could mount a gun were seeking a letter of marque and put to sea as their fathers had done during the Revolution. Within a matter of months, more than 150 privateers were on the prowl—carrying ten thousand sailors and a thousand guns, a considerable augmentation of a navy whose seventeen vessels altogether carried fewer than 450 guns. By the end of 1812, Warren was reporting that no fewer than six hundred letters of marque had been issued.

Though sturdily patriotic, most privateers kept an eye cocked for profit, too. *Highflyer* from Baltimore snagged prizes valued at $187,000 in a matter of weeks before being snapped up by a 74-gun ship-of-the-line. In five months, the Salem-based *America* brought in six prizes worth $158,000. And on two cruises—one between July and October and the other from December to March—*Comet*, also from Baltimore, had cut such a swath through British merchant shipping that she was fast making her captain—Thomas Boyle, epitome of the charming rogue—a very feared man indeed.

But as valuable as they might have been, there were also problems with privateers. They were largely outside the Navy's control—metaphorically loose cannons—and the more unscrupulous captains and crews verged on outright piracy—overhauling, boarding, and plundering vessels without distinction. That's what Captain John Sinclair of *General Armstrong* accused his crew of doing after they mutinied on him. The crew, however, had its own grievance, put to paper on March 18, 1813, when, eleven days out of the Cape Verdes and short on food, they handed Sinclair a written protest sealed with sixty-three signatures.

> Great discontent (and God knows not without sufficient cause) which has for some time past prevailed on board, among officers and men. STARVATION now staring us in the Face, for we are fully convinced your intention is to go on the coast of Africa. Langor and weakness already having possession of half of the crew . . . induces us to apprise you that we are aware of the situation we are likely to be placed in . . . Why did you not purchase (for you said you could) sufficient supplies at Brava? And not attempt to gull us with the story of a "British Squadron being off those Isles" . . . [T]he first law in nature bids us shape our course home . . . The crisis demands that we go to the Westward and the prospect far better, both for owners and crew . . . [W]e trust you will shape our course toward the United States . . . in so doing, we are willing and at all times ready to obey your commands.

But they didn't obey his commands, for when *General Armstrong* docked at Wilmington, North Carolina, on April 17, Sinclair was in chains. Eventually, the crew was arrested, but they managed to escape prosecution anyway.

Privateers were also prone to making deadly mistakes. Commodore John Rodgers was just back from his second cruise when Boston merchants, their coasting trade under the menace of a British privateer from Nova Scotia, raised funds to build *Commodore Hull*, which was given to Rodgers as an auxiliary naval vessel while *President* underwent refitting. But because there was no agreed-upon signaling system between government and private vessels, *Commodore Hull* was fired upon by privateer *Anaconda*, which mistook her for an enemy vessel, *Liverpool Packet*. A mutineer from *America* was also turned over to Rodgers; that privateer's captain had stamped out the insurrection while in the West Indies, chaining the chief malefactor below decks for several months until he returned to Salem. Rodgers demanded that he be given one hundred lashes for "Seditious and Mutinous Words."

The figurehead of the privateer *General Armstrong*. Late in the war, while taking on water and supplies in the neutral Azorean port of Fayal, Captain Samuel Reid was forced to scuttle his vessel when he found her suddenly surrounded by British warships. As the crew abandoned ship, a few defiant sailors stayed behind to rescue their old general. Under fire, they hacked him down and carried him to safety ashore. A kind of superstition surrounded figureheads, and sailors often chiseled away little fragments from these ornamental carvings to pocket as mementos or good luck charms. Damage to, or loss of, a figurehead was a bad omen, and sailing on a ship that lacked one made many a tar uneasy.

Opposite, left: Privateer recruiting posters similar to this one, which happens to be from the momentous year of 1776, could have been found in taverns, haberdasheries, and public squares up and down the Eastern Seaboard—Salem, Baltimore, and Norfolk were hot spots—during the second war of independence. Privateering kept the town of Salem, Massachusetts, afloat during the Revolution, and its merchants were quick to turn to that familiar enterprise when the War of 1812 broke out, arming and crewing almost a dozen vessels within days of receiving the war news.

Opposite, right: A standard letter of marque authorizing the private schooner *Lucy* to "subdue, seize and take any armed or unarmed British vessel, public or private, which shall be found within the jurisdictional limits of the United States ˙ or elsewhere on the high seas . . ."

"DEVILISH FAST"
The Baltimore Clipper

A model of an early Baltimore clipper, *Ann McKim*, named after her owner's beloved wife and launched in 1833 for the China tea trade. She is often thought of as the first true clipper.

Opposite: Renowned English ship portraitist James E. Buttersworth (1817-1894) created this striking scene of the Baltimore clipper *Flying Cloud* sailing off the Needles in the Isle of Wight, redolent of what writer Stephen Crane called "the silvered passing of a ship at night."

"Beautiful beyond anything then known in naval construction," in historian Henry Adams' opinion, the Baltimore clipper—sharp-hulled, clean-lined, and capped with long, raking masts—was the most famous privateer of the War of 1812. According to George Little, who captained several of them during the course of a long life at sea, the Baltimore clipper was "well armed and manned, and possessed a pair of heels, as report had it, that would outstrip the wind."

Although its origins have been variously traced to seventeenth-century prototypes in England, Bermuda, and Jamaica, the lithe vessel that Baltimore shipyards excelled at building stemmed directly from colonial antecedents common around the Chesapeake Bay. Though it was initially intended for coastal trade and voyages to the West Indies, commerce was only one of the two forces that shaped the clipper's evolving design. The other force was war—the incessant wars between England and France, which guaranteed that any merchantmen daring enough to trade American grain for West Indian sugar or rum would be menaced by one of these great naval powers, each ruthlessly trying to exterminate the other's colonial trade.

That placed a premium on a merchant's speed and elusiveness. The Baltimore clipper developed as a response to this need for swiftness. Its immense fore-and-aft rig, capped with topsails and even topgallants, was hoisted on whip-like masts, and its sharp-cut bows, low freeboard, and deep-set hull enabled it to sail close to the wind while "clipping" over the waves at a spry twelve knots.

These were also the qualities that made it an ideal blockade runner and privateer, roles it admirably fulfilled during the American Revolution. By the War of 1812, some Baltimore clippers stretched over one hundred feet in length and mounted upward of 16 guns. They raided British commerce with impunity because they could usually escape a pursuing warship by simply bending on more canvas. "The schooner," as Adams put it, "if she could only get to windward, laughed at a frigate."

Baltimore-built vessels became the scourge of British shipping. In only six days during the autumn of 1814, *Kemp*, off the North Carolina coast, took four of seven ships from a British convoy despite the best efforts of a Royal Navy frigate to protect them. Between 1812 and 1814, *Comet*, commanded by the famed Thomas Boyle, made twenty-seven captures on three cruises. During the final six months of the war, Boyle took command of *Chasseur*, the "Pride of Baltimore," capturing several dozen more prizes and, while cruising off the British Isles, issuing his famous one-ship blockade of the United Kingdom, which sent London's shipping insurance rates soaring.

One of the more celebrated warships of the young U.S. Navy was even a Baltimore clipper. Hardly had the 12-gun schooner *Enterprise* come down the ways at the Fells Point shipyard in 1799 when she was in the West Indies netting nineteen vessels during the Quasi-War with France. The only non-frigate to survive the naval cuts of 1801, *Enterprise* went on to serve with distinction throughout the First Barbary War. After she was rebuilt in 1809, however, one officer noted dolefully "that only an expert would have recognized in her the trim, fleet-winged schooner of 1801." Her tall, rakish masts had been removed and substituted with the "squat rig of a brig." That didn't stop her from defeating HMS *Boxer* on September 5, 1813, off the coast of Maine, although the action killed both commanding officers.

For decades following the end of the war, the Baltimore clipper led a lingering, if not slightly depraved, existence, becoming the choice vessel for pirates and smugglers, carrying illicit cargoes of opium to China and slaves to the Caribbean. Though it ceased being built around the midcentury, it bequeathed much of its character to ships with names like *Flying Cloud* and *Sea Witch* and *Lightning*—tall-sparred, sharp-lined, deep-drafted ships that, crowded with canvas and heeling to the wind, carried the clipper name into legend.

THE PRIVATEERS

"Militia of the Sea"

Hardly had war been declared in the summer of 1812 when all over the East Coast the owners of fast-sailing schooners and brigs were soon installing cannons, taking on crews, and putting to sea to fight the British. These private vessels had been commissioned to do so by the U.S. government, for each carried the one instrument that distinguished it from a pirate ship: an imposing, duly signed and stamped "Letter of Marque and Reprisal."

Since at least the sixteenth century, such official warrants, sanctioned by international law, had been issued by warring nations to augment their navies. Most of the world's major maritime powers—Great Britain, France, the Netherlands, Spain, all of which were incessantly fighting each other—authorized the arming and outfitting of privateers. During the American Revolution, such fleets greatly extended the reach of the tiny Continental Navy, and during the War of 1812, Yankee seamen weren't the only ones who were taking out letters of marque. Canadian sailors were, too. But operating from a base in Halifax, Nova Scotia, they were fighting for the British.

By 1812, a rough distinction was often made between letter of marque vessels—merchantmen authorized to mount guns mostly, though not exclusively, for self-defense while otherwise carrying on business as best they could—and true "privateers"—those who had gone to sea primarily to attack enemy commerce, motivated as much by the prospect of profit as patriotism. Provided he had that signed and stamped document in his possession, a privateer could lawfully claim any enemy ship he captured as a prize, subject to adjudication by a duly constituted prize court. The potential value of even a single merchant ship and cargo, much less a number of them, could be very alluring, for half of such proceeds would go to the ship's owners, and half would be divided among the captain, officers, and crew. In order to ensure that nothing hampered such payments, some owners chose to reinforce the rules already stipulated by the letter of marque. The captain of *General Armstrong*, for example, was enjoined to be "very particular in strictly prohibiting any plunder or depredations on neutrals or other vessels."

Though privateers slipped out of harbors up and down the coast, they were especially associated with New York and Baltimore. New York alone provided 102 ships, mounting 698 guns and manned by nearly 5,900 men. In one seven-month period, these ships captured some seven hundred prizes. In one cruise lasting longer than a year, the New York-based *Scourge* captured twenty-seven prizes. *General Armstrong* was not far behind with twenty-four prizes. But no port was as closely associated with privateering as was Baltimore—that "nest of pirates" to the British. Even George Washington owned a share in a Baltimore privateer during the Revolution. Joshua Barney had been a young officer in the Continental Navy during that war; by the summer of 1812, he was the 53-year-old dean of privateers, captain of the Baltimore-built *Rossie*, which by October had seized prizes worth $1.5 million, plus more than two hundred prisoners. The jaunty Thomas Boyle, perhaps the most famous of the war's privateers, captured twenty-nine prizes in *Comet* before moving, in 1814, to the larger *Chasseur*, which after numerous exploits, including the capture of seven ships in one day, was crowned the "Pride of Baltimore."

Boyle would become famous for proclaiming a mock "blockade" of the British Isles enforced by *Chasseur* alone. But in truth swarms of privateers infested those seas, where the merchant pickings were best. In just one month in the summer of 1813, for example, *True-Blooded Yankee* captured twenty-seven vessels off the British Isles, ranging impudently into the bay of Dublin, briefly capturing an island off Ireland, and seizing a town in Scotland.

Privateers dared to be so bold because they could flee from any British warship, unless the weather was blowing from a quarter favoring the larger sails of a man-of-war. Though some indeed fell prey to the Royal Navy, others, surprisingly, acquitted themselves quite well.

Captain Dominique Diron, the rumbustious Frenchman, commanded the Charleston privateer *Decatur*, carrying six 12-pounder carronades, one 18-pounder long gun, and 103 men, "chiefly if not all Blacks & Mulattoes," according to one British account. In August 1813, *Decatur* became one of only a few privateers to take a Royal Navy vessel mostly by boarding. In a furious hand-to-hand battle resembling something out of a pirate tale, Diron's men captured HMS *Dominica*, killing or wounding three quarters of her crew.

On February 27, 1815, Thomas Boyle and *Chasseur* captured a Royal Navy sloop-of-war—by accident. Boyle had closed within pistol shot of what appeared to be a lightly armed merchantman in the Florida Strait. The potential prize suddenly opened a row of ten gun ports and fired a broadside, proving that she was instead HMS *St. Lawrence*, her men concealed behind bulwarks. Yet in the short but severe fight that followed, Boyle managed to outshoot and outmaneuver his opponent, watching the "blood run freely from her scuppers," as he noted in his log, before accepting her surrender.

Another shadowy French privateersman, a certain Captain Ordronaux, commanded the 17-gun *Prince de Neufchâtel*. This sleek vessel, which had outrun numerous Royal Navy warships in her career, was off Nantucket Shoals on October 11, 1814, when she encountered the 50-gun frigate HMS *Endymion*. Both vessels were becalmed by nightfall, so *Endymion*'s captain, under cover of darkness, attacked the raider with 120 men in five boats. *Prince de Neufchâtel* was quickly surrounded, and the British

Cutter	Jefferson	30 m	Capt.	
Sch	Fame	30 m	"	Webb
	Fair Trader	35 m	"	
Cutter	Polly	60 m	Capt.	Samuel C. Hardy
Sch	Dolphin	50 m	"	Jacob Endicott
Sch	Regulator	50 m	"	Mansfield
Sch	Buckskin	50 m	"	Bray
Sch	Active	25 m	"	Pattison
Ship	John	160 m	"	John Crowninshield
Sch	Alfred		"	Williams
Sch	Dart		"	Davis
Brig	Montgomery		"	Hollis Breed
Ship	Tickler		"	
Sch	Fame		"	Skipper Green
				Chapman
Ship	Alexander	155 m	"	Millman
Brig	Thorn	148	"	
Ship	America		"	Ropes
Sch	Revenge		"	Sinclair
Sch	Growler		"	Saml B Graves

No. 216 — PORTSMOUTH.

Share in Privateer brig Portsmouth.

THIS CERTIFIES, That *Thomas Sullivan* will be entitled to *One eighth* Share of half the prizes which may be taken, or Prize Money which may accrue on the *Second* cruize of the Privateer Portsmouth, according to the stipulations made in the articles of agreement between the Officers and Crew of said Portsmouth, provided the said *Thomas Sullivan* goes out in said brig and performs his duty during the cruise.

This Certificate is transferable in whole or in part, to the order of the said *Sullivan*.

Wm Shaw } AGENT

I do hereby sell, assign and convey the above *One eighth* Share to *Roger Moran* ———— having received *Twenty five* dollars ———— cents therefor.

Portsmouth, *Oct 31* 1814

Attest *Patrick T. Cahill*

Thomas Sullivan

attempted to board—only to meet an eye-gouging, cutlass-wielding, hand-to-hand resistance from her thirty-seven defenders, who killed or wounded more than twice their own number before driving the British off and managing to escape. She was captured two months later, though it took four British frigates to do so.

In the most celebrated tale of privateer valor, Captain Samuel Reid had taken *General Armstrong* into the port of Fayal in the Portuguese Azores when, on September 26, 1814, she was trapped there by a Royal Navy squadron, happening by on its way to join the fleet assembling for the invasion of New Orleans. With no time to blockade the privateer in the port, the British simply violated Portuguese neutrality and attacked the American vessel where she was berthed. Yet day after day, Reid and his men, employing everything from cannon and grapeshot to pikes and pistols, repulsed hundreds of boarders, inflicting frightful losses each time. Enraged, the British kept coming, forcing Reid to scuttle his ship and retreat to an abandoned convent. There he fought them off for several more days before being saved by Portuguese intervention. It was once widely believed that this heroic stand so delayed the British squadron from meeting the fleet that Andrew Jackson had time to prepare his defenses. Though some historians doubt that was the case, Old Hickory himself declared, "If there were no battle of Fayal, there would be no battle of New Orleans."

Despite such instances of bravado, the issuing of letters of marque was already on the ebb. Although privateers were sometimes called the "Militia of the Sea," in truth they weren't often employed in defensive roles. Even as raiders they often fell short. At least 526 American privateers operated during the war, but only 207 ever captured a prize. Then again, perhaps half of the 1,344 merchantmen that were taken were soon recovered by the British. Many privateers didn't even clear their expenses, leading an exasperated Congress to relax customs duties on prize cargoes to help tide them over. On balance, therefore, the U.S. Navy cruisers, few though they were, performed more admirably as commerce raiders.

By 1856, when the Declaration of Paris was signed, most of the world had agreed that privateering caused naval powers more trouble than the letters of marque were worth, and with that international agreement the system was largely abolished. But because privateers had still formed an invaluable seagoing auxiliary in the War of 1812, the Navy Department long granted the equal of navy pensions to citizen-sailors who had been disabled in that struggle, as well as to the widows and orphans of those who had lost their lives.

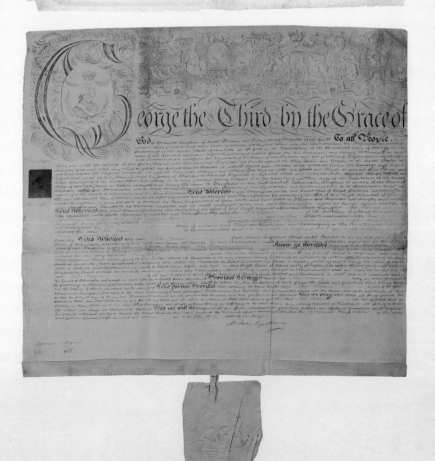

George the Third by the Grace of
To all People

HEAVY WEATHER

In early 1813, though, Rodgers was more concerned with the Navy, and with his own professional embarrassment. He had cruised "upwards of 13,000 miles—indeed actually circumnavigated the whole western Atlantic Ocean," he wrote to Minerva, without managing to find or capture more than a few British ships. "I am mortified," he admitted, "particularly in times like the present when a man's merit is measured by his good luck."

Rodgers, however, was exactly the kind of commander that the new secretary of the Navy, William Jones, would come to value. President James Madison had selected the Philadelphia merchant, former congressman, and prominent War Hawk to replace the outgoing Paul Hamilton not only because of his administrative ability but also because he had actually trod the quarterdeck as a sea captain, having been a privateer during the Revolution.

Jones, who had no patience for individual heroics, also had no illusions about the challenges he faced. A force already stretched too thin would have to stretch even more. Although Congress had authorized the construction of four 74-gun ships-of-the-line—including *Franklin* at Philadelphia, *Washington* at Portsmouth, and *Independence* at Charleston—and upward of six more 44-gun frigates, with such triumphal names as *Guerriere* and *Java*, that would prove a real burden to yards that would also have to supply men and material for a frantic shipbuilding race on the Great Lakes.

The war at sea would prove equally challenging. The British would attempt to capture or confine to port what few cruisers his little navy possessed. Those still at sea were starting to return. He would have to get them out again, but they would all need extensive refitting first, none more so than *Argus*.

Argus had struggled back into New York in early January, ten weeks after parting company with *United States* in mid-October in the mid-Atlantic. Since then it had been, as Master Commandant Arthur Sinclair reported, "a long, unpleasant, and, considering the track I have taken, unsuccessful cruise."

At first he had set a course far to the windward of Barbados, hoping to fall in with British merchantmen sailing north from Brazil who might not yet know a war was on. But the closer he had approached Cape St. Roque, the fewer the sails on the horizon, so he had turned about and, running low on water and provisions and under orders not to reprovision except in a homeport, struck out for the United States. Met, however, by "one continued and heavy gale of Wind," *Argus* began showing her age in every joint, leaking all over the place, even in the magazine, wardroom, and captain's quarters. Her provisioning situation had become dire; men and officers both were down to four ounces of bread every twenty-four hours. The water was even more strictly rationed. "Thirty of forty of those poor improvident fellows have resorted to drinking saltwater," Sinclair reported, "which has completely knocked them up, and some of them have been rendered delirious."

It was a bad time to encounter a squadron of six British frigates and ships-of-the-line. But somehow, after a nerve-wracking three-day chase, which took *Argus* several hundred miles off course, the sloop, throwing her boats and spars overboard, had managed to elude them—as she did so snapping up one of them as a prize. Then she had lain hove-to outside New York for days until the gales subsided long enough for her to limp into port.

A PLUME FOR JAMES LAWRENCE

Then Rodgers had to swallow another tale of triumph. On March 19, after some 145 days, *Hornet* returned home.

In early January, Bainbridge and *Constitution* had left Master Commandant James Lawrence and *Hornet* blockading *Bonne Citoyenne* in the harbor at Salvador, Brazil. They had maintained that station for nearly three more weeks, the British captain meanwhile refusing Lawrence's challenges to come forth and fight, until on January 24 the ominous bulk of HMS *Montague*, a 74, hove into view. *Hornet*, too, scurried for the safety of a neutral harbor, but when darkness fell she made good her escape.

Having gained the open sea, Lawrence managed to capture a small British brig sailing from Rio, and before burning her removed her cargo, including $23,000 in specie, perhaps some consolation for having to abandon *Bonne Citoyenne* with a treasure chest worth half a million pounds. Then he was cruising past the steamy, jungle-choked, reef-strewn coast of Surinam, on a course for the West Indies and home, when he encountered, on February 24, just outside the fort guarding the entrance to Demerara—soon to become Georgetown, Guyana—a Royal Navy brig at anchor. Hardly had that registered when his lookouts descried a second one, approaching close-hauled to the wind from the northeast.

Quickly clearing for action and hoisting his colors, Lawrence had recovered sufficiently to exchange broadsides with the oncoming foe as the two ships passed. He then wore round and managed to loosen his starboard broadside before both were running before the wind. Lawrence then simply outmaneuvered his opponent, gaining his starboard quarter and pounding him with one devastating broadside of grapeshot after another while marksmen in the tops poured down withering volleys of musket balls. The British vessel simply couldn't bring her guns to bear, and she was decimated in less than fifteen minutes. A waving hat signaled her surrender, as the masts bearing her colors had been knocked down.

She turned out to be HMS *Peacock,* and she was sinking fast. Her captain,

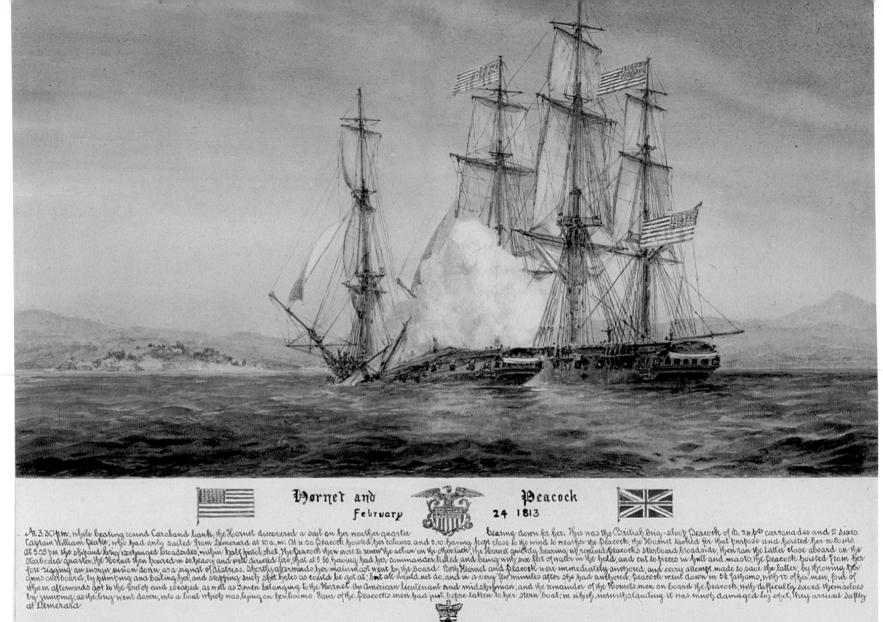

Hornet and Peacock
February 24 1813

At 3.30 p.m, while beating round Caroband bank, the Hornet discovered a sail on her weather quarter, bearing down for her. This was the British brig-sloop Peacock of 16, 24-pdr carronades and 2 sixes. Captain William Peake, who had only sailed from Demerara at 10 a.m. At 11.20 Peacock hoisted her colours, and 5.10 having kept close to the wind to near her the Peacock, the Hornet tacked for that purpose and hoisted her colours. At 5.25 p.m she ship and brig exchanged broadsides, within half pistol shot, the Peacock then wore to renew the action on the other tack, the Hornet quickly bearing up received Peacock's starboard broadside, then ran the latter close aboard on the starboard quarter, the Hornet then poured in so heavy and well directed fire, that at 5.50 having had her commander killed and being with six feet of water in the hold, and cut to pieces in hull and masts, the Peacock hoisted from her fore-rigging an ensign, union down, as a signal of distress. Shortly afterwards her mainmast went by the board. Both Hornet and Peacock were immediately anchored, and every attempt made to save the latter, by throwing her guns overboard, by pumping and bailing her, and stopping such shot holes as could be got at; but all would not do, and in a very few minutes after she had anchored, Peacock went down in 5½ fathoms, with 13 of her men, four of whom afterwards got to the fore top and escaped, as well as 3 men belonging to the Hornet. An American lieutenant and midshipman, and the remainder of the Hornet's men on board the Peacock, with difficulty saved themselves by jumping, as the brig went down, into a boat which was lying on her booms. Four of the Peacock's men had just before taken to her stern boat: in which, notwithstanding it was much damaged by shot, they arrived safely at Demerara.

William Peake, had been wounded by splinter and ball before a solid shot instantly ended his life. Much of his crew had also been killed or wounded. Though she mounted sixteen 24-pound carronades, it would turn out that the appropriately named Peake had ordered no gunnery practice for the last three years. Those guns were being tossed overboard as fast as possible anyway, as were the anchors and anything else of weight while men pumped and plugged in the fast-descending tropical twilight. They didn't make it; *Peacock* went under, carrying with her thirteen British and three American seamen.

There was nothing to be done for them, so *Hornet*'s crew repaired their own vessel and escaped before dawn arrived and that other brig came into action. She was now carrying 277 men, including prisoners and redeemed American privateers that *Peacock* had been carrying—but as *Hornet*'s own men had already been on a two-thirds allowance of rations, and the holds held only 3,400 gallons of water, Lawrence had no choice but to head straight home, finally docking in New London to a hero's welcome.

That left one American cruiser still at sea.

FEMALE MARINES AND SAILORS
Legend and Real

The idea of women serving in the military struck Americans of the time as a curiosity, and so an 1815 booklet entitled *The Female Marine* circulated soon after the war. Ascribed to Lucy Brewer, it pretended to tell the story of a young woman who joined the Marines, dressing as a man and calling herself George Baker, to escape a Boston brothel. The pamphlet describes her service through a full stint in the Marines without being found out. Her story and several sequels became bestsellers; young women saw Baker as a pioneering heroine. Later, it was discovered that Brewer's story was a fiction written by a Boston scribe named Nathaniel Coverly. The original 1815 pamphlet, bound on thin paper and smaller than a four-by-six index card is held by the Library of Congress.

The Lucy Brewer fiction notwithstanding, there are authenticated cases of women who did serve in the war, although some of their names have been lost to history. As early as September 1812, navy surgeon Usher Parsons, accompanying sailors headed for service on the Great Lakes, noted in his diary, "We this day discovered among the crew a female clad in sailor's apparel." He did not give her name.

Later, among the American squadron captured on Lake Champlain in 1813, Eliza Romley of Ipswich, New Hampshire, showed up on a list of prisoners in the prisoner-of-war camp at Québec. As Prisoner No. 240, Bromley was described as nineteen years old; five feet six inches tall; with brown hair, blue eyes, a tan complexion, and a scar on her upper lip. She arrived at the camp with other sailors taken from *Growler* and *Eagle* after a hard-fought battle on June 3, 1813. Romley spent weeks in detention with the other prisoners before British officers discovered she was a woman and released her.

A third American woman sailor documented in the book *In the Midst of Alarms*, by Dianne

ANNE JANE THORNTON,
THE
FEMALE SAILOR.

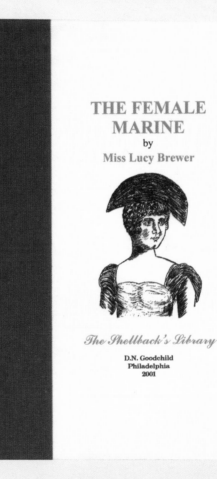

THE FEMALE
MARINE
by
Miss Lucy Brewer

The Shellback's Library

D.N. Goodchild
Philadelphia
2001

Left: *The Female Marine*, first published in 1815. A peculiar piece of early Americana, this puzzling little booklet, more than just a pamphlet but neither a novel nor a short story, eludes literary classification. It is the spirit in which Lucy Brewer's tale is told, however, that gives it a lasting quality.

Far left: Lucy's British counterpart, Anne Jane Thornton, a real woman from Donegal who posed as a boy to go to sea in pursuit of a lost lover. Thornton was eventually found out, but the captain of the London-bound ship aboard which she masqueraded as sailor Jim Thornton later sang her praises. "She did the duty of a seaman without a murmur and had infinitely a better use of her hands than her tongue," the captain reported. "She performed to admiration. She would run up the topgallant sail in any sort of weather and we had a severe passage. Poor girl, she had a hard time of it, she suffered greatly from the wet but she bore it all excellently and was a capital seaman."

Graves, served with the American privateer *Revenge*, captured by the British in 1813. "She has about $200 in wages and prize money and wants to be sent home to the United States," reported *Niles' Weekly Register*. "She has a comely face, sunburnt as well as her hands; and appeared when in men's clothes, a decent well-looking young man."

While women could not serve openly in the military then, they could by the end of the war serve as nurses. Stephen Decatur was among the first officers to authorize female nurses in Navy vessels, and two women, Mary Marshall and Mary Allen, served aboard the U.S. frigate *United States* in that capacity for several months. Their names can be found in the ship's log for May 10, 1813.

She was a Salem vessel from stem to stern—built and paid for by the citizens of Salem and surrounding Essex County in 1799—and because Salem rivaled neighboring Boston as one of the country's most prosperous seaports, its proud merchant fleets returning laden with goods from around the world, any Salem-built vessel would surely prove to be a wanderer.

The U.S. subscription frigate *Essex*, with 32 guns, had quickly lived up to expectations. In 1800, she had been the first ship in the Navy to sail south of the equator and around Africa's Cape of Good Hope. Thirteen years later— hatches battened down, guns lashed in the hold, tossing under bare poles with only the jib set, the towering seas crashing over her decks—she also became the first one to beat her way around Cape Horn, embarked on the most extraordinary voyage of the war.

A bone model of the frigate *Essex* made by a French prisoner of war in the early nineteenth century.

It had started as a stormy one. After escaping from the Delaware River in October 1812, *Essex* had encountered heavy gales, shipping so much water that many barrels of provisions were spoiled. So by the time she reached the Cape Verdes off Africa a month later, she was already in desperate need of reprovisioning, a problem that would dog her captain, David Porter, for the rest of the voyage.

Porter's orders had called for him to rendezvous at sea with the other ships—the frigate *Constitution* and the sloop *Hornet*—that made up Commodore William Bainbridge's squadron. Together they were going to round the Cape of Good Hope and raid British commerce in the Indian Ocean. But when *Essex* eased into Porto Praya, the chief port of the Cape Verdes and one of the assigned rendezvous points, there was no sign of *Constitution*. Since the Cape Verdes belonged to Portugal, nominally an ally of Britain, Porter felt fortunate enough to be able to stock his ship with a bounty of provisions, though casks of water were scarce. They took plantains, cocoa nuts, and scurvy-staving oranges, lemons, and limes, as well as pigs, sheep, fowl, and fine turkeys. More than a few monkeys and goats also found their way aboard, as pets, and when *Essex* stood off for Brazil, her little menagerie along for the ride, "she bore no slight resemblance . . . to Noah's ark."

Weeks without taking the first prize—after capturing ten of them during the war's opening weeks—soon began to gnaw at a crew that many in the Navy dismissed as being full of "hard cases." They did pick up a British packet, HMS *Nocton*, with $55,000 in specie, but that was it. The farther down the coast of Brazil *Essex* sailed, the fewer had been her prizes; the greater had been her unceasing need to replenish food and water (the water-guzzling pigs and goats were soon ordered slain, Porter receiving a flood of petitions "to save from slaughter a favorite kid, or a pig that had been destined for a Christmas dinner"); and the more elusive had been the news of *Hornet* and *Constitution*. Porter finally picked up rumors that an American sloop had been captured and that a great sea battle had been won by an American frigate, which had then turned north for home. If true, *Essex* was isolated deep in enemy-patrolled seas.

The Boston-born Porter, forty-two, did not panic easily. He had been in the Navy since 1798, had served aboard *Constellation* during her remarkable West Indies cruise against the French, and had been thrown into a Tripolitan dungeon during the Barbary Wars. What's more, he was an independent sort, forever in trouble with the naval establishment. Nevertheless, in February 1813, off the coast of Argentina, Porter had concluded that the only way to ward off starvation or capture was to press around the Horn and into the Pacific. There he might make war on the numerous British whalers—whose casks of oil lit the lamps of London—plying the waters between South America and the Galápagos Islands. The Pacific anyway had always called to him. He had read the accounts

of Cook and Dampier and d'Entrecasteux and all those Pacific explorers from a generation earlier. He, too, had a yearning to explore that all-embracing sea. A memo soon circulated among his crew.

SAILORS AND MARINES!

A large increase of the enemy's force compels us to abandon a coast that will neither afford us security nor supplies; nor are there any inducements for a longer continuance there. We will, therefore, proceed to annoy them, where we are least expected. What was never performed, by a single ship, we will attempt. The Pacific Ocean affords us many friendly ports. The unprotected British commerce, on the coast of Chili, Peru, and Mexico, will give you an abundant supply of wealth; and the girls of the Sandwich Islands, shall reward you for your sufferings during the passage around Cape Horn.

D. Porter

Meanwhile, a ship that had already sailed in all of the world's oceans was outfitting in Portsmouth, England. HMS *Phoebe*, captained by James Hillyard, was to escort an East Indies-bound convoy as far as Brazil. After that, her mission was to proceed to Oregon, where the Northwest Company feared American encroachment on its fur empire. That would bring her around the Horn into the Pacific, too.

Above: Shortly before the outbreak of war, Captain David Porter penned this letter in support of William P. C. Barton's protracted campaign to make citric juice a mandatory antiscorbutic—in place of pickles and vinegar—aboard U. S. Navy vessels. In preparing *Essex* for her cruise, Porter acquired as much lime juice as his frigate could stow. Nevertheless, it would prove trying to keep scurvy at bay during the long cruise.

Left: An oil portrait of a stoic-looking Captain David Porter, possibly painted by renowned Revolutionary War artist John Trumball.

ASHORE AND AFLOAT
Procurement and Its Challenges

"In truth, a man-of-war is a city afloat," wrote Herman Melville in the 1840s, recalling his service aboard the frigate *United States*, a city "with long avenues set out with guns instead of trees, and numerous shady lanes, courts, and by-ways." On any given day there was visible "every trade in operation on the gun-deck—coopering, carpentering, tailoring, tinkering, blacksmithing, rope-making, preaching, gambling, and fortune-telling." The quarterdeck resembled a "grand square, park, or parade ground, with a great Pittsfield elm, in the shape of the mainmast, at one end, and fronted at the other by the palace of the Commodore's cabin." There were even bells to toll the hours, eight bells meaning a change of the watch—and a meal.

The crewmen wolfed their gruel and downed their grog on canvas tarpaulins spread between the guns. The boatswain, carpenter, sailmaker, gunner, and other hands-on warrant officers—the sergeants of the ship—messed together in their quarters. The captain dined by himself in splendor, while his lieutenants took their meals in the wardroom, joined by the sailing master and the ship's three civil officers: the surgeon, the chaplain, and the purser—the man whose job it was to ensure that everyone aboard was fed.

Though he wore the uniform of a naval officer, all the provisions and supplies on the ship, for which he alone was responsible, had been bonded to his personal account. If he did not keep scrupulously accurate books, his own livelihood was subject to forfeit. But he was more than a mere seagoing shopkeeper. All the ship's getting and spending was his preserve; as the ship's banker, financier, and paymaster, he was the arbiter of that little city's entire economy. He embodied afloat the complex network of activity ashore that had built, outfitted, and supplied the ship in the first place.

Up and down the coast, wherever a navy yard was found, a civilian naval agent was responsible for all of the yard's procurement. Harnessing a vast web of manufacturers large and small, from mills and foundries to chandlers, bakers, and seamstresses, the agent ordered, ensured delivery of, and paid for all of the cordage, cables, sails, paints, tar, naval stores, tools, anchors, spars, candles, clothing, and hammocks, as well as all of the casks of salted meat, dried vegetables, and "ship's bread," as the flattened, saucer-shaped biscuits that constituted the sailor's staff of life were called—most everything, that is, except for the weapons and ordnance needed to equip a warship.

Captains might come and go, but a purser often remained with a particular vessel. The entire system funneled down to him. He provisioned his ship, and once his ship put to sea, all her procurement needs fell on his shoulders.

Every week when under sail, the purser inspected hundreds of barrels of beef and pork, tons of stored ship's bread, crates of candles, and thousands of gallons of casked water, spirits, vinegar, and molasses that were stowed in the holds. He reported on their condition to the captain and was tasked with purchasing or otherwise obtaining fresh provisions whenever needed—and at sea, they were always needed, for the enemy was within as well as without.

Ship's bread, for instance, was usually infested with squirming weevils that resembled maggots, though they "only in a slight degree altered its qualities," as Captain David Porter blandly noted, facing far steeper procurement challenges than a few weevily biscuits during his seventeen-month cruise with the frigate *Essex*. Seamen chewing their ship's bread just had to accept the slimy, squiggly texture before hastily swallowing a mouthful. While beetles proliferated in the bread barrels, rats gnawed through every kind of container, ruining bread, meat, dried peas, and cartridges alike. Seawater, too, seeped into the holds,

A fine linen dress shirt that once belonged to Chew. It exhibits all the construction techniques typical of the period, including narrow felled seams, efficient use of selvedges, fine gathering, and minute stitches.

Opposite, right: A piece of nineteenth-century ship's bread, the staff of a sailor's life. The survival of this rock-hard biscuit is a testament to both its unpalatibility and its resistance to spoilage. A merchant sailor once wrote that "biscuits would make good protection for house roofs instead of slates that [are] commonly used, being much harder and consequently more durable." Nevertheless, hardtack was far from impervious to the gnawing of weevils and vermin.

United States Navy Department
To Samuel Thwing Jr. Dr.

1803.

To Bread d'ld for Frigate Constitution Viz.

July 27. To 50.0.0 Ship Bread @ 4.75 ... 237.50 ... $430.44
" " 42.3.14 ditto ... ditto @ 4.50 ... 192.94
92.3.14 All the above Bread
Jn'o S Deblois Purser

Boston July 30. 1803. Received from Samuel Brown Naval Agent Four hundred thirty Dollars 44/100 in full for the above Account for which I have signed duplicate Receipts —

Samuel Thwing jun'r

No.

BOSTON, Commonwealth of Massachusetts,

Sept 30. 1798

RECEIVED of HENRY JACKSON, Naval Agent for the United States, at Boston, Eight Dollars and Twenty nine cents in full for Surveying timber in the U S Navy yard Boston per bill —

for which I have signed triplicate Receipts of the same tenor and date.

Benj White

Right: Chew bought these moccasins while serving at Sackets Harbor. Abigail wrote to her husband in 1814 requesting that he pick up a present for their young son, James Lawrence, named after *Chesapeake*'s much-lionized captain, who'd died in his purser's arms. "If you can get little socks or the Indian shoes for him he would like some." It is likely that these moccasins are the ones that Chew managed to obtain. They are made of deerskin with integral cotton leggings.

spoiling even more rations. Wastage of approximately seven percent of stored provisions came to be expected; the purser might be held accountable for anything above that.

Then there was the shadow of scurvy, which haunted all ships at sea. Though they might embark with holds full of antiscorbutic fruits, vegetables, and lime juice, those supplies were quickly depleted and needed replenishing at every likely port of call. Onions, apples, pears, plantains, yams, lemons, melons, bananas, coconuts—whatever faraway land produced, the purser had to haggle for it with canny locals who had traded with many a hungry ship. Porter managed to postpone scurvy for most of his long voyage; Captain Charles Stewart, however, curtailed his early 1814 cruise with *Constitution* partially because the first signs of the disease began appearing among the crew after only three months.

Sometimes the decks more nearly resembled those of Noah's Ark, as Porter noted, rather than those of spit-and-polished naval vessels, so crammed were they with pigs, poultry, goats, sheep—and on *Essex*, giant Galápagos tortoises—as no chance to supplement salted provisions with fresh meat was missed. But stock needed to be fed and watered, too, and when water ran short, they were often slaughtered en masse.

The demand for water simply eclipsed all other needs. "Water, water everywhere, Nor any drop to drink," the poet Samuel Taylor Coleridge had famously written in "The Rime of the Ancient Mariner" a little more than a decade earlier; it was a grim irony only too apparent at sea. Capturing rainwater was uncertain at best; after one period of squally weather, *Essex* had only obtained a paltry

No.

BOSTON, *Commonwealth of Maffachufetts,*

Septr 3 1798

RECEIVED of HENRY JACKSON, Naval Agent for the United States, at Boston, *Six hundred Twenty*

Seven Dollars Eight cents in full for a Ten hundred Fifty pounds of Powder for use of the US Frigate Constitution, proving Cannon &c Per bill

for which I have figned triplicate Receipts of the fame tenor and date.

for Mungo Mackay

ribbons, soap, tobacco, pipes, combs—incidental to government-issued supplies were called. Only the purser was allowed to charge a small markup, fixed by regulation at no more than twenty-five percent above cost. To many tars, this was no better than institutionalized fleecing. "The purser is a conjuror," Melville wrote. "He can make a dead man chew tobacco." The writer was insinuating that the vessel's chief financial officer might be making fraudulent charges even on the accounts of dead sailors. But the provisions and stores that the purser provided had originally been charged to him at cost. He was thus financially at risk, and as an added incentive for managing them well he was allowed to take a small profit.

If the crewmen didn't always trust him, the captains usually did. Thomas Chew was *Constitution*'s purser in 1812; he not only kept the keys to the storeroom, bread room, and spirit room but also was entrusted with the key to the powder magazine. Transferred in the spring of 1813 to *Chesapeake*, Chew was present during the battle between that frigate and HMS *Shannon*—an action in which his British counterpart was killed. After witnessing the death of *Chesapeake*'s captain, James Lawrence—some say Lawrence died in Chew's arms—and being held briefly as a prisoner of war in Halifax, Chew was returned to Boston on a cartel ship, bearing the surviving lieutenant's official report of the defeat.

Minerva Rodgers' brother, Henry Denison, spent more than a year as a prisoner of war in England. He had been the purser on *Argus* when in August 1813 that famous raider was defeated off the coast of Wales by HMS *Pelican*. Alongside the surgeon, it was Denison who kept the long vigil beside the bedside of the *Argus*' dying captain, William Henry Allen. David Porter relied on his purser, John Shaw, to an extraordinary degree, even making him on one occasion the prize master of a captured vessel—though admittedly, running short on officers, he once made the chaplain a prize master, too.

And when it all came down to the sharp end—combat at sea—the purser often volunteered to take up a station on the quarterdeck. When the Battle of Lake Erie was raging toward its climax and Oliver Hazard Perry departed his flagship *Lawrence* for the nearby *Niagara*, he left behind him not only decks strewn with the carnage of his crew but also the one gun still left firing, and that was being served by the chaplain and the purser, until the purser, too, fell gravely wounded.

sixty gallons. Even when on reduced rations—both Porter and Stewart often had their thirsty sailors subsist on a barely survivable two quarts a day—a typical frigate's crew of between 350 and 450 men consumed hundreds of gallons every twenty-four hours. Every few weeks, therefore, a warship would head for some port or for some desolate beach to replenish her water. The source, usually a spring or stream, was not always easily accessible, which meant that the heavy casks—a fifty-four gallon hogshead full of water weighed an eighth of a ton—had to be rolled back to the beach, sometimes beneath a blistering sun, manhandled into the boats, and ferried back through heavy surf to the ship. After one such ordeal, Porter worried that only five thousand gallons had been obtained—at best a three-week supply. No wonder he was delighted to discover, in the holds of one captured whaling vessel, not only abundant provisions but also a hundred tons of casked water.

Sometimes such water stayed fresh for months. When rounding Cape Horn, Porter recorded that "a live mullet, nearly three quarters of an inch in length, was this day pumped from a cask filled with the water from the river Delaware" six months earlier. But sometimes the water was bad, not only slimy with dead insects—perhaps the only water available—but also infected with invisible parasites that made everyone on board queasily sick.

Whenever supplies of food or water ran short at sea, the captain was allowed to reduce rations whose size was otherwise stipulated by regulation. Under such circumstances, as when *Essex*'s crew was put on half or even quarter rations, the purser compensated the men in cash for their undrawn portions. With that money, however, they often turned around and bought from the purser certain "slops," as a variety of small miscellaneous items—extra clothing, pocketknives, bottles of mustard, hair

In March, acknowledging that the Royal Navy was going to "harass the seaboard" that year, Secretary Jones wrote to his commodores that "our great inferiority in naval strength does not permit us to meet them on this ground without hazarding the precious Germ of our national glory."

> [W]e have however the means of creating a powerful diversion, & of turning the Scale of annoyance against the enemy. It is therefore intended, to dispatch all our public ships, now in Port, as soon as possible, in such positions as may be best adapted to destroy the Commerce of the enemy, from the Cape of Good-hope, to Cape Clear, and continue out as long as the means of subsistence can be procured abroad, in any quarter.

Commerce raiding—as for specifics, Jones suggested the West Indies, suspecting that those islands would be stripped of British cruisers called off on blockade duty. He deferred, though, to his commodores, Charles Stewart, Stephen Decatur, and John Rodgers, who all preferred to hunt in the North Atlantic as well. Rodgers identified four stations that might intercept the four great streams of British commerce: the Grand Banks off Newfoundland, which lay along the trade routes to and from the West Indies; the seas between the southern cape of Norway and the northern tip of Denmark, which lay along Britain's Baltic Sea trade; those lying squarely beneath the equator, between Brazil and Africa, through which funneled all her East Indiamen; and the approaches to the English Channel. Each frigate was to cruise by itself along one of these trade routes.

It was April before the icy weather gripping Boston relented enough for refitting work to resume. It was a busy month. On the ninth, *Chesapeake* slipped back into port after a four-month cruise that had taken her to the Cape Verdes and back, though she only took four prizes. Captain Samuel Evans soon requested sick leave. His replacement was the recently promoted James Lawrence, who, having to leave *Hornet*, had been assigned to the New York Navy Yard. Because his wife, Julia, was ill, he was hoping to win *Constitution*, which would still be some months refitting. He was given *Chesapeake* instead.

While Rodgers completed *President*'s refit, Minerva longed to spend more time with him, a yearning that other Navy wives well understood, including Mrs. Chauncey, whose own husband, Commodore Isaac Chauncey, was off leading the Navy's effort to win the Great Lakes. "My Dearest Husband," Minerva wrote in April, while visiting New York City, "I shall go over to see Mrs. Chauncey in the morning. I am told she is in bad spirits. I sympathize with her most sincerely."

Minerva was able to visit the refurbished *Macedonian*, anchored in New York Harbor. "I went on board the *Macedonian* with George," she wrote to her husband. "She appears to be a large ship but very much out of order."

Rodgers was ready to leave by mid-April. But for several weeks he kept a weather eye on the two British frigates patrolling Massachusetts Bay. The 38-gun *Shannon* had been commanded by Captain Philip Bowes Vere Broke for seven years—the same Broke whose squadron had chased Rodgers on his first cruise nine months earlier. Rodgers had eluded him then, and Broke was determined it would not happen again. Alongside the sister ship *Tenedos*, he was keeping close inshore waiting for *President*—the readiest to sail of the four frigates in Boston. Rodgers bided his time. Then, on April 30, a nor'easter brought fog and rain and heavy winds, which drove the British frigates off station. *President* and *Congress*, which had been beating about in the bay for days, made a run for it and got away.

A week later, on May 8, having in the meantime chased a British brig and passed to windward of what they suspected was a Royal Navy frigate accompanying a 74, the two American ships had cleared George's Bank, and, running along the southern edge of the Gulf stream, the two captains, who had cruised together nearly the circumference of the earth within the past year, parted company.

Rodgers set a course that passed south of the Grand Banks, hoping to intercept any passing West Indian convoys. All he met with, however, were several American merchantmen returning from runs to Lisbon and Cádiz, so he turned the helm to the north, only to find more days of featureless sea. Another loop to the south, toward the Azores—still nothing, though another passing American merchantman reported encountering a West Indian convoy four days back. Bearing off before the wind, *President* ran for the northeast. But all she picked up were four stragglers; once again, he had missed the convoy proper.

Rodgers, as it turned out, was the only commodore to escape that spring. Charles Stewart could not get to sea because *Constellation* remained blockaded in Norfolk, so in May he was given command of *Constitution* instead, Bainbridge opting to wait for one of the 74s then under construction. *Constitution*, however, would not be ready for sea for some months yet.

On May 22, Stephen Decatur, with *United States*, *Macedonian*, and *Hornet*, tried slipping out of New York. At first, they stood out toward Sandy Hook, the southern gate to New York Bay, but neither the right weather conditions nor the presence of a British ship-of-the-line, the 74-gun *Valiant*, and her accompanying frigate, *Acasta*, promised an easy escape.

So Decatur tried the back way. His squadron retreated to the Brooklyn Navy Yard, only instead of mooring there the ships continued up the East River, threading the crooked passage that eventually led into the western end of Long Island Sound. The trickiest stretch, Hells Gate, was subject to strong tides, and its rocky bottom was notoriously shallow. *United States* actually grounded there for an alarming few minutes, but the tide lifted her off and she remained unscathed.

When the tide was right the trio came out into the Sound, and they then dashed eastward toward its outlet. Arriving on June 1 between Montauk Point and Block Island, however, in the area called the Race, they encountered yet again *Valiant* and *Acasta*. Seeing that he was also about to be taken in flank, Decatur had no choice but to retreat to nearby New London, Connecticut—where he realized he was trapped. His three vessels soon moved six miles up the Thames River, while fortifications were hurriedly thrown up against possible British raids or even attacks in force.

THE MAINMAST TOPPLED

When he was a rear admiral during the Civil War, David Farragut recalled the James Lawrence he had known as a boy midshipman half a century earlier: "He was as splendid-looking a sailor as I ever saw."

Lawrence was one of those quiet yet ardent men who impressed everyone he met. Born in New Jersey, he was among the many youths who had joined the new Navy during the Quasi-War with France, when French privateers ravaged American shipping. He had been second-in-command of the raiding party, led by Stephen Decatur, that had ventured into Tripoli harbor that memorable night and burned *Philadelphia* down to her keel. As commander of *Hornet*, he had sailed with Rodgers on the first cruise of the war, and with Bainbridge across the equator and into the South Atlantic. His subsequent victory over *Peacock* had then won him nationwide acclaim. At thirty-two, he was a man gifted with a tall, broad-shouldered physical presence, and he was also unshakably high-minded. As Decatur said, "He had no more dodge in him than the mainmast."

Lawrence only hesitantly accepted the command of the frigate *Chesapeake*. He was anxious about his wife's health and would have welcomed some time spent with her. But there was a war on, and Jones had ordered him to cruise in the Gulf of St. Lawrence, where he could disrupt British commerce and prey upon troop transports. He was rushing to put to sea, but the challenge of running the blockade was more complicated than usual.

Every Bostonian knew that, outside the harbor, two of the king's frigates, HMS *Shannon* and HMS *Tenedos*, ceaselessly patrolled, and that *Shannon*'s captain, Broke, had issued a standing challenge to any American frigate commander in Boston to test his mettle in a trial of arms, a ship-to-ship duel. Like Rodgers, one could ignore this challenge and, when the night was dark and the wind high, slip out to sea to harry the enemy's trade routes. Many naval officers, however, felt almost honor-bound not to resist a challenge. It was bred into the service, like the code of chivalry of knights of old.

Lawrence was a man of spirit. He had orders to put to sea forthwith. He knew that Broke knew it, too, for his preparations were all too obvious. Lawrence

A portrait in oils by J. Herring (1794–1867) of star-crossed Master Commandant James Lawrence.

also sensed the air of expectancy hanging over Boston. A man who has no dodge in him cannot easily take the furtive way out. "It was the old story of Scylla and Charybdis in a new dress," Admiral Albert Gleaves, his biographer, later wrote. "If he went out and lost, he would be censured for bad judgment. If he remained in port while the *Shannon* unmolested flaunted her flag in his face, there would

A modern rendering by artist Robin Brooks of the disastrous duel between USS *Chesapeake* and HMS *Shannon* on June 1, 1813. The crushing defeat of the American frigate brought a stinging end to the early streak of victories in single-ship actions that had galvanized the American public and shaken Britain's sense of its navy's invincibility.

be uglier reasons assigned for his passiveness. No one knew better than Lawrence that public opinion always applauds boldness and dash, but never forgives timidity."

On the evening before his departure, he was said to have walked all night in the public squares. What he thought about can only be guessed, but the next morning, June 1, 1813, he was ready.

Early that morning, *Shannon* had dared to approach as close as the Boston Light. There she remained, hove-to, long enough for the challenge to be unmistakable. Lawrence, at the center of the harbor in the deep anchorage called President Roads, had no need to read the note Broke had just scribbled to him. "As the *Chesapeake* appears now ready for sea," the scion of an ancient lineage in East Anglia had penned, "I request that you will do me the favor to meet the *Shannon* with her, ship to ship, to try the fortunes of our respective flags."

In a missive astonishing for its candor, Broke described his disappointment in Rodgers' escape without a trial of arms. He explained the positions and needs of every British ship in the vicinity, only to assure his antagonist that it would be but a ship-to-ship duel; no other British frigates would intervene.

> You must, sir, be aware that my proposals are highly advantageous to you, as you cannot proceed to sea singly in the *Chesapeake* without imminent risk of being crushed by the superior force of the numerous British squadrons which are now abroad where all your efforts, in case of a *rencontre*, would, however gallant, be perfectly hopeless. I entreat you, sir, not to imagine that I am urged by mere personal vanity to the wish of meeting the *Chesapeake*, or that I depend only upon your personal ambition for your according to this invitation. We have both nobler motives . . . Choose your terms, but let us meet.

Lawrence never saw that note. He didn't have to. The mere sight of *Shannon* now standing back out to sea was summons enough.

In the early afternoon, *Chesapeake*, too, was passing the Boston Light. Every hilltop and every roof was soon crowded with people hoping to witness a historic victory, but the trial would take place too far out at sea. Those who realized this fact had headed for the wharves, where among a multitude of craft a packet boat was soon heaving off, filled with hopeful sightseers, including thirty-five-year-old George Dodd from Connecticut, who soon afterward described it all to a friend.

> On Tuesday Morning last I went from Long wharfe in a Packet with about forty Gentlemen down this Harbour to see the U.S.S. Frigate *Chesapeake* go to Sea as 'twas probable she would in consequence of the British Frigate Shannon being close in. . . the *Chesapeake* her three topsails were loose her Ensign flying at her Gaff end, and a white Flagg at her Fore top gallant royal masthead with the words "Sailors Rights & Free Trade" in large letters there.

An engraving by Henry Bryan Hall after a painting by Alonzo Chappel depicting the fatally wounded James Lawrence being carried below deck to the cockpit, where in despair and defiance he repeatedly cried out his final command: "Don't give up the ship!"

Thirty miles east of the Boston Light, *Shannon* lay hove-to, waiting.

The weather was pristine, but the air was heavy with foreboding. Broke had donned his top hat and buckled on his broadsword. He had been in command of *Shannon* for nearly seven years. He knew his ship and he knew his crew, whom he had drilled relentlessly in gunnery. Next to Nelson's *Victory*, *Shannon*, it was said, was the most respected ship in the Royal Navy.

Lawrence looked even more resplendent. He wore his blue-laced coat with gold epaulettes, his white trousers tucked into high black boots, his cocked hat. But he had been in command for only a matter of weeks, and his ship, the "unlucky" *Chesapeake*, had been hard to man, not many seamen wanting to serve with her. He'd had to depend on drafts from *Constitution*. Nevertheless, she looked smart in her fresh coat of paint, while *Shannon* showed all the wear of months spent on station.

All swords are slashing in this colored aquatint illustrating *Shannon*'s riled-up crew boarding the vanquished *Chesapeake*. The bloody aftermath of this scene left civilian witnesses aghast. When *Chesapeake* arrived in Halifax, her decks had yet to be scrubbed clean, and Judge Haliburton, better known by his nom de plume, "Sam Slick," recorded the sight in lurid detail. "The coils and folds of rope were steeped in gore as if in a slaughterhouse," he wrote. "Pieces of skin with pendant hair were adhering to the sides of the ship, and in one place I noticed portions of fingers protruding as if thrust through the outer wall of the frigate, while several of the sailors to whom liquor had evidently been handed through the portholes by visitors in boats were lying asleep on the bloody floor as if they had fallen in action and had expired where they lay."

Heath del.   M. Dubourg sculp.

BOARDING and TAKING the AMERICAN SHIP CHESAPEAKE,

by the Officers & Crew of H.M. Ship Shannon, *Commanded by Capt. Broke, June 1813.*

Published & Sold July 1, 1816, by Edwd. Orme, Publisher to His Majesty, & the Prince Regent, Bond Street, corner of Brook Street, London.

Lawrence closed with great skill, maneuvering his frigate ever nearer but at such an angle that the British gunners could not bring their pieces to bear. They were under orders anyway not to fire "whilst the gallant fellow kept his head toward us." One British tar turned to Broke and said, "I hope, sir, you will give us revenge for the *Guèrriere* today." To this, his captain replied, "You shall have it, my man; go to your quarters."

Shannon was now underway, too, but in the heart-pounding final few seconds, *Chesapeake*, only a pistol shot away, came gliding up alongside her. Then Lawrence put his helm down, came quickly to the wind, and at 5:50 p.m., just as *Chesapeake*'s foremast came abreast of *Shannon*'s mizzenmast, the veteran British gunners fired. The boom of their guns was instantly answered by one from *Chesapeake*, and then all was smoke and pandemonium. But the British had been a split second faster. That first volley had swept *Chesapeake*'s spar deck, killing or wounding two-thirds of the men stationed there in one appalling salvo. For the next six minutes, as the ships continued on parallel courses, pounding each other with broadsides, the Americans never regained the initiative. Lawrence, staggered by a pistol ball to his right knee, clung to the binnacle and kept issuing commands, but one after another his officers fell around him, one with his head blown clean off, another with his leg severed, two more killed instantly, and several more down with mortal wounds. No officers were left on the spar deck, and only two remained on the gun deck when a grenade hurled from *Shannon* exploded in a box of ammunition left out on *Chesapeake*'s poop—witnesses on the Bay thought her magazine had blown—and fire was soon sweeping over her quarterdeck, only adding to the scrim of smoke.

Though her headway had soon brought *Chesapeake* even with *Shannon*, in those deadly few minutes her jib sheet, fore-topsail, spanker braces, tiller ropes, and wheel were all shot away or severely damaged, and her head soon turned with the wind, driving her helm a-lee and sending her stern crashing into her foe, her poop rail catching in *Shannon*'s sheet anchor and main chains. Thus she hung there, locked up at nearly right angles to the British frigate, whose expert gunners were suddenly raking her at will, the surviving Americans unable to respond. In the midst of this storm of grape, canister, and solid shot—which pulverized everything in its path so that, to British riflemen in *Shannon*'s tops, it resembled "a mist of debris, as the mist of spoon drift in a pelting gale"— Lawrence was seen limping forward calling for boarders, as the bugler, petrified, had deserted his station. There was no mistaking the figure in the cocked hat, and one of the British sharpshooters took aim. Lawrence crumpled, the musket ball having plowed through his groin. As he was being carried down the hatch, he was heard crying, "Don't surrender the ship!"

Broke, meanwhile, was vaulting over *Chesapeake*'s taffrail, calling, "He who can, follow me!" Swarms of British marines and boarders followed his outline, sword in hand, as it plunged through the smoke down the length of *Chesapeake*'s

decks. The big guns fell silent as the battle became a clashing hand-to-hand melee. Having reached the American forecastle, Broke was clubbed to the deck by musket butt and saber. Essentially leaderless, though, *Chesapeake*'s men were soon tumbling down the hatches, their captain lying in the wardroom groaning out commands: "Go on deck; order them to fire faster! Fight the ship till she sinks!" "Never strike! The flag shall wave while I live." "Don't give up the ship! Blow her up!"

It was too late. Above decks, the British were already hoisting their flag over the American ensign.

The battle had lasted only fifteen minutes, but they were perhaps the bloodiest fifteen minutes of the war. Even George Dodd, watching in stunned silence from two miles away, could tell that. "[W]hen the smoke cleared off the ships were separated a very short distance & I saw the British Flagg, with the American Flagg reversed under it," he wrote to his friend.

> I am of the opinion from every Circumstance that I saw, that the Chesapeake was boarded and carried in ten minutes from the time the first gun was fired. The fight was a dreadful one and her being captured so soon makes it very lamentable there is no doubt a Great Slaughter was made on board both Ships . . . Capt. Lawrence commanded the Chesapeake & had 400 souls on board, the ship was provided for a cruise of six months & was in every way in compleat order—and the British got her with a little or no damage—'tis too much—yet so it is, and it must be borne.

In Boston, where it had all been muted thunder, hushed crowds gathered at street corners, unwilling to believe the reports being delivered from the returning boats. The crowds still lining the cliffs at Cape Ann, however, saw, just as twilight fell, the two ships pass barely three miles away—on the way to Halifax.

It proved to be a difficult three-day voyage to Halifax, the pair of damaged ships being commanded by a twenty-two-year-old lieutenant. Hundreds of unruly prisoners were chained in the holds, and the British officers' nerves were on edge, fearful that at any second John Rodgers and *President* would come heaving vengefully out of the fog. Among the scores of writhing, dying men in desperate need of attention, the two officers lay apparently mortally wounded. Broke's skull had

This gold dirk, which belonged to Edward N. Thayer, a *Chesapeake* midshipman, was taken as a trophy by *Shannon*'s crew. Officers and midshipman often carried dirks on board as badges of rank. Uniform regulations, however, forbade men from bringing the weapons ashore, as the daggers frequently found their way into brawls.

been laid open and his brains exposed, while Lawrence muttered incoherently until midnight on June 4, when he drew his last breath.

As the two ships finally wove their way into the harbor at Halifax, bells were ringing at the news, but as far as the eye could see, the rigging on all the ships was crowded with sailors, all of them silent out of respect for Lawrence, who had won their reverence for his magnanimous treatment of *Peacock*'s men. Among those ships was His Majesty's brig *Boxer*, captained by Samuel Blyth. Four days later, when Lawrence was buried with the full panoply of ritual that the Royal Navy could muster—the houses in Halifax draped in black, the three hundred soldiers of the guard of honor lining the route to St. Paul's Church, the six companies of infantry preceding the hearse, the surviving officers of *Chesapeake* following it— Blyth was among the six senior naval officers selected to be pallbearers.

While bells pealed in London at the news, and the guns at the Tower were fired in honor of the triumph—"Not the victory of the Nile nor of Trafalgar inspired more excitement, joy, and exultant pride in England . . .

AN

ACCOUNT

OF THE FUNERAL HONOURS BESTOWED

ON THE REMAINS OF

CAPT. LAWRENCE AND LIEUT. LUDLOW,

WITH

THE EULOGY

PRONOUNCED AT SALEM, ON THE OCCASION, BY

HON. JOSEPH STORY.

To which is prefixed,

AN ACCOUNT OF THE ENGAGEMENT BETWEEN THE CHESAPEAKE
AND SHANNON, WITH DOCUMENTS RELATIVE TO THE SAME,
AND BIOGRAPHICAL AND POETICAL NOTICES.

" A nation's tears bedew the hero's grave."

BOSTON:

PRINTED BY JOSHUA BELCHER.

1815.

CARD
CATALOGUED.

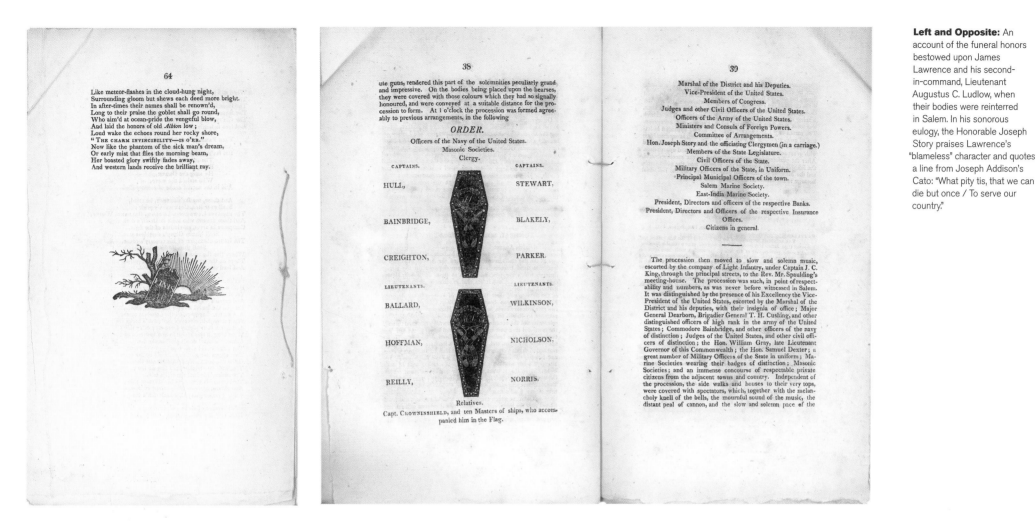

No greater tribute was ever paid to the fair fame of the Navy of the United States than the acclaim with which the English people greeted the capture of the *Chesapeake*," rhapsodized one historian a century ago—the cloud of melancholy that had lifted off the Royal Navy settled across the Atlantic. Richard Rush, one of President Madison's advisors, recalled its descent many years later.

I remember, what American does not! the first rumor of it. I remember the startling sensation. I remember at first the startling incredulity. I remember how the post offices were thronged for successive days by anxious thousands, how collections of citizens rode out for miles in the highway, accosting the mail to catch something by anticipation. At last, when the uncertainty was dispelled, I remember the public gloom; funeral orations, and badges of mourning bespoke it. "Don't give up the ship!"—the dying words of Lawrence—were on every tongue.

Broke, against all odds, would recover, but the aftereffects of his wound still killed him thirty years later. Lawrence would be buried many times. In August 1813, under a flag of truce, his body was removed from Halifax and carried to Salem, where all the flags on all the ships in the harbor stood at half-mast, and there reinterred, his pallbearers then including Isaac Hull, Charles Stewart, William Bainbridge, and Johnston Blakeley.

In September it was moved yet again, to New York, thirty thousand people lining the route taken by the cortege, from the Battery to Wall Street, dirge bells tolling mournfully, soldiers tramping dolefully, to a final resting place in Trinity Churchyard and a shrine in American naval myth. For Lawrence had "passed before the public eye like a star," as Washington Irving wrote, "just beaming on it for a moment, and falling in the midst of his brightness."

MIDNIGHT SUN

By early June, the greatly feared John Rodgers and his frigate were on course to pass just to the west of the British Isles. Though skirting the Royal Navy's home waters, he did not meet a single ship until he encountered some Danish vessels off the Shetland Islands. By that point, however, his provisions and water were running low, so he steered for the forbidding fjords of Norway and on June 27 dropped anchor in the harbor at Bergen, the largest town in a country still the unwilling vassal of Denmark, now an ally of Napoleon's.

As *President* was the first American warship to visit a Norwegian port, the whole bay was soon alive with the boats of the curious. "Indeed it appeared as if their curiosity could never be gratified," Rodgers confided to his journal, "as the only pleasure the inhabitants of the city and surrounding country appeared to take was in rowing round the ship; and this they continued to do night as well as day from the hour of our arrival until the moment of our departure."

Meanwhile, Rodgers and his officers were whirled off into a steep-gabled old town, where they paid courtesy visits to the governor, the bishop, and the local commander of military forces. They, in turn, were received with glittering hospitality, dining in palaces and mansions—but since a nationwide famine had devastated Norway only a year before, there were precious few provisions to spare for the ship. So having filled his casks with water, Rodgers departed a few days after arriving, firing his guns in salute and returning to war.

By the middle of July, he was on his way toward the North Cape of Norway, where the Atlantic merged into the encircling Arctic Ocean. In that region with neither a sunrise nor a sunset, for high summer in those latitudes brought with it the midnight sun, dancing around the horizon for weeks at a time, he lurked for a British convoy rumored to be sailing from Archangel in Russia and escorted by only two Royal Navy sloops. He did not wait alone, for on July 18 a sleek fore-and-aft rigged schooner hove into view. It was *Scourge*, an American privateer out of New York, and for the next several days the two far-rovers kept each other company. Before too long they spotted two sails to the southwest.

But they did not belong to the convoy. It was hard to tell at some distance, but as they stood toward them, every officer on *President*'s quarterdeck, from the commodore on down to midshipman Matthew Calbraith Perry, whose older brother was at that moment readying a war fleet on Lake Erie, saw at the far end of their spyglasses both a British frigate and a 74-gun ship-of-the-line. *Scourge* soon took to her heels and disappeared. Rodgers hauled by the wind on the opposite tack to avoid them. It was too late, and soon they were in pursuit— a long, fearful, agonizing pursuit, as hour after fleeting hour *President*, crowding all sail, made for the northwest, but with the winds light and variable, Rodgers was not able to outsail them; at times, indeed, they seemed to be gaining on him. Moreover, with the sun remorselessly gamboling around the horizon, there was

no darkness to cloak a change in direction.

For more than three days this continued, then the breeze freshened, and Rodgers was able to outrun them at last. Subsequently, it was determined that his pursuers were in reality a frigate and a sloop, but in the far northern haze, objects at a distance can loom larger to the perceiving eye, a well-known phenomenon of polar exploration.

Having never glimpsed the convoy, an impatient commodore instead steered for Scotland, skulking about the Shetlands and Orkneys, ranging to windward of the Hebrides, prowling for prizes. These were dangerous waters, the coast of Great Britain itself occasionally heaving into view on his larboard quarter. Outside the North Channel of the commerce-crowded Irish Sea, long a favorite haunt of privateers, Rodgers captured a ship, a barque, and a brig, sending two as cartels with his prisoners to England and burning the third. Though he could not know that on July 10, fearful of Rodgers on the loose somewhere nearby, the Sea Lords had reiterated that none "of His Majesty's Frigates should attempt to engage, single handed, the larger Class of American Ships," instead awaiting "some other of His Majesty's Ships with whose assistance the Enemy might be attacked with a reasonable hope of success," he did catch wind that he was now being pursued by a squadron.

Provisions nearly exhausted, in mid-August the commodore set a course for Newfoundland and home. At that very moment, though, at the southern entrance to the Irish Sea, one of his protégés was engaged in the single most destructive U.S. Navy cruise of the war.

A PRIZE TOO MANY

In 1798, when he was thirteen years old, William Henry Allen had been swept up in the excitement provoked by the outbreak of the Quasi-War with France, and though he was a general's son—his father, a Revolutionary War hero, was head of Rhode Island's militia—he was from that point on a true-blue Navy man. In the dozen years since he first became a midshipman in 1800, he had served on most of the ships and with most of the commanders whose names would subsequently garland the early history of the fleet.

In 1800, when still wet behind the ears, he had accompanied William Bainbridge when George Washington carried the dey of Algiers' tribute to the Ottoman sultan in Constantinople. He was a midshipman with *Philadelphia* before that frigate was captured by the Tripolitan corsairs during the First Barbary War. He was a lieutenant when *Chesapeake* was fired upon by HMS *Leopard* in 1807 and the only American officer to fire a gun in return. And he had been the first lieutenant aboard *United States* when Stephen Decatur won his great victory over *Macedonian*; Henry Allen, in fact, had been prize master of *Macedonian*, outsailing the Old Wagon across the Atlantic. Above all, however, it was Rodgers who had made the deepest impression on the younger officer. He had served with Rodgers aboard both *Constitution* and *Essex*; while on station in the Mediterranean the two had even toured the classical ruins of Sicily and Southern Italy together, marveling at excavated Pompeii and Herculaneum.

So in the spring of 1813 it was with Rodgers as his mentor that he relieved William Sinclair at the helm of the once-proud *Argus*, which both Stephen Decatur and Isaac Hull had previously commanded. The leaky, dilapidated brig that Sinclair had brought home in January was newly patched, caulked, and refitted, for on June 18 she slipped out of New York on a diplomatic mission, carrying William H. Crawford, the new U.S. minister to France, to take up his post with Napoleon's French Empire. Less than a month later, after a stormy passage, Lieutenant Allen brought her safely into L'Orient.

Then began the second part of his mission. Filtering back through the British blockade, Allen brought *Argus* into the open waters of the English Channel. Here was the great funnel through which all British maritime trade from both the East and West Indies eventually converged. But to mount the kind of commerce raid that Allen envisaged was tantamount to bearding the British lion in his den. Not only were the waters of the Channel patrolled by English squadrons blockading France, but those same waters also lapped the shores of such massive Royal Navy installations as Portsmouth and Plymouth. Nonetheless, in a remarkable three-week period—July 23 to August 13—Allen darkened the skies over the Channel with the smoke of no fewer than nineteen burning ships.

East Indiamen in the China Seas.

a large ship carrying goods from Greenock in Scotland to Newfoundland. The next day, Friday the thirteenth, *Argus* ran down a brig laden with West Indies sugar for Dublin, a sloop laden with pine lumber, and a brig bound for London from Dublin with linen and wine. Allen burned most of them, and throughout the long summer twilight, telltale plumes of smoke marked *Argus*' passage.

But Jones would not have applauded what came next. A British brig, HMS *Pelican*, had been hunting the American raider; her captain not only saw those plumes but also glimpsed *Argus* just as darkness fell. This was the time, the secretary might have urged his captain, to make good an escape, to continue what was already the single most destructive cruise of the War of 1812. But as day dawned over the burning wreck toward which *Pelican* had been steering, it revealed *Argus*, still in place, hove-to, awaiting the test of combat.

Allen misjudged his opponent. Captain John Maples was a seasoned veteran of both Trafalgar and Copenhagen, and at half past five, when his crew gave three cheers and the battle commenced, he handled his vessel with practiced skill. Scarcely had the first broadsides thundered when a solid shot ripped Allen's leg off at the hip. He was taken below to be worked on by the ship's surgeon, James Inderwick, a "heavy set" twenty-three-year-old with skillful hands but no formal medical degree. A mere half hour later, though weak from loss of blood, he was back on deck. By then, however, *Pelican*, which had been raking *Argus* along all her vulnerable spots, had come alongside and was preparing to close with the cutlass when Allen struck his colors.

He died four days later, an hour before midnight, according to Inderwick's journal entry, at the Mill Prison Hospital in Plymouth, where his surviving crewmen were imprisoned for the duration of the war. Before their captain had been hoisted off the ship into a waiting launch, the last of *Argus*' men had gathered around him for a final farewell. Though he had been drifting in and out of delirium, he latched onto a moment of lucidity. "God bless you, my lads," he said. "We shall never meet again."

It was exactly the kind of naval war, using exactly the vessel, that Secretary William Jones had envisioned: small nimble warships making brutally destructive raids on enemy commerce and melting away before larger frigates could hunt them down. Allen even had the temerity to poke his bow into coves along the coast of Devon and Cornwall, Royal Navy home grounds if there ever were such; he prowled halfway up Ireland's Shannon River almost to Limerick. Maritime insurance rates in London soared twenty-five percent.

Jones would have applauded the actions of Thursday, August 12, when Allen, in St. George's Channel between Britain and Ireland, captured a Welsh brig carrying slate and woolens to London, a Portuguese brig bound for Cork, and

Above: Made shortly after his death, this stipple engraving of William Henry Allen is the only surviving portrait of the captain and was probably based on a pencil or pen-and-ink sketch drawn by Allen himself.

Left: A list of the contents of William Henry Allen's four trunks and a receipt documenting payment from *Argus*' purser, Henry Denison, for the shipment of these personal effects. Allen was buried in the churchyard of St. Andrew's, his hearse attended by eight of *Argus*' seaman, all wearing black crape armbands tied with white ribbons. One of *Argus*' officers pulled a brass button off his uniform jacket and left it behind for the stonecutter, who used the American eagle stamped upon it as a model for the engraving on Allen's headstone.

Opposite: A hand-colored aquatint illustrating the capture of the brig *Argus* on August 14, 1813.

SPOILS OF WAR
The Prize System in the War of 1812

An enemy vessel striking her colors after an encounter at sea was a sight naturally welcomed by every ship's captain during the age of fighting sail. Except in the very worst of battles, what that captain did not want to see was the enemy vessel sinking, for he could not then claim her as a prize.

Patriotism aside, once war was declared, the lure of profit is what compelled many a privateer and many a naval officer to weigh anchor and hoist sail. For more than a century, in every maritime nation washed by the Atlantic, whenever there was a war at sea the considerable proceeds from the sale of condemned enemy vessels and their cargoes had been given to those captains and crews who had captured them as prizes. Numerous British admirals had in this way become very wealthy indeed, but the prospect of riches had stirred every man, of whatever rank, who fought at sea. It made for happier ships altogether; sailors were more prompt in discharging their duties, more cheerful, even more eager for battle—while the absence of prize-taking opportunities could leave them dejected and uninspired.

Yet the stipulations regarding the disposition of prizes had grown out of a complex system of international law and were very exacting. After his opponent had struck his colors, and while the battle smoke was still clearing, our victorious captain was supposed to be manning the captured vessel with a prize crew detached from his own ship's complement. The captured ship's sailors—prisoners of war, if the vessel was a warship, but not if it was a merchantman—were stowed below decks, while a prize master took the vessel into the most convenient port for adjudication, although weeks might elapse before this proviso could realistically be met.

Adjudication, or the passing of legal judgment on the fate of a captured ship, was the prerogative of courts of admiralty—"prize courts," for short—found in most major ports, ruling on all manner of maritime issues. After entering such a port, the prize master's first duty was to give notice of his arrival to the admiralty judge or his commissioners. He then submitted the ship's papers—passport, license, bills of lading, invoices, manifest, muster roll, and logbook—to the court registry, on his oath that none were forged or fraudulent.

The ship would then be consigned to the custody of the court, and if a merchant vessel—as were the vast majority of prizes—its cargo holds and hatches were sealed. The original master, officers, and any other witnesses to the seizure were subjected to a series of standardized depositions, called "interrogatories," touching on every point that might affect the resolution of the case. Meanwhile, the captors—or, more likely, proctors acting on their behalf—filed a "prize libel" against the vessel, asserting that she was the subject of prize rights, and then applied for a hearing. A "monition" was then issued, summoning anyone who could show just cause why the property should not be condemned as a prize to appear in court on a given date. In American ports, a copy of the monition was posted on the mast of the vessel in question.

On the day of the hearing, if no one contested the libel, and if the court deemed the vessel to be a lawful prize and was satisfied that the captor, if a privateer, had abided by the conditions stated in his letter of marque, then the vessel and her cargo were forthwith condemned and arrangements would be made for their sale.

Unlikely as it might seem during a war, however, a claim for restitution of the prize might be made at the hearing, perhaps by the ship's master, her owner, or someone holding a lien on her who happened not to be an enemy citizen. Or the court could decree—and its authority was absolute in such matters—that the captors were guilty of misconduct, negligence, or fraud, in which case the prize might be confiscated or, if a merchant vessel, even restored, with punitive damages, to her original owners.

Prize law could be hedged about with legal quibbles. In 1807, when the British attacked Copenhagen to prevent the Danish fleet from falling into Napoleon's hands, the Royal Navy spirited away eighteen Danish ships-of-the-line, fifteen frigates, five brigs, and twenty gunboats, altogether estimated to be worth four and a half million pounds. Yet a British court of admiralty decreed that, since there had been no formal declaration of war, the captors were not entitled to any prize money. The livid officers and men were instead mollified by an eight-hundred-thousand-pound payoff.

Once a ship was condemned, appraised, and sold, any prize money going to a victorious privateer would then be divvied up according to previous arrangements made between that captain and owner. If the prize happened to be an enemy naval vessel captured by an American naval one, the government would simply appropriate the condemned ship, but it dared not be stingy to the victorious crew. Those officers and men would still receive the appraised prize money according to a set rate, the captain receiving nearly a fifth of the whole, and then scaling down the ranks, even the meanest tar in the forecastle receiving his due share.

Captain Isaac Hull swiped this dinner plate from the cabin of the conquered *Guerrière.* Most likely, it was one of many spoils quickly seized in a general sweep before the Americans set the trounced vessel on fire and consigned her to the waves. The ten-inch plate is made of soft paste porcelain decorated with a blue transfer print and red overglaze. The print is of chinoiserie snakes and dragons, interspersed with four pastoral scenes featuring tents and domed buildings.

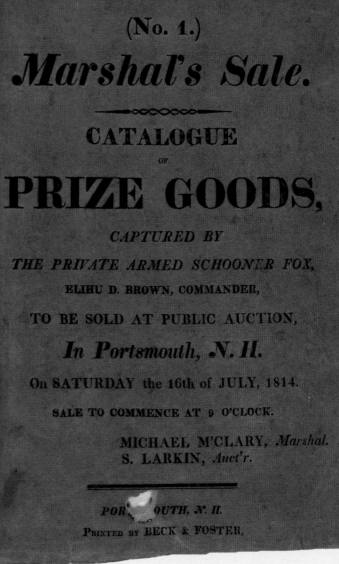

Nevertheless, the disbursement of prize money was not always straightforward. There might be "multiple captors" as claimants, since everyone even marginally involved in the seizing of a ship hoped to grab a share of the spoils. In the U.S. Navy, the money was doled out "according to the number of men and guns on board each ship in sight" of the capture, which might add up to a large number if a fleet action was underway. In 1814, the year following the Battle of Lake Erie, for instance, Congress purchased the captured British vessels—the famous "two ships, two brigs, one schooner, and a sloop"—for $250,000. This money was eventually distributed among the 596 men who took some part in the victory, Isaac Chauncey and Oliver Hazard Perry walking away with over $12,000 apiece.

Clearly there was a premium paid for single-ship victories versus fleet ones. After Stephen Decatur brought the defeated *Macedonian* into New York, the Navy took the ship while the $200,000 that was her appraised value was distributed by Decatur's agent to the several hundred members of the victorious *United States'* crew—making a nice haul for each man. The odds might be even better for a smaller warship. In 1814, the U.S. sloop-of-war *Peacock* captured the British sloop *Epervier*, and as a result her 140 officers and men not only shared the subsequent prize money but also shared the $118,000 in specie that *Epervier* was carrying.

Left: A prize certificate entitling Thomas Sullivan, a crewman with the privateer *Portsmouth*, to a portion of any prizes taken during the brig's second cruise.

Above: A catalog of the privateer *Fox*'s loot, sold at auction in Portsmouth on July 16, 1814.

By the summer of 1813, after a year of war, the Royal Navy presence off the coast of North America had grown from 83 warships to 129—a formidable and imperious presence, especially around the indented shores of eastern Long Island, just across the Sound from New London, where Stephen Decatur's squadron remained bottled up.

Beside himself to get back to sea, Decatur was willing to try anything that would create—or more probably blow—a hole through the Royal Navy's confining wall. Bulking large among his foes was HMS *Ramillies*, the 74-gun flagship of the squadron commander, Captain Thomas Hardy, who had been one of Nelson's closest friends and was one of the most experienced officers in the Royal Navy.

On June 25, as *Ramillies* stood in the Sound across from New London, an American schooner was seen trying to run along the shore. Out came Hardy's boats, and though a volley or two of musketry was loosened from the shore, they easily captured the schooner. They were anyway in the habit of requisitioning such trading craft, which often carried agricultural produce badly needed in the larders of the patrolling warships. Such craft were usually brought alongside to be unloaded. This particular schooner was found to be carrying valuable naval stores, no doubt meant for Decatur's flotilla—which would never get them now.

The tide, however, was running so strong that the boats had difficulty making it back to *Ramillies* with their prize. So instead they unloaded the schooner where they stopped, one store after another—only they didn't notice, until it was too late, that as they moved one particular hogshead, a cord fastened to the striker of a gunlock was tugged, which sparked a train of black powder that flared to an enormous load hidden beneath the naval stores. The resulting explosion, one American gleefully reported, "*distroy'ed every Soul* as well as the Launches." In fact, ten seamen and one officer, as an incensed Warren informed the Admiralty, had been killed "by a Diabolical and Cowardly contrivance of the Enemy."

Decatur found no shortage of men willing to risk their lives in such infernal schemes, for Congress in March had passed the Torpedo Act, promising any individual who managed to burn, sink, or destroy a British warship half the value of the vessel and its guns and cargo.

Understandably suspicious, Captain Hardy soon caught wind of another attempt on his flagship. A native Long Islander, it seemed, was outfitting a boat with a torpedo, as all underwater mines or explosive devices were called at the time, and had already made a failed approach or two. This person, he had learned, had been recommended to Decatur "as a fit person to be employed on a particular service by him, and that he has for some time been entered on the books of one of the frigates at $40 per month." Furthermore, several officers aboard *Ramillies* reported having seen him aboard with clams and fruit, allegedly for trade but "of course as a spy to collect information on our movements." This perpetrator was none other than Joshua Penny, the same Joshua Penny who had once been impressed into the Royal Navy and had escaped in Cape Town to live in the caves like an animal.

Outwardly, Penny was living peaceably enough in his East Hampton home, but he had never ceased meditating revenge.

I was in my own coasting vessel at New York when WAR was declared against Great Britain! I immediately sold my vessel, and resolved to put myself in an attitude to annoy the enemy of my country, and the scourge of the terrestrial globe. I returned to my home at Three Mile Harbour, in the township of East Hampton, determined to avail myself of the first opportunity of doing mischief to those who had so long tortured me. The British landed frequently on Gardiner's Island, in sight of my house, on the opposite side of Gardiner's Bay.

The enemy could not have come much closer to him. He had to act.

[Admiral Decatur] ordered four boats to proceed under my direction as pilot, and crossed the Sound in the night of the 26th of July, 1813 . . . We perceived by our glasses that they were fitting out nine of their boats . . . They fired on us for about half an hour, and threw shot in all directions about us, while we were rowing in our whaleboats. Their last 18-pound shot struck about six feet from the boat's stern, and threw water all over us, when the lieutenant ordered us to "avast oars and give the British three cheers for that shot " . . .

A short time after this, a stranger from New York came to me and said that he had been advised to make application for my assistance in a torpedo, to explode the craft which infested our bays and harbors. I agreed without hesitation . . . and conducted him to places where we might unobserved watch the motions of the enemy . . .

The next morning, Sunday, August 20, 1813, a boat was discovered taking sounding near my house, in the creek . . . I had made the application for a guard and expected it, but thought to take a short nap before it should arrive. I had been sleeping about half an hour, when the house was surrounded by people who had lain in ambush among my corn . . . My wife, three little boys, old Robert Gray and a female Indian, composed, with myself, the family . . . The first salutation was three spiteful raps with the fist, at the door . . . "Decatur's people," was their answer— "Mr. Penny, we want you to get up immediately." I was satisfied, however, that they were the Prince Regent's people—sprang out of my bed, and in my shirt ran for my gun. I had to pass through two doors before I reached the kitchen where my gun was hanging . . . they burst in the door and surrounded me . . . Lieutenant Lawrence, 1st of the Ramillies . . . presented a pistol to my nose, and attempted to shoot me. I never saw more fire issue from a lock in my life—it flew in my eyes—it rolled on the floor; but as luck would have it, missed fire!

In the summer of 1813, while Commodore Stephen Decatur's ship, *United States*, was blockaded in Connecticut's Thames River, Decatur gave considerable thought to innovations in naval warfare and corresponded with noted inventor Robert Fulton, who'd presented myriad ideas to the Navy with varying degrees of success. (Commodore John Rodgers, for one, thought he was a madman.) Among the devices they discussed in regard to adapting steam power to warships were torpedo schooners, slow-moving ships with guns arranged so that they could be fired in any direction. Fulton wrote this letter to Decatur detailing the workings of the proposed vessels.

Hustled under guard to *Ramillies,* Penny was taken below decks, clapped in irons, and left there in the late summer heat, fed only bread and water, for the eighteen days it took the 74-gun ship-of-the-line to reach Halifax. Meanwhile, Hardy wrote to Major Benjamin Case, the Royal Navy's agent for prisoners, refusing to release the prisoner.

> I now beg leave to inform you I had received certain information that this man [Penny] conducted a detachment of boats, sent from the United States squadron, under the command Com. Decatur, now lying in New London, from that port to Gardiner's Island on the 26th of July last, for the express purpose of surprising and capturing the captain of H.B.M.'s frigate *Orpheus* and myself, and having failed in that undertaking, but making prisoners of some officers and men belonging to the *Orpheus,* he went with the remaining boats to Three Mile Harbor . . . I cannot think of permitting such an avowed enemy to be out of my power, when I know so much of him as I do. He will, therefore, be detained as a prisoner of war until the pleasure of the commander-in-chief is known.

In early September, the seizure and harsh treatment of a civilian had outraged a different commander in chief. President James Madison was so infuriated that he told Secretary Jones on the sixth that the "putting [of Penny] in Irons for the cause alleged, should be instantly retaliated, and notice given to the British Commander." Penny, who had been thrown into Halifax's notorious Melville Island prison, was paroled and released nine months later.

This set of nineteenth-century leg irons is typical of those used to restrain prisoners like Joshua Penny. The metal bar was turned and withdrawn and the two horseshoe-shaped irons fitted around the ankles.

THE ENCHANTED ISLES

By early spring 1813, David Porter and *Essex* had rounded Cape Horn. "Although we deemed ourselves more fortunate than other navigators had been, in getting around the Horn, we had not been without our share of hardships," Porter wrote in his journal.

The weather had, for some days, been piercing cold; this, with the almost constant rains and hails, and the water shipped from the heavy seas, and from leaks, kept the vessel very uncomfortable, and the clothes of the officers and crew very uncomfortably wet. The extremities of those who had formerly been affected by the frost became excessively troublesome to them, so much so as to prevent some from doing their duty; from this cause, I myself was a considerable sufferer. Many, also, felt severely the great want of shoes, and the necessary quantity of woolen clothing. Their allowance of provisions was barely sufficient to satisfy the cravings of nature, and as to refreshments of any kind, they were entirely out of the question.

When they had passed the seventy-seventh degree of west longitude, however, they "saw a speedy end to all our sufferings and anxieties, and tasted, in pleasing anticipation, our delightful cruise in the Pacific." After drying out, warming up, and collecting wild pigs on the island of Mocha, they sailed up the towering coast of Chile. Porter was worried about the reception he might find when he steered into the harbor at Valparaíso, the country's chief port, because Chile was a Spanish possession and Spain was now allied with Britain against Napoleon. But his worries evaporated after being warmly welcomed on all sides. It turned out—rather uncomfortably for a captain who was soon feted at glitzy diplomatic receptions—that Chile had just declared its independence, and *Essex*'s stopover had been deemed an official visit of friendship from the U.S. government.

Therefore, as soon as possible, he stood back out to sea and set a course for the Galápagos Islands. He had picked up only a worthless prize or two by the time *Essex* first entered that lost world, and though whales abounded, there was not the first sign of British whalers. "There were few on board the ship who did not now despair of making any captures about

the Gallapagos Islands," Porter wrote in his journal. "I determined not to leave the Gallapagos so long as there remained a hope of finding a British vessel." Then his astonishing streak of luck began.

At daylight on the morning of the 29th, I was roused from my cot, where I passed a sleepless and anxious night, by the cry of "sail ho!" "sail ho!" which was re-echoed through the ship, and in a moment all hands were on deck. The strange sail proved to be a large ship, bearing west, to which we gave chase; and in an hour afterwards we discovered two others, bearing south-west, equally large in their appearance. I had no doubts of their being British whale ships; and as I was certain that toward mid-day, as usual, it would fall calm, I felt confident we should succeed in taking the whole of them. I continued my pursuit of the first discovered vessel, and at 9 o'clock spoke her under British colors. She proved to be the British whale ship Montezuma, captain Baxter, with 1400 bbls. of sperm oil on board. I invited the captain on board; and while he was in my cabin, giving me such information as was in his power respecting the other whale ships about the Gallapagos, I took his crew on board the Essex, put an officer and crew on board the Montezuma, and continued in pursuit of the other vessels.

He would pick up a dozen more of them before he departed. He found them to be "fine vessels, of from 250 to 400 tons burthen, mounting from 6 to 18 guns, and manned with from 25 to 35 men, abundantly supplied with whaling gear, casks of a superior quality to contain the oil, large copper

Captain John Percival (1779–1862), known as "Mad Jack" or "Roaring Jack" for his hotheaded exploits against French, British, and Caribbean pirates, once owned this brass lamp whose design follows the centuries-old type of grease lamp known as a "Hanging Betty." It was usually whale oil that fueled the cotton, flax, or hemp wick. Depending on the type of oil he used, Percival could fill his cabin with either a pleasant smell or a noxious one. Spermaceti oil burned slowly, without a disagreeable odor, and produced a bright glow, so it was widely regarded as one of the best oils for illumination.

Below left: A nineteenth-century whaling flenser, also known as a blubber spade.

Below right: A nineteenth-century whaling harpoon gun.

Opposite: The frigate *Essex* under full sail.

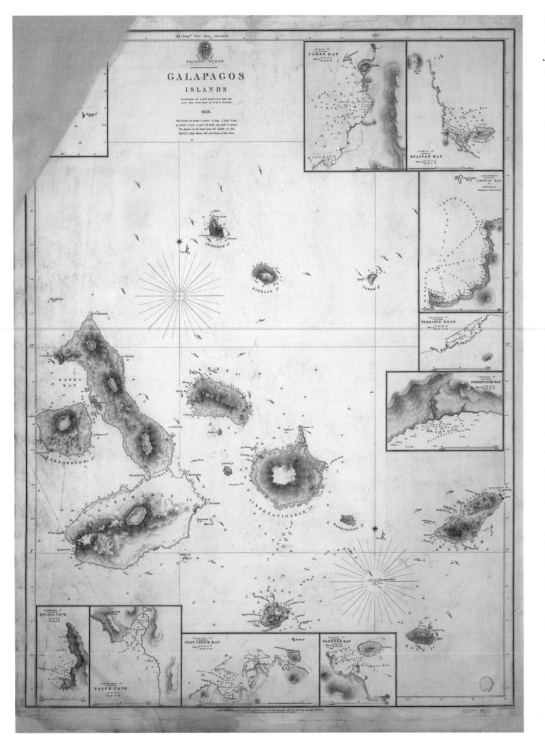

tanks, iron boilers, skimmers, tubs, leather hose for starting the oil, spare whale boats, frames, plank, &c. &c." Some of them—*Atlantic*, which he renamed *Essex Jr.*, *Seringapatam*, and *Sir Andrew Hammond*—he essentially commandeered and outfitted with captured guns, thereby creating his own makeshift fleet. Others he sent back to the mainland with prize crews. He even had his twelve-year-old foster son, midshipman David Farragut, serve as one of the prize masters. By then, most of the murmurings about taking no prizes had vanished, perhaps speeded by the note Porter had posted on that first day that they took *Montezuma*.

SAILORS AND MARINES,

Fortune has at length smiled on us, because we deserved her smiles, and the first time she enabled us to display *free trade and sailors' rights*, assisted by your good conduct, she put in our possession nearly half a million of the enemy's property.

Continue to be zealous, enterprising, and patient, and we will yet render the name of the Essex as terrible to the enemy as that of any other vessel, before we return to the United States.

For six months—April to September 1813—the lurking *Essex* stalked whalers throughout the strange world of the Galápagos. The Spanish had called the islands *encantadas*—enchanted—for they seemed to shift their positions, resisting accurate charting, and their currents balked any attempt to escape the bewildering maze. With their smoking volcanoes, spectral trees, hideous iguanas, and lumbering giant tortoises, they seemed the very picture of primeval desolation, yet generations of hungry mariners had been wading ashore to fetch those tortoises, though they might weigh several hundred pounds apiece. They were the seafaring epicure's delight, approximating the "tenderest veal," as Porter wrote in his journal. *Essex*'s crewman, who had supplemented their diminished rations when rounding the Horn with ship's rats and Brazilian monkeys ("so great was their desire for fresh provisions," Porter had written in his journal, "that a rat was esteemed a dainty, and pet monkeys were sacrificed to appease their longings") could not gather enough of them. In addition, they removed eight hundred giant tortoises from captured British whalers. Porter had them stowed in the hold, presuming that they would stay alive for eighteen months, even without food and water.

In the Galápagos, it was but a short step from provisioning a vessel to reflections on natural history. Indeed, the Navy's proud tradition of scientific exploration might be said to have its origins in the observations David Porter made aboard *Essex* in 1813. While his crew went about clubbing to death the unresisting birds and beasts, he pondered over the marvelous world surrounding him. He was one of the first visitors to the Galápagos to intuit something approaching the modern understanding of the archipelago's dynamic geology, noting that the easternmost islands were old enough to have started accumulating

that "those of James' Island appear to be a species entirely distinct from those of Hood's and Charles' Islands." That was an observation noted with some interest by Charles Darwin when he read Porter's book, for the great British naturalist made the study of species distribution in the Galápagos the key to his theory of evolution. In fact, to historian Edward Larson, Porter's journal "had an impact on the awakening interest in Galápagos natural history second only to Darwin's *Journal of Researches.*"

In the autumn of 1813, however, natural history studies were merely incidental. By Porter's reckoning, he had effectively destroyed the British whale fishery in the eastern Pacific, taking a dozen prizes during the six months *Essex* cruised the archipelago. But the ship badly needed refurbishing and refitting.

Meanwhile, HMS *Phoebe*, along with the sloops *Cherub* and *Raccoon*, had rounded the Horn and were making their way up the coast of Chile. While in Rio, Captain James Hillyar had learned that his orders were altered. He was now to stalk and capture *Essex* "at all costs."

But by the time his frigates entered the maze of the Galápagos to hunt the American raider down, she had long since disappeared.

soil, while the westernmost ones were still "composed of ashes and lava, all apparently fresh." Quite likely they had "not long been thrown from the bowels of the ocean." Porter was also among the first to recognize that the distribution of its animal life might have significant scientific implications. He observed that some of the bird species seemed to be "peculiar to those islands." And having collected fourteen tons worth of giant tortoises on James Island, only to find them decidedly inferior in taste to the delectable ones gathered elsewhere, he concluded

GETTING THERE AND BACK AGAIN
Navigation in the War of 1812

This hourglass, used on board *Franklin*, a 74-gun-ship-of-the-line built in 1815, contains enough sand to mark ten-minute intervals.

Made by Gedney King & Son, a Boston-based nautical instrument manufacturer, this nineteenth-century sextant has a triangular ebony frame that is arced at the bottom, a reinforced brass index arm, and an ivory name plate. Along the arc is an ivory scale that is graduated every five minutes from -5 degrees to 135 degrees and read by vernier with tangent screw to single minutes of arc. The top of the arm has a peephole that lines up with two reflecting mirrors. In addition, there are three colored lenses fixed between the two mirrors. It is precisely the type of instrument that was used on board ships in the eighteenth and nineteenth centuries. Used for finding one's location north or south of the equator, the sextant was much more accurate than the earlier quadrant, astrolabe, or backstaff. As such, it was an integral part of the maritime world—and it was extremely expensive. This one is shown with its wooden case, which not only protected it but also preserved its accuracy.

From the moment an American warship weighed anchor and embarked upon a cruise, no detail of her handling, from the stowing of her hold to the making and shortening of her sails, escaped the sharp eye of the sailing master. This warrant officer, who fell somewhere between the lieutenants and the midshipmen in the ship's hierarchy, was responsible for more than just the vessel's trim and balance. As the chief navigator, he was as likely to be poring over charts alongside the captain as he was to be scrutinizing how the ship heeled to the wind.

The captain might set the course, but the sailing master plotted it on those charts as a series of legs, taking as his "departure" some obvious landmark, like the Boston Light or Sandy Hook. That was not always easy at night or in bad weather, the best conditions for slipping past the British blockade, but every subsequent course the ship steered would stem from this baseline point. Chartrooms were thus as well stocked as were magazines and bread rooms, for without their geographic and oceanographic data, overlaid with an indispensable grid of parallels of latitude and meridians of longitude, and without an associated cache of navigational instruments, there could be no getting there and back again no matter what the enemy might do.

To plot the ship's progress on the charts, the master always had to keep track of her ever-changing speed and position. Every hour, therefore, the midshipman and quartermaster of the watch went aft to the taffrail and ordered the log line, or chip line—a triangular chip of wood (not an actual log), attached to the end of a long line in which knots had been tied every eight fathoms, or forty-eight feet—to be cast overboard. When the chip hit the water, the quartermaster turned a twenty-eight-second sandglass. As the ship surged forward, the knots sang off the reel and flew into the ship's wake until, the sands of time having run out, the quartermaster called, "Mark!" As the line was reeled back in, the midshipman would count the number of knots that had gone overboard. Eight and a half knots meant pretty fair speed; twelve or thirteen meant fast. Whatever the speed, it was chalked onto the slate kept near the wheel.

The determination of position was the central navigational ritual of the day. Shortly before high noon, the sailing master, one of his mates, and the midshipmen retrieved their quadrants and sextants from their felt-lined cases. They would then take successive "fixes" of the sun just as it approached its zenith. As it topped out in the sky, the master would cry, "Mark!" and they would all note the altitude—the angle between the sun and the horizon—their instruments had just measured. At the same time, the quartermaster would turn the ship's half-hour glass over, thereby bringing the little world of the ship into harmony with that of the heavens, for at sea the day officially began at noon, twelve hours earlier than the corresponding time on land.

After master and mate went below and compared their readings, correcting for any small inaccuracies, they could determine their latitude. That told them where they were between the equator and the pole. But to pinpoint their relative location east or west—their longitude—they needed a fixed reference point that was not only a *where* but also a *when*,

for times of day and night were ceaselessly shifting depending on where in the sky the sun or stars happened to be wheeling. For much of maritime history, determining longitude had been a matter of guesswork, reckoned from how far and how fast one had come. By the 1760s, however, a feverish race to better calculate longitude at sea culminated with the invention of two new and remarkably accurate methods.

One of them also depended on the sextant, only not to shoot the sun but rather the moon. Calculating by "lunar distances" meant measuring the angle between the moon and a nearby celestial object, the sun if it was still in the sky, or any of certain stars ranged along the ecliptic. That measurement was then checked against corresponding tables of lunar distances and times published in almanacs, from which one could calculate the exact time it was at the Royal Observatory in Greenwich near London, where the method was developed. Greenwich time thus became the fixed reference *when* for determining longitude, while lunar distances were accurate to within about ten or fifteen miles, which on the open ocean was generally deemed to be a close enough longitude reading.

The other method entailed a vessel's carrying Greenwich time aboard it. A marine chronometer might look like a fancy mantelpiece clock, only it was not intended to keep ship's time, which was still regulated by the flipping of half-hour and four-hour sandglasses and the ringing of bells, but rather to keep Greenwich time, however many oceans away from the Royal Observatory that ship happened to be. Only a sophisticated, finely calibrated mechanism, encased in heavy brass and often mounted on gimbals, could be guaranteed not to lose

seconds or minutes as it wound down, or to be jarred out of order by the ceaseless motions of the ship.

Employed properly, a marine chronometer allowed a master to determine longitude more accurately than any other method. But since they were very expensive, they had not yet been widely adopted in the early nineteenth century. The U.S. frigate *Constitution* received her first one only in the autumn of 1812. Perhaps her officers trusted the science behind their celestial observations more than they did blind mechanics, for they utilized the exquisite machine for little more than recording ship's time in the log. David Porter, on the other hand, carried a "very accurate chronometer" aboard *Essex* on his voyage to the Pacific in 1813 and was willing to put it to its proper use. But, worried that it was damaged during the stormy passage around Cape Horn, he tended to rely more on lunar observations to establish longitude—as well as to check the chronometer's accuracy, the one instrument that was soon to eclipse the lunar method altogether.

Whenever clouds or haze obscured the sun or fog reduced visibility, the master fell back on dead reckoning, the age-old way of estimating position and direction by plotting past courses and speeds. Long before there were sextants and chronometers, Columbus and Magellan had relied on simple traverse boards, where wooden pegs marked each change in a ship's forward progress, to supplement their compasses. Yet, even when mounted on gimbals to reduce motion and housed in a binnacle before the wheel, a compass could not always

be taken at its face value. The needle was subject to variation caused by the difference between the magnetic north pole and the geographical one. If not closely monitored, a variation of six percent would, if accumulating unchecked over a few days, send a vessel well off her course. And then there was the effect of current and leeway, or the way a ship was always being pushed sideways by the wind, to guard against as well.

A variation of dead reckoning widely practiced during the War of 1812 was "latitude sailing," hewing closely to a nearby parallel of latitude, especially when crossing vast tracts of ocean on an east-west axis. It simplified navigation until a landmark was approached, in which case a ship might just jump to another latitude and keep going. When approaching land, however, the leadline—a rope, tied to a lead weight, marked along its length in fathoms, or six-foot segments—would be used to avoid grounding in the shallows. As the ship eased forward, a seaman, standing in the forechains, would continually be casting this line, and each time the weight hit bottom he would call out, or "sound," the fathom mark. In 1814, Commodore John Rodgers, knowing that the British blockading fleet was out in deeper water, steered *President* up the Florida coast "on soundings," meaning he kept to the shallows within the hundred-fathom mark, well to shoreward of the enemy cordon, but carefully so as to avoid grounding the big frigate.

Perhaps no achievement in dead reckoning during the war surpassed that of twenty-two-year old U.S. Marine Lieutenant John M. Gamble, who escaped the enraged tribesmen at Nuku Hiva in the Marquesas with only eight sailors in the captured whaler *Sir Andrew Hammond*. Though mutineers had taken his spyglass, charts, and nautical instruments, he somehow managed to "run the trade winds," following only compass readings, over 1,800 miles to the northwest, and after a seventeen-day voyage was lucky enough to avoid disaster and reach the Hawaiian Islands. If not blockaded, captured, or sunk by the British, and if not grounded or becalmed to the point of starvation, the most likely event to delay or prevent a U.S. Navy vessel's homecoming was a storm. Storms, sometimes lasting for days on end, might buffet and hurl a ship far off course. They could also arise with terrifying suddenness. The

most reliable early warning—a falling barometer—was a relatively new signal aboard ships at this time. Although barometers had been around for more than a century, they could not be used at sea until mechanisms were devised to prevent the column of mercury from oscillating with every motion of the ship.

Even a gimbal-stabilized barometer could not have predicted the immense wave that struck *President* abeam in December 1812. It not only broke the lower studding-sail boom but also smashed many of the gunports, killed two sailors, and poured a vast quantity of water down the hatchways. Lighting once struck the mainmast of the frigate *United States*—"in its course it had cut away the pendant," wrote author Willis J. Abbott, "shot into the doctor's cabin, extinguishing that worthy's candle, to his vast astonishment; then, gliding away, broke through the ship's hull near the waterline, and plunged into the sea, after ripping off a few sheets of copper from the ship's bottom."

An unexpected squall blew the schooners *Hamilton* and *Scourge* onto their beam ends, promptly sinking them in the deep waters of Lake Ontario. And some combination of wind and wave no doubt led to the foundering of the corvette *Wasp* in late 1814; she simply disappeared and was never seen again. A few months earlier, in the inscrutable way of the sea, her namesake, the original sloop *Wasp*, captured by the British and renamed *Peacock*, had also foundered in a storm.

But whether calm or storm, wind or current, the factors that might speed or delay an ocean passage were still imperfectly understood. Each swell, each current, seemingly each ripple that *Essex* encountered was duly noted in the ship's log. Each island not found where the chart had placed it was painstakingly resurveyed using celestial observations, for Porter hoped to correct "erroneous" data laid down often many years earlier by pioneering mariners and explorers. Within a generation or two, however, navigation at sea would be vastly improved, thanks to the efforts of the U.S. Navy, which in the 1840s produced the first amalgamated wind and current charts for the world's major oceans. That, too, stemmed in part from the War of 1812, for the man responsible for such advances, the "Pathfinder of the Seas," Lieutenant Matthew Fontaine Maury of the U.S. Naval Observatory, had been inspired to join the Navy by an older brother who had met *Essex* at Nuku Hiva and fought in the Battle of Lake Champlain.

Faced with such an unremitting blockade, William Jones persuaded Congress in March to approve the construction of six sloops of war, which he believed would make more adept commerce raiders and would be better at diverting blockaders from their stations. These new sloops—*Argus*, *Wasp*, *Peacock*, and *Frolic*—would prove to be every bit as famous as their older sisters, the frigates, and like the frigates they would be more powerfully built and armed exemplars of their class than anything else then afloat. They also meant opportunity for many junior officers. Johnston Blakeley, for instance, would command *Wasp*, leaving the brig *Enterprise* to Lieutenant William Burrows.

Meanwhile, at Portsmouth, New Hampshire, Isaac Hull was worried about protecting the 74-gun ship-of-the-line that he was building at the Navy Yard. British privateers frequented the coast to the north and east, menacing the coastal trade, while a frigate and a sloop were often stationed just offshore. On August 21, therefore, he ordered *Enterprise* to cruise along the bay-indented, island-studded coast of Maine, staying as close inshore as possible to avoid those larger warships, peering into the coves and protecting the coastal trade.

A thirteen-year veteran of the Navy, the twenty-seven-year-old Burrows was the son of the Marine Corps' first commandant and had just been released from a British prison in Barbados. His new assignment demanded a sharp eye and fine judgment, as enemy privateers might be disguised as small fishing boats or coastal lighters. Furthermore, many outwardly loyal New Englanders were still trading with the enemy, some for commercial motives, others to avoid the fate being visited upon the Chesapeake Bay that summer. In Cape Cod Bay, where British warships sheltered from storms, a kind of truce existed; a Spanish flag run up the mast meant they were willing to pay for wood, food, and water. In Maine, where the island of Monhegan had reportedly declared itself neutral, some citizens, even a general of militia, were willing to reach an accommodation with a certain British brig—as Burrows discovered when he heard the rumor in Portland.

On the morning of September 5, as *Enterprise* approached Pemaquid Point, Burrows indeed saw a brig in the bay, and what's more, she fired her guns to summon her shore parties quickly back on board. She was none other than HMS *Boxer*, and her captain was thirty-year-old Samuel Blyth, who had been one of James Lawrence's pallbearers in Halifax. Blyth, who had been personally decorated for bravery by Admiral Sir James Yeo after the storming of Cayenne in French Guiana, had only the previous evening expressed the wish to "make a prize honorable to his profession." No doubt, as he made straight for the American warship, he saw his chance. The two brigs were evenly matched. *Enterprise* was only a little stronger, relying on fourteen 18-pound carronades, while *Boxer* had only ten. But as the two vessels hauled the wind to stand out of the bay, Blyth nailed his colors to the mainmast, asserting that they should "never be struck" while

he still possessed life. Meanwhile, Burrows, moving one of his two long 9-pounders from the bow to the stern, declared, "We are going to fight both ends and both sides of this ship as long as the ends and the sides hold together."

As the two brigs stalked each other from Pemaquid Point to Monhegan, people flocked to the rocky shores to watch. Even one minister, it was said, cut short his service to rush to an overlook. By midafternoon, having approached to within half a pistol shot of each other, the two brigs opened a booming fire. Blyth had barely uttered the cry, "Great God! What shots!" when an 18-pound solid shot ripped him in half. Moments later, Burrows, was hit by canister that tore through his leg and lodged in his groin. For more than half an hour, it was broadside for broadside in the smoke until—masts broken and hanging overboard, braces and rigging shot away, and *Enterprise* maneuvering for the killing rake—*Boxer*'s surviving lieutenant hailed that he was striking because the colors were nailed to the fallen mast. Only her quarterdeck guns were still manned, and they were being directed by the purser. When offered Blyth's sword, the dying Burrows only waved it off, wishing instead that it be sent to the dead man's family. "I am satisfied, I die contented," he managed to mutter. Lieutenant Edward McCall, now in command, then took the two battered brigs with their ghastly freight of wounded and dead into nearby Portland, Maine, where a sizeable crowd had gathered.

American newspapers were soon glorying in "another brilliant naval victory." Even Secretary William Jones let his enthusiasm run away with his judgment. "For brilliancy and decision," he told the chairman of the Naval Affairs Committee, the victory "has never been surpassed in naval action." The English, however, were again downcast. The Americans "have some *superior mode of firing*," opined one London paper, "and we cannot be too anxiously employed in discovering to what circumstances that superiority is owing."

Two days after the battle, seemingly everyone in Portland and many from the surrounding district were lining the streets, hanging from upper story windows, and gathering on rooftops as two black-draped barges, like something out of Arthurian saga, carried the coffins bearing the dead captains to shore. As a pair of hearses wended their way up the hilly streets, they were followed by both American and British officers in stately procession while bells rang solemnly and minute-guns fired reverberantly. In Portland's Eastern Cemetery, the two were buried side by side in a plot overlooking the sea. It all made a deep impression on six-year-old Henry Wadsworth Longfellow, who recalled it many decades later in his paean to his hometown, "My Lost Youth."

> I remember the sea-fight far away, / How it thundered o'er the tide! / And the dead sea-captains, as they lay / In their graves, o'erlooking the tranquil bay / Where they in battle died.

Opposite: A satirical print by William Charles commemorating the victory of *Enterprise* over *Boxer*. As Winifred Morgan points out in *An American Icon*, Charles' portrayal of the Brother Jonathan figure "stresses republican simplicity in contrast with John Bull's monarchical trappings—a crown on his head and fussy braid on his coat."

A BOXING MATCH, or Another Bloody Nose for JOHN BULL.

All throughout September, no fewer than twenty-five British warships, on station from the Grand Banks of Newfoundland to the Chesapeake Bay, were under orders to be on the lookout for one lonely frigate, *President*, which might try to run their gauntlet.

On the twenty-third day of the month, HMS *High Flyer* was cruising off Nantucket Shoals when her lookouts spotted a frigate on the horizon. Her lieutenant quickly hoisted a recognition signal. When he saw that it was satisfactorily answered, he approached and hove to beneath the larger warship's stern, down the ladder of which an officer neatly attired in a British uniform soon descended. *High Flyer* made him every courtesy, for the frigate towering beside him, the lieutenant was told, was none other than HMS *Sea Horse*. The resplendently dressed officer, with a copy of *High Flyer*'s signal book in hand so as to check her bona fides, then invited the lieutenant on board. There he was presented to the captain, an imposing gentleman who after exchanging formalities asked what the young man could tell him about this man Rodgers who had everyone in such a stir. The lieutenant merely replied that around the fleet the American was considered "an odd fish and hard to catch."

The captain seemed taken aback. "Sir," he demanded, "do you know what vessel you are on board of?"

"Why, yes, sir," the lieutenant replied. "His Majesty's Ship *Sea Horse*."

"Then, sir, you labor under a mistake," the captain glowered. "You are on board the United States frigate *President*, and I am Commodore Rodgers."

John Rodgers might have been a lion among men, but he was also a fox. All that dangerous way back from Ireland he, too, had been especially watchful. Off the Grand Banks he had captured two additional vessels, learning from one that HMS *Bellerophon*, a 74, and HMS *Hyperion*, a frigate, were only a few miles distant. He simply stood farther out to sea and sailed around them, not glimpsing another sail until he approached Nantucket Shoals toward the end of September. His provisions now quite literally exhausted, he had no choice but to run for the nearest friendly port—which might have led him straight into the arms of the Royal Navy were it not, by great good fortune, that he encountered *High Flyer* and, knowing a few of the British signals, drew her into his snare instead.

From that signal book he gleaned enough about the position of the British squadrons to forego Boston altogether and strike out rather for Rhode Island where, on September 26, the captured *High Flyer* alongside, *President* glided into the harbor at Newport.

While Admiral Warren had to admit to the Admiralty that Rodgers had once again eluded their trap, the commodore was writing his wife—repeatedly, as he was impatient for an answer.

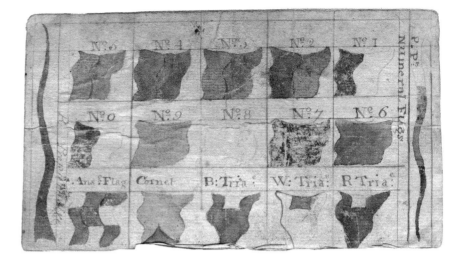

U.S.S. *President*
Near Providence, Oct. 3d 1813
My beloved my adored wife, Having informed you of the uncertainty of my stay here, and having left it entirely to yourself whether or not you will honor me with a visit, it is impossible to describe the anxiety I shall experience until I hear from you. The determination of going to sea again in so short a time should the disposition of the Secretary be such as not to prevent it will I apprehend cause you some pangs which Heaven knows I would make any sacrifice short of self reproach to avoid; you must therefore not refuse for this is something which whispers me that fate will yet gratify my best wishes so that I have only one more trial to make to receive her favors and return with the reward to enjoy the caresses of my beloved wife and children.

Minerva, however, was answering them as soon as the letters reached her.

October 5, 1813
My Dearest Husband,
I shall have here to make my way to Providence . . . [Y]our letters only reached me yesterday—and the second <u>this</u> moment. You have left it to my belief therefore I do not hesitate . . . I do not in any way wish to influence you . . . should you deem it expedient to depart ere I reach Providence! God knows the blow would be extreme but I should endeavor to bear it as becoming the wife of a hero. Ever yours most tenderly, M. Rodgers

The commodore, however, did not feel like a hero. Though he had nearly circled the British Isles and sailed over more than half the distance around the globe on his three cruises, he had yet to encounter a British frigate that was not

Should a single light be displayed above any of the figures, it is to be understood that a point of the Compass is refered to; and on the discovery of any objects as land, danger, ships &c or any other thing necessary to be pointed out by signal that may require its bearing shewn, it will be done in the following manner, viz.

Single For N. No. 1 will be displayed with a signal light over it. For N. E. No 2 with the same light above. For E. No. 3 For S. E. No 4 For S. No 5 For S W. No 6 For W. No 7 For N. W No. 8, all with the light above as before. But should any intermediate points be required, it will only be necessary to repeat the signal once for each point, allowing for each repetition one point to the *right hand*. For example, should N. by E. be required, make the signal for N. and as soon as it is answered (which is done by hoisting a single light) repeat it; and so on for the number of points you wish to designate.

For a half point more, you will shew a single light after having made the point, which is to be considered the half point more to the right hand.

By this simple mode you can express the whole compass with care and distinctness, and when those numbers are displayed with the single light over them, and previous to any other signal, such as, land—danger, ships, &c the *course* you are to steer until further orders is pointed out.

The first six occurrences requiring great rapidity of execution, are not numerically arranged; but merely placed opposite such signs as can be shewn immediately in the moment required. A single light is the answer to these signals.

also accompanied by a 74. Yet as the senior officer in a service that put an undue premium on individual heroics, Rodgers felt that he, too, should also be covered in the glory that only victory at sea could bring. Secretary Jones demurred; he had little patience for naval heroics and was delighted that his senior commander had so thoroughly harassed British commerce that his name had become a byword among the Royal Navy, which then had to spin off more and more of her resources trying to hunt him down.

As events would prove, his record stood third to only two other American ships, neither of which would survive its cruise. One had been *Argus*, and the other, far away though she might be, was *Essex*.

THE FARAWAY ISLES

By late October, *Essex* was tucked away where winter would never find her. Before leaving the Galápagos, Porter had studied his charts and, stirred by the old yearning, had steered his little fleet 3,500 miles to the west, to the distant, seldom-visited Marquesas Islands of Polynesia. They had passed pods of whales and immense shoals of flying fish before the first jagged peaks, covered in luxuriant tropical vegetation and streaked with waterfalls, first loomed into view. Crashing breakers marked an encircling coral reef, but after picking their way through its tangles, the makeshift American flotilla dropped anchor in a palm-fringed bay surrounded on all sides by rugged cliffs and hills—the island of Nuku Hiva.

This was home to the Te I'i, who, understandably wary of these intruders, had to be bought off with gifts of trinkets and small tools before they bestowed their friendship. That bit of diplomacy aside, over the next seven weeks, *Essex* was unloaded, stripped, careened on that coralline beach, and scraped. Her holds were smoked with charcoal, killing nearly 1,500 rats. Her seams were caulked and her hull repainted. Her decaying main topmast was replaced. A small village grew up around these activities, with a cooper's shop for making new water casks, a sail loft for repairing canvas, an infirmary, a guardhouse, and even a makeshift fort, all built with the islanders' help.

At the same time, Porter's men were enjoying the "relaxation and amusement" that their captain had promised them during the difficult passage around the Horn. They feasted on succulent pork, fresh fruit, coconuts, taro, plantain, and twenty varieties of bananas. There was never a need to open a single cask of salted provisions, and even the Galápagos tortoises were turned loose to amble off into the jungle. But feasting was not the only activity they enjoyed on those soft, star-flocked tropic nights. Scarcely had *Essex* dropped anchor in Nuku Hiva Bay when the island's women were swarming over the decks. "When the ship was moored, the shore was lined with the natives of both sexes," Porter recorded in his journal. "But the females were most numerous, waving their white cloaks or *cahoes* for us to come on shore." As far as the visitors were able to determine, among the Te I'i, the younger women were free to bestow their favors on whomever they pleased, and the men willingly yielded themselves up to temptation. Even Porter found it necessary, "from motives of policy," to pay court to an eighteen-year-old princess. "All was helter skelter, and promiscuous intercourse," he admitted, "every girl the wife of every man in the mess, and frequently of every man in the ship." Subsequently, he acknowledged letting matters get out of hand, conceding that if there were

Mouina.
Chief Warrior of the Taychs.

Drawn by Capt Porter   Engraved by W. Strickland

An engraving after a drawing by Porter depicting the chief warrior of the Te I'i, Mouina, whom Porter described as a "tall, well-shaped man, of about thirty-five years of age, remarkably active, of an intelligent and open countenance, and his whole appearance highly prepossessing." Porter detailed the dress of the warriors at length: they wore ornamental plumes fashioned from the feathers of man-of-war birds, cloaks made of tree bark, and necklaces strung with whales' teeth. They carried a "black and highly polished spear" or a "club richly carved," and their bodies were "highly and elegantly ornamented by tattooing, executed in a manner to excite our admiration."

Dating from the late eighteenth or early nineteenth century, this *'u'u* club from the Marquesas Islands looks remarkably similar to the one that Mouina is holding in Porter's drawing. The club is made mostly out of ironwood, a very tough and heavy wood known as *toa*, which is also the Marquesan word for warrior. Carved into either side of it at the top are a number of faces, which were thought to provide the owner with added protection. It has a handle bound with coir and human hair. The rich, dark patina is believed to have been achieved by soaking the club in taro swamps and polishing it with coconut oil.

"any crime" in such liaisons, "the offense was ours, not theirs; they acted in compliance with the customs of their ancestors."

While his men thus luxuriated in this South Pacific idyll, their captain indulged a taste for cultural anthropology, filling his journal with descriptions of tattooed, stilt-walking islanders, headdresses made of frigate bird feathers, spears and slings and canoes, forts and temples and ceremonies. He also, unavoidably, became embroiled in the island's wars. On an island with so many hidden, inaccessible valleys, each of Nuku Hiva's several tribes had become inveterate enemies of the others. As the Te I'i were being threatened by the Happahs, Porter sent a detachment of men with a 6-pounder and some muskets into the hills, and the resulting smoke and thunder quickly brought the Happahs to heel. The Typees, whom Herman Melville would later make famous, were more difficult to subdue. Porter's little sailor army had to accompany two thousand Te I'i warriors

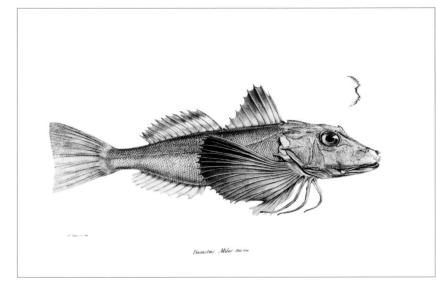

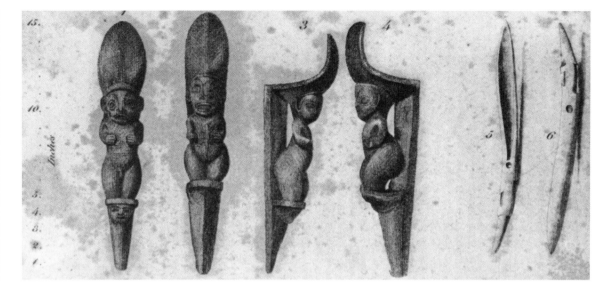

JEUNE FILLE DE L'ILE MADISSON.

An original 1843 hand-colored woodblock print of a young woman of Nuku Hiva.

Left, top: Darwin's drawing of a Galápagos gurnard, from *The Zoology of the Voyage of HMS Beagle*. Fish also interested Captain David Porter, although perhaps more from a subsistence standpoint. He noted with special interest the flying fish he saw flitting over the waters surrounding the Marquesas, observing that they were unusually large and red-winged.

Left, bottom: *Essex* in Huku Hiva Bay.

An illustration from Porter's journal depicting the intricate stilts of the Polynesian islanders. "The natives of Santa Christiana make a very dexterous use of their stilts, and would, in a race, dispute the palm with our most experienced herdsmen in stalking with theirs over the heaths of Bordeaux," Porter penned. "The pains taken by the former in ornamenting with sculpture, those which they had invented, may prove that they set on them a great value, for this work, executed on a very hard wood, with the sort of tools which they employ, must cost them much trouble, and require a very considerable portion of time. Besides, they are seen amusing themselves in keeping up the habit of walking with stilts; this exercise enters into their games, and constitutes a part of their gymnastics."

across the mountains on a punitive raid against the Typees, laying waste to their valley before they came to terms.

Porter's policy was to dominate the warlike tribes by demanding tributes of provisions from each, the natural outcome of which was a desire to dominate the entire island. During an improvised ceremony, complete with the firing off of some cannons, he grandiosely proclaimed Nuku Hiva— which he dubbed "Madison Island" in honor of the president—to be a U.S. protectorate. It was an attempt at annexation that neither the chief executive nor his secretary of state, James Monroe, would ever acknowledge.

"EVERY SHIP IN CHACE"

As 1813 drew to a close, Admiral Sir John Borlase Warren was back in Bermuda, taking stock of the Royal Navy's position off the coasts of North America. Although his squadrons had captured 115 ships, mostly trading schooners, between April and November, he had also extended the blockade to the coasts of Connecticut. Quite simply, he wanted more ships. Several hurricanes had swept through the West Indies that season, damaging vessels on station there; one had even struck Halifax, ripping nearly sixty warships from their anchors and driving them onshore. Meanwhile, as he told the Sea Lords, the "Americans are building a very large Class of Corvette Ships"—the sloops *Peacock, Wasp,* and their sisters—while "every exertion is making at New York, Philadelphia, and Baltimore to prepare Vessels of War, the rapidity with which the Americans build and fit out their Ships is scarcely credible."

He also wanted more ships to forestall the hordes of privateers still easily stealing through his wooden cordon, even from heavily blockaded Charleston. Baltimore clippers were still escaping from the Chesapeake Bay. When nights were dark and winds were high, they were impossible to stop—several of them, it seemed, "passing out in a Squadron and outsailing every Ship in Chace."

Secretary Jones, on the other hand, was issuing cruising orders again. He ordered the brigs *Enterprise* and *Rattlesnake* to the West Indies, emphasizing that they were to stay together, as that might make them more formidable should they encounter a heavier British foe. *Siren* was to escape Boston and strike out for Africa, nosing into the ports along the way before rounding the Cape into the Indian Ocean, where a surprised enemy might be caught loading cargoes of "Elephant teeth, Gums, rich Woods, and Gold Dust." He prohibited all of his commanders at sea from giving or receiving an enemy's challenge. "The Character of the American Navy," he insisted, "does not require those feats of Chivalry." Neither were they to reduce their crews by manning prizes. They were to burn them instead. "With every patriotic Officer, private motives will yield to considerations of public good, and . . . the great object and end of our public force is to harass and distress the enemy." After all, "His Commerce is our true Game, for there he is indeed vulnerable."

In mid-December, *Congress* limped through the winter gales to the safety of Portsmouth, New Hampshire. It was not enemy action but rather the rigors of wind and sea that were wearing her down. It had been eight months since that day in the mid-Atlantic when Captain John Smith signaled farewell to John Rodgers and set a course for the south. Though mostly lurking between the Cape Verdes and Brazil, she had taken only four prizes, returning exhausted of supplies, her bowsprit decayed, her caulking loosened.

The same day, that weather abated long enough to allow her into the Navy Yard. *Constitution,* now refitted and ready for duty, was easing out of Boston, waiting for the weather to worsen to make her break for freedom. It was the last day of the year—a year to the day, in fact, since *Java* had gone up in flames.

President was in the mid-Atlantic again. Before he had slipped out of Newport in early December, Commodore John Rodgers had written a note.

My beloved Wife!
The *President* is this moment launching her head into old Neptune's domain with a fine breeze from the NW. Do not suffer your repose to be disturbed by idle rumors during my absence. The wind is fresh and I have only time to say God bless. I remain your, Jn Rodgers

Only God knew where *Essex* was.

Commodore John Rodgers' portable writing box—the laptop of the era—and his inkwell.

GEMS OF ART.

Admiral
PORTER.

Rear-Admiral
FARRAGUT.

UNP1863sf-1

Porter's son, David Dixon Porter, and adopted son, David Farragut, who became a midshipman at the frighteningly young age of ten. Long after his naval adventures with *Essex* in the War of 1812, Farragut would become a hero of the Union Navy in the Civil War, helping to break the Confederate hold over the Gulf of Mexico's ports. Showing some of his father's pluck on August 5, 1864, he refused to back down when one of the Union fleet's lead ships struck a mine while attempting to sail into the channel. In reply to the warning, "Torpedoes ahead!" given by the forward ships, Admiral Farragut called out, "Damn the torpedoes!" and took the lead with his flagship.

As it happened, by early December, with *Essex* refurbished and refitted, her decks loaded with coconuts and hogs, David Porter was preparing to return to his own war. Uncertain what he might find, though, when he ventured back into the East Pacific, he ordered Marine Lieutenant John Gamble to remain behind at Nuku Hiva with three of the prize vessels—*Greenwich*, *Seringapatam*, and *Sir Andrew Hammond*—instructing him to rendezvous with *Essex* six months later at Valparaíso if he did not soon return with a British squadron on his heels. Before giving the final order to weigh anchor and shake out sails, however, Porter assembled *Essex*'s crew in the ship's waist. It would be too much to expect men to willingly forsake delightful days and soft nights spent beneath tropic stars. He had caught wind of a conspiracy to seize the ship and remain forever in that palm-shaded paradise. So, crew assembled before him, he announced that at the first sign of mutiny, he would fire the powder magazine, blowing the entire vessel and everyone aboard to kingdom come. Nobody dared call his bluff.

Instead, *Essex* and *Essex Jr.* stood out to sea, and after a six-week voyage reached the soaring Andean-capped coast of Chile. Once more they called at Valparaíso, where once more they enjoyed the hospitality of the local grandees— that is, until the day HMS *Phoebe* glided up next to the moored *Essex*.

As Farragut later remembered it, when *Phoebe* and *Cherub* "made their appearance off the port, one third of our crew were on shore on liberty, which was one watch, our crew having been divided into three watches."

> The mate of an English merchant ship that lay in port went immediately on board the *Phebe* and stated to Capt. Hyllar that one half of our crew were on shore, and the ship would fall an easy prey. The ships hauled into the harbor on a wind, the *Phebe* made our larboard quarter, but the *Cherub* fell to leeward, about a half mile. When the *Phebe* had gained our quarter, she put down her helm and luffed up on our starboard bow, within 10 or 15 feet of our ship.

But *Essex* had been warned just in time and had fired a gun recalling her missing crewmen. So what *Phoebe* found was not a frigate caught by surprise but rather one cleared for action and manning her guns. "Boarding was our forte, and every man was prepared for it, with a dirk made by our armourer out of an old file, a cutlass that you might shave with, and a pistol," Farragut recalled. It was the British who were caught by surprise. Were it not that Valparaíso was a neutral port, a rash powder monkey might have ignited a fight that *Essex* had every chance of winning.

> While the [*Phoebe*] was alongside within 20 yards, and all hands at quarters the Powder Boys were stationed, with matches to discharge the guns as the men

boarded in the smoke. This boy saw someone from the [*Phoebe*], as he imagined, grinning at him. "D—n you my fine fellow," said he, "I'll stop your laughing or making faces at me." When as he was in the act of firing his gun, Lt. McKnight saw him and with one blow sprawled him on the deck. Had that gun been fired, I am convinced the *Phebe* would have been ours. But it was destined otherwise.

Three weeks later, on March 28, 1814, having been challenged to come out and battle both *Phoebe* and *Cherub*, which were ceaselessly patrolling outside the harbor, *Essex* made a break for it when the wind was right. She almost made it. She had gained the offing and was standing out to sea, outracing her adversaries— possibly to recross the Pacific, possibly to raid her way through the Indian Ocean and home—when a white squall hit her, laid her over on her beam ends, and tore off that troublesome main topmast. Left crippled outside the harbor, her carronades useless against foes who stood off and pounded her with their longer-range guns, *Essex* was shot to splinters, and more than half of her crew killed or wounded.

The men left behind at Nuku Hiva fared no better. Faced with growing restiveness among the islanders and renegade deserters from his detachment, Lieutenant Gamble fled to sea in *Seringapatam*, but on May 7, 1814, even that shorthanded crew mutinied, tossing him into a small boat alongside a mere handful of loyal sailors. While *Seringapatam* sailed away, never to be seen again, Gamble managed to navigate his way back to Nuku Hiva. There, after a desperate fight with both the natives and the deserters, he commandeered *Sir Andrew Hammond*, and with only eight men, most of them wounded, and no instruments or charts, somehow sailed across two thousand miles of open ocean to the Hawaiian Islands—only to be scooped up by the waiting *Cherub*. The British squadron that soon nosed into Nuku Hiva Bay discovered that the Marquesans had massacred the few remaining Americans.

David Porter and the other survivors were paroled and eventually returned to the United States, where they received a hero's welcome and were honored with grand dinners, parades, and rallies. The battered Salem-built frigate, however, was towed all the way to Plymouth, England, and there taken into the Royal Navy. *Chesapeake* might have been broken up in 1820 and her timbers used in an English mill, the beams, joists, and floors still bearing the scars of grapeshot, but *Essex* ended her days as a prison ship, a dismasted hulk moored in the harbor of Kingstown (now Dún Laoghaire), Ireland, holding convicts awaiting transportation to the other side of the world, to the penal colonies in distant Australia.

Anticipating ship-to-ship combat with *Cherub* and *Phoebe* in Valparaíso, Porter sent these detailed engagement instructions to Lieutenant John Downes, his executive officer, on January 10, 1814. Unfortunately, the rendezvous with destiny didn't happen on his terms.

Right: Lieutenant John Downes' dirk.

Opposite: George Ropes' rendering of *Essex*'s capture by the frigate *Phoebe* and the sloop *Cherub* in the bay of Valparaíso.

CAPTURE OF THE U.S.FRIGATE ESSEX BY HIS B.M.FRIGATE PHOEBE & SLOOP CHERUB IN THE BAY OF VALPARAISO

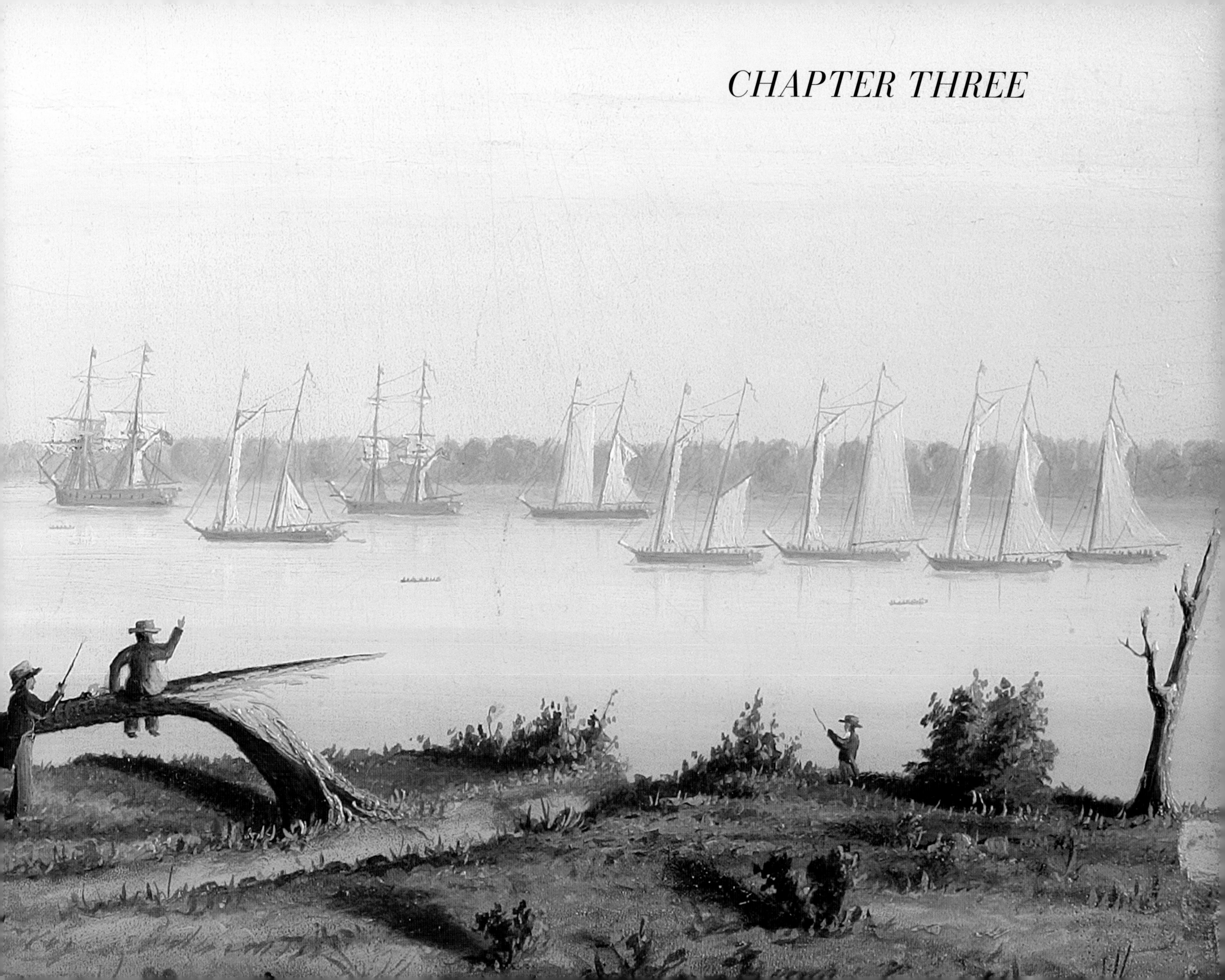

CHAPTER THREE

Perry's battle flag bearing the motto "Don't Give Up the Ship"—the dying command of Captain James Lawrence, Perry's close friend. To sew the flag, Perry's purser engaged a local Erie woman, Margaret Foster Steuart, who enlisted the help of her daughters and nieces. Due to a conservation treatment in the early 1900s, it is commonly believed that the original color of the flag was blue, but it may have been red, brown, or even black ("black, the color of death, with Lawrence's last words . . . inscribed on it, in white letters," as Edward Chauncey Marshall described it in 1862). The flag, made of a single layer of finespun wool, the linen letters stitched to both sides, is shown here in its true state, stripped of its blue façade.

Overleaf: Perry's fleet in Put-in-Bay on the morning of the Battle of Lake Erie.

"OUR ONLY SAFETY"

THE GREAT LAKES

1812–1813

"WE MUST HAVE A NAVY NOW TO COMMAND THE LAKES,
IF IT COSTS US 100 SHIPS OF THE LINE; WHATEVER BECOMES OF THE OCEAN."

~ John Adams to Thomas Jefferson

Born in Québec, reared in Halifax, his father a British veteran of the American Revolution, Ned Myers came to America to be a sailor.

The Canadian's stint with the Navy as a "common Jack" began in New York Harbor only a short time before war was declared and started unpromisingly—he was assigned to a gunboat, No. 107, one among many nameless Jeffersonian gunboats in the harbor's large flotilla. Bogged down with heavy guns, the little boats tipped over at even a whisper of wind and were "such ill-conditioned craft," as Theodore Roosevelt later wrote, "that the best officers might be pardoned for feeling uncomfortable in them."

As the threat of war began to materialize, Myers and his new mates found themselves in the New York Navy Yard at the behest of its commandant,

Captain Isaac Chauncey, whose artificers needed help overhauling the Salem-built subscription frigate *Essex*. Defective spars were stymieing her sailing speed, and her worm-eaten hull, encrusted with weeds and barnacles in the hundreds of pounds, had to be scraped thoroughly clean. The work was accomplished at a breakneck pace, but war came faster. Word of its declaration arrived on a cloudless Saturday in New York City two days after the fact. Though it arrived too late to make the morning papers, and no extras hit the presses, the streets were soon abuzz with the news. "On this occasion I got drunk, for the second time in my life," Myers told his old friend James Fenimore Cooper many years later. "A quantity of whiskey was started into a tub, and all hands drank to the

A map of the Great Lakes region as it appeared in 1812.

Right: A full hull model of a gunboat, circa 1808, built in bread and butter construction. The model is decked and fully equipped, including a bilge pump, a mast tabernacle and crutch for lowering the sailing rig, and side benches.

Opposite: An Americanized portrayal of the legendary Shawnee leader Tecumseh, whose name fittingly meant "the shooting star."

And so a young man who had dreamed of going to sea as a boy found himself heading deep into the wilds to fight on the watery frontier between the country of his birth and that of his adoption.

CONTESTED WATERS

The Great Lakes had always been a frontier, always contested waters—between Huron and Iroquois, English and French, British and American. Lower Canada, or Québec, which stretched along the St. Lawrence River, still retained the imprint of three centuries of French colonization. Upper Canada, or Ontario, was lapped by the waters of the Great Lakes.

After the American Revolution, the border between the British Empire and the new republic reached right across Lakes Ontario, Erie, Huron, and Superior until, vanishing in an immensity of forestland, it was only a line drawn on maps. Along Lakes Ontario and Erie, however, there was a clear divide between loyalists to the north and revolutionaries to the south—a divide still simmering with hostility.

Yet the Lakes were also a great unifying feature. They were the water highway of the continent, carrying people and trade goods through a world that was otherwise wilderness. In the seventeenth century, La Salle followed the stepping stones that were the Lakes deep into the continental interior, and then, after a short portage, canoed down a stream that proved to be the Mississippi River. With one sweep of his arm, he claimed the whole expanse to the west for his monarch, King Louis XIV, and New France, including "Louisiana," nominally embraced all the chief waterways of the continent, from the Gulf of St. Lawrence to the Gulf of Mexico.

In 1803, President Thomas Jefferson had purchased Louisiana from a cash-strapped Napoleon. That had only complicated matters with Great Britain, which had its own designs on the Northwest. It had really complicated matters with the Native American tribes, who believed that the land between the Great Lakes to the north, the Ohio River to the south, and everything west of the Mississippi belonged to them by treaty. Because Britain sponsored this idea of a "Great Indian Reserve"—

success of the conflict." Soon after, on July 3, 1812, *Essex* weighed anchor, and Myers returned to his gunboat—but not for long.

After the *Essex* was fitted out, the flotilla cruised in the Sound, and was kept generally on the look-out, about the waters of New York. Toward the end of the season, our boat, with several others, was lying abreast of the Yard, when orders came off to meet the Yard Commander, Captain Chauncey, on the wharf. Here, this officer addressed us, and said he was about to proceed to Lake Ontario, to take command, and asking who would volunteer to go with him. This was agreeable news to us, for we hated the gunboats, and would go anywhere to be quit of them. Every man and boy volunteered. We got twenty-four hours' liberty, with a few dollars in money, and when this scrape was over every man returned, and we embarked in a sloop for Albany.

which its policymakers, who viewed the American Revolution as but a temporary setback, saw as a buffer that might blunt the ambitions of the new republic—the tribes were in alliance with the king and empire. They rallied around the magnetic, compelling, visionary Shawnee warrior Tecumseh, who before countless council fires had exhorted the chiefs of the Wyandot, Delaware, Potawatomi, Piankashaw, Kickapoo, Menominee, and other tribes tumbled together by the advance of European civilization to join in one great confederacy, perhaps even an independent nation, that might halt the tide of American expansion. Tecumseh was soon wearing the red coat and epaulettes of a British brigadier general.

Even the elements collided over those inland seas. Great gales swept across their surfaces, kicking up whitecaps and piling huge waves against the rocky, pine-clad shores, leaving behind only a detritus of old canoes and broken schooners. In 1812, with the drumbeat of war so clearly approaching, it was remarkable that on such an expanse of contested waters the British Empire had only five warships— under the auspices of the Provincial Marine, a holdover from the Seven Years' War—and the U.S. Navy but a solitary brig still in active service.

LAKE ONTARIO, EARLY SUMMER 1812

The 16-gun *Oneida* had taken shape under the persnickety hands of a master shipwright named Henry Eckford—who'd marked, felled, and hauled her timbers himself—in the tiny hamlet of Oswego, New York, in 1808. Eckford, owner of the most flourishing shipbuilding firm on New York City's East River, had built the brig for Lieutenant Melancthon Taylor Woolsey, who by 1812 was marking his twelfth year in the Navy.

By nature sturdy and athletic, Woolsey carried himself with a "pleasing mixture of gentleman-like refinement and seaman-like frankness," according to James Fenimore Cooper. A midshipman sent to the Lakes at the commencement of *Oneida*'s construction, Cooper had cultivated a friendship with the affable lieutenant, whose years on the frontier had put him at ease with all kinds of people. Cooper remembered him as lacking "the grimace" of authority but not "the substance," adding, "A better-hearted man never lived."

Oneida, which Woolsey once fondly dubbed "the handsomest vessel in the Navy," was built to snuff out smugglers during the trying months of Jefferson's 1807 Embargo Act, which shut down all American foreign commerce in a misguided attempt at the "peaceable coercion" of Britain and France. Though the act was soon repealed, Washington's power players deemed it wise to have an active naval presence on the Lakes anyway.

Left to his own resources, since the government provided him precious little, the young lieutenant began to cobble together a base. In the northeast reaches of the Lake, he found a sheltered harbor with deep waters and softly

Constructed in the "admiralty style," this model of *Oneida*, armed with sixteen 24-pounder carronades and two long 6-pounder guns, depicts her as she appeared in the spring of 1813. Built in 1:48 scale by Colonel Clayton F. Nans, USMC (Retired), of Sackets Harbor, the model is based on surviving plans and data from the Naval Records Group of the National Archives, as well as on archeological information gleaned from the remains of War of 1812 vessels by Dr. Kevin J. Chrisman of Texas A&M University.

A contemporary portrait of Melancthon Taylor Woolsey.

sloping shores that was perfectly suited for a shipyard. Though it was perilously close to the British naval base in Kingston, which was only forty-five miles away on the other side of the St. Lawrence River, Woolsey still persuaded the Navy Department to purchase it, paying Augustus Sacket, a potash and pearl ash runner, $5,000 for what came to be called Sackets Harbor. In 1810, Woolsey sailed *Oneida* to her new base.

With war about to break over the Lakes in early June 1812, Woolsey was patrolling Ontario's American shore, on the lookout for smugglers—Congress had issued a final warning to the British in the form of a ninety-day embargo—when he netted his first prize near the Genesee River: *Lord Nelson*, a Canadian merchantman whose master could show no papers. Not lacking initiative, Woolsey impounded the schooner and wasted no time in converting both it and *Julia*, another laker, into gunboats—though he lacked guns to arm them, men to man them, and money to do either.

The declaration of war, when Woolsey caught wind of it, only made him work harder. With the responsibility for his nation's defense on Lake Ontario resting squarely on his solitary shoulders, he closely monitored the British vessels moored off Kingston. Though the might of the Provincial Marine remained embarrassingly herculean by comparison, he still tried scaring up a force that wouldn't be laughed off the lake. Down the St. Lawrence, eight American merchantmen had been bottled up by the British in the harbor of a little village called Ogdensburg. Fearing how the vessels might be put to use if they fell into enemy hands, and desirous of boosting his own spartan squadron, Woolsey set his sights on safeguarding the lakers.

"All our merchantmen except three are down the river St. Lawrence," he reported to Secretary of the Navy Paul Hamilton on July 4. "Two schooners have been taken and burned by the enemy. How the others will fare God only knows. I am now fitting out the schooner *Julia* as a Gun Boat to carry the thirty-two pounder originally intended for the *Oneida*." He scribbled an urgent postscript: "The whole amount of Ordnance that I can muster is one Thirty two and Three six pounders." (That 32-pounder, it was said, had some time before been carried to the harbor's land battery and all but abandoned, Woolsey having no means to do anything useful with it. The neglected gun had sunk so far down into the muck that its carriage disappeared and only its slick black cannon poked through. The townspeople, thinking it suggestive of a mud-caked, pot-bellied pig, started calling it the "Old Sow.")

Though dispatches took up to ten days to reach Washington, and a reply could take three weeks or longer, Woolsey continued to plead for support. He was keenly aware of his own vulnerability. Isolated, *Oneida* might not withstand a push from the British, who were sure to act. "I have no doubt but that an attempt will be made by them on the *Oneida*," he wrote. "I shall watch them narrowly."

This watercolor by nineteenth-century landscape painter Hugh Irvine (active between 1800 and 1830) depicts the British naval facilities at Point Frederick in Kingston. The small loyalist town on Lake Ontario's north shore was home to the Provincial Marine and later formed the heart of the Royal Navy's shipbuilding operations.

LAKE ERIE, SUMMER 1812

Three hundred miles to the northwest, tiny Mackinac Island, guarding the deep strait where Lakes Huron and Michigan meet, had long been an emporium for the fur trade. At three o'clock in the morning on July 17, 1812, however, a fleet of bateaux and war canoes packed with a motley crew of French Canadian voyageurs, Indian warriors, and British regulars crossed over from Canada and assaulted the island's stronghold, which sat high atop a limestone bluff. Before dawn, the three hundred raiders had surrounded the thirty American soldiers stationed there. After confirming the declaration of war, British general Isaac Brock had launched a preemptive strike on this strategic locale, soon obtained its surrender, and detained the sole American merchant ship anchored there: a salt droger aptly called *Salina*.

Salina's owner and captain was a lakeman by the name of Daniel Dobbins, who had come to Mackinac to trade for furs. Born on the Pennsylvania frontier, Dobbins had lived for sixteen years in the tiny hamlet of Erie, where he had arrived on foot as a nineteen-year-old surveyor. He had then found it to be a desolate place, consisting of only a single tavern, a tannery, and a forlorn scatter of log cabins. "All the rest," he later wrote, "was wild, gloomy forest; and these few hardy pioneers of the woods, with the Indians, disputed their right to the soil with the bear, the wolf, and the panther."

Dobbins, not just a roughhewn son of the wilderness, was one of the best navigators on the Lakes. Since becoming master of his own vessel in 1803, he had traded salt, furs, feathers, whiskey, and *mococks* (the Algonquin word for birchbark boxes containing maple sugar) up and down Lakes Erie and Huron.

Now, in the blink of an eye, he was about to lose his ship.

He had suspected something was amiss after arriving in Mackinac's harbor and finding no other traders moored there. The American commander had advised the few citizens to gather inside the fort for protection, but Dobbins hurried back to his ship instead. He prepared to "cut and run" with his vessel, but a British brig, *Caledonia*, blocked his path.

The island's captives—including Dobbins, his crew, the soldiers, and the civilians—were soon ordered to either take an oath of allegiance or give their word of honor that they wouldn't take up arms against the British. Dobbins twice refused. Despite such outright defiance, he was allowed to keep *Salina*, which would serve as a cartel ship, ferrying the prisoners, himself included, to Fort Malden in Amherstburg, Ontario, across the Detroit River from the American town of that name. There they would remain on parole until they could be properly exchanged.

Salina passed down Lake Huron to where it poured through the St. Clair and Detroit Rivers into Lake Erie. Before reaching his intended destination, however, Dobbins made a beeline for Detroit, where he took up with Colonel Lewis Cass' division of General William Hull's Army of the Northwest. When

Hull surrendered that force on August 16, Dobbins again found himself in British hands and was herded into Fort Malden. There he was betrayed by an informant who knew that he had violated his parole by participating in Detroit's defense—an offense punishable by death. Fortunately, Dobbins ran into an old friend—a fellow Freemason—who alerted him to his predicament and slipped him a signed pass to Cleveland.

A painting of Daniel Dobbins.

Opposite: Commissioned around 1820 by Lieutenant Colonel Robert C. McDouall (1774-1848), the British commander of Fort Mackinac during the War of 1812, and painted by William Dashwood, this is the oldest known painting depicting Mackinac Island and Fort Mackinac. The scene shows the fort later in the war, following the 1814 battle in which American forces attempting to retake the island were repulsed. The captured prizes *Tigress* and *Scorpion* are being brought into Haldimand Bay. McDouall had himself added to the painting—he's in the left center ground, wearing his stove-pipe shako and the distinctive green uniform of the Glengarry Light Infantry Fencibles.

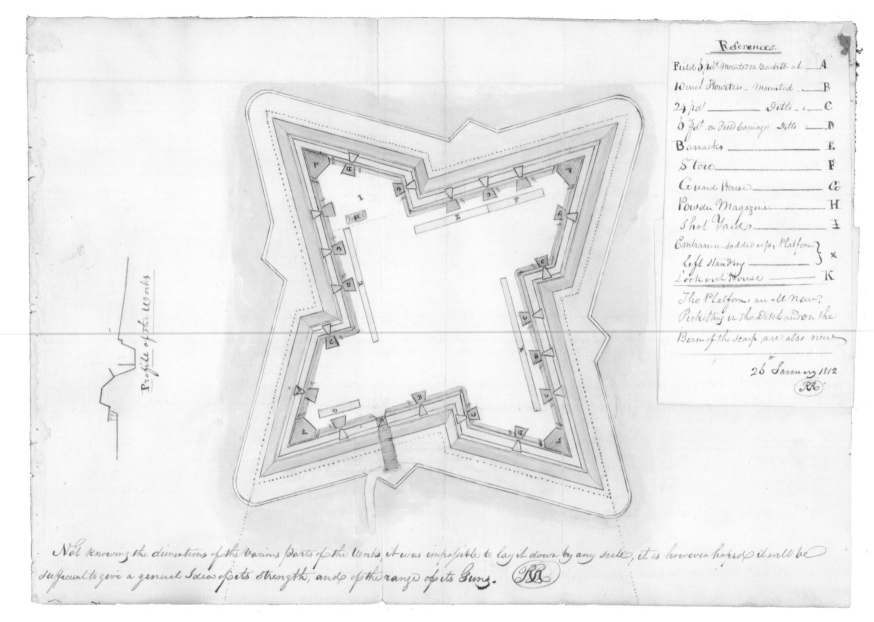

It proved all the same to be a most eventful escape. He took refuge in a rotted, sunken gunboat "with but little more room in the hold where I was than to keep my head out of water." A reward was soon posted for his capture, dead or alive. Learning of the price on his head, Dobbins risked venturing down the Detroit River. In a roundabout getaway that saw him go by dugout, then horseback, then foot, then dugout again, he finally made it to Presque Isle, the sheltered harbor that served Erie. There his eyewitness report of the surrender at Detroit was the first to reach the ears of General David Meade, who urged him to carry it on to Washington as quickly as possible. The long ride through the forests to Pittsburgh, then down the military road to Baltimore, was draining, but he made good time. Near Hagerstown, Maryland, he passed Cass, who was also on his way to deliver the demoralizing news, his blood still boiling over Hull's gutlessness. The colonel had been so angry, it was said, that he'd snapped his sword across his knee rather than surrender it to Brock.

Meanwhile, on the morning of July 19, Woolsey was on *Oneida*'s quarterdeck when he spied five sails in the offing beating up for Sackets Harbor. The Provincial Marine was closing in, but the American brig failed to gain the open lake before the British warships blocked the way. Mooring *Oneida* with one broadside of nine guns facing the enemy, Woolsey had the remaining guns taken off the ship and quickly moved to the land battery's emplacements. But he faced daunting odds. Arrayed against him were *Royal George*, 20 guns; *Seneca*, 18 guns; *Prince Regent*, 16 guns; *Earl of Moira*, 14 guns; and *Duke of Gloucester*, 10 guns. Their 78 guns against his 16 (plus the few manned by the local militia and the 32-pound Old Sow) were enough to make good their threat of razing the town to the ground if Woolsey failed to relinquish *Oneida* and *Lord Nelson*, or even if he dared to fire a single shot.

An artillery duel erupted anyway, lasting for two deafening hours. Some say the Old Sow fired the first shot, though with no ordnance heavier than 24 pounds anywhere to be found, the crew resorted to stuffing patches of carpet around the cannonballs so that they could carry down the barrel. The first round fired in this way was met with peals of laughter from the British decks. Retaliatory shots landed on the bluffs. One ball plowed the earth like a mole for many yards before coming to rest; it was immediately retrieved and volleyed back. The battle ended abruptly when one well-timed solid shot raked the length of *Royal George* just as she was wearing about to deliver another broadside, killing eight men. At this, the British signaled retreat and turned tail for Kingston. A band on shore struck up "Yankee Doodle" in celebration, and Woolsey's men filled the still-smoky air with their cheers.

Despite the cards stacked against him, Woolsey kept up a spirited resistance. "I have no doubt but that another attack is contemplated and that they are only waiting for a more favorable wind," he wrote to Hamilton. Meanwhile, he laid plans to rescue the American merchantmen trapped at Ogdensburg, the possession of which might help him rule the lake. He sent his only lieutenant, Henry Wells, down the St. Lawrence after them. "We were not able to accomplish our object," Wells reported back after one failed rescue attempt, but "as long as light continued we kept our guns aplaying." Though *Julia* continued to fight her way downriver, the vessels all returned upriver safely enough, for in August, Major General Henry Dearborn, commander of American troops from the Niagara River to New England, had arranged a ceasefire on his far-flung front.

Lieutenant Woolsey's lonely vigil was about to end anyway. On August 25, just as he took up his quill to inform Hamilton that, with the imminent arrival of the released merchantmen, he wanted "guns, and in fact every thing necessary for the military equipment of eight vessels," he learned that Detroit had fallen nine days earlier. "Sir," he wrote, "it is with much regret that I inform you that news has arrived here today that Govr Hull is defeated."

Three days later, a bone-weary James Madison and his wife, Dolley, were bound for their plantation in the Virginia Piedmont and had stopped in Dumfries, Virginia, when an express rider came galloping into town, his tin horn blowing, his satchel brimming with handbills announcing the surrender of Detroit. The president abruptly turned around and was back in Washington the next day. In the meantime, a travel-stained Dobbins had walked into the office of Secretary of War William Eustis, who hadn't an inkling of the disaster until he heard Dobbins' story.

Madison called an emergency meeting of his cabinet. The mood was head-splittingly tense. Everyone, however, urgently agreed that the situation was calamitous. Yet the only way to reverse it was to somehow regroup and resume the march on Upper Canada. The British line of supply and communication, stretching down the Great Lakes to the St. Lawrence, had to be severed. A wedge had to be driven between them and their Indian allies. Failing to do so would mean losing not merely the war but the entire Northwest. It was absolutely critical, therefore, to win command of these watery highways. This meant the Navy, and the Navy would need warships—fast.

"There is one thing to be done," Madison concluded. "We must gain control of the lakes. Therein lies our only safety."

This broadside of William Hull's proclamation to the people of Canada, urging them to side with the United States, was printed in *The Western Intelligencer* on Monday, July 20, 1812. Despite his boast of a force that could "look down all opposition," Hull's actions far from lived up to his words. He hastily withdrew from Canada after learning of the capture of Fort Mackinac, and he would never live down his spineless surrender of Detroit. James Madison's comptroller, Richard Rush, publically denounced him as a "gasconading booby."

"DEPOTS OF LIVING DEATH"
American Prisoners in Britain

A French prisoner of war made this full-hull model of a 12-gun sloop circa 1800. The entire model is carved from ivory and is presented in a wooden carrying and display case, decorated both externally and internally with dyed inlay straw work. Silvered mirrors inside the case reflect light onto the model, giving the set ivory sails an almost translucent effect. Typically, such models were not made to scale, as accurate scale plans were not available, and tools were limited.

When war broke out between Great Britain and the United States in 1812, Americans still remembered the horrors of the prison ships moored off Brooklyn during the American Revolution. Thousands of men had died in those floating coffins, many unnoticed for days in the dark, crowded, fetid conditions.

Though in 1812 more humane treatment and a better prisoner exchange system—called a cartel—were soon agreed upon, neither side would escape censure for its handling of prisoners of war. But whereas the Americans mainly captured British soldiers during the battles along the frontier, throwing them into abysmal penitentiaries alongside murderers and thieves, the British usually seized mariners and privateers, most of whom, at one time or another, were cast into the holds of prison ships.

Sometimes that was only a temporary confinement, for the war at sea was so widely dispersed that prisoners might end up in Bermuda or Barbados, Jamaica or Halifax. Furthermore, whenever a prisoner exchange was agreed upon, many of the captives would be returned to American shores by cartel ships, white flags of truce fluttering as they entered the harbors of New York and Boston. Less fortunate men, however, found themselves being hauled back to Britain, where an estimated seventy thousand French prisoners, captured in the wars with Napoleon, were already being held. Their fate then depended on their rank.

Masters and first mates of privateering vessels with 14 guns or more might be paroled, according to the longstanding system whereby officers—and occasionally enlisted men, too—pledged their word of honor not to fight again until properly exchanged. They might have to spend an uncomfortable night or two in, say, Mill Prison near Plymouth, but then they were sent to one of the numerous country villages already crowded with paroled French majors and privateer captains enjoying the "freedom of the town," though eking out an existence on the slenderest of resources.

Lesser ranks, and those officers who chose to stay with their men, were sent to the hulks, those rotting warships, long past their prime, now dismasted and altered into the worst kind of floating hells. In peacetime, somewhere around four hundred convicts could be confined in a single hulk. In wartime, double and even triple that number were jammed into those festering, verminous holds. There they were confined from before sunset to after sunrise, with all the ports battened tight for security. Below decks the air became so foul that candles would not burn, and when the ports were unlatched in the morning, they were nearly blown open by the force of the putrid stench. One French prisoner, newly arrived on a hulk outside Portsmouth, recalled being handed a hammock, hair mattress, and thin, holey blanket before wading down into a crowd of "dead people come out for a moment from their graves, holloweyed, earthy complexioned, roundbacked, unshaven, their frames barely covered with yellow rags, their bodies frightfully thin." Americans who returned on cartel ships also "had the appearance of having made their escape from a churchyard."

No hulks inspired more fear than those moored up the Medway River near Chatham, thirty miles east of London. Surrounded by an expanse of marsh only occasionally interrupted by distant church steeples, fourteen crumbling ships-of-the-line were holding thousands of French prisoners before hundreds of American prisoners, including mariners trapped in England when the war broke out—and even some impressed sailors who had refused to fight—began arriving at the point of the bayonet. They proved a tough lot for their captors, endlessly jeering the guards and ceaselessly trying to escape. Some of them managed to cut a hole through the side of one hulk, hiding their deed behind the ship's copper sheathing, and sixteen

An unbroken line of prison hulks floating drearily in the harbor of Portsmouth. To the right, other ships, their pennants fluttering in the stiff breeze, are also anchored "in ordinary," including what appear to be two large Spanish prizes. A swathe of pink cloud dominates the scene and symbolically progresses from dark immediately above the hulks to a more brilliant light over the channel leading to the open sea. This painting was created circa 1810 by Parisian Ambrose Louis Garneray (1783-1857), who was all too familiar with his subject. A seasoned sailor, he was serving aboard a privateer when he was taken prisoner by the British in 1806 and interned on various "pontons" (prisons made from the hulks of captured and disabled French ships moored in the mud) off Portsmouth. He honed his artistic gifts by painting portraits of his captors in exchange for petty privileges.

men slipped out one night. Four more—in the middle of the day—commandeered a small boat moored to the accommodation ladder of another hulk. Gaining the shore, they fled across the fields, most quickly recaptured, except for a big Narragansett man, who led several hundred British marines on a wild chase over the countryside, only to be caught after he sprained his ankle. Such malefactors were confined in the six foot-square "Black Hole" in the very bowels of each ship, where there was hardly any air and certainly no light.

Both men and morals quickly degenerated in the Chatham hulks. "Such a sink of vice, I never saw, or ever dreamt of, as I have seen here," one survivor later recalled with a shudder. In one three-month period, eighty-four of his fellow Americans died of "ship fever" and were buried in the marsh.

Soon the pressure on the hulks was such that the British Transport Authority, responsible for prisoners, began moving American captives to what was, if possible, an even more shuddersome destination. "From the autumn of 1812 to April of 1813," wrote British historian Francis Abell, "there were 900 American prisoners at Chatham, 100 at Portsmouth, 700 at Plymouth, most of them destitute of clothes and swarming with vermin." On April 2, 1813, the Transport Board ordered them all to Dartmoor, no doubt because of their ceaseless attempts to escape from the hulks.

They were horrified, for they knew it to have the reputation of being the worst prison in England.

Situated high on the wild, treeless, sparsely inhabited moor for which it was named, the grim, granite Dartmoor Prison, swept by bitter winds or shrouded in dense fog, was built in 1809 to hold French prisoners of war. Nearly five thousand of them—ranging from officers still possessing shreds of their customary élan

A single iron handcuff, circa 1810.

Below: A commemorative Horatio Nelson domino box, created sometime between 1803 and 1814. The inside is decorated with a British sailor mourning at a bust of Nelson. This was a common theme on souvenirs and commemorative pieces after the Battle of Trafalgar. Prisoners of war often supplemented their wages by crafting objects like this, which they could sell for a pittance. They would use beef or mutton bones left over from their meals and other available materials to create these intricate pieces. Some prisoners became so well known for their work that they were commissioned to make particular items and would be supplied with finer materials, such as ivory and mahogany.

Right: Seaman Thomas Sullivan kept this illustrated diary while serving aboard the privateer *Portsmouth*, which set sail at the end of 1814, and throughout his imprisonment at Dartmoor. He describes at length the dreariness of the place and the "harsh and injurious" treatment of the detainees. His final entry is a fulmination on the massacre. "O shame where is thy blush!" he rails against the British militia. "O cowardice where is thy shrinking confusion! But know ye bloody butchers of our slaughtered countrymen that millions of free born sons of Liberty shall ere long revenge their murdered brethren!" He goes on to lament the loss of his companions and the sorrow that will cast its shadow over their bereft loved ones. "Ye helpless orphans," he says, referring to the massacred men's children, "no more shall ye receive the tender caresses of your Father; he sleeps beneath the gloomy walls of Dartmoor! No more shall ye be dandled on his knee, or receive from his glowing lips the kisses of parental affection! Ye sons of Columbia, the blood of your slaughtered brethren cries to you from the ground, revenge our Deaths."

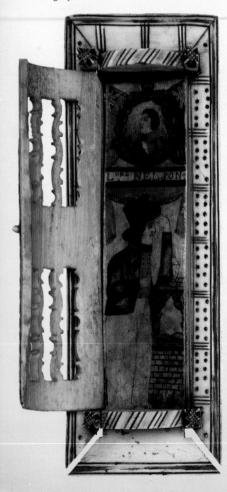

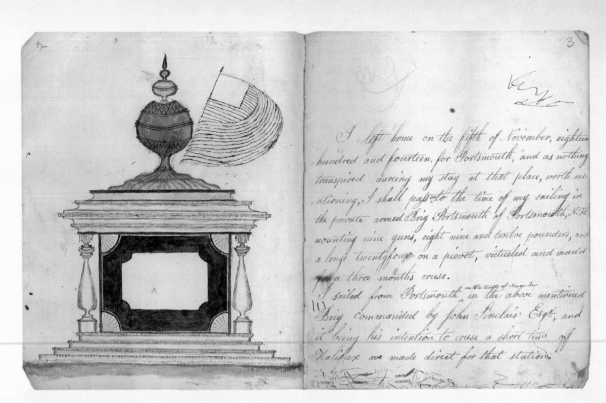

to depraved wretches possessing no shreds whatsoever, having gambled even their clothes away—crowded the thirty-acre compound of this "depot of living death" when the first Americans arrived.

Adjusting to dank, overcrowded stone barracks, with barred windows open to all kind of weather, the newcomers not only endured but also prospered. They became tobacco traders, schoolteachers, dance instructors. They played in makeshift bands and acted in amateur theatricals. A strapping African American, "King Dick," who was six foot five even before donning a huge bear-skin cap, opened a boxing academy. Some men plaited straw hats or carved wooden figurines or crafted elaborate domino boxes and exquisite scale models of frigates from bone fragments. Others, of course, dug tunnels.

Several attempts were made to tunnel out of the horrid place. All were foiled in the end, the British having been alerted by informants. Anyone deemed guilty of trying to escape was punished by confinement in Dartmoor's version of the "Black Hole," the *cachot*, a lightless and virtually airless stone chamber all too closely resembling a tomb. Nevertheless, after peace was made with France in May 1814, some five hundred French prisoners marched out to freedom—and intermingled with them were some daring French-speaking Americans.

In late 1814, while diplomats in Ghent, Belgium, were negotiating an end to the war, five thousand more Americans had joined their freezing countrymen in Dartmoor, where even fireplaces were forbidden. Though winter turned to spring, and peace was signed and duly ratified, the prisoners saw no change in their confinement, thanks to the shilly-shallying of officials in arranging for their transport home. Discontent finally boiled over on April 6, 1815, when nervous guards, fearing for their lives, fired on a mob of prisoners. Seven Americans were killed and perhaps sixty wounded in what many in the United States would later decry as a massacre.

Only days later, the first 263 American captives were led out to freedom. The remainder followed over the next few weeks, until the last handful marched out of the gates in July. At the same time, nearly 2,500 French prisoners—captured during the Waterloo campaign in the last flare-up of the Napoleonic Wars—were beginning to arrive, guarded by only three hundred English militiamen. For the departing Americans, even though their war was over, the rule remained inflexible: one guard to each man.

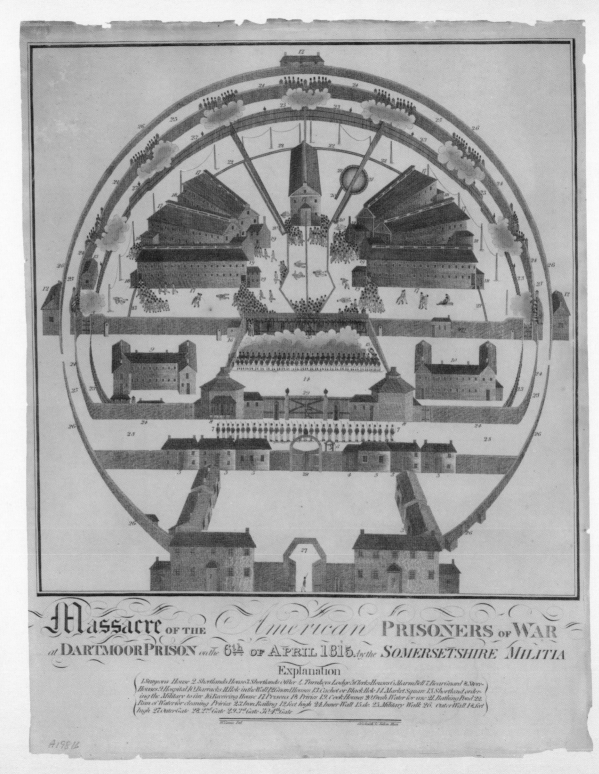

Massacre OF THE American PRISONERS OF WAR at DARTMOOR PRISON on the 6th OF APRIL 1815, by the SOMERSETSHIRE MILITIA

This print, published in Salem in 1815, shows an aerial view of Dartmoor Prison during the massacre, which occurred on April 6, 1815. Prisoners, seen in blue and brown standing outside their prison cells, are being fired upon by the British military, seen in red. Numbers denote the various prison erections, including a bathing pond and the ominous *cachot*, or black hole.

An oil portrait of Commodore Isaac Chauncey by Gilbert Stuart, painted circa 1818.

Opposite: A modern painting by Marine Colonel Charles Waterhouse depicting the grueling undertaking of ship-building at Sackets Harbor in the deep winter of 1813.

In the flurry of orders and directives that followed, three, in particular, stood out.

One set of orders, signed by Hamilton and dated August 31, soon arrived at the New York Navy Yard, where they were opened by Captain Isaac Chauncey.

> The season has arrived, when your Country requires your active Services. The President of the United States has determined to obtain command of the Lakes Ontario & Erie, with the least possible delay—and the execution of this highly important object is committed to you.
>
> With respect to the means to be employed, you will consider yourself unrestrained, minor interests must yield to the greater. The object must be accomplished; and all the means which you may judge essential, must be employed.

A prosperous farmer's son, the forty-year-old Chauncey had gone to sea by the age of twelve; taken command of his first ship, one of fur mogul John Jacob Astor's merchantmen, by nineteen; and earned the coveted rank of master commandant by thirty-two. At one time or another he had served aboard the frigates *President, John Adams, Chesapeake,* and *Constitution.* For the past five years the well-connected, "steady if not brilliant" Chauncey had been helming the New York Navy Yard, where he had become thoroughly acquainted with all of the challenges posed by the construction and maintenance of warships and the procurement of supplies. He was just the experienced and authoritative officer needed to build a naval establishment in the wilderness.

He set to work immediately. In a month of frenzied activity he emptied the navy yard's warehouses and assembled more than a hundred cannons and thousands of swords and small arms. He persuaded New York's leading shipbuilders, Henry Eckford and his neighbors, Noah and Adam Brown, to lend him 140 shipwrights and carpenters. He mustered hundreds of officers and men—volunteers all, including Ned Myers of gunboat No. 107—from the naval vessels that had been undergoing repairs or refittings under his watch. And he gathered wagonloads of supplies—warm clothing, watch coats, slops, surgical tools, cordage, canvas, and countless other essentials. This mass of men and material was shipped up the Hudson River to Albany, disembarked, transferred to barges and flatboats, sent west up the Mohawk River, and then taken by oxcart over indescribably bad roads to the shores of Lake Ontario. Some of it was dispatched westward to the Genesee River and Buffalo, but most of it went to Sackets Harbor, which Chauncey had chosen as his headquarters.

Woolsey was more relieved than rankled at having been superseded. He couldn't have held the lake by sheer intrepidity much longer, although his

opponents had proved ineffective enough. Falling somewhere between a transport service and a true navy, the Provincial Marine was led by officers in their dotage. "Our Navy . . . is worth [less] than nothing," wrote Reverend John Strachan, York's Anglican bishop and one of the most influential members of Upper Canada's ruling oligarchy. "The Officers are the greatest cowards that ever lived, and would fly from a single Bateau."

Chauncey arrived in Sackets Harbor in early October. Eckford's crew was well underway in building the 26-gun *Madison*, which would be finished in forty-five days and launched in November. Soon they would lay the keel of the 28-gun *General Pike*. In the meantime, other men were busy converting the merchant vessels that Woolsey had acquired into armed schooners. By November 8, Chauncey thought them ready to "sweep the lake," though Myers, who had been assigned to *Scourge*, formerly *Lord Nelson*, found her almost as insufferable as the gunboat he'd left behind. "This craft was unfit for her duty, but time pressed, and no better offered," Myers later recalled. "Her accommodations were bad enough, and she was so tender, that we could do little or nothing with her in a blow. It was often prognosticated that she would prove our coffin."

Scourge did not venture out that season, but Myers saw action aboard *Oneida*, which he described as "a warm little brig . . . but dull as a transport." Sluggish as *Oneida* might have seemed, she chased her British counterpart, *Royal George*, straight off the lake that November. "We gave her nothing but round-shot from our gun," Myers recounted, "and these we gave with all our hearts."

In only three months, Chauncey had gained control of Lake Ontario. He did not relax his vigilance, though, even after the onset of winter left everything locked up in ice. He dreaded the prospect of British troops tromping over the frozen lake from Kingston to put Sackets Harbor to the torch. "I am really alarmed, Sir, for the safety of our little Fleet collected here," he wrote to General Dearborn. "I trust you will deem their preservation of so much importance to our future operations against Canada, as to induce you to order to this post as soon as convenient 1000 additional regular Troops: the militia

will not do." Myers remembered some other defensive measures and the intervals of recreation that broke the tedium of labor: "Around each [frozen-in] craft . . . a space was kept cut, to form a sort of ditch, in order to prevent being boarded. Parties were regularly stationed to defend the Madison, and, in the days, we worked at her rigging, and at that of the Pike, in gangs . . . The winter lasted more than four months, and we made good times of it. We often went after wood, and occasionally we knocked over a deer."

Chauncey, meanwhile, could only await the breakup of the ice—and the arrival of the Royal Navy, which was bound to appear with spring. "What John Bull was about [that winter] is more than I can say," Myers recollected, "though the next season [would show] he had not been idle."

LAKE CHAMPLAIN, AUTUMN 1812

On September 28, a second man to open a set of Navy orders in the wake of the summer's military bungles was commanding a squadron of gunboats at Portland, Maine. Lieutenant Thomas Macdonough must have blinked upon reading them.

> The President of the United States, has selected You, to command the vessels, on Lake Champlain & You are required to proceed to that Lake, & assume the Command accordingly, without a moment's delay.

Macdonough, twenty-eight, had only recently rejoined the Navy, having taken a leave of absence in 1810 for a higher-paying job at the helm of a British merchant ship bound for India. He had first joined the service back in 1799, after a seafaring older brother had lost a leg in the Quasi-War with France. Though orphaned by the age of eleven, the Delaware native had harnessed his prominent family's wealth of contacts to secure a commission as a midshipman. He then served with distinction in the First Barbary War and followed that with a stint commanding *Wasp*. When war was declared in June 1812, he had quickly returned to uniform, and by October he'd arrived on the shores of Lake Champlain.

Set in the trough between the rugged Adirondacks of New York and the Green Mountains of Vermont, the long, sinuous lake dominated the northern stretch of the arrow-straight natural passageway leading from Montreal to New York City. In 1755, during the Seven Years' War, a French army had marched down this age-old invasion route, only to be stopped in the Battle of Lake George farther to the south. In 1776, British redcoats followed in their footsteps—first ensuring, however, that a makeshift British fleet controlled the waters of Lake Champlain, which lapped along their flank for a hundred miles. An equally makeshift American fleet, however, had delayed the British advance long enough so that it met defeat in the Battle of Saratoga.

Despite such ominous historical parallels, Macdonough found only two dilapidated gunboats awaiting him, one partially sunk and the seams on both cracked wide. Six additional vessels—about all that remained on the lake—had already been purchased by the War Department for the use of soldiers stationed there.

Nevertheless, by October's end Macdonough had managed to wrest two of the sloops out of the hands of the U.S. Army, one of which, the 6-gun *President*, he considered to be "the largest and best vessel on the Lake." He had also nearly finished refurbishing the two gunboats, mounting on each a 12-pounder. Unfortunately, he was still running into problems with the hard-pressed New York Navy Yard, from which he was to draw men and supplies. None had reached him yet. Meanwhile, the British had established a base on the Isle aux Noix at the head of the Richelieu River, through which the lake's waters flowed north into Canada. And there they were building a fleet.

A portrait by Orlando S. Lagman of Commodore Thomas Macdonough, only a lieutenant when he was ordered to Lake Champlain in the fall of 1812.

Opposite, left: Dismayed by a lack of clear, official orders, and eager to show his progress, Daniel Dobbins penned this letter to "Commodore Chauncey or the commanding officer of the lake at Buffaloe" on September 28, 1812.

Opposite, right: Secretary of the Navy Paul Hamilton issued this sailing master's warrant to Daniel Dobbins on September 16, 1812.

The third man to receive an important set of naval orders was none other than Daniel Dobbins. While still in Washington, this man who knew Lake Erie's "ways, winds, and waters" better than anyone else had paid a visit to the secretary of the Navy. While discussing the situation on that front, Dobbins had suggested to Hamilton that Presque Isle was a relatively safe place for building a fleet without harassment from the enemy. By the time he left Washington on September 16, 1812, he had been appointed a "Sailing Master" and carried in his pocket a note from Hamilton, couched as instructions.

> You will proceed without delay to Presque Isle, on the Lake Erie, and there contract for, on the best terms in your power, all the requisite timbers & other materials for building four Gunboats—agreeably to the dimensions, which you will receive from Commre Tingey; and if in your power you will contract for the building of those boats, but such contracts must be submitted to Commre Chauncey, or the officer that may be appointed by him to command the naval forces on the Lake Erie.

Dobbins was under no illusions about the challenges confronting him. For one thing, he was far from the shipyards of the East River, with their troves of maritime staples and their supplies of timber: masts from New England, ribs and elbows from Southern forests, timbers and planking from South America. But when it came to building warships in the wilderness, timber was the one thing he didn't need. Though he had no experience as a shipwright apart from refitting his own packet ship, as a gesture of principle, upon his return to Presque Isle, he felled and hewed the first tree—a massive oak—himself.

On September 28, he wrote to Chauncey, assuring his new commander of progress.

> Sir,
> I have the honour to transmit to you (the inclosed) a Coppy of My instructions from the Secretary of the Navy and asure you Sir that I Stand Ready to execute any order that you May be pleased to Issue. I have Made arrangements for the timber and Iron work. Steel for axes I have been oblided to Send to Meadville for as there was not any at this place that is good for any thing. I intend going to Pittsburgh soon for the purpose of procuring Rigging and Cables, anchors I believe I Can get likewise the Riging can be got there Cheaper and that is good. Be pleased to let Me hear from you at your arival so that I May Regulate my future Proceeding by your instructions. I have been obliged to hire the Men by the day and Shall be obliged to hire the hands the Same way. Any farther arrangements that I May Make I will inform you of.

A few weeks later he received a brusque, discouraging reply, sent not by Chauncey but by his second in command, Lieutenant Jesse D. Elliot, who had been busy establishing a shipyard at Black Rock, just north of Buffalo on the Niagara River, for exactly the same purpose: to build a fleet for Lake Erie.

> It appears to me utterly impossible to build Gun Boats at Presqu'ile; there is not a sufficient depth of water on the bar to get them into the Lake. Should there be water, the place is at all times open to the attacks of the Enemy, and in all probability when ready for action will ultimately fall into the hands of the Enemy, and be a great annoyance to our force building and repairing at this place. From a slight acquaintance I have with our side of Lake Erie, and with what information I have obtained from persons who have long navigated the lake, I am under the impression Lake Erie has not a single harbor calculated to fit out a Naval expedition, and the only one convenient I am at present at, which is between Squaw Island and the main, immediately in the mouth of Niagara River. I have no further communication to make on the subject.

Though Chauncey was wrapped up in his enterprises at Sackets Harbor, he was also responsible for Lake Erie—on paper at least. ("Your operations must be simultaneous—let the work of preparation go on at both places at one & the same time," Hamilton had instructed him.) Unaware of Hamilton's arrangements with Dobbins, however, Chauncey had dispatched Elliott to take charge of the other lake. Though he was arrogant and alienating, Elliott was no slouch as a naval officer—he would soon lead a daring raid into those waters and capture two British brigs, *Caledonia* and *Detroit*—but he was nearly worn ragged by the rigors of establishing a shipyard at Black Rock under conditions of severe privation.

Dobbins replied confidently that he believed the water at Presque Isle to be deep enough for their purposes but protected from heavily armed British ships by being no deeper. The French had named Presque Isle ("almost an island") aptly: the slender peninsula curved like a bow around the protected bay. Dobbins knew that the British wouldn't be able to circumvent that sandbar without the help of a local pilot. Furthermore, Dobbins wrote, "I have made my arrangements in accordance with my own convictions, for the purpose of procuring the timber and other materials for their construction. I believe I have as perfect a knowledge of this lake as any other man on it and I believe you will agree with me, were you here."

That was the last he heard of the matter. Until he got official approval from Chauncey, he couldn't get to work. But he could begin preparations. He set about procuring men and supplies, though a tightening blockade had

Sir

I have the honour to transmit
to you the inclosed a Copy of My instruct
-tions from the ~~Secretary~~ the Secretary of the
Navy and assure you Sir that I S am Ready
to execute any order that you May be pleased
to Issue I have Made arrangements for the
timber and Iron work Stud for ones
I have been abledged to Send to Mead
-ville for as there was not any at this
place that is good for any thing.
I intend going to Pittsburgh soon for the
purpose of procuring Rigging and Cables, and as
I believe I can get the ~~likewise~~ the Rigging can
be got ther Cheep and that that is good
be pleased to let Me hear from you at
your arival So that I May Regulate my
future Proceedings by your instructions. I have
I been abledged to hire the men by the day
and I shall be abledged to hire the hands the
Same way any further arangements that I
May Make I will inform you of I am with
Respect yours

Lee S[ep]t. 28th 1812   Daniel Dobbins
                                    Master U.S. Navy

NAVY DEPARTMENT,
16. Sep.r 1812

SIR,

HEREWITH you will receive a warrant as a *Sailing master*
in the Navy of the United States,
dated *this day* —
I enclose a copy of the Navy rules and regulations, a copy of the uniform;
and the requisite oath, which you will take and return to me.

This appointment must be accepted by letter, from the date of which letter
your pay will commence.

For Paul Hamilton
C. W. Goldsborough

Mr. Daniel Dobbins
of Erie Present
Pennsylv.

sent the prices for materials soaring, and hundreds of nearby militiamen had driven the costs for food and lodging similarly skyward. It was two hundred miles to the nearest shipwright; he would have to begin with some house carpenters instead.

In early 1813, when Chauncey showed up to tour the construction site, Dobbins already had the makings for several gunboats and a small brig, putting to silence those who had questioned whether his activity would add up to much. The veteran naval officer must have liked what he saw, because he gave his approval, to Dobbins' relief, and ordered that a second, larger brig be constructed as well. He was concerned, however, about the lack of skilled workers; a master shipwright from Buffalo soon agreed to help. "I shall make it a point to do all that is in my power to facilitate the business," Dobbins promised the departing Chauncey.

Then he got to work. The hills around Erie abounded in timber—chestnut, walnut, ash, oak, and pine—with a going rate of one dollar a tree. Other necessities—cannons, muskets, powder, and shot; ship fittings, anchors, anchor chains, iron for braces, gun mounts, and pivots; canvas, paint, barrels of pitch, and tools of the trade—had to be hauled in by sled across packed snow or by wagon over trails boggy with snowmelt mud. Dobbins had been told to draw supplies from the Philadelphia Navy Yard, but Philadelphia was very far away. Pittsburgh, a little over one hundred miles south, was the closest town of any size that had enough forges and shops to be of real use. But that was a difficult hundred miles, part wilderness track, part

rapids-strewn river. Dobbins had to improvise. For caulking, he needed a substitute for oakum; he settled on a novel use of tea lead. Most of the rigging—more than eight thousand pounds of cable, four and a half inches thick—came from John and Mary Irwin's family business in Pittsburgh. Scrap iron—ranging from old wagon rims to rusty barn door hinges—was gathered from the few shops, warehouses, and stores and eventually welded together. With time at such a premium, Dobbins had no choice but to use unseasoned timber, held together in many cases with wooden trunnels, since iron for handwrought nails was scarce. By necessity, different woods were used side by side, with ribs of poplar alternating with those of oak and ash. As historian Max Rosenberg has noted, often a tree standing in dawn mist one morning was by sunset of the same day felled, milled, and part of a ship.

Deck spikes and a wooden dowel and nail from Perry's flagship, Niagara.

A nineteenth-century broad axe, its blade offset, used for hewing and shaping shipbuilding timbers.

Handle, or "box," of a pit saw. Made by J. Moody, this wooden saw holder consists of a two-handed handle with a wedge clamp for the lower end of the pit saw. Though Erie had three saw mills at the time that Perry's fleet was built, pit saws were likely used for the larger timbers.

Caulking mallet, mid-nineteenth century. Caulkers would have used such a tool to pound oakum—or tea lead, in Dobbins' case—into seams between timbers or deck planks.

Augers like this one were used to bore holes for wooden dowels.

This hawsing iron was unearthed by Clinton Bebell around 1940 in Erie, just offshore from where Perry's fleet was built. Hawsing irons were used for caulking deck seams. The long handle enabled one caulker to stand holding the iron while another swung the mallet against the head of the iron, driving the caulk deep into the seam.

A ship's carpenter would have used this hand-forged adze as a finishing tool for smoothing wooden beams and timbers.

The ice broke up later on Lake Ontario than it did on Lake Erie, so before the first fissures appeared, a naval strategy for the year 1813 was in place. The British wanted to reassert their control over all the Lakes, including the southern shores, a control that it had enjoyed prior to the American Revolution. The coming struggle for Lake Erie might determine the future development of North America. A British victory there could split the United States' western territories from its eastern states—a wedge that in turn might blunt the Americans' thrust into the Old Northwest, provide the Native Americans with a buffer state, and restore the British Empire's influence over the interior of the continent.

For the Americans, the plan was to reverse the military disasters of the previous year—not just the loss of Mackinac Island and Detroit but also the humiliating repulse of General Stephen Van Rensselaer's invasion at Queenston Heights in October—by renewing the offensives into Upper Canada with even more vigor. That depended, though, on seizing control of Lakes Erie and Ontario before the snows fell again come autumn. It also meant that the U.S. Army and the U.S. Navy would have to cooperate; joint operations would be crucial.

The capture of Kingston, of course, would mean victory on all the Lakes, but that base was deemed too well defended to attack. So in late April, the ice having finally disappeared, Chauncey's squadron of fourteen ships set a course for York, the provincial capital of Upper Canada. On board were 1,700 troops led by Brigadier General Zebulon Montgomery Pike, the thirty-four-year-old Western explorer for whom Pike's Peak would be named, as well as his superior, Major General Henry Dearborn. From the moment the first soldiers landed—early in the morning on April 27, supported by the fire of the ships—until sometime in the afternoon, when surrender negotiations commenced, the battle went the Americans' way, their forces sweeping past one defended position after another until their advanced units were running

through the streets of the town. The only setback was the firing of an immense powder magazine, which killed Pike, among dozens of others.

The surprise raid on York was a qualified success in other ways, too. Forcing their way into the dockyard, the Americans captured a brig, *Duke of Gloucester*, and seized or destroyed numerous 24-pounder carronades along with many other stores that, it turned out, were destined for the British fleet on Lake Erie. Unfortunately, for nearly three days the soldiers—and, regrettably, some of the sailors as well—ran riot in the town, looting and plundering at every turn. The burning of the Legislative Assembly, the printing office, and other government buildings and private houses would not be forgotten when British soldiers advanced on Washington, D.C., a year later.

For the moment, though, it was all uproar and abandon, and Ned Myers of *Scourge* found himself swept up in it.

We found the place deserted. With the exception of our own men, I found but one living being in it. This was an old woman whom I discovered stowed away in a potato locker, in the government house. I saw tables set, and eggs in the cups, but no inhabitant. Our orders were of the most severe kind, not to plunder, and we did not touch a morsel of food even. The liquor, however, was too much for our poor natures, and a parcel of us had broke bulk in a better sort of grocery, when some of the officers came in and stove the casks . . .

I ought to feel ashamed, and do feel ashamed of what occurred that night; but I must relate it, lest I feel more ashamed for concealing the truth. We had spliced the main-brace pretty freely throughout the day, and the pull I got in the grocery just made me ripe for mischief. When we got aboard the schooner again, we found a canoe that had drifted athwart-hawse and had been secured. My gun's crew, the Black Jokers, wished to have some fun in the town, and they proposed to me to take a cruise ashore. We had few officers on board, and the boatswain, a boatswain's mate in fact, consented to let us leave. We all went ashore in this canoe, then, and were soon alongside of a wharf. On landing, we were near a large store, and looking in at a window we saw a man sitting asleep, with a gun in the hollow of his arm. His head was on the counter, and there was a lamp burning. One of the blacks pitched through the window, and was on him in a moment. The rest followed, and we made him a prisoner. The poor fellow said he had come to look after his property, and he was told no one would hurt him. My blacks now began to look about them, and to help themselves to such articles as they thought they wanted. I confess I helped myself to some tea and sugar, nor will I deny that I was in such a state as to think the whole good fun. We carried off one canoe load, and even returned for a second. Of course such an exploit could not have been effected without letting all in the secret share; and one boat-load of plunder was not enough . . . Some riflemen came in, too, and I succeeded in getting my jokers away.

An 1858 print by Alonzo
Chappel depicting the American
capture of Fort George in 1813.

CAPTURE OF FORT GEORGE.

(COL. WINFIELD SCOTT LEADING THE ATTACK.)

From the original Painting by Chappel, in the possession of the Publishers.

Johnson, Fry & Co Publishers, New York.

Entered, according to act of Congress AD 1859 by Johnson, Fry & Co in the clerks office of the district court of the southern district of New York.

The recklessness of sailors may be seen in our conduct. All we received for our plunder was some eight or ten gallons of whiskey, when we got back to the harbour, and this at the risk of being flogged through the fleet! It seemed to us to be a scrape, and that was a sufficient excuse for disobeying orders, and for committing a crime. For myself, I was influenced more by the love of mischief, and a weak desire to have it said I was foremost in such an exploit, than from any mercenary motive. Notwithstanding the severity of the orders, and one or two pretty sharp examples of punishment inflicted by the commodore, the Black Jokers were not the only plunderers ashore that night. One master's-mate had the buttons taken off his coat, for stealing a feather bed, besides being obliged to carry it back again . . .

I walked over the ground where the explosion took place. It was a dreadful sight; the dead being so mutilated that it was scarcely possible to tell their colour. I saw gun-barrels bent nearly double. I think we saw Sir Roger Sheafe, the British General, galloping across the field, by himself, a few minutes before the explosion. At all events, we saw a mounted officer, and fired at him. He galloped up to the government house, dismounted, went in, remained a short time, and then galloped out of town. All this I saw; and the old woman in the potato locker told me the general had been in the house a short time before we landed. Her account agreed with the appearance of the officer I saw; though I will not pretend to be certain it was General Sheafe.

I ought to mention the kindness of the commodore to the poor of York. As most of the inhabitants came back to their habitations the next day, the poor were suffering for food. Our men were ordered to roll barrels of salt meat and barrels of bread to their doors, from the government stores that fell into our hands. We captured an immense amount of these stores, a portion of which we carried away. We sunk many guns in the lake; and as for the powder, *that* had taken care of itself. Among other things we took was the body of an English officer, preserved in rum, which, they said, was General Brock's. I saw it hoisted out of the Duke of Gloucester, the man-of-war brig we captured, at Sackett's Harbour, and saw the body put in a fresh cask. I am ashamed to say that some of our men were inclined to drink the old rum.

The next battle, however, was an unqualified success. No sooner, it seemed, had Chauncey and Dearborn left York in ruins than they were dropping anchor off the Niagara River, under the protective guns of Fort Niagara. Standing on the bluffs on the far side of the stream was Fort George, the northernmost of the two bastions defending the thirty-five miles of the river's Canadian shore. On May 25, the Americans began a two-day bombardment of their British opponent. Fort George's defenders prepared for both a frontal assault from across the river and a flank attack from the lakeshore—which, when the fog dissipated on the morning of the twenty-seventh, proved to be a nearly flawless amphibious operation that led General John Vincent to abandon Fort George and, ultimately, Fort Erie as well. The Niagara Peninsula had fallen to the Americans.

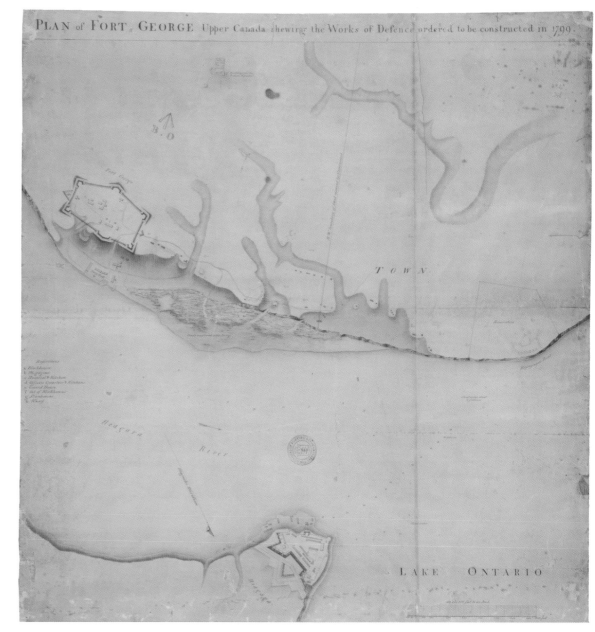

It was a sensational victory, the first one that American arms could justly celebrate, and it was largely made possible by that successful amphibious landing. As the American troops had stormed ashore, they were met with the point of the bayonet, but American gunboats had come inshore and, directed by a young naval officer, kept up such a withering fire of grape and canister that the defenders were driven off. That officer's name was Oliver Hazard Perry.

This turn-of-the-century plan of Fort George shows its military buildings, including its blockhouse, magazine, hospital and kitchen, officers' quarters, guardhouse, and stonehouses.

LAKE ERIE, EARLY SPRING TO LATE SUMMER 1813

Right: A painting of Commodore Oliver Hazard Perry by American artist and museum keeper Rembrandt Peale.

Below: Perry's epaulette. Commodores wore these showy "swabs," as they were informally dubbed, on both shoulders, each epaulette adorned with a star, while master commandants wore only one, on the right shoulder. Perry wore this one, therefore, when he was a master commandant.

Though his wife called him her "cup of felicity," Perry was always a study in contradictions: exacting yet generous; ambitious yet modest; hot-tempered yet warmhearted; a man of few words who loved voluminous books— biographies, histories, the works of Shakespeare. Above all, he was a man who loved the sea—its ever-shifting moods, its infinite promise, its certain peril— with incurable abandon.

Born into a seagoing Rhode Island family that had seen its share of financial distress, Perry, like so many of his fellow officers, had joined the Navy in 1799 during the Quasi-War with France. As a midshipman he had served with the U.S. frigate *General Greene,* then commanded by his father, Christopher Raymond Perry, who'd been a privateer during the American Revolution. Oliver had begun to step out of his father's shadow during the First Barbary War, but his career began to stall after he was ordered to oversee the construction of seventeen gunboats for the protection of Newport. He was still commanding that squadron when the War of 1812 broke out. Fearful that he might be left languishing in the war's backwaters and frustrated by the Navy Department's refusal to grant him a posting at sea, he had opted to transfer to the Great Lakes, where he might have a command of his own. "I hope, Sir," he'd written to Hamilton in November 1812, "you may have some situation for me more active than my present command."

On January 20, 1813, as he sat bundled up and encircled in ice at Sackets Harbor, Chauncey penned a dispatch for Newport. "You are the very person I want for a particular service," he asserted, "where you may gain honor for yourself & reputation for your Country."

In late March 1813, the twenty-seven-year-old master commandant arrived at Presque Isle and assumed supervision of the shipbuilding. He found that four gunboats were well underway and that the keels of the brigs had been laid. Most importantly, shipbuilder Noah Brown had arrived from New York with a party of skilled workmen.

Perry was nevertheless amazed to find that not a single gun, rope, or sail had yet arrived. Only two of five blacksmiths had turned up, and one of them was only the other's assistant. The fifty ship's carpenters dispatched from Philadelphia had been lost for nearly a month. When they did come stumbling in from Pittsburgh, they had no tools. Those had been shipped separately and were still somewhere en route. The blockmakers were also reportedly lost. To hurry things up, Perry himself journeyed down the by now well-traveled post road to Pittsburgh, where he hovered about the foundries and workshops, hastening everything forward, speeding up the stalled deliveries of ropes, cables, sails, anchors, guns, and muskets.

Through relentless determination and sheer willpower, the two men—for Perry had kept Dobbins on as supply officer, purchasing agent, and adviser—heaved and strained against circumstance until everything finally started pulling together. Skilled workmen, some from as far away as Newport, began arriving, lured by rumors that an experienced ship carpenter could earn up to $1.75 a day, while loggers received about 50¢ a day and blacksmiths commanded up to four times that much. The men lived in two large barracks or boarded in log houses nearby. Militiamen were now everywhere, and batteries were being dug into the bluffs.

The work sped up, only subsiding when virulent outbreaks of malaria prostrated the men. By early May, the three gunboats had been launched, and the brigs were being planked with oak. The hammers rang from dawn to dusk and sometimes deep into the night. "It appeared that every man was engaged as if he was on a strife," Noah Brown observed. Two weeks later, even the brigs were launched, to a round of cheers from the assembled workers, villagers, and militiamen.

Meanwhile, needing to confer with Chauncey, Dobbins and Perry had undertaken an expedition of sorts.

This copper spike from one of Perry's ships bears a "U.S." stamp.

Slipping out of Erie one night in a four-oared open boat, they stealthily made their way to Buffalo, then continued on a dicey journey down the Niagara River, often within musket shot of the British lines. Landing at Fort Schlosser, they walked two miles to Niagara Falls, soaked to the skin in the pelting rain. There, for three dollars, they were able to acquire an old nag of a horse, but since it was the "only one to be got," Perry prepared to complete the journey alone. "I soon got the commodore mounted on this old horse . . . and off he started," Dobbins later wrote. "Next morning, not feeling satisfied at his going alone in this way, mounted on a miserable old horse, and himself in full dress, a fine mark for the scattering Indians and scouting parties on both sides of the river, I ventured contrary to orders to follow him on foot."

And so Dobbins thus ensured Perry's safe arrival at Fort Niagara, where the officer found Chauncey and his fleet preparing the attack on Fort George—the battle in which Perry would earn, as one local writer later put it, "the first twig of the cluster of laurels so soon to adorn his brow."

Perry carried this 1808 flintlock pistol made by Joseph Henry of Philadelphia.

Sailmaker's packet and needles, stamped "USN 1858." Sailmaker's needles were specially shaped so that they didn't cut the canvas threads as they were being used.

A stippled bust portrait of the swashbuckling Sir James Lucas Yeo.

In mid-May, while Chauncey was anchored off Fort Niagara preparing the assault on Fort George, a ship had sailed out of the St. Lawrence and entered Lake Ontario. It was the Royal Navy finally heaving into view.

Aboard, wearing the puffed-up title of Commodore and Commander of His Majesty's Forces on the Lakes of Canada, was Sir James Lucas Yeo, a "long, thin, sulky-looking chap," in C. H. J. Snider's memorable description, "with a chin as hard as the peak of an anchor, and eyes that spat black lightning." Only thirty years old, he was already a man with a well-established reputation for bravado, his most famous exploit having been a swashbuckling raid on the French garrison at Cayenne in Guiana that had helped expel Napoleon's forces from South America. Made a post-captain at twenty-five, he was commanding the frigate *Southampton* when he captured the U.S. brig *Vixen* on November 22, 1812, in the Bahamas—only to strike an uncharted reef shortly afterward and have his ship sink beneath him. Salvaging some sails, a pound of pork, and a hatful of soggy, sand-crusted bread, the British crew and the American prisoners became castaways together, marooned in tolerable amity on a desolate cay visited only by nesting seabirds and the occasional wandering sea turtle. It was a subject that the 465 officers and seamen accompanying Yeo to Canada dared not mention.

Yeo had hardly been in Kingston a fortnight when he launched an attack on Sackets Harbor. On May 28, his six-ship squadron, carrying eight hundred British infantrymen, approached what had been only a quiet little station a year earlier but now hummed with the din and clatter of shipwrights at work. It was also defended by fortifications manned by several thousand regulars and militiamen employing several pieces of artillery. The battle on May 29 was a confused melee, swinging one way and then another, as a British midshipman described in a letter to his mother.

The American Fleet lay in Sackets Harbour about 45 Miles from Kingston, which place we attacked 3 Weeks ago, the reason was this, their Fleet went away with Soldiers to take Fort George at the Head of the Lake, we immediately Embarked 900 Soldiers and attacked Sackets intending to burn the Ship which was on the Stocks and all the Publick Stores, but they were to Strong for us. We landed at day Break under a most destructive fire of Cannon & Musquetry, the Country being very woody their Riflemen picked us off without being Hurt or perceived, the Action lasted 4 Hours and I suppose a Hotter never was for the time it lasted, We burnt their Stores but not the Ship, I commanded a Gun Boat, but my boat being soon filled with Killed & Wounded and I myself wounded in the leg the Boat being no longer able to act I landed with & fought with the Soldiers and luckily escaped any further damage.

A. Buck. pinxt.   H. R. Cook. sculp.

ESTO PERPETUA

CAPT.ʳ SIR JAMES LUCAS YEO. KN.ᵗ

CONSTANO

Published Nov.ʳ 1.1810. by T. Gold. N.º 103 Shoe Lane. Fleet Street.

In the end, the defenders managed to stave off the attackers, and Yeo's squadron withdrew, notwithstanding the efforts of an overly excited American lieutenant who, fearing the day was lost, had set fire to *General Pike*, the 28-gun sloop still on the stocks, to prevent her from being captured—nearly succeeding in what the British had set out to do but had failed to accomplish.

Chauncey's flotilla returned the next day and remained in the battered little harbor for the next six weeks, refitting and repairing damages. When not standing offshore waiting for his foe to emerge from behind the safety of his fortifications, Yeo cruised the lake unopposed. Like a pirate he swooped down on American depots on the Genesee River, where his marines disembarked and seized all the stores, and on Sodus Bay, where he made off with six hundred barrels of flour and pork.

After Yeo returned to Kingston in late June to refit, a midsummer torpor fell over Lake Ontario, enlivened by rumors of espionage and derring-do. So close were the rival bases that deserters frequently appeared in the American camp. "But so many deserters coming over at this time," Chauncey wrote to William Jones, the new secretary of the Navy, "created in my mind a suspicion that a part if not the whole of them had been employed by the enemy as spies and incendiarys." His paranoia was further inflamed by reports that a native New Yorker was secretly working for the British. Samuel Stacy, who hailed from nearby Ogdensburg, had been lurking about Sackets Harbor a little too frequently, it seemed, as Chauncey informed Jones.

> When he left Ogdensburgh he said that he was going to Utica upon important business. He told others that he was going into the Western Country to collect Money, instead of which he came to the Harbor without any ostensible business and made a great many inquiries respecting the Fleet—when they would sail—and the force of the new Ship &c. &c. &c.; I therefore thought it my duty to detain this man for trial. I can prove his frequent intercourse with the Enemy, at any rate I shall deprive the Enemy of the information which he would have conveyed to him which is all important at this time.
>
> It would be very desirable to hang this Traitor to his country—as he is considered respectable in the country in which he lives and I think that it is full time to make an example of some of our Countrymen who are so base, and degenerate as to betray their country by becoming the Spies & Informers of our Enemy.

More intriguing were reports that Yeo had resumed his swashbuckling habits. He had been seen in the nearby woods, at the head of several hundred picked men, preparing to mount a night raid on the American base, and had only retreated upon being found out—to which Jones, agreeing that "impetuosity" was that Englishman's salient characteristic, opined that "copious phlebotomy"—bloodletting—would be "the best cure for Knight Errantry."

LAKE CHAMPLAIN, SUMMER 1813

The spring of 1813 was a hopeful season for Macdonough on Lake Champlain. In February, fifteen ship's carpenters had arrived from New York, followed a month later by his naval ordnance. Soon, three large sloops—*President*, *Eagle*, and *Growler*—were overhauled and refitted so that they could carry even more guns. By May, Macdonough was moving his burgeoning little fleet from its station at Burlington, Vermont, across the lake to Plattsburg, New York. Although the British at Isle aux Noix had reportedly fitted out three sloops in addition to their galley-like gunboats, the odds were now more favorable. He waited only for a detachment of sailors to man his vessels—sailors, he emphasized in his correspondence with Jones, for "[s]oldiers are Miserable creatures on shipboard."

Then came the first setback. In early June, while *President* was being repaired, Macdonough dispatched *Growler* and *Eagle* to patrol the lake's northern reaches and cow the British gunboats from leaving the Richelieu River. Unfortunately, an overeager lieutenant led them too close to Isle aux Noix, where, trapped by the British in the turbulent Richelieu, they ran aground. Both of the sloops, and a hundred crewmen to boot, fell captive.

Suddenly reduced to *President* and two small gunboats, Macdonough was forced to purchase two additional sloops, which he renamed *Commodore Preble* and *Montgomery*, and set about rebuilding his fleet.

Then the second blow fell. Between July 29 and August 3, a British squadron sailed into the lake and attacked American blockhouses, arsenals, barracks, and storehouses with impunity. Macdonough was caught refitting his ships and could only respond by deploying his guns as fixed batteries. His report detailing these embarrassing events brought a stern rebuke from Jones.

> You are to understand that upon no account are you to suffer the enemy to gain the ascendancy on Lake Champlain, and as you have now unlimited authority to procure the necessary resources of men, materials, and munitions for that purpose, I rely upon your efficient and prudent use of the authority vested in you.

It promised to be a long autumn for the young officer.

Navy Depart.^t
June 18. 1812

Sir

I apprize you that war has this day been declared between "the United Empire of Great Britain and Ireland and their dependencies" and the United States of America. You are to consider the vessels under your Command as entitled to every belligerent right, as well of attacks as defence — For the present, it is — desirable that, with the force under your Command, you remain in such position as to enable you most conveniently to receive further more extensive, and more particular orders, which will be conveyed to you through New York, but as it is understood that there are one or more British Cruisers on the Coast, in the vicinity of Sandy hook You are at your discretion, free to strike at them — returning immediately after into port — you are free to — Capture or destroy them — Extend these orders to Comme Decatur —

Respectfully yrs —

Paul Hamilton

Comme Jno Rodgers —
NYork —

In 1812, the Admiralty in London, which administered the Royal Navy, had its headquarters in a sprawling, pillared neoclassical building approached through an elegant arch flanked by winged seahorses. Its maze of chambers housed dozens of scribbling secretaries, while the Sea Lords themselves met in a tastefully appointed board room complete with large globes and a fireplace surmounted by exquisitely carved nautical instruments.

Its American counterpart, the Navy Department, occupied just three rooms on the second floor of a crowded brick building, shared with both the War and State Departments, standing just west of the White House. There, the secretary of the Navy labored with only a handful of civilian clerks to help him. His file depository was the attic, which to one observer was filled with books, old papers, and letters "in great disorder."

There wasn't even a Navy Department in the United States until four years after its navy was founded. In May 1798, President John Adams had persuaded Congress to detach naval matters from the War Department and appointed Benjamin Stoddert, a merchant and key political ally, to be the first secretary of the Navy. Stoddert not only had to face the outbreak of the Quasi-War with France on the high seas but also had to boost an officer corps from fifty-nine to seven hundred men, most of whom he interviewed personally in makeshift headquarters dispersed across Philadelphia. While the infant Navy acquitted itself remarkably well in the West Indies, Stoddert—the first in a series of secretaries with little seafaring experience but plenty of drive and energy—established the nation's first six navy yards and urged the construction of twelve frigates.

By 1801, with the national capital now rising from its new site on the banks of the Potomac, President Thomas Jefferson selected Robert Smith, a Maryland legislator, to head the Navy Office. These were the years of retrenchment, however, when both Congress and the administration preferred to defend the nation's seacoast with strong, U.S. Army-built forts and small, lightly-armed Navy gunboats rather than protect its commerce on the open ocean. Somehow, Smith managed to steer his department through these headwinds, directing the First Barbary War against the Tripolitan pirates in the Mediterranean—and serving as attorney general with only four clerks to help him. One was "a virtual Assistant Secretary," a historian later wrote, "another was a sort of one-man Bureau of Naval Personnel; another handled the central procurement of supplies; and only the fourth concentrated on correspondence." The men serving at sea would anyhow commemorate the secretary in their "Bob Smiths," as they called their twice-daily grog ration, for during those years of trade restrictions and even trade embargoes with the West Indies, Smith had substituted cheaper, more readily available American rye whiskey for the traditional rum—and the sailors approved of the change.

Hard drink apparently helped undo his successor, former South Carolina governor Paul Hamilton, whom President James Madison tapped in 1809 after kicking Smith upstairs to be his first secretary of state. Hamilton,

with no experience of ships or the sea, often seemed out of his element, and his enemies in Congress seized on rumors that he was drunk at his desk every afternoon to hound him out of office by December 1812. But Commodore John Rodgers found him a "most zealous friend of the Navy," and whatever his shortcomings, Hamilton pushed through the landmark Naval Hospitals Act of 1811 and helped lay the Navy's wartime strategy: defense of the Great Lakes, commerce raiding at sea, and sorties by small, frigate-centered squadrons. Moreover, during the first six months of fighting, while his neighbors in the War Department were in despair over the U.S. Army's initial disasters, his was the service that won victory after surprising victory against the most formidable navy in the world.

Former congressman William Jones, who took the helm in 1813, had at least served on warships in his youth. Fortunately, he had a huge capacity for work, for he was concurrently serving as secretary of the treasury, and though he tried reforming the department's inefficient administration—up to twenty civilian clerks were now carving out miniature fiefdoms—his was the watch during which the British attacked Washington. Although the department's files and valuables were removed to safekeeping before the redcoats put the crowded brick building to the torch, Jones could not save the Washington Navy Yard. Reluctantly, he gave the order to burn it, with its stock of prime live oak timber and the nearly finished 44-gun frigate on the stocks, before it fell into enemy hands. He found some redress, though, by helping lead the counterattack on British forces during their withdrawal from nearby Alexandria, Virginia.

By the time Benjamin Crowninshield became secretary in early 1815, the conflict had drawn to a close—and so had the years of haphazard naval administration. The War of 1812 had finally persuaded the nation that its navy was too vital to be further skimped and stinted.

Crowninshield, a scion of New England's most famous shipping family, had hardly taken office before he was supervising the completion of several 74-gun ships-of-the-line and ensuring that never again would so many crucial functions, ranging from shipbuilding and procurement to the standardization of equipment and procedures, be entrusted solely to civilians without the benefit of professional advice. So he established a three-man Board of Naval Commissioners (beginning with John Rodgers, David Porter, and Stephen Decatur) to provide the secretary with the seasoned advice of men who had struggled firsthand with the stresses of life at sea and, what's more, knew the cannon's roar—veteran postcaptains, not unlike the Sea Lords of the Admiralty, who might steer an expanded U.S. Navy into the future.

Meanwhile, on the other side of the Adirondacks, both of the opposing fleets had now left their harbors. Yet each commodore was still wary of the other, still hesitant to risk everything on a fleet action that would not be entirely to his liking, each knowing, as one British midshipman put it, that the "Fate of upper Canada depends on our being the Conquerors or the Conquered."

On storm-swept Lake Ontario, though, it wasn't always the enemy that needed careful watching.

On August 7, the two fleets closed on each other near the western end of the lake. With *Wolfe*, his flagship, Yeo was accompanied by *Royal George, Earl of Moira, Prince Regent,* and *Simcoe.* Chauncey, with *General Pike,* had a large force, including *Madison, Oneida, Governor Tompkins, Conquest, Ontario, Pert,* and the schooners *Lady of the Lake, Growler, Julia, Hamilton,* and *Scourge.* The decks of the last two were overburdened with heavy guns, having twice as many as were mounted on the other schooners, making them twice as unsteady, considering their shallow draft.

The opposing sides spent the day angling for position, but the wind fell, and by evening all the ships were becalmed, separated by not much more distance than could be covered by a cannon shot. Aboard *Scourge,* therefore, Myers and his mates prepared to bed down at their guns.

It was a lovely evening, not a cloud visible, and the lake being as smooth as a looking-glass. The English fleet was but a short distance to the northward of us; so near, indeed, that we could almost count their ports. They were becalmed like ourselves, and a little scattered . . .

Mr. Osgood said . . . , "I think we may have a hard night's work yet, and I wish you to get your suppers, and then catch as much sleep as you can, at your guns." He then ordered the purser's steward to splice the main-brace. These were the last words I ever heard from Mr. Osgood . . .

I was soon asleep, as sound as if lying in the bed of a king. How long my nap lasted . . . I cannot say. I awoke, however, in consequence of large drops of rain falling on my face. Tom Goldsmith awoke at the same moment. When I opened my eyes, it was so dark I could not see the length of the deck. I arose and spoke to Tom, telling him it was about to rain, and that I meant to go down and get a nip, out of a little stuff we kept in our mess-chest . . . Tom answered, "This is nothing; we're neither pepper nor salt." One of the black men spoke, and asked me to bring up the bottle, and give him a nip, too. All this took half a minute, perhaps. I now remember to have heard a strange rushing noise to windward as I went toward the forward hatch, though it made no impression on me at the time. We had been lying between the starboard guns, which was the weather side of the vessel . . . One hand was on the bitts, and a foot was on the ladder, when a flash of lightning almost blinded me. The thunder came at the next instant, and with it a rushing of winds that fairly smothered the clap.

The instant I was aware there was a squall, I sprang for the jib-sheet. Being captain of the forecastle, I knew where to find it, and throw it loose at a jerk . . . All this time I kept shouting to the man at the wheel to put his helm "hard down." The water was now up to my breast, and I knew the schooner must go over . . . The flashes of lightning were incessant, and nearly blinded me. Our decks seemed on fire . . . [T]he schooner was filled with the shrieks and cries of the men to leeward, who were lying jammed under the guns, shot-boxes, shot, and other heavy things that had gone down as the vessel fell over . . .

I succeeded in hauling myself up to windward, and in getting into the schooner's fore-channels. Here I met William Deer, the boatswain, and a black boy of the name of Philips, who was the powder-boy of our gun. "Deer, she's gone!" I said. The boatswain made no answer, but walked out on the fore-rigging, toward the masthead . . .

I now crawled aft, on the upper side of the bulwarks, amid a most awful and infernal din of thunder, and shrieks, and dazzling flashes of lightning; the wind blowing all the while like a tornado. When I reached the port of my own gun, I put a foot in, thinking to step on the muzzle of the piece; but it had gone to leeward with all the rest, and I fell through the port, until I brought up with my arms. I struggled up again, and continued working my way aft. As I got abreast of the main-mast, I saw someone had let run the halyards. I soon reached the beckets of the sweeps . . . I then crawled quite aft, as far as the fashion-piece. The water was pouring down the cabin companion-way like a sluice; and as I stood, for an instant, on the fashion-piece, I saw Mr. Osgood, with his head and part of his shoulders through one of the cabin windows, struggling to get out. He must have been within six feet of me. I saw him but a moment, by means of a flash of lightning, and I think he must have seen me. At the same time, there was a man visible on the end of the main-boom, holding on by the clew of the sail. I do not know who it was. This man probably saw me, and that I was about to spring; for he called out, "Don't jump overboard! Don't jump overboard! The schooner is righting."

I was not in a state of mind to reflect much on anything. I do not think more than three or four minutes, if as many, had passed since the squall struck us, and there I was standing on the vessel's quarter, led by Providence more than by any discretion of my own. It now came across me that if the schooner should right she was filled, and must go down, and that she might carry me with her in the suction. I made a spring, therefore, and fell into the water several feet from the place where I had stood. It is my opinion the schooner sunk as I left her. I went down some distance myself, and when I came up to the surface, I began to swim vigorously for the first time in my life. I think I swam several yards . . . until I felt my hand hit something hard. I made another stroke, and felt my hand pass down the side of an object that I knew at once was a clincher-built boat. I belonged to this boat, and I now recollected that she had been towing astern. Until that instant I had not thought of her, but thus was I led in the dark to

Artist Richard Schlecht's representation of Ned Myers abandoning ship in *Scourge*'s final moments. Myers was one of only eight crewmen from *Scourge* and *Hamilton* who escaped with their lives.

the best possible means of saving my life. I made a grab at the gunwale, and caught it in the stern-sheets. Had I swum another yard, I should have passed the boat, and missed her altogether! I got in without any difficulty, being all alive and much excited.

My first look was for the schooner. She had disappeared, and I supposed she was just settling under water. It rained as if the floodgates of heaven were opened, and it lightened awfully. It did not seem to me that there was a breath of air . . .

My only chance of seeing was during the flashes . . . I now called out to encourage the men, telling them I was in the boat. I could hear many around me, and occasionally I saw the heads of men, struggling in the lake . . .

I kept calling out, . . . and presently I heard a voice saying, "Ned, I'm here, close by you." This was Tom Goldsmith, . . . the very man under whose rug I had been sleeping, at quarters. He did not [need] much help, getting in . . . "Ned," says Tom, "she's gone down with her colours flying, for her pennant came near getting a round turn about my body, and carrying me down with her. Davy [Jones] has made a good haul, and he gave us a close shave; but he didn't get you and me."

The top-heavy *Hamilton* and *Scourge* had both foundered in the sudden squall, sinking like stones. Within fifteen minutes, a seventh of Chauncey's fleet vanished, taking along the lives of more than seventy sailors. Two days later, as the Americans escaped eastward, Yeo scooped up two additional U.S. schooners, *Julia* and *Growler*. Chauncey had now lost nearly a third of his force, without it ever coming to action.

The cat-and-mouse game continued, each commodore scanning the horizon for the telltale sails of his adversary. Along the shore thousands of soldiers shifted anxiously, for new campaigns were afoot. Meanwhile, Chauncey bombarded Jones—who already had his hands full dealing with the tightening British blockade and the raids up and down the seaboard and in the Chesapeake Bay—with ever more requests for sailors to man the vessels he was so feverishly constructing at Sackets Harbor. Across the water, in Kingston, Yeo was similarly informing the Admiralty of "how inadequate" his force seemed in comparison to that of his opponent. "The Officers, and Men, which come from England," he wrote, "are scarcely sufficient to Man the Squadron on this Lake."

Neither commander, it seemed, had anything to spare for Lake Erie.

LOST ON THE LAKE

Finding *Hamilton* and *Scourge*

Above, right: National Geographic engineer Alvin M. Chandler attaches a bracket to the remotely piloted vehicle. A sector-scanning sonar seen above Chandler's wrists enabled operators to surmount the barrier of ten-foot visibility by providing an acoustical picture of the wrecks from as far away as three hundred feet.

Below, left: An artist's view of the exploration of the sunken *Scourge*.

Below, right: The remotely piloted vehicle that was used to positively identify the wrecks discovered on the lake bottom as *Hamilton* and *Scourge*.

Opposite: An underwater view of Diana, *Hamilton's* figurehead, made wraithlike by the ravages of water and time.

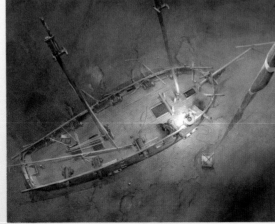

After two armed schooners, *Hamilton* and *Scourge*, foundered on Lake Ontario that stormy night of August 8, 1813, the Buffalo *Gazette* gasped with dismay: "In a moment 100 of our brave fellows were plunged into the wave, and two of our best schooners lost to the service."

More than 160 years later, those schooners were found again, thanks to the determined efforts of a Canadian dentist and underwater archaeologist named Daniel Nelson. Having long been fascinated by the story of the two ships, Nelson, who lived in nearby Hamilton, on the shores of Lake Ontario, had often looked out over the serene surface of the water wondering where the ships might lie. In 1971, working with the Royal Ontario Museum in Toronto, he began searching for them in earnest.

Happening upon an entry in the logbook of HMS *Wolfe* made the morning after the storm, which mentioned the location of the "enemy squadron," Nelson was able, in 1973, to narrow the probable area of the shipwrecks to a zone a few miles north of present-day Port Dalhousie. The Canadian government loaned him a research vessel equipped with side-scan sonar capable of mapping large areas of the lakebed. He also leased a magnetometer, hoping,

as his team quartered back and forth over likely spots, to pick up traces of iron that might mean cannons were resting somewhere beneath them. That instrument instead located a pile of bridge girders that had slipped off a freighter, as well as some old artillery shells from a World War II firing range. Shortly before he and his team had to knock off for the winter, though, the sonar detected a large object on the lakebed, nearly three hundred feet down in the quiet abyss, that could very well be a ship.

This tantalizing glimpse was the only one Nelson got for another two years. Then, in July 1975, his reading was confirmed, and what's more, there seemed to be another object nearby. Both indeed seemed to be ships. In November, the team was able to send down a remotely tethered vehicle equipped with a television camera. Watching topside, Nelson saw a ghostly stern swim eerily into view. Then he saw spars on the deck, followed by the grim specter of a human skeleton, and lastly the strange sight of a box of cannonballs, propped open.

It was clearly a warship. There were oxidized cannons still on deck and even cutlasses hanging in their proper places along the bulwarks. He was looking at *Hamilton*, unseen for a century and a half.

Over the next few years, a number of exploratory dives were made to the ships. In 1980, even famed French oceanographer Jacques Cousteau couldn't resist having a peek, for the vessels, with most of their masts still upright, were remarkably well-preserved. The lightless, near-freezing water at that depth had retarded decay. Though visibility was not much better than ten feet in those murky regions, a National Geographic remotely piloted vehicle still managed to take dramatic color close-ups of the "ghost ships," the carved figureheads looming out of the blackness with an otherworldly aura.

The ships still lie on the bottom of Lake Ontario. They are owned by the city of Hamilton, the U.S. government having given over to that municipality the title to its former warships. They are also protected

by Canadian law, not only because of their historical significance but also because the vessels still contain human remains. Though they might repose in the deep, these "three dimensional blueprints of their time," as Nelson once described them, continue to provide scholars and archaeologists with valuable insights into how ships were constructed and outfitted for the War of 1812.

During the heyday of work on the Presque Isle fleet, Noah Brown had happened upon a carpenter who was being a little too painstaking in his labors. "We want no extras," he chided the man. "Plain work is all that is required; they will only be wanted for one battle; if we win, that is all that is wanted of them."

The two brigs were almost ready for that one portentous battle between hastily built, improvised warships. By mid-June, they were looking like real ships. "One of the brigs is completely rigged, her battery mounted," Dobbins reported on June 27. "The other will be equally far advanced in a week." Almost the same size—being about 110 feet long and 16 wide—they would mount two long 12-pounders and eighteen 32-pound carronades. One would be named *Lawrence*, after Captain James Lawrence, who had just lost his life and his frigate, *Chesapeake*, in a single-frigate duel with Captain Philip Bowes Vere Broke's *Shannon* off Boston. The other would be christened *Niagara*, celebrating the recent American victories on that peninsula. They were sleek and handsome brigs—only they had no extras; even their wooden bulwarks were paper thin.

On the evening of June 18, an exhausted Perry had returned to Presque Isle from his adventure at Fort George. He came in from the lake, shepherding no fewer than five vessels to add to his budding fleet. With the fall of Fort George, the British had evacuated Fort Erie, whose guns had dominated the juncture between the Niagara River and Lake Erie, thus keeping the ships that Jesse Elliott had assembled and refitted blockaded in the Black Rock dockyard—the brig *Caledonia*; the schooners *Somers*, *Tigress*, and *Ohio*; and the sloop *Trippe*. Not having to worry about dodging the fort's guns, however, had not made the trip to Presque Isle any easier. It took two weeks and the backbreaking labor of several ox teams, augmented by some two hundred soldiers, to pull the five heavily laden vessels against the turbulent current of the Niagara River. Once he had gained the Lake, Perry and his little flotilla then had to face choppy waters, violent headwinds, and a Royal Navy squadron hunting especially for them.

That squadron was commanded by Lieutenant Robert Heriot Barclay, a one-armed, ginger-haired veteran of Trafalgar, a new arrival on the Lake Erie station. Arriving in early June at the naval base in Amherstburg, across the river from Detroit, he soon took over the squadron that had unsuccessfully tried to capture Perry—the 17-gun *Queen Charlotte*, the 13-gun *Lady Prevost*, the 10-gun *Hunter*, and the schooners *Little Belt* and *Chippewa*—the only squadron, in fact, on the Lake. That was the one advantage he had over Perry—possession of a fleet—and he hoped to keep it that way.

Back at Presque Isle, Perry's efforts to build his own fleet had only encountered more obstacles. The order for anchors from

Pittsburgh had been delayed, and he was getting desperate. Even more worrisome was the lack of skilled sailors. He didn't have enough men to fit out one brig, much less the nine sloops and gunboats he now had on hand. So he badgered Chauncey, sending him urgent requests for more men. "I know you will send them as soon as possible," he wrote, "yet a day appears an age."

When seventy sailors did finally arrive, Perry complained about the "motley set of Negroes, soldiers, and boys." Bristling at this, Chauncey retorted heatedly: "I have yet to learn that the color of the skin, or the cut or trimming of the coat, can affect a man's qualifications or usefulness. I have nearly fifty blacks on board of this ship, and many of them are among my best men."

Perry, stung, his nerves worn raw by the grueling pace of things, promptly sent a letter of resignation to Jones. Fortunately, he withdrew it, but it had been that kind of a summer. Soon afterward, Jesse Elliott arrived with 150 picked seamen.

If anything, Barclay was facing even steeper odds. At twenty-six, only a year younger than Perry, he depended on a longer and more uncertain supply line. He was also beset by equally pressing personnel challenges. Only a few Royal Navy officers and men had accompanied him to Amherstburg. To man his ships he depended on large drafts of soldiers—landsmen—many of whom had never set foot on anything larger than a ferry. "I have to state that there is a general want of stores of every description at this post," Barclay soon wrote to General Henry Procter, British commander on the Detroit frontier.

The *Detroit* may be launched in ten days, but there is no chance of her being ready for any active service until a large proportion of stores, and guns are sent here— And even admitting that she could be equipped—there is not a seaman to put on board her—The absolute necessity of Seamen being immediately sent up is so obvious that I need hardly point it out to you—The Ships are manned with a crew, part of whom cannot even speak English.

A 20-gun sloop, *Detroit* promised to be the finest warship on the lake once she was completed, but the carronades she was due to receive had been captured by the Americans during the raid on York in April. Therefore, Barclay would outfit her armament with a range of long guns, of any and every caliber imaginable, taken from the casemates of Fort Malden. Some of them, it was said, could only be fired by snapping flintlock pistols over their vent holes.

At Presque Isle, Dobbins and Perry had another problem to contend with: getting the vessels out of the harbor. A shift in the prevailing winds and unusually low water had reduced the clearance over the sandbar from six feet to something less than five—about four feet shallower than the draft required by both *Niagara* and *Lawrence*. What's more, in late July, Barclay's squadron turned up to blockade

This small compass was once owned by Perry. Not intended for navigation, it was used to take a quick bearing on other ships or landmarks. It passed through the family to one of Perry's cousins, Aseph, who acquired it in 1838.

the harbor, and was even willing to spar with shore batteries on the cliffs. If Barclay couldn't stop Perry from building ships, he could try to stop him from launching them.

Then one morning he was gone. Perhaps he had needed to reprovision or resupply, or maybe with a storm brewing over the lake he had sought a safer anchorage to ride it out. Whatever it was, it took Barclay away for four days.

This was Perry's chance to get his ships over the bar and into the lake. The shallow water, however, presented a challenge. Anticipating this problem, Brown had built "camels." When these huge, watertight wooden cradles were submerged, a ship could be maneuvered into them. Pumped dry, these cradles naturally floated, raising the ship whose hull they gripped. Because the camels were of a shallower draft than their cargo, they could then be towed over the bar, resubmerged, and their wooden-walled passenger released back into a sufficient depth of water.

But this foot-by-foot process of plugging and pumping and pulling was slow and painstaking work—it took nearly two days to get *Lawrence* alone over the sandbar, and a ship being maneuvered in this way, with all guns and ballast removed in order to lighten her, was a sitting duck. Fortunately, *Niagara* went over the bar slightly faster. By midday on August 6, all the new vessels were safely out of the harbor and onto the lake—just as Barclay's ships hove into sight. Barclay took one look at the American warships, arranged in a line of battle, and stood back offshore.

There were now two fleets on the lake. Both of them soon set courses to the west, Perry to meet with General William Henry Harrison, whose Army of the Northwest lurked behind breastworks near Detroit, and Barclay to Amherstburg, where he was at wit's end to find experienced sailors who could man *Detroit*. Perry, similarly desperate, was taking on soldiers from Harrison's

army—some of them Kentucky riflemen whose skillful marksmanship might prove useful, others militiamen who didn't know a rope from a halyard.

Barclay's most acute problem, though, was the rapid diminution of every kind of supply, especially naval stores, without which he simply could not continue operations. The American seizure of the Niagara Peninsula and Chauncey's activities on Lake Ontario had reduced the supply of men and material to a trickle. Procter's army, along with its several thousand Native American auxiliaries led by Tecumseh, was stationed in a region where rivers and forests were plentiful but farmland scarce. It depended entirely on a steady supply of government provisions to survive. By late summer, these had run so low that the British army actually tried to seize supplies from the American-held Fort Meigs.

By August, a bad situation was made much worse when Perry's little flotilla effectively blockaded Barclay in Amherstburg. The specter of starvation then reared its ugly head; it was critical that the water highway to the east be reopened. The young Royal Navy lieutenant could no longer resist the pressure to give battle. Off Malden, the Americans staked out his operation, finding him and his men hard at the task of making preparations for engagement. *Detroit* was almost, but not quite, ready. Some of Perry's officers recommended striking them unawares, but Perry wouldn't have it. "No," he said. "I will take no dishonorable advantage of them, but wait until they get in readiness, and meet them fairly and openly on the lake."

On the night of September 9, Perry's squadron had dropped anchor in the snug little harbor of Put-in-Bay in the Bass Islands twenty miles to the south. It was a full-moon night, "one of those beautiful autumnal evenings peculiar to the lake region," as William Dobbins, Daniel's son, gleaned from his father's reminiscences. Aboard his flagship *Lawrence*, Perry was still recovering from a ravaging bout of "lake fever," a distant cousin of typhus. Though the sickness had also stricken many of his men, and had left him "shaky as an aspen," a showdown with Barclay was inevitable. Summoning his officers to the quarterdeck, he gave them their battle orders and then unfurled an eighteen-foot-long motto flag that left no mistake for whom his flagship was named: he had James Lawrence's stirring final words—"Don't give up the ship!"—emblazoned on the bunting in capital letters three-feet high. When that banner was run up the mainmast, he told them, it was the signal to close for action.

Left: Perry composed this letter to General William Henry Harrison on September 5, 1813, five days before the epic Battle of Lake Erie. In it, he outlines plans for meeting his foe on the lake, professing that he won't be able to "seize a favorable moment to make a dash at the enemy."

Perry's signal lantern, made of tin with windows of scraped horn.

The next morning, September 10, 1813, lookouts spied Barclay's six sails on the horizon. The Americans beat to quarters and were soon standing out of the harbor. The sun, recalled David Bunnell, then a teenaged sailor with *Lawrence*, "rose in all his glory . . . but before it set, many a brave tar on both sides was doomed to a watery grave, and many a jovial soul who had 'led the merry dance on the light fantastic toe,' the evening previous, never danced again."

The squadron fell into its assigned places in the line of battle. The schooners *Scorpion* and *Ariel* took the van. Then came the three brigs: *Lawrence*, her big motto flag not quite snapping as the breeze was so light; the little *Caledonia*; and *Niagara*, commanded by Jesse Elliott. Bringing up the rear were the remaining schooners, *Somers, Porcupine, Tigress,* and *Trippe.*

The enemy's ships were plainly visible now, stretched out in their own line of battle—the schooner *Chippewa*, then Barclay's flagship, *Detroit*, followed by the brig *General Hunter*, the sloop *Queen Charlotte*, the brig *Lady Prevost*, and the sloop *Little Belt*— all on a course to the southwest, keeping the wind, blowing around seven knots, on their starboard quarter. Barclay was holding the weather gauge.

"I don't care," Perry reportedly said. "To windward or leeward—they shall fight today."

As the opposing lines slowly began to close, men began scattering sand over the decks to give them better footing once the blood began to flow. They set out water buckets to stanch fires at the guns and to slake their desperate thirst once the cannonading began.

"The word 'silence' was not given," Bunnell recalled. "We stood in awful impatience—not a word was spoken, not a sound heard, except now and then an order to trim a sail, and the boatswain's shrill whistle . . . This was a time to try the stoutest heart. My pulse beat quick . . . [T]he dart of death hung as it were trembling by a single hair, and no one knew on whose head it would fall."

Then the wind shifted, favoring Perry. The motto flag flew to the masthead, and *Lawrence* closed for action, angling toward the British ships, now lying hove-to and beginning to fire their guns.

Lawrence was soon the epicenter of a tremendous racket and roar. As Perry tried narrowing the gap sufficiently to bring his ship's short-range carronades into action, *Detroit*'s disparate assortment of long guns hurled a devastatingly precise

Lawrence's surgeon, Dr. Usher Parsons.

hail of iron into his path. Those of *Hunter* and *Queen Charlotte* immediately joined in, and though the American schooners *Scorpion* and *Ariel,* their own long guns booming, were in close support, the combined firepower of the three British warships remained unerringly aimed at *Lawrence*. For twenty minutes, the deadly fusillade of solid shot and grape continued unchecked, smashing into her hull, holing her sails, splintering her flimsy bulwarks, pulverizing her rigging, dismantling her guns, and tearing her crew to pieces. Even when she was close enough to begin firing back, and even when the other American vessels joined furiously in the engagement, *Lawrence* remained the favorite target of British broadsides. For two hours, the pummeling continued, until nearly every man aboard had been hit; so many gunners went down that surgeon's assistants had to step up and take their places. Even Perry, dressed in a plain blue round jacket so as to be inconspicuous, was manning *Lawrence*'s last functioning gun, with help from the chaplain and ship's purser, since nearly four-fifths of the crew had by then been killed or wounded. By some miracle—his compeers later coined it "Perry's Luck"—he was barely scratched, even though the ships were now so close that musket balls had joined the rain of solid shot, grape, and canister. Bunnell vividly described the terrible scene on deck.

During the action a shot struck a man in the head, who was standing close by me; his brains flew so thick in my face, that I was for some time blinded, and for a few moments was at a loss to ascertain whether it was him or me that was killed.—We had peas boiling for dinner—our place for cooking was on deck, and during the action a shot had penetrated the boiler, and the peas were rolling all over the deck,—we had several pigs loose on deck, and I actually saw one of them eating peas that had both his hind legs shot off—and a little dog belonging to one of the officers, that was wounded, ran from one end of the vessel to the other, howling in the most dreadful manner.—A hardy old tar who acted in the station of "Stopperman," (when any of the rigging is partly shot away, they put a stopper on the place, to prevent it from going away entirely) discovering our main stay partly shot away, jumped and began to put a stopper on, and while in the act, another shot cut the stay away below him, which let him swing with great force against the mast—He very gravely observed,—"Damn you, if you must have it, take it."—A shot from the enemy struck one of our guns, within a quarter of an inch of the caliber; little pieces of metal flew in every direction, and wounded almost every man at the piece. One man was filled full of little pieces of cast iron, from his knees to his chin, some not bigger than the head of a pin, and none larger than a buck shot.

Bunnell, who had enlisted in the Navy for the "opportunity of settling some small accounts with John Bull," stayed at his gun until it "got so warm

In 1857, artist William Henry Powell (1823-1879) was commissioned by his home state, Ohio, to paint this scene for the rotunda of the Ohio Statehouse. Nearly ten years later, he was asked to replicate this work on a larger scale so that it could hang in the Senate wing of the Capitol. As his subject, Powell chose the dramatic moment when Perry abandoned his ravaged flagship, *Lawrence*, and made his way by rowboat through enemy fire to reach the unscathed *Niagara*. Powell couldn't resist enlarging the crew of the boat, showing six oarsmen (some wounded, with blood seeping through their bandages), a helmsman, Perry, and Perry's thirteen-year-old brother, Alexander, who served as Perry's midshipman and may or may not have actually accompanied his brother in the rowboat. To the right, a doomed figure drifts in the flotsam. In another instance of artistic license, Perry does not carry his battle flag; instead, Powell chose to fly Old Glory from the bow.

In addition to the brief, well-known battle report he sent to General William Henry Harrison, Perry also penned two slightly longer dispatches, both identical in wording, to Secretary of the Navy William Jones and Commodore Isaac Chauncey before the ink had even dried on his letter to Harrison. In these moments, as historian Bancroft has noted and as the overtones of the message suggest, "a religious awe seemed to come over [Perry] at his wonderful preservation in the midst of the great and long continued danger." Shown here is that dispatch.

that it jumped entirely out of its carriage, which rendered it useless." Around him, the crack of fire had gone quiet, but he "looked up to see if our flag was still flying, and with pleasure beheld, partly obscured by smoke, the star spangled banner yet waving." Soon, though, that flag would wave no more, as Sailing Master William Taylor wrote in a tumultuous letter to his wife.

> Judge the scene at 1/2 2 PM when 22 Men & officers lay dead on decks & 66 wounded, every gun dismounted carriages knock'd to pieces—every strand of rigging cut off—masts & spars shot & tottering overhead & in fact an unmanageable wreck. I say at this time when not another gun could be worked or fir'd or man'd Capt. Perry determined to leave her—got a Boat alongside haul'd down his own private flag which we fought under with the last words of Lawrence on it—Don't give up the Ship—& bore it in triumph on board of the *Niagara*—leaving Lts. Yarnell, Forrest & myself to act as we thought proper we at this time all wounded—about 10 minutes after he got on board the *Niagara*—we concluded as no further resistance could possibly be made from this Brig & likewise to save the further effusion of human blood as at this time they kept up a galling fire on us, agreed to haul down our colours—many poor fellows men as well as officers that lay wounded on our decks, shed tears of grief saying Oh don't haul down our colours—No ship my dear girl this war has been fought so obstinately & suffer'd so much as the *Lawrence*.

The sight of Perry, sword in one hand, motto flag in the other, being rowed through the smoke from the wrecked, body-strewn *Lawrence*—grape and canister and musket balls screaming and plunging all around him—to the unscathed *Niagara* marked the most dramatic moment of the battle. Though every other vessel in the American squadron had been swept up in the combat—even the gunboats bringing up the rear had made telling use of their long guns—Elliott, for reasons never entirely made clear, had kept *Niagara* to windward of the line of battle, screened by her sister ships. When the wrecked *Lawrence* started drifting out of control, some aboard *Niagara* even thought that Perry had been killed. He then turned up very much alive, clambering aboard and commandeering their brig as a substitute flagship. "Two-thirds of my men are either killed or wounded and the *Lawrence* can provide no further assistance," one witness remembered Perry telling Elliott. Insisting that they could yet win the day, Elliott descended into the rowboat to guide the remaining U.S. gunboats through the battle smoke, leaving Perry in command of *Niagara*.

Both the British and American ships were now fast disintegrating in the hailstorm of iron. Barclay was hit in the leg, and his officers were falling in droves. When the American gunboats then drew nearer, their raking fire began to have telling effect on *Lady Prevost*, which also soon drifted out of control. At this instant, Perry brought *Niagara* slicing across the British line, at the moment she crossed releasing both of her broadsides at once. The carronades had been charged with canister, and the resulting carnage on Barclay's vessels was ghastly.

In response, Barclay tried wearing ship to bring his own starboard broadside into action, but damaged as she was, *Detroit* collided with *Queen Charlotte*, and their spars and rigging became inextricably entangled. Thus helpless and exposed, the intertwined ships were raked from one direction by *Niagara* and from the other by the gunboats. Barclay went down, his good

We have met the enemy and they are ours: Two Ships, two Brigs one Schooner & one Sloop.

Yours, with great respect and esteem

O H Perry.

arm now maimed. All of his commanders were either dead or wounded, and all of his ships were being shot to slivers. A raking broadside from *Niagara* quite literally swept the decks of *Lady Prevost*, and those sailors it didn't blow away tumbled down the hatchways, leaving only her dazed captain standing alone.

Detroit and *Queen Charlotte* struck their colors around three o'clock. Their sister ships soon followed. Bunnell never forgot the elation he felt in those first few minutes after the last gun fell silent.

> What a glorious day to my country—and how rejoiced I was to find the battle ended—victory our own, and myself safe, except a slight wound, and much deafened. I did not recover my proper hearing for a year afterwards.

Before an hour had passed, Perry was rowed back to the battered *Lawrence*. "It was a time of conflicting emotions, when the commodore returned to the ship," wrote the ship's surgeon, Dr. Usher Parsons, who'd been in the grips of the fever and had to make his rounds carried on a cot. "The battle was won and he was safe … Those of us who were spared approached him as he came over the ship's side, but the salutation was a silent one—not a word could find utterance."

Perry penned a quick note to Jones, and then, for Harrison, he scribbled on the back of an old envelope the terse message that would echo so resoundingly down the years:

> We have met the enemy and they are ours: Two Ships, two Brigs, one Schooner, & one Sloop.

Among the most magnificent pieces of early American silver, this tureen was given to Perry by the citizens of Newport, Rhode Island. Crafted in sterling by Thomas Fletcher and Sidney Gardiner of Philadelphia, the dish is engraved with a detailed scene of the battle. Heads of Neptune guard the handles, and the cover is topped by an early American eagle perched on an anchor. Perry wrote a letter to the people of Newport, thanking them for the lavish gift.

Lawrence's decks, where Perry, now wearing his undress uniform, chose to formally accept the British surrender, were intentionally left a bloody shambles when the surviving British officers in solemn procession picked their way across to tender their swords to Perry, who refused to take them.

That night, most of the sixty-five men who had been killed in the action were lashed in hammocks and committed to the waters of the lake, a 32-pound shot added to speed them to eternity. Two mornings later, after the ships had been patched up enough to limp to the Bass Islands, the slain officers were buried. The tattered colors of both nations hung at half-mast as another solemn procession, British and American officers marching side by side, made its way over the wet sand of the beach and crossed to the suitably wild and desolate spot not far from Put-in-Bay that had been selected for a burying ground. There the shrouded bodies were laid to rest, British and American again alternating with one another as the respective chaplains intoned the burial service. A volley of musketry concluded the ceremony.

The battle that had claimed those lives had been judged significant before the first shot was ever fired. Daniel Dobbins and Noah Brown could congratulate themselves that their fleet, in which seemingly every tree in the American forest had a share, outlasted its British counterpart in the one pivotal encounter for which it was built to fight. The battle's wider consequences, though, soon became apparent. With the British fleet entirely swept away, Procter's vital link to the East was finally sundered. He had no choice but to retreat, and retreat meant abandoning all the territory in the Northwest, from Mackinac to Detroit, that had so swiftly been won by Brock in the opening days of the war. Procter also needed to retreat fast, for starvation was now a real possibility. That meant abandoning his Native American allies, most of whose homes lay to the north and west, and the American reconquest

Top: Wood from Perry's flagship, *Lawrence*, was used to make this courtly walking cane, inscribed with the officer's laconic battle report, now famous, to General William Henry Harrison: "We have met the enemy and they are ours . . ."

Above: A report of ships taken prize in the Battle of Lake Erie.

An oil painting by Louis Bennett Chevalier (1823-1889) depicting the burial of the officers killed in the Battle of Lake Erie.

PERRY'S Victory.

Auld Lang Syne.

Hail Columbia!

William

Of the Ferry.

Sold Wholesale, at No. 198, Race Street, Philadelphia.

of the Michigan Territory would be the wedge that split the British-Native American alliance. Those warriors who were attached to Procter's army, just as dependent on government provisions as were their British comrades, had to retreat east with him or starve. Tecumseh, in a moment of loathing, had sneered, "We must compare our Father's conduct to a fat animal that carries its tail upon its back, but when affrighted, it drops it between its legs and runs off." But he went with them nonetheless.

Perry's victory also ensured that not only Detroit but also Amherstburg would fall without firing a shot when Harrison's forces stormed across the border two weeks later—thanks to Perry's unhindered ability to transport his men and supplies across the Detroit River. Harrison quickly caught the retreating Procter and, on October 5, destroyed his army in the Battle of the Thames. It was the battle in which Tecumseh was killed, and with his death died the dream of an independent Native American Confederacy.

To be sure, the Royal Navy was soon laying plans to build another fleet and retake Lakes Erie and Huron. That was one reason why Chauncey and Yeo still fought for control of Lake Ontario. Another was the Americans' need to safeguard an invasion of Canada. The leaves were on the turn when the two fleets encountered each other off Burlington Heights near York on September 28.

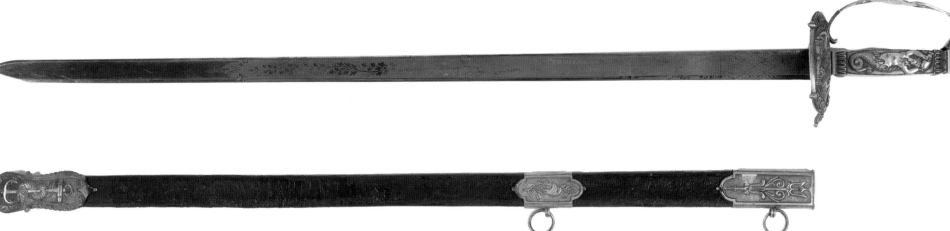

This sword was presented to midshipman James Bliss for heroic action in the Battle of Lake Erie.

Maneuvering back and forth in what became known as the "Burlington Races," they actually closed with each other, but though some broadsides were exchanged, the dismasting of many ships on both sides, which ended the day, was due not to cannon fire but—once again—to a Lake Ontario gale.

Thus, American general James Wilkinson, who was planning a two-pronged attack on Montreal, didn't get the "pleasure [of seeing] Chauncey give the vaporing dog [Yeo] a sound drubbing." Chauncey had been keeping Yeo away from hampering that attack. The original plan was to assail Kingston, but this was deemed too risky. Wilkinson's eight thousand men were instead transported down the St. Lawrence, but because Lake Ontario was still being contested, Chauncey could neither protect them from the British gunboats that harried their voyage nor prevent those same gunboats from playing a role in Wilkinson's defeat at Crysler's Farm on November 11.

The second prong of the attack, led by General Wade Hampton, had departed Burlington on Lake Champlain, and thanks to Thomas Macdonough, whose own gunboat flotilla was back in operation by August, it made a safe passage across those waters to Plattsburgh. But as it advanced down the dusty highway leading straight to Montreal, that army encountered too many enemy troops and thus veered off into the mountains—soon to meet their own defeat at Chateauguay. Those enemy troops along the road to Montreal spelled trouble for Macdonough once the ice on Lake Champlain melted in the spring.

The war for the eastern lakes would continue into 1814, but the battle for Lake Erie was effectively over. The Royal Navy would never return there in force. Perry was celebrated up and down the East Coast and toasted for decades after his early death because, as one biographer put it, in no other engagement "were the consequences to the whole country of such momentous character." For those limitless square miles of mountain and forest and desert stretching westward to Oregon were won not by an army but by a navy.

This wood snuff box, inlayed with mother of pearl, was presented to Perry in honor of his stirring victory.

CHAPTER FOUR

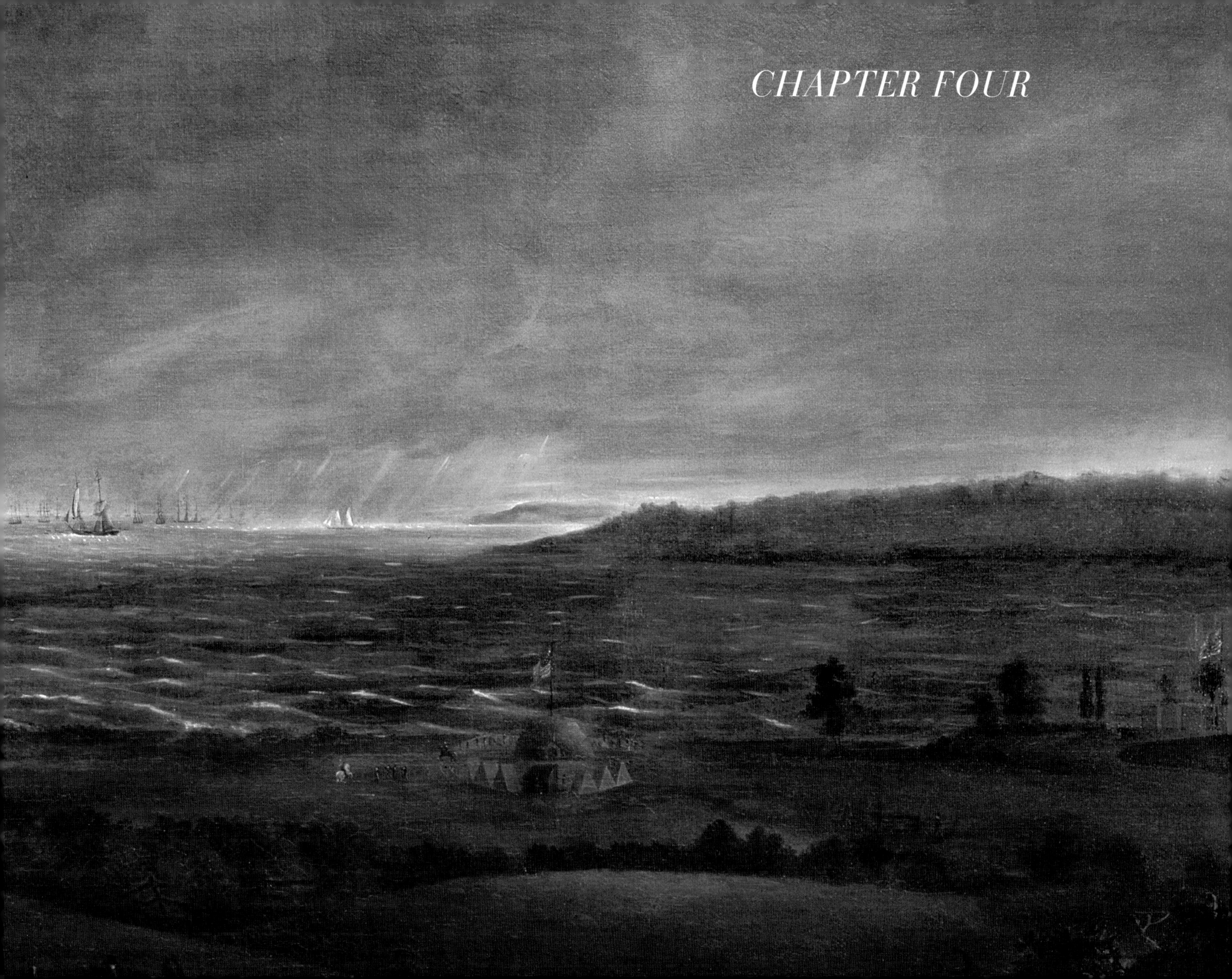

This vivid, undated wash drawing captures the utter chaos that ensued in the wake of the torching of the capital by the British on August 24, 1814. The White House, engulfed in flames and spewing pillars of black smoke, is seen in the background.

Overleaf: Alfred Jacob Miller's monumental panorama of the bombardment of Fort McHenry. In the spring of 1829, eighteen-year-old Miller, the son of a sugar merchant and grocer who'd aided in Baltimore's defense, unfolded his easel on old Look-Out Hill (modern-day Riverside Park) and began to paint "the awful grandeur" of that scene, which he captured transcendently. "His painting is marked by a beautiful richness of coloring," a *Baltimore Gazette* critic noted, "and a graphic faithfulness in the delineation of the shores of the bay, the British fleet, the smoke of the cannon, and the bombs "bursting in air" over the Fort.

"FIRE ON THE HEAVENS"

A BLAZE IN WASHINGTON AND FLAMES OVER BALTIMORE

1813–1814

"I MARCHED WITH THE TROOPS OF BARNEY FROM BENEDICT TO BLADENSBURG, AND TRAVELED
NEARLY THE WHOLE DISTANCE THROUGH HEAVY FORESTS OF TIMBER OR NUMEROUS AND DENSE CEDAR THICKETS . . .
I STOOD AT MY GUN, UNTIL THE COMMODORE WAS SHOT DOWN."

~ Charles Ball, Navy sailor and freedman

"I SAW THE CAPITOL IN FLAMES . . . A SIGHT SO REPUGNANT TO MY FEELINGS,
SO DISHONORABLE, SO DEGRADING TO THE AMERICAN CHARACTER, AND AT THE SAME TIME, SO AWFUL—
ALMOST PALSIED MY FACULTYES."

~ Mordecai Booth, Navy clerk

In May 1813, the war arrived on John and Minerva Rodgers' doorstep. Their hometown of Havre de Grace came under siege by the nineteen-barge fleet of Admiral George Cockburn, fresh from the Napoleonic Wars and on the rampage in the Chesapeake Bay. Having attacked Frenchtown, Maryland, only days before, Cockburn, a well-groomed protégé and favorite of the legendary Horatio Nelson, crossed to Havre De Grace, a settlement of about fifty homes,

and began shelling its warehouses and docks, his rocket boat sending Congreves hissing through the air with a chilling shrillness.

The next morning, May 3, Cockburn's forces landed and swiftly mowed past the town's defenses: two small batteries on Concord Point. One lone militiaman, Second Lieutenant John O'Neill, a nervy Irishman, owner of the area's nail manufactory, remained at the Potato Battery—so called because

ADMIRAL COCKBURN BURNING & PLUNDERING HAVRE DE GRACE

on the 1ˢᵗ of June 1813. done from a Sketch taken on the Spot at the time.

1. *Cockburn.*
2. *Westfall 1ˢᵗ Lieut of the Marlborough.*
3. *Weyburn Capt of Marines.*
4. *Lieut Carter.*

5. *Machine for throwing Rockets.*
6. *A New Coach part of the Plunder.*
7. *Mrˢ Seers Tavern.*
8. *A British Officer endeavouring to ride over 2 of the Citizens.*

of the size of the shot lobbed by its guns. Though he had no one to serve the vents, he manned the cannons to the last. When wounded by one's sharp recoil, he was taken prisoner, while the rest of the local defenders retreated across town. The invaders sacked and torched most of the buildings, a fiery scene described by a woman visiting from Philadelphia.

Such a scene I never before experienced. On the report of guns we immediately jumped out of our beds; and from the top of the house could plainly see the balls and hear the cries of the inhabitants. We ran down the road, and soon began to meet the distressed people, women and children, half naked; children inquiring for their parents, parents for their children, and wives for their husbands. It appeared to us as if the whole of the town was on fire.

The enemy robbed every house of everything valuable that could be carried away, leaving not a change of raiment [clothing] to one of ten persons; and what they could not take conveniently, they destroyed by cutting in pieces or breaking to atoms ... Mrs. Rodgers (wife to the commodore), Mrs. Pinckney, and Mrs. Goldsborough took shelter at Mr. Pringle's. When a detachment was sent up to burn that elegant building, Mrs. Goldsborough told the officer that she had an aged mother in it, and begged it might be spared. The officer replied that he acted under the admiral, and it would be necessary to obtain his consent. Mrs. G. returned with the officer and detachment and obtained the permission that the house should be spared; but when she reached it, she found it on fire, and met two men, one with a sheet, the other with a pillowcase crammed full, coming out, which she could not then notice, but ran upstairs, and found a large wardrobe standing in the passage, all in a flame. William Pinckney, who was with her, and two of the marines, by great exertion saved the house; but some of the wretches, after that, took the cover from the sofa in the front room, and put coals in it, and it was in flames before it was discovered.

A beautiful Madonna, which the commodore had been offered one thousand dollars for, they were about destroying, but ... they wrapped it up in the burning sofa cover, and left it as a mark of their valor.

An officer put his sword through a large elegant looking glass, attacked the windows, and cut out several sashes. They cut hogs through the back, and some partly through, and then let them run. Such wanton barbarity among civilized people, I have never heard of.

Cockburn himself came ashore and directed the looting and burning, in his words, "to cause the Proprietors ... to understand and feel what they were liable to bring upon themselves by acting in a hostile manner." Referring directly to the shots fired from the town that morning—though they were fired in defense— and obliquely to the Americans' plunderous attack on York the previous month, he had taken it upon himself to settle the score and appeared eager to put a match to every last house. In newspaperman Hezekiah Niles' magniloquent description, he "stood like Satan on his cloud when he saw the blood of man from murdered

This page from Commodore John Rodgers' journal is dated Friday, May 28, 1813. Rodgers was out at sea, cruising with *President*, when his hometown came under attack. After news of the depredations reached him, he took to his journal to vent his outrage. "By this ship [*General Hamilton*], I received a newspaper containing an account that a part of Admiral Warren's squadron had penetrated as far as the head of the Chesapeake," Rodgers wrote, "and that they had laid in ruins the poor little harmless unprotected and unoffending village of Havre de Grace, having carefully in their way thence avoided every place that was protected by a single gun. History does not record such another instance of wanton and dastardly barbarity ..."

Opposite: This hand-colored engraving, done from a drawing sketched on the spot at the time, shows Admiral Sir George Cockburn and his troops burning and plundering Havre de Grace on June 1, 1813.

Abel first crimson the earth, exulting at the damning deed." Though he clearly relished in the despoilment, the marauder nevertheless left a few homes standing, including Sion Hill, when implored by Minerva and the other women sheltered at the Pringle residence. The estates were not left entirely untouched, however.

Spiriting away Minerva's beloved pianoforte and Rodgers' handcrafted carriage (the former later turned up in the living room of Admiral Sir John Borlase Warren, commander of the North American Station, who was also spotted riding about Halifax in the pilfered buggy), Cockburn returned to his ship and continued on, proceeding to capture and destroy a cannon foundry on Principio Creek, as well as the towns of Fredericktown and Georgetown on the Eastern Shore. Each raid seemed to unravel more barbarically than the last.

BID DEFIANCE

Three months earlier, in January 1813, when Cockburn was still far away in Bermuda, the first British warships had sailed into the Chesapeake Bay. The two ships-of-the-line, three frigates, one brig, and a schooner had hardly passed the Virginia Capes when a sail was spotted standing toward them. It wasn't long before she was made out to be an American frigate—and not just any frigate.

Constellation was one reason why the British were invading the Bay. They were hoping to capture or destroy what had been, before the summer of 1812, perhaps the most famous of American warships and certainly the only one that had ever outfought not just one but two frigates of a first-rank naval power. She had come off the slips in Baltimore in September 1797 and was soon off to the West Indies to protect American commerce during the Quasi-War with France. In February 1799, off the island of Nevis, she had defeated and captured the French frigate *L'Insurgente*. Exactly a year later she encountered the 52-gun *La Vengeance* and, after a fierce and stormy battle, had nearly subdued her, only to have her escape into the night.

Though officially rated at only 38 guns as compared to the 44 of her larger sister frigates *President*, *United States*, and *Constitution*, she had proved to be a dangerous and versatile warship. Because she had outpaced *L'Insurgente*, reputedly the fastest ship in the French navy, she had also won the sobriquet "Yankee Racehorse." In January 1813, therefore, having just completed an extensive refit at the Washington Navy Yard, *Constellation* was one ship that the British were determined not to let escape to sea.

It was the Royal Navy's good fortune, and Charles Stewart's misfortune, that each encountered the other near the gates of the Chesapeake Bay. Stewart, *Constellation*'s capable captain, had hoped to break into the open Atlantic before the inevitable blockade clamped down. Realizing it was too late, he altered course for nearby Hampton Roads, where the waters of three rivers—the James from

the northwest, the Nansemond from the southwest, and the Elizabeth from the southeast—met in one common estuary. Up the Elizabeth River lay Norfolk, Virginia's principal seaport, and the Gosport Navy Yard. Both were protected by forts flanking the river.

Stewart made for the protection of those forts. But the Elizabeth was a shallow river, and *Constellation* had to partially kedge her way to safety before a rising tide floated her in. It was too shallow, and the channel was too uncertain for the British to follow. Though their fleet could not enter, the American frigate could not leave.

Weeks passed. Both Cockburn and Warren arrived in the Bay. Both went marauding up the tobacco coasts to Havre de Grace and back. Warren soon departed for Bermuda, carrying forty prizes in tow. All the while, Stewart feared the blockading vessels might attempt a cutting-out expedition using boats or shore parties. Though the Virginia militia was ringing Norfolk with hastily improvised defenses, Stewart initially placed more trust in the river. He anchored *Constellation* in the middle of the channel, flanked on either side by a line of nineteen gunboats stretching from the eastern bank to sandy Craney Island, which abutted its western shore. He took no chances. He fastened up her lower gun ports. He set nets, boiled in pitch until they were as hard as wire, to repel boarders. He had the carronades jammed to the muzzle with musket balls and depressed so as to sweep the approaches to the vessel. Even so, on at least two occasions, large British raiding parties were discovered stealthily approaching the frigate. Having lost the element of surprise, however, they returned in the darkness.

By the time *Constellation* was returned back upriver for safekeeping behind the Norfolk forts, Stewart had departed for Boston to take up his new command at the helm of the frigate *Constitution,* having done what he could to arrange defenses so that, as he stated to Secretary of the Navy William Jones, "we might bid defiance to their operations by water." In his place, Master Commandant Joseph Tarbell took the temporary captaincy of the frigate now hemmed in at Norfolk. Very quickly he was put to the test. On June 20, thirteen British warships—including four ships-of-the-line and four frigates—were back in Hampton Roads. Warren had returned from Bermuda with reinforcements.

The Americans could clearly see that troops were being prepared for landings. That evening, though, squalls interspersed with calms seemed to offer an opportunity to take the initiative. So Captain John Cassin, commandant of the navy yard, ordered Tarbell to attack HMS *Junon*, a frigate anchored a little to one side of the rest of the fleet. In the pre-dawn darkness, fifteen gunboats stood toward the enemy. But they were soon spotted, and then a breeze sprang up, allowing *Junon* to leisurely move out of range while a second frigate, *Barossa*, moved in with disconcertingly accurate gunnery. The gunboats were lucky to beat a retreat by sunrise, with only one vessel crippled and one damaged.

The Americans were clearly facing an overwhelming force. Outside of the now-shaken gunboats, their only remote hope of repelling a British attack lay in the batteries that the militia was planting on Lambert Point and especially on Craney Island, where they had a miscellaneous assortment of artillery, ranging from 6-pounders to 24-pounders. Craney Island, it was soon apparent, was the key to Norfolk, but with something under six hundred men manning its lines, it seemed worrisomely vulnerable. So at 11:00 p.m., Tarbell contributed one hundred of *Constellation*'s sailors and fifty of her marines. They would man an 18-pounder on the northwest corner of the island.

They arrived just in time, for at dawn on June 22, every man in those lines could see numerous ships' boats, no doubt full of Royal Marines and soldiers, gliding over the water to land off to the west, near the mouth of the Nansemond River. They looked, in the tremulous eyes of the Americans, to be several thousand strong. Soon those units had made their way to the narrow strait separating Craney Island from the mainland. And there they were stopped, unable to ford the strait in the face of the galling fire from the island's gunners. They soon fell back into the thickets to regroup.

Meanwhile, the men in the seaward-facing batteries were grimly watching a massive force of fifty barges, bristling with troops, approaching them in two long columns, led by *Centipede*, Warren's own barge, a brass 3-pounder mounted in her bow. All along the line the Americans held their fire. It wasn't until the boats were almost upon them that the militia commander gave a signal. Matches were applied, lanyards were pulled, and the guns bucked and roared. The water was swept by a fusillade of flying metal, smacking and thudding into the oncoming vessels. *Centipede* was halted on a shoal, and three more boats were holed so badly that they quickly sank. While the island's gunners kept up their brisk, withering rate of fire, a daring midshipman, with some of *Constellation*'s crew in tow, splashed into the river, secured the abandoned boats, and wrested away some forty prisoners floundering about in the shallows. Those not collared by the Americans were clambering into the remaining barges, some of which were already turning back. Others had managed to gain the shore, but heavy fire soon forced their men back to the rear of the island. Though they managed to launch some Congreve rockets, they had fallen within range of the gunboats, and soon they were driven off altogether.

The firing slackened, then ceased. While prisoners and deserters were rounded up, the British assault wave receded. As the long summer twilight began to descend, the defenders also saw, rounding the point from the distant Nansemond River, the boats of the first landing party returning to their ships, too.

If there were hurrahs at this point, they were well deserved. Seven hundred men had repulsed a force at least twice, if not three times, their size—had indeed caused them nearly a hundred casualties, while not losing a man of their own. "[T]he officers of the *Constellation* fired their 18 pounders more like riflemen than

An oil portrait, circa 1817, of the swaggering, enigmatic Admiral Sir George Cockburn, shown glorying in his most memorable deed—the burning of Washington. He wears his undress coat and hat (1812-1812 pattern), breeches, and Hessian boots.

Artillerists," Cassin wrote glowingly to Jones. "I never saw such shooting and seriously believe they saved the Island yesterday." Every gun on that island, however, must have been well-served to drive off British assault troops so quickly. As Theodore Roosevelt later put it, if the American seamen "could get *out* to the boats, the British ought to have been able to get *in* to the battery."

Although Norfolk's defensive measures only intensified, neither Warren nor Cockburn deemed a further attempt worth the effort. *Constellation* might be left unmolested, but blockaded as she was, she would never put to sea. The Yankee Racehorse would have to sit this one out.

Several days later, the British fleet weighed anchor and stood across the Roads, where on June 25 its assault troops landed at Hampton, Virginia. Once again, Congreve rockets shrieked through the air, and as the British rolled over the local militia, the town went up in flames. Soon, matters got out of hand. This was more than Cockburn's usual "petty larceny kind of warfare," as Jones had once described it; real atrocities were committed, which soon made even British cheeks hot with shame. "Every horror was perpetrated with impunity—rape, murder, pillage," Lieutenant Colonel Charles Napier admitted to his diary, "and not a one was punished." Cockburn blamed the vilest deeds on the *Chasseurs Brittanique*, former French prisoners of war who had been scraped out of the prison hulks moored in England in exchange for fighting the Americans. Yet all charges of misconduct were dismissed, much to the outrage of the American public.

The whole crusade was merely a prelude—Cockburn's fleet would return the following year with an even fiercer vengeance.

TERROR ON THE TOBACCO COASTS

Early on in 1813, British naval planners had begun to study the Chesapeake Bay with keen interest. As American troops multiplied, surging north to the Canadian frontier, the vast watershed to the south—a direct artery to the nation's capital—loomed ever larger in their machinations. Here, along the hundreds of miles of undefended coastline, raids might create an effective diversion, stoppering the flow of northward-bound forces, while eroding American morale and wreaking even greater economic havoc upon the lifeblood of Tidewater Maryland and Virginia—their cash crop, tobacco, which in a twist of classic irony had subsidized the creation of the very ships that now brought terror to their shores.

Though the blockade had put a crimp in the canvas of many a tobacco schooner, the seamen of this region were a hardy, elusive lot. Their sharp sails still dotted the waters, and beyond the sprawling oyster reefs, the storehouses along the planters' wharves remained hubs of activity, hogsheads packed with dried tobacco leaves rolling in daily by the dozens. Warren, whom the Sea Lords had entrusted with the momentous tasks of capturing the remaining "Rascally" frigates, intercepting the mischief-making privateers, and successfully blockading most of the United States' eastern coastline, failed to meet their expectations, as unrealistic as they might have been, and found even the trade ships—"particularly good Sailing Vessels"—slipping through his grasp, especially the Chesapeake runners, which broke through the blockade "in spite of every endeavour and of the most vigilant attention of our Ships to prevent their getting out."

In November 1813, the Lords, their feathers in a ruffle, gave Warren the boot. His performance had been less than lackluster, in their opinion, and they couldn't seem to light a fire under him. They sent a notice via packet ship informing Warren that his services were no longer needed at the North American Station. He'd made a big to-do of it, so his replacement, Vice Admiral Sir Alexander Cochrane, didn't take over until April 1, 1814. Cochrane, whose ill-starred elder brother had been decapitated by a cannonball during the Revolution, bore a deep-seated grudge against the Americans, and his rancor made him zealous and electric where Warren had been uninspired and insipid. Furthermore, his second-in-command, Cockburn, was all too willing to do his bidding. (By then, Cockburn was so reviled for his pillaging ways that one fed-up Virginian had run an ad in a local paper offering rewards for a trio of grisly trophies—$1,000 for Cockburn's head and $500 for each of his ears.)

From his post among the thick cedars of Bermuda, Cochrane ordered a tightening of the blockade and officially extended it to New England. He also instructed Cockburn to keep up his raids with unflagging gusto and to establish a base of operations on the Chesapeake. To Cochrane's disliking, Cockburn picked Tangier Island, a remote stretch of swampy marshland twelve miles west of Virginia's Eastern Shore, but time pressed, and he needed a training ground—it would have to do.

One of Cochrane's first orders of business had been recruiting slaves, enticing runaways with the promise of emancipation and the opportunity to serve with British forces—an appeal to their natural desire for retribution against former captors. The tactic, which had first been employed during the Revolution, was nothing new, and since the previous summer slaves had been escaping in droves to the asylum offered by the British Crown. Cochrane's motives, however, were very pointed, and he made no effort to hide them—he intended to storm Washington, and he needed an army to do it. His new Corps of Colonial Marines, drawn almost exclusively from the local slave population, would form a small branch of that army, and a camp of sorts was soon erected on Tangier Island.

The recruitment of slaves also stirred up more economic trouble for the Americans. In the Tidewater's deeply stratified society of flush plantation owners, beleaguered freed people, and slaves, the latter made up more than a third of the population, and the tobacco trade, which had been built on their backs, depended upon their labor. Fleeing lives of toil in the fields, hundreds responded to Cochrane's succinct proclamation.

This is therefore to Give Notice, that all those who may be disposed to emigrate from the UNITED STATES will, with their Families, be received on board of His Majesty's Ships or Vessels of War, or at the Military Posts that may be established, upon or near the Coast of the UNITED STATES, when they will have their choice of either entering into His Majesty's Sea or Land Forces, or of being sent as FREE Settlers to the British Possessions in North America or the West Indies, where they will meet with all due encouragement.

Freedman Charles Ball found himself amid the uprising. Born a slave around 1780 in Calvert County, Maryland, he had been sold as a young boy— separated from his parents and sent to South Carolina in chains. He later escaped to freedom, and when the war broke out, he was working at a fishery— a temporary job—in his native town, where he witnessed the mass exodus of enslaved residents to British ships, as well as "many of the evils that followed in the train of war, before I assumed the profession of arms myself."

In the spring of the year 1813, the British fleet came into the bay, and from this time the origin of the troubles and distresses of the people of the Western Shore may be dated. I had been employed at a fishery near the mouth of the Patuxent, from early March until the latter part of May, when a British vessel of war came off the mouth of the river and sent her boats up to drive us away from our fishing ground. There was but little property at the fishery that could be destroyed, but the enemy cut the seines to pieces and burned the sheds belonging to the place. They then marched up two miles into the country, burned the house of a planter, and brought away with them several cattle that were found in his fields. They also carried off more than twenty slaves, who were never again restored to their owner; although, on the following day, he went on board the ship, with a flag of truce, and offered a large ransom for these slaves.

These were the first black people whom I had known to desert to the British, although the practice was afterwards so common. In the course of this summer and the summer of 1814, several thousand black people deserted from their masters and mistresses, and escaped to the British fleet. None of these people were ever regained by their owners, as the British naval officers treated them as free people.

In October 1813, shortly before Napoleon's crushing defeat in the Battle of Leipzig drove the second stake into the heart of the Little Corporal's quest for empire, Ball, an ocean away, humbly went about his day-to-day affairs. After a local widow had arisen one morning to find all of her slaves' cabins deserted, he'd offered to help and went aboard a "vast castle" of a ship to negotiate the return of the escapees, or to persuade them to return on their own volition, as the woman had always been kind to them. He "went amongst them, and talked to them a long time, on the subject of returning home, but found that their heads were full of notions of liberty and happiness in some of the West India Islands."

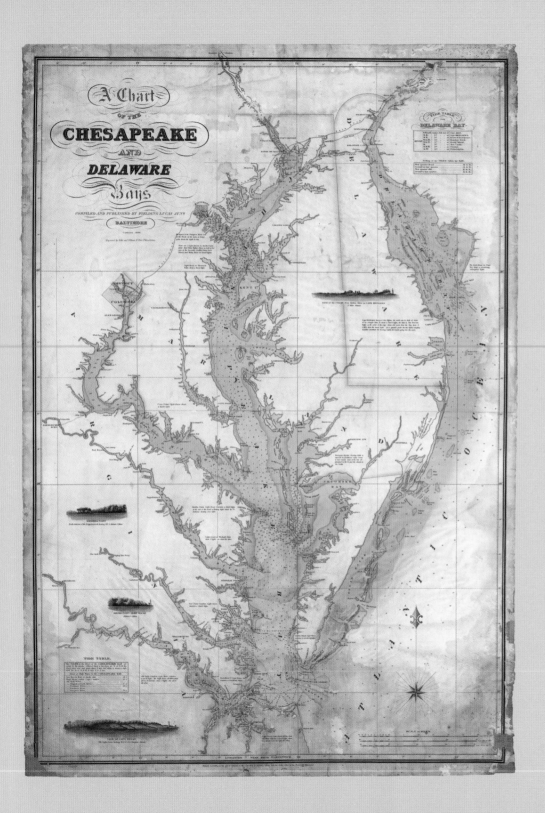

He politely refused their invitation to go along. "I returned many thanks for their kind offers," he remembered, "but respectfully declined them, telling those who made them that I was already a freeman."

Ball spent two weeks aboard the 74, during which time he observed several dramatic scenes, including the breakout—in broad daylight—of two daring Baltimore privateers, as well as a frantic British effort to recapture escaping American prisoners. After disembarking, Ball went back to his quiet life in Calvert County, picking up odd jobs here and there, in Maryland's farms and fisheries, while war's vicissitudes unfolded around him, and thousands of miles distant Napoleon's mighty scepter crumbled into dust.

That winter, a new opportunity presented itself—"an honorable and comfortable situation," as promised the oversized ad that appeared in the pages of Baltimore's *American and Commercial Daily Advertiser* on Christmas Day 1813.

THE FLYING SQUADRON

The advertisement had been taken out by Joshua Barney, who was seeking recruits for his newly formed Chesapeake flotilla. The native Baltimorean was getting on in years, but behind his unassuming façade lay a story of intrigue and high-seas adventure; of lost and gained fortunes; of nascent American enterprise and independent ingenuity; and of patriotism at its best.

In his boyhood, Barney had gone to sea against the wishes of his parents, landlubbers who thought an ordinary sea life was beneath him, though no ordinary sea life did it turn out to be. He cut his teeth on merchant voyages across the capricious Atlantic, and by sixteen he was wearing a lieutenant's epaulette in the Continental Navy. His plucky exploits during the Revolution— he took part in thirty-five naval engagements—were the stuff of storybooks. Surviving five defeats, three captivities (some of which he escaped by donning elaborate disguises), two shipwrecks, one mutiny, and a daring operation with *Hyder Ally* that James Fenimore Cooper labeled "one of the most brilliant that ever occurred under the American flag," Barney had emerged from the whirlwind of war with a congressional invitation to join the new navy as one of its first six captains. In a moment of youthful hubris, Barney, not liking where his name fell on the officers' list—fourth out of six—declined the coveted opportunity, relinquishing that spot in time's records, and took to the West Indies trade, until he was tempted by another naval offer—this time from the French navy, which presented him with a commodoreship. Motivated by the high rank and the good pay, his acceptance of the commission drew the ire of some of his countrymen when the Quasi-War with France found him on the wrong side, though he adamantly refused to harass America's merchantmen.

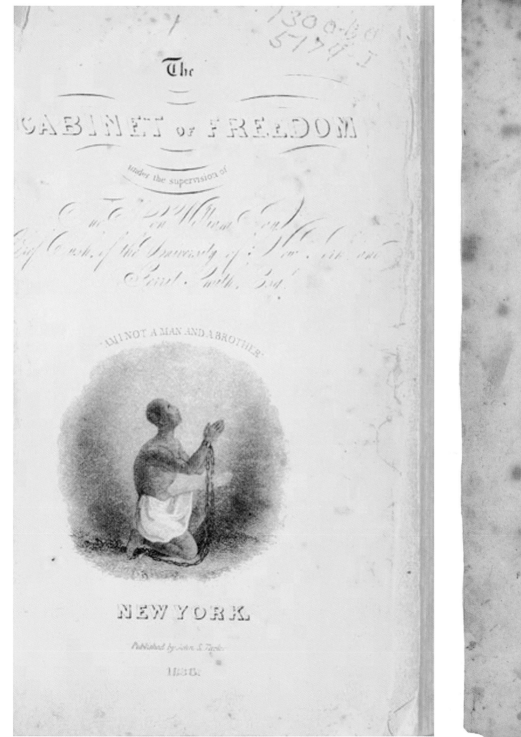

The
CABINET of FREEDOM

under the supervision of

AM I NOT A MAN AND A BROTHER.

NEW YORK

Published by John S. Taylor

1837

Opposite: An 1840 chart of the Chesapeake and Delaware Bays.

Left: The frontispiece to the 1837 edition of Charles Ball's autobiography, *Slavery in the United States: A Narrative of the Life and Adventures of Charles Ball, A Black Man.* The illustration of a black man in chains accompanied by the slogan "Am I not a man and a brother?" is a variation of the image on the Society for the Abolition of the Slave Trade's seal, which was popularized by prominent abolitionist Josiah Wedgewood, who mass produced cameos bearing this image. Wedgewood's friend, Thomas Clarkson, noted, "Ladies wore them in bracelets, and others had them fitted up in an ornamental manner as pins for their hair. At length, the taste for wearing them became general, and thus fashion, which usually confines itself to worthless things, was seen for once in the honorable office of promoting the cause of justice, humanity, and freedom."

Right: From *An Historical and Practical Essay on the Culture and Commerce of Tobacco* (London, 1800), this engraving shows various stages in the processing of Tidewater tobacco, the planting and harvesting of which relied heavily on slave labor. As this illustration depicts, the leaves were air dried in an open tobacco house; pressed into casks called hogsheads, a procedure known as "prizing"; and stored for inspection. After the crop was carefully examined, the hogsheads were rolled overland and loaded onto tobacco schooners.

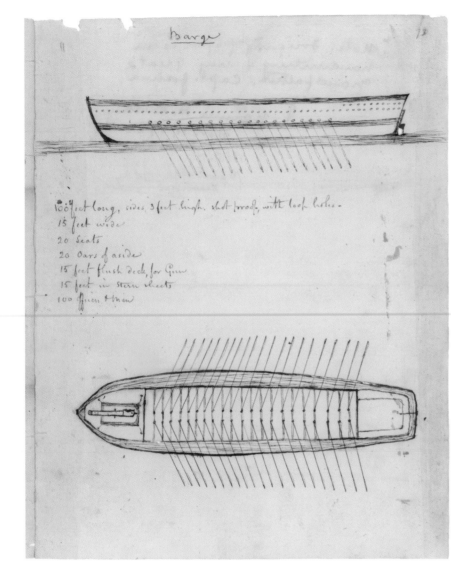

Dated July 4, 1813, Barney's defense proposal included this rough blueprint of the barges that would form his flying squadron.

Right: A painting by Polish native Stanislav Rembski of adventurous citizen-sailor Joshua Barney.

Resigning his commission in 1802, crestfallen by charges against his loyalty, he returned to the United States and tried to restore his image as a patriotic American. But he seemed to have hexed future opportunities with his own navy, to which he offered his services multiple times over the next decade only to be overlooked.

Thus, when the War of 1812 broke out, Barney had gone the more lucrative route of a privateer. His ninety-day cruise on the schooner *Rossie* was so successful that once it came to an end, he retired to his farm near Elkridge, Maryland, pocketing an enviable $18,195 in prize money. By then, Barney had lived at least nine

lives, among them master mariner, escape artist, emissary, quick-thinking merchant, political dabbler, gentleman farmer, and privateersman. Nevertheless, he had yet to grab his slice of history.

Come summer of 1813, in the wake of Cockburn's depredations, Barney had not sat idly by. At the time, he was volunteering on a three-man committee tasked with designing a morale-boosting banner for the American troops stationed at Baltimore's Fort McHenry. They had been drilling without letup on the parade ground, preparing for an impending attack by sea. "We, Sir, are ready at Fort McHenry to defend Baltimore against invasion by the enemy," Major

George Armistead, the garrison's commander, had penned to General Samuel Smith, who was heading the defense of Baltimore. "That is to say, we are ready except we have no suitable ensign to display over the Star Fort, and it is my desire to have a flag so large that the British will have no difficulty in seeing it from a distance." As Barney saw to it that Armistead's request was granted, he also found time to draft an inventive proposal for an oar-powered defense force that he hoped might save the Chesapeake from further British irruptions, which loomed in the offing. With a single motive—to protect his homeland— he sent the well-thought-out plan to Secretary Jones, complete with a rough pen-and-ink sketch of the barges as he envisioned them.

> The Avowed object of the Enemy is the distruction of the City & Navy yard, at Washington, the City and Navy yard at Norfolk, and the City of Baltimore . . . Frigates, Sloops of War, Schooners with Barges, and small craft will be employed against those places . . . The question is, how to meet this force with a probability of success. Our ships (two frigates) cannot act, our old gunboats will not answer, they are too heavy to Row, and too clumsy to sail, and are only fit to lay moor'd, to protect a pass, or Assist a Fort. I am therefore of the opinion the only defence we have in our power, is a Kind of Barge or Row-galley, so constructed, as to draw a small draft of water, to carry Oars, light sails, and One heavy long gun, these vessels may be built in a short time, (say 3 weeks) Men may be had, the City of Baltimore could furnish Officers & men for twenty Barges . . . Let as many of such Barges be built as can be mann'd, form them into a flying Squadron, have them continually watching & annoying the enemy in our waters, where we have the advantage of shoals & flats throughout the Chesapeake Bay, the Enemy could be followed by such boats in every direction, without danger, their force would be respectable, and the enemy dare not dispatch Small ships, Brigs, or Schooners upon any expedition whilst such a force lay near them . . . Add to this squadron three or four, light fast-sailing vessels, prepared as fireships, which could with ease (under cover of the Barges) be run onboard any of the enemy's ships, if they should attempt to anchor, or remain in our Narrow rivers, or harbours . . . The expense of these Barges would not be great, they would cost about $3000 each, and after the service was performed might be sold for Coasters, having only a deck to put on them . . . [O]ur Bay harbours and Cities lay exposed to the fury of the Enemy. This is the outline of a plan of Defence & offence, the details can be better explained verbally than in writing, when all the advantages could be pointed out, in fact we have no other mode of defence left us.

In late August, he received a response. Jones had not only eagerly endorsed the idea but also assigned Barney himself to lead the venture, though in the seniority-sensitive early Navy, Barney's prior turndown of a captaincy precluded Jones from being able to commission him at the rank the endeavor warranted. Nevertheless, a solution was found.

> The President of the U. States, in order more effectually to accomplish the objects of the Legislature . . . has determined to select, for the special command of the Flotilla, on the upper part of the Chesapeake, a Citizen, in whose fidelity, skill, local knowledge, and commanding influence with the Mariners of the district, reliance may be placed, in cases of great emergency. I have, therefore, the pleasure to offer to you that Special Command . . . It is not intended, because it would be incompatible with the rights of others, to appoint you, by Commission, to any regular and permanent rank in the Navy of the U. States; but, for the purpose and direction of your command, you will be considered as an Acting Master Commandant, in the Navy of the U. States.

At age fifty-six, Barney was, for all intents and purposes, back in the uniformed service. Through the fall and winter, the flying squadron took shape under his meticulous oversight, though he was beset by countless challenges, including the lack of a purser—not a small dilemma, as it left him buried in mounds of paperwork. Still, as Jones had urged him, he made "every possible exertion . . . during the Winter to meet the Enemy with Vigor in the Spring." In fact, his little flying squadron would be the only thing standing between the British and Washington.

Above: A receipt, dated April 26, 1814, for three signal pendants sewn by Sarah Stiles, the wife of a marine lieutenant, for Barney's barges.

Barney kept this marbled journal while he was cruising with the rakish *Rossie*, the first privateer to sail from Baltimore in 1812.

By mid-April, British sails had begun to pop up near Tangier Sound, compelling Barney to investigate. A series of shakedown cruises, however, revealed that his flying squadron had serious flaws. Frustrated with his "miserable tools," he directed repairs but was so eager to see what Cockburn was up to and so "anxious to be at them" that he jumped the gun and set sail on May 24 with eighteen vessels—his flagship, *Scorpion*, a sloop-rigged floating battery; thirteen barges; two gunboats; a scout boat; and a galley.

On June 1, Barney's flotilla encountered Cockburn's scouting party, led by Captain Sir Robert Barrie, near Drum Point, where the Patuxent River enters the Chesapeake. Barrie sighted the flotilla close to shore and frantically fired his signal guns to alert the scattered vessels of his comrades. Barney, pursuing the advantage of surprise while it held, made chase. Soon, however, HMS *Dragon*, a 74-gun ship-of-the-line that had been skulking about in the Potomac River, heeded Barrie's signals and came to the rescue. The advantage turned to the British.

As the Americans rushed for cover in the Potomac, an unfortuitous squall came up, putting Barney's mariner skills to the test, as they were forced to change course for the Paxtuent, the British fast on their heels. One gunboat, No. 137, lagged gallingly behind—carrying all of their provisions and supplies. Not willing to lose her, Barney stopped to fight, gallantly turning his guns on the British, while the straggler was towed to safety. Fatigue and Mother Nature soon got the best of both sides, and the engagement ended in a deadlock.

On June 10, Barrie's forces, augmented by the brig *Jaseur* and the frigate *Loire*, tried again to crush the pesky "mosquito flotilla," which had gone up St. Leonard Creek to the safety of the shallow, shoal-riddled waters—unfortunately, also a dead end. With the flying squadron bottled up, Barrie sent his barges up the narrow inlet to assail them. But Barney was prepared. His son, William Barney, manned *Scorpion*, while he took over another vessel. When one of the British rockets struck Barney's flagship, scorching three men and leaving the vessel aflame, William leaped over the side and doused the fires within sight of his father.

Soon, Barrie's barges were met with the unrelenting fire of Barney's fearless flotillamen,

sending the ships into rapid retreat, one schooner fleeing in such a hurry that she ran aground on a shoal. Among these men was freedman Charles Ball, who served "sometimes in the capacity of a seaman, and sometimes as cook of the barge." That day, he was a seaman.

Though the counterattack was successful, quelling any further attempt by Barrie to enter the Americans' little lair, Barney and his flotillamen remained hemmed in at St. Leonard Creek. All they could do now was watch and wait. By midsummer, however, with enemy forces growing, Jones decided that protecting the "bare Hulls" was not worth the number of men it took to do so; these men, after all, could be guarding Washington and Baltimore instead. At one point, Barney received orders to destroy the flotilla, which left him in a terrible "depression of Spirits" and injured the now flagging morale of his men. After recovering from his stunned disbelief, he began dismantling the barges, until he received another order reversing the first. Frustrated, Barney restored the flotilla and decided he'd had enough of the waiting game. Before dawn on June 26, he created a diversion: U.S. batteries fired on the warships from the headlands, which allowed the flotilla to slip out of the creek and rush upriver to Nottingham.

Meanwhile, Cockburn was mapping a plan for capturing Washington.

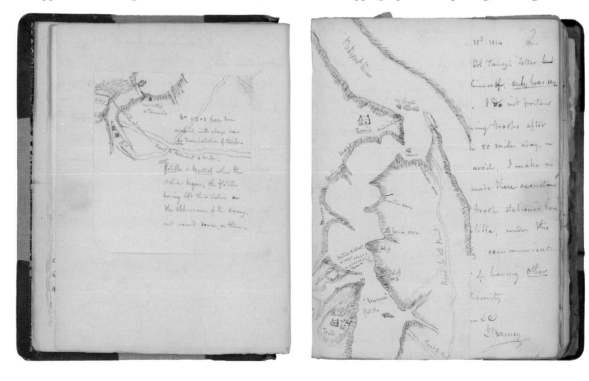

On June 10, 1814, Barney made these two hasty sketches of the British and American positions on St. Leonard Creek.

Opposite: This painting by Tom Freeman shows Barney's barges in action during the Battle of St. Leonard Creek on June 10, 1814.

"ALWAYS SO GREAT A BLOW"

With Napoleon's exile to Elba in early April 1814, the British had found themselves with both hands free to come down hard on the Americans. Feeling betrayed by kinsmen who had struck against their former protector in a time of peril, they prepared to give the Yank upstarts a "complete drubbing." Droves of reinforcements, fresh from the European battlegrounds, embarked for the continent across the pond. While many set off for Canada, the others—several thousand of "Wellington's Invincibles" under the command of General Robert Ross—headed straight for the Chesapeake Bay. Cochrane and Cockburn awaited their arrival with jubilant anticipation. "Mr. Madison," Cochrane said, "will be hurled from his throne."

Cockburn masked their intentions—and attempted to lure Barney out—with raids south on Leonardtown and Chaptico at the end of July. The latter Maryland village had no strategic significance, and one eyewitness reported the senseless pillage that took place there.

> [T]hey got about thirty hogsheads of tobacco and no other plunder, the inhabitants having moved all their property out of their grasp. Yet here they made a most furious attack on every window, door, and pane of glass in the village, not one was left in the whole . . . They picked their stolen geese in the church, dashed the pipes of the church organ on the pavement, opened a family vault in the churchyard, broke open the coffins, and stirred the bones about with their hands in search of hidden treasure.

A pair of epaulettes worn by Napier.

By mid-August, the British plans had matured, and the capital was ripe for the taking. It would be a two-pronged effort. Cockburn, with Ross' reinforcements, would head up the Patuxent, stamp out Barney's troublesome flotilla—the one obstacle in their path—and proceed on to Washington. Sir James Alexander Gordon, a resilient one-legged veteran of the Napoleonic Wars, would take a fleet of bomb ketches up the Potomac, obliterate Fort Washington, and then support the British withdrawal from Washington once they had taken the city. Baltimore would be their next target.

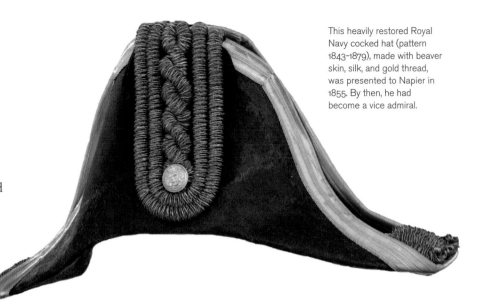

This heavily restored Royal Navy cocked hat (pattern 1843-1879), made with beaver skin, silk, and gold thread, was presented to Napier in 1855. By then, he had become a vice admiral.

On August 16, Cockburn's convoy was spotted menacingly making its way up the Paxtuent with its landing force of Wellington's Invincibles, four thousand strong. As the mighty warships passed upriver, they startled witnesses on shore with the eerie sight of "a large fleet stalking through a wood." No ships of that size had ever attempted to penetrate so far up the Chesapeake's headwaters.

By then, Washington knew the threat was real. In the weeks and months previous, the defense efforts of Madison's cabinet had been plagued by inertia, disorganization, and a false belief that the British wouldn't really concoct designs on such a strategically trivial location. But as the persuasive Cockburn had told his fellow officers, possessing the capital was "always so great a blow to the government of a country."

Now, Jones acted more swiftly and surely than anyone else. He sent Master Commandant John O. Creighton on a reconnaissance mission to scout out Gordon's squadron, which had made its appearance on the Potomac, and he dashed off letters to three of his luminaries—John Rodgers, David Porter, and Oliver Perry—soliciting their much-needed help. "The enemy has entered the Patuxent with a very large force indicating a design upon this place which may be real, or it may serve to mask his design upon Baltimore," Jones wrote to Rodgers on August 19, when Cockburn's troops had landed at Benedict. "In either case it is exceedingly desirable to collect in our vicinity all the disposable force within reach as soon as possible. You will therefore, with the least possible delay, proceed to Baltimore . . . where the further orders of the Department will await you."

A day later, Jones sent a message to Barney instructing him to send the flying squadron "with as few men as possible" as far up the Patuxent as it could go—and to scuttle the whole flotilla if the enemy advanced on it in force. In the meantime, Barney was to "retire before the enemy toward this place [Washington], opposing his progress as well by your arms, as by falling trees across the road, removing bridges, and presenting every other possible obstacle to his march."

THE FLOTILLA IN FLAMES

On August 22, Barney's flying squadron met its end at Pig Point, a quiet bend on the Patuxent where shoals prevented it from going any farther. Cockburn closed in on the flotilla, coming in view just in time to see the vessels erupt in flame. "I plainly discovered Commodore Barney's broad pendant in the headmost vessel . . . and the remainder of the flotilla extending in a long line astern of her," Cockburn wrote to Cochrane. "Our boats now advanced toward them as rapidly as possible but on nearing them we observed the sloop bearing the broad pendant to be on fire, and she very soon afterwards blew up. I now saw clearly that they were all abandoned and on fire with [fuses] to their magazines, and out of the seventeen vessels which composed this formidable and so much vaunted flotilla, sixteen were in quick succession blown to atoms."

Weighed down with supplies and lugging several cannons in late summer's unusually sweltering heat—so scorching, in fact, that heat exhaustion would fell many of Ross' Invincibles on their long march to the capital—Barney and his four hundred flotillamen were long gone westward. Their final destination would be Bladensburg, but Barney and his men almost didn't make it there.

Reaching Woodyard, Maryland, Barney joined up with General William Winder's troops and acquired a contingent of marines, handed off to Barney per Jones' request. As Barney soon discovered, Winder's forces—Washington's primary hope for defense—were largely composed of hastily assembled militiamen, dressed in civilian duds, who appeared more like jumpy bystanders.

Winder spent two fretful nights dithering over where Ross' forces would attack—Annapolis, Bladensburg, Washington via the Eastern Branch bridges, he couldn't decide. Men were shuffled about from place to place with no clear orders, and on the morning of the twenty-fourth, when it was finally revealed that Bladensburg would be the spot, Barney's flotillamen and marines found themselves posted at a little bridge near the Navy Yard, far from where the action would be. As an anecdote related by Barney's daughter-in-law goes, President Madison chanced by in his coachee, and Barney beseeched him to let them go on to Bladensburg, saying that a midshipman with half a dozen men would be able to keep the enemy from crossing simply "by blowing up a few of the timbers." Madison couldn't argue with this, and Barney and his men were off.

A full-length, nineteenth-century oil portrait of Sir Charles Napier standing on a rocky coast, gesturing toward an unnamed fortress in the distance. He is wearing a frock coat, white waistcoat, and trousers. As ostentatious as he might appear here, Napier was anything but. Anticipating widespread, bloodthirsty despoilment, he had had strong qualms about the British expedition into the Chesapeake Bay. "I will, with my own hand," he vowed to his journal, "kill any perpetrator of brutality under my command." Exhibiting the quaint sense of humor that marked his character, he added, "Nevertheless, a pair of breeches must be plundered, for mine are worn out, and better it will be to take a pair than shock the Yankee dames by presenting myself as a *sans culotte*."

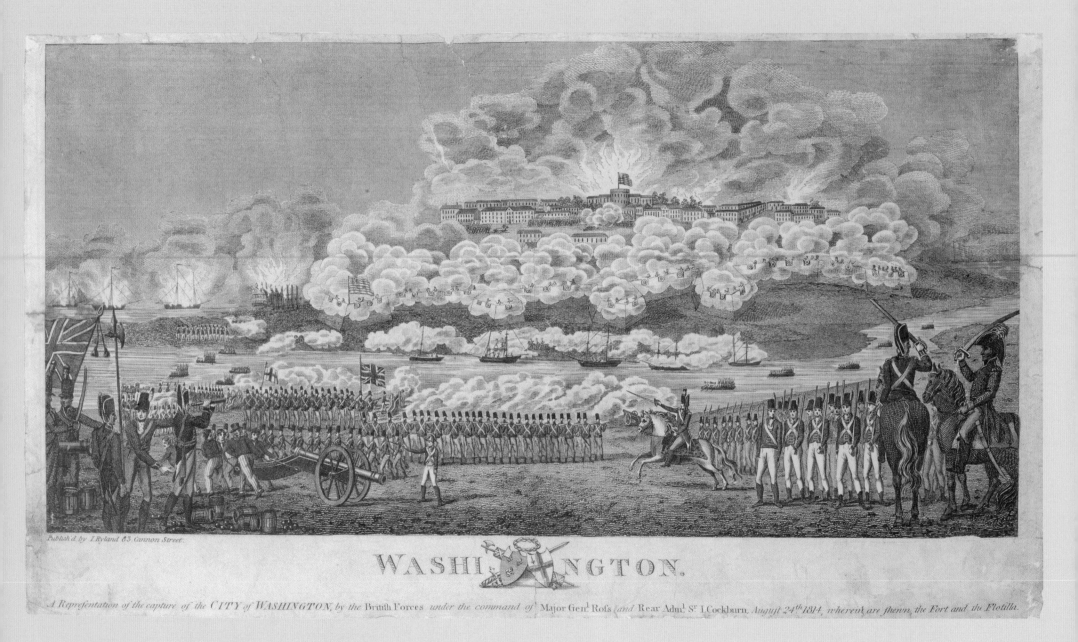

Publish'd by I.Ryland 83.Cannon Street.

WASHINGTON.

A Representation of the capture of the CITY of WASHINGTON, by the British Forces under the command of Major Gen¹ Ross and Rear Adm¹ S⁺ I.Cockburn, August 24ᵗʰ 1814, wherein are shewn the Fort and the Flotilla.

"I TOLD YOU IT WAS THE FLOTILLAMEN!"

Bladensburg was a quiet crossroads on the main post road down the coast. Its sole renown derived from a clearing, shaded by alders, near the stage-coach road where duels took place outside the boundary of Washington, dueling being illegal there. On August 24, by the time Barney and his flotillamen arrived, having walked miles carrying their guns in that terrible heat, they were, in Barney's words, "very much crippled from the severe marches . . . many of them being without shoes." Defensive lines had already been set up, and Winder ordered them to the third line—the last line of defense. Though the ragtag American troops outnumbered the invaders, a charge by Ross' battle-hardened soldiers unnerved the defenders, and Winder quickly lost control of his troops. The British plowed across a ravine and through the militia on high ground to Barney's right flank; the militia fled.

Barney responded quickly. He trained an 18-pounder on the British and drove back their advances on the main road. The flotillamen took his lead, but they soon found themselves running out of rounds, with the drivers of the ammunition wagons nowhere to be found. Brandishing cutlasses, they rallied on with a familiar sea cry: "Board 'em! Board 'em!" Then, when another British unit advanced from behind them, a shot struck Barney in the thigh. Bleeding profusely, he was helped to his feet by three of his flotillamen. Seeing their position was untenable, Barney urged them to save themselves, but they refused to leave their leader until he made it an order, and even that did not sway all of them. The British raced in, spearing their way through the stalwarts with swords and fixed bayonets. Soon, Cockburn and Ross came for Barney. In the finery of their uniforms, they had stood out during the battle, Ross losing his beloved Arabian horse.

"Well, Admiral, you have got hold of me at last," Barney told Cockburn. The admiral was so impressed by Barney's doughty performance that he was inclined to show some uncharacteristic compassion. "Do not let us speak on that subject, commodore," he said. "I hope you are not seriously hurt." A surgeon and a stretcher were sent for, and Barney was carried off the field. Cracking a sly smile, Ross purportedly turned to Cockburn and said, "I told you it was the flotillamen!" Cockburn had to concede that Ross was right: " Yes! They have given us the only fighting we have had."

Charles Ball vividly remembered these events and later recounted them in his memoir, first published in Pennsylvania in 1836 under the title *Slavery in the United States: A Narrative of the Life and Adventures of Charles Ball, A Black Man*, an account that would become one of the leading slave narratives published before the Civil War.

I was present when the flotilla was blown up, and assisted in the performance of that operation upon the barge that I was in. The guns and the principal part of the armament of the flotilla were sunk in the river and lost.

I marched with the troops of Barney from Benedict to Bladensburg, and traveled nearly the whole distance through heavy forests of timber or numerous and dense cedar thickets. It is my opinion, that if General Winder had marched the half of the troops that he had at Bladensburg down to the lower part of Prince George county and attacked the British in these woods and cedar thickets, not a man of them would ever have reached Bladensburg . . .

When we reached Bladensburg and the flotilla men were drawn up in line, to work at their cannon, armed with their cutlasses, I volunteered to assist in working the cannon that occupied the first place on the left of the Commodore. We had a full and perfect view of the British army, as it advanced along the road, leading to the bridge over the East Branch, and I could not but admire the handsome manner in which the British officers led on their fatigued and worn-out soldiers. I thought then, and think yet, that General Ross was one of the finest looking men that I ever saw on horseback.

I stood at my gun, until the Commodore was shot down, when he ordered us to retreat, as I was told by the officer who commanded our gun. If the militia regiments that lay upon our right and left could have been brought to charge the British, in close fight as they crossed the bridge, we should have killed or taken the whole of them in a short time, but the militia ran like sheep chased by dogs.

In the meantime, Gordon's squadron had been sailing up the Potomac on the second prong of the attack. Lieutenant Colonel Charles Napier, aboard one of the vessels, later described that tricky ascent and the scene, from a distance, of the great conflagration in the captured city.

The River Potomac is navigable for frigates as high up as Washington, but the navigation is extremely intricate and nature has done much for the protection of the country, by placing one third of the way up very extensive and intricate shoals called the Kettle Bottoms. They are comprised of Oyster Banks of various dimensions, some not larger than a boat, with passages between them.

The best channel is on the Virginian shore, but the charts gave us mostly very bad directions, and no pilots could be procured. A frigate had attempted some time before to effect a passage, and after being frequently aground, gave it up as impossible . . .

The wind was light, and several boats ahead sounding. As long as the soundings were good, no apprehension was entertained, but . . . the *Euryalus* opened the ball and struck . . . and boats and hawsers were sent to assist in getting her off.

SIFTING FOR SCORPION

This pharmaceutical vial and rusty pair of surgical scissors belonged to Thomas Hamilton, the flotilla's surgeon, who kept his instruments neatly stowed in a white pine field kit. In an irony of war, he purchased part of his kit from Hague and Nowill, an English firm.

The weather service predicted that day in July of 2010 to be the summer's hottest day. Perfect for digging through two centuries of silt for the ruins of an ill-fated flotilla.

At the boat landing stood Bob Neyland, the chisel-featured pro who leads the Navy's underwater archaeology unit. That day, he would explore what he believed was the U.S. gunboat *Scorpion*, Joshua Barney's flagship, a vessel that was "blown to atoms" along with the rest of Barney's Chesapeake flotilla in the summer of 1814 as the British bore down on Washington. Neyland's team loaded up their twenty-two-foot Boston Whaler with diving tanks, helped by J. B. Pelletier, a fireplug of a contractor with URS Corporation who has supported many wreck dives. They soon headed upriver to the site they mapped about a mile above the Route 4 bridge, where the Patuxent was a narrow brown ribbon between poplars. Not where a naval wreck might be expected.

After years of planning, a three-agency partnership to find *Scorpion* was finally getting into the water. But those agencies weren't sure what they'd find.

The summer of 1814 was a scorcher too, Neyland observed as they cruised upstream past the feathery-topped grasses that thronged the shore by Mount Calvert plantation. He noted how annoyed the British empire had to be to send the world's most powerful navy across the Atlantic, straight from defeating Napoleon, into this disease-ridden back-water. "The British forces based their forward operations at the plantation," he said with a nod toward the brick mansion up the slope. From there they watched the sky glow with the flotilla's flames.

This two-week expedition—led by Neyland; Susan Langley, an archaeologist with the Maryland Historical Society; and Julie Schablitsky, an archaeologist with the Maryland Highway Administration—aimed to confirm as much as possible about the wreck's identity and location, including its orientation and any surrounding field of debris. The team would handle and preserve artifacts as needed. Back in the 1970s, Donald Shomette and his colleagues at Nautical Archaeological Associates and the Calvert Marine Museum in Solomons surveyed the upper Patuxent with a grant from the U.S. Department of the Interior, looking for *Scorpion*. Their first dive turned up only a broken turtle shell, but Shomette returned later and found well-preserved jetsam, including a tin cup, several glass vials, and surgical clamps. Based on those artifacts, probably the Navy's earliest medical instruments, historians have speculated that *Scorpion* served Barney as both hospital and flagship.

The longer-term goal is to open to the public the most complete 1812-era wreck in the Chesapeake Bay watershed. By the summer of 2012, the Navy and its partners aim to place a coffer dam of roughly one hundred feet by fifty feet over the hull, allowing visitors to see the ship directly, unobscured by the Patuxent's impenetrable sediment.

As the temperature climbed that afternoon, Neyland and Schablitsky donned scuba masks and dropped into the murky shallows near the west bank while Langley and Pelletier mapped the river floor by sonar. On the shore, highways surveyor Terry Blomquist bushwacked through thorns to nail down land-based coordinates.

Pelletier brandished their first instrument of exploration: a long length of copper pipe. From the foredeck, he knelt and, gripping a T-handle, pressed the pipe into the muck. Attached to a hose pumping water, the pipe looked clumsy, but as a hydroprobe it helped to overcome the complete lack of visibility. By listening to how the water column cut through the silt, he could tell whether it was hitting wood, metal, or ceramic. Langley noted on the map points where the probe scored two metal and wood hits. It helped them hone in on the ship's outline.

At the afternoon's end, two white buoys marked the points roughly seventy feet apart that sonar showed to be the wreck's bow and stern, buried under five to eight feet of river bottom. They also located a second obstruction just downriver, possibly another vessel in the flotilla.

The vials Shomette retrieved from the Patuxent wreck not only suggested *Scorpion* but gave physical testimony to navy medicine in the 1800s. The best-known seafaring bonecutter from that era is probably the fictional Stephen Maturin in Patrick O'Brian's swashbuckling *Master and Commander* novels. *Scorpion*'s Dr. Hamilton kept his nostrums in a white pine field kit, along with a crude tooth extractor that suspiciously resembles a corkscrew.

Historians have studied the wreck's tin cup and found markings much like African American cultural symbols. It may have belonged to Caesar Wentworth, the ship's cook, and if it can be authenticated, said Langley, there's a good chance the wreck is *Scorpion*.

A week into the expedition, the site was swarming with activity. A sixty-foot barge held a shipping container for field headquarters and three large blue dumpster-like containers for dredged material. The crew would pump the sediment through sieves in two troughs for artifacts before being pumped again into the containers. The job turned out to be bigger than expected: they'd have to dredge deeper to reach the ship's hull, and the heat and recent rains were taking a toll. A patch of green carpet on the deck served as a heat mitt for the divers against the barge's frying pan. That day they were finally ready for a first-hand river-bottom survey.

Going first, Pelletier suited up and stepped down the ladder. According to the week's soundings, the wreck's ribs appeared to be in good shape.

Langley supported Pelletier by Buddy phone. Visibility underwater was nil, and the current was so strong that Pelletier wore a belt of forty-pound lead weights plus two five-pound ankle weights to keep from being swept downstream.

"Diver on the bottom," Langley announced. The stream of whitish bubbles churning up from the murk tracked Pelletier's progress upstream as he checked a taut baseline, marked at meter intervals by plastic loops, toward the buoy at the wreck's stern. It was slow going, as if he were crossing centuries. He reached the stern, tugged on the buoy, then retraced his baseline on a slow march back to the bow, confirming that stretch. Branches and muck floated past on the surface.

After fifty minutes, he surfaced and pronounced the scene below "beautiful."

Brown soup beautiful? Mainly the silence, he admitted. After centuries undisturbed, the wreck seemed to cling to oblivion.

Neyland and the others continued the dive and in the following days, more details surfaced. The team mapped planking, iron pins, and what appeared to be the edge of a ship's hold. No smoking gun, but a steady accretion of evidence. They aim to continue the job and hydroprobe what may be a second wreck just downstream. This all leads to 2012, said Neyland, and a clearer view of the flotilla. Then *Scorpion*'s tale of a dozen small craft that faced the Royal Navy before erupting in a pyrotechnic sky display over Maryland, weeks before Key's bomb-lit stint in Baltimore harbor, will likely get its due.

"Why is it important?" Langley asked. Because after the Revolution, the War of 1812 was America's first conflict fought on the home front. It galvanized Americans, she said, and for many "crystallized a unity that had been extant in name only."

Hamilton used this spatula and these Philadelphia-made apothecary bowls to mix drugs for sick or wounded flotillamen.

Left: Caesar Wentworth, the gunboat's cook, drank his daily grog ration from this tin-plated mug. Wentworth served with the Navy from September 1813 until the war ended.

Below: The discovery of this small pick, used by the officer or petty officer in charge of firing the gunboat's cannon for cleaning the artillery pieces' touchholes, proves that the gunboat carried lighter artillery pieces in addition to her two large cannon.

This ink and watercolor drawing, created circa 1814 by George Munger (1781–1825), shows the ruins of the U.S. Capitol. The British were awestruck by its soaring grandeur, and to many, the task at hand felt like an act of desecration, as Captain Harry Smith, junior adjunct to General Robert Ross, recalled. "I had no objection to burning arsenals, dockyards, frigates building, stores, barracks, etc.," he wrote, "but well do I recollect that, fresh from the Duke's [Wellington] humane warfare in the South of France, we were horrified at the order to burn the elegant Houses of Parliament [the Capitol] and the President's house." Admiral George Cockburn didn't share this sentiment. Smith noted that he "would have burnt the whole," and story has it that he sat in the speaker of the House's chair and jeered, "Shall this harbor of Yankee democracy be burned?"

No one could tell where she hung; there was abundance of water astern, ahead, all around, and yet the ship was immovable. A diver went down, and found, to the astonishment of all on board, that an oyster bank, not bigger than a boat, was under her bilge. The boats had missed it with the lead, and the *Sea-Horse* had passed by a few feet on one side.

After some hard heaving, we floated, and the squadron weighed. We proceeded with great caution, having several boats abreast of each other, with leads going ahead of the ships; but notwithstanding all this care, the *Sea-Horse* grounded on a sand-bank . . .

[After] five days, during which the squadron warped upwards of fifty miles, and on the evening of the fifth day anchored off Maryland Point. The same day the public buildings at Washington were burnt. The reflection of the fire on the heavens was plainly seen from the ships, much to our mortification and disappointment, as we concluded that that act was committed at the moment of evacuating the town. It was, nevertheless, decided to proceed, and as the next reach was sufficiently wide to beat through, although the water was very shoal, we anticipated some relaxation from our toils.

The following morning to our great joy, the wind became fair and we made all sail up the river, which now assumed a more pleasing aspect. At five o'clock in the afternoon, Mount Vernon, the retreat of the illustrious Washington, opened to our view, and shewed us for the first time, since we entered the Potomac, a gentleman's residence. Higher up the river, on the opposite side, Fort Washington appeared to our anxious eyes; and to our great satisfaction, it was considered assailable.

A little before sunset the squadron anchored just out of gunshot; the bomb vessels at once took up their positions to cover the frigates in the projected attack at daylight next morning, and began throwing shells. The garrison, to our great surprise, immediately retreated from the fort; and a few moments after, Fort Washington was blown up—which left the capital of America, and the populous town of Alexandria, open to the squadron, without the loss of a man.

STOKING THE FLAMES

Only two days before, in the ill-fated metropolis, a Navy clerk named Mordecai Booth set about preparing for what looked increasingly inevitable, based on reports from the front. Booth had been the clerk of Thomas Tingey, commandant of the Navy Yard, since June 1811, with a salary of $1,000 dollars a year. Ordered by Jones to prepare the yard's lumber stocks for burning in order to keep them from the enemy's grasp, he first scouted British movements as they approached the Capitol, risking swift execution if he were to be discovered. When he was certain about the threat, he rushed back, reporting to Tingey what he'd seen: "But Oh! My Country! And I blush Sir! to tell you—I saw the Commons Covered with the fugitive Soldiery of our Army—running, hobbling, Creeping, & apparently pannick struck."

A portrait of the first commandant of the Washington Navy Yard, Thomas Tingey, who ordered the yard burned when it became heartbreakingly clear that the capital had fallen into British hands. "I was the last officer who quitted the city after the enemy had possession of it, having fully performed all orders received, in which was included that myself retiring, and not to fall into their possession," Tingey later wrote to his daughter. "I was also the first who returned and the only one who ventured in on the day on which they were peaceably masters of it."

The life-size Gilbert Stuart portrait of George Washington that Dolley rescued from imminent destruction. "Save that picture!" Dolley demanded of two visitors, friends of the Madisons who had come to her aid. "Save that picture if possible. If not possible, destroy it. Under no circumstances allow it to fall into the hands of the British!" When she saw that it was taking too long to dismount the painting from the wall, she ordered the frame sundered so that the canvas could be removed. Ultimately, it was the Madisons' door-keeper, Jean-Pierre "French John" Sioussa, who saved the day—he drew a penknife from his pocket and deftly cut the weighty twill canvas out.

Booth led a frenetic effort to remove the stockpile of gunpowder from the Navy Yard to the safety of a farm across the Potomac in Virginia. He reported to his superior about his desperate rides through the city to secure wagons for the task, as one citizen after another fled in fear. Booth called the scene of the city in flight "the Most to be regretted of my life." He breathed easier only late on August 23, when he reached a tavern at Falls Church and found his family safe there.

> Tuesday 23rd. Today I was in the yard before sunrise—and proceeded to have the Teams appraised &c: and as soon as practicable, got off Thos: Cowthon and Wm. Barnett with provisions for Commdr. Barney.—The Other four . . . I caused to go to the Magazine, where they were loaded with one hundred and twenty four Barrels, and two quarter Casks of Powder . . . Before I left the City, I impressed the Waggon & team of four horses of John Bair, an old Dutchman—to whom I gave a Certificate of impressment, and got him into the Yard. I then followed the Waggons with the powder, and overtook them before they cross'd the Potomac Bridge. On the South side, and as I was about to ascend the ridge from the Causeway, I met Colo. Minors Redgment of Fairfax Militia—The Colo. recommended six persons as a competent guard to take charge of the powder, and that night, I reached Wren's Tavern at the falls Church, late at night, within one mile of the farm of Daniel Dulany Esqr., where the powder was to be deposited. This Night a little before day, Captn. Smallwood & family, with my Daughters and Son.—reached Wrens—The Acct: given me of the retreat of our troops, and the advance of the British, and the consternation of the Citizens—was to me truly distressing, but the Seeing my Children out of the reach of a ferocious and vandal enemy— was delight indeed.

First Lady Dolley Madison had decided to defy the invaders and host a dinner party at the White House on August 23; it had to be canceled when none of the invitees showed up. Even on August 24, with reports that the British were on their way from Bladensburg, she had a table set for the return of her husband and a few "military gentlemen" from the front. Only when a family friend, an officer, came and urged her to seek safety did she round up several of the country's most prized heirlooms, including a Gilbert Stuart portrait of George Washington, for safekeeping and flee the city for Little Falls, Virginia. All this she told her sister in a letter penned that very day, up to the last moment.

> My husband left me yesterday morning to join General Winder. He inquired anxiously whether I had courage or firmness to remain in the President's house until his return on the morrow, or succeeding day, and on my assurance that I had no fear but for him, and the success of our army, he left, beseeching me to take care of myself, and of the Cabinet papers, public and private. I have since received two dispatches from him, written with a pencil. The last is

alarming, because he desires I should be ready at a moment's warning to enter my carriage, and leave the city; that the enemy seemed stronger than had at first been reported, and it might happen that they would reach the city with the intention of destroying it. I am accordingly ready; I have pressed as many Cabinet papers into trunks as to fill one carriage; our private property must be sacrificed, as it is impossible to procure wagons for its transportation. I am determined not to go myself until I see Mr. Madison safe, so that he can accompany me, as I hear of much hostility toward him. Disaffection stalks around us. My friends and acquaintances are all gone, even Colonel C. with his hundred, who were stationed as a guard in this inclosure. French John (a faithful servant), with his usual activity and resolution, offers to spike the cannon at the gate, and lay a train of powder, which would blow up the British, should they enter the house. To the last proposition I positively object, without being able to make him understand why all advantages in war may not be taken.

Wednesday Morning, twelve o'clock.—Since sunrise I have been turning my spyglass in every direction, and watching with unwearied anxiety, hoping to discover the approach of my dear husband and his friends; but, alas! I can descry only groups of military, wandering in all directions, as if there was a lack of arms, or of spirit to fight for their own fireside.

Three o'clock.—Will you believe it, my sister? We have had a battle, or skirmish, near Bladensburg, and here I am still, within sound of the cannon! Mr. Madison comes not. May God protect us! Two messengers, covered with dust, come to bid me fly; but here I mean to wait for him . . . At this late hour a wagon has been procured, and I have had it filled with plates and the most valuable portable articles, belonging to the house. Whether it will reach its destination, the Bank of Maryland, or fall into the hands of British soldiery, events must determine. Our kind friend, Mr. Carroll, has come to hasten my departure, and is in a very bad humor with me, because I insist on waiting until the large picture of General Washington is secured, and it requires to be unscrewed from the wall. This process was found too tedious for these perilous moments; I have ordered the frame to be broken, and the canvas taken out. It is done! and the precious portrait placed in the hands of two gentlemen of New York, for safe keeping. And now, dear sister, I must leave this house, or the retreating army will make me a prisoner in it by filling up the road I am directed to take. When I shall again write to you, or where I shall be tomorrow, I cannot tell!

The spunky Dolley snatched up a few pieces of silverware, tucking them into her little reticule, before being hustled out the door and into a waiting carriage. As she bumped along Pennsylvania Avenue, it must have been a strange sight to behold, for the presidential butler followed not far behind in Madison's mercurial coachee, a feather bed strapped to the back. Jean-Pierre "French John" Sioussa, the last person to vacate the White House, set out a few buckets of water and wine to quench the thirst of any retreating soldiers who might straggle by and fled with Dolley's darling pet mackaw in tow.

An issue of the *National Intelligencer* from Thursday, July 28, 1814, chockfull of war news. The name at the top right-hand corner, inked in by a subscription clerk, belonged to the recipient. Unflinching in its support of the war effort, the *Intelligencer* was a hot target for the August invaders, who were intent on wiping it out completely. Dyed-in-the-wool Yankee grit saw it up and running again mere days after the redcoats left town.

That evening Cockburn and Ross strode through the streets of Washington, the insolent Cockburn atop a white mare, her foal tottering along behind them. At the sight of this, a few shots of defiance rang out, prompting Cockburn, in his typical modus operandi, to torch the houses from which they came. Giving orders to burn the Capitol and the Library of Congress, he headed for the offices of the *National Intelligencer* to personally orchestrate their destruction. Cockburn had voraciously devoured the headlines he made, and the country's first national newspaper had vilified him more vituperatively than any other; now he would take his revenge. The offices were gutted completely—reams of paper scattered to the wind, a decade's worth of files fed to the licking flames of a bonfire, the printing presses dashed to pieces, the little blocks of type chucked out the shattered windows. "Make sure that all the Cs are destroyed," Cockburn purportedly told his underlings, "so that the rascals can have no further means of abusing my name."

As bystanders swooped in to salvage what little remained, the raiders proceeded up Pennsylvania Avenue to the White House, where Cockburn's staff found the dinner left by Dolley for her husband's return: wines in cut-glass decanters waited on the sideboard, with ale and cider in coolers, and forty place settings lay on the table. Cockburn poured himself a glass and with his officers drank a toast to "Jemmy's health," a sarcastic reference to the president. Cockburn's men smashed the windows and on the admiral's signal sent torches through the broken glass, sending the White House up in flames.

At the Navy Yard, Tingey, Booth, and Creighton had set a preemptive fire of their own to keep the ships and timber out of enemy hands. In giving the orders, Tingey had wavered for a moment, sickened by what they had to do. After it was done, Tingey thought to note the time—8:20 p.m.—before bidding goodbye to his loyal clerk, as though it were a final farewell.

The night sky glowed for miles around with the flames from Washington's inferno, which Napier saw miles downriver on the Potomac.

Mary Hunter, a Washington resident, heard the cannon fire from the direction of Bladensburg, then saw the Union Jack flying from Capitol Hill. That night, looking out toward the Navy Yard, Hunter beheld an "almost meridian brightness" in which the whole city was lit as brightly as a drawing room. "Few thought of going to bed," she wrote, as "they spent the night in gazing on the fires and lamenting the disgrace of the city."

The news traveled as fast as the light from the flames and galvanized Americans in a way the divisive war had not previously. "Every American heart is bursting with shame and indignation at the catastrophe," wrote Baltimore editor George Douglass, a militia member.

"The most disastrous news reached us," Minerva Rodgers wrote to her husband. "I have just heard that Washington is in ashes. I am bewildered & know not what to believe but am afraid to ask for news . . . May God preserve and bless you!"

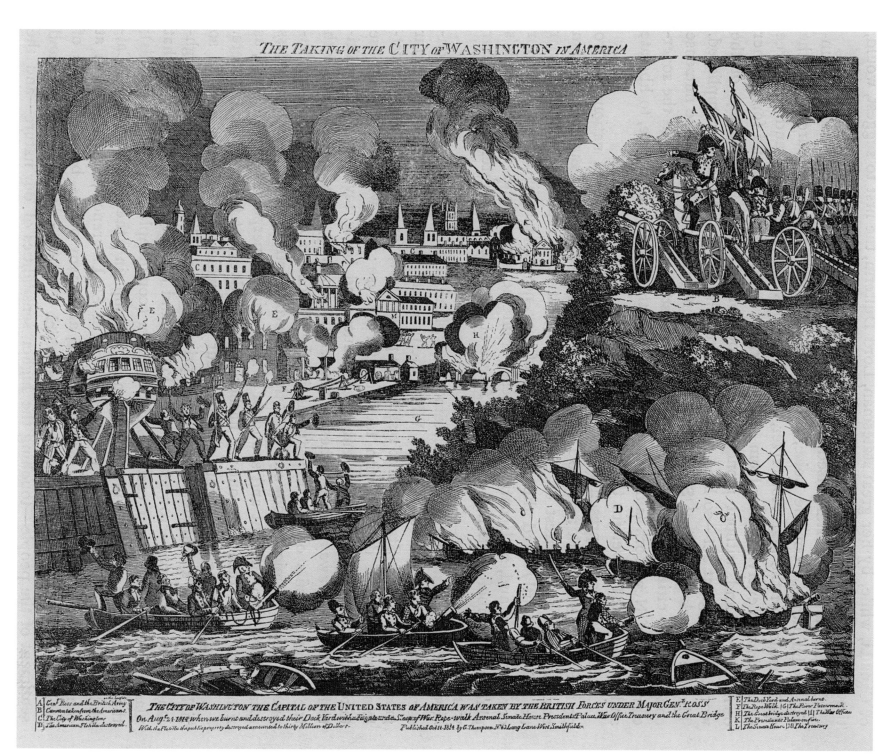

The Taking of the City of Washington in America

A | Gen.ʳ Ross and the British Army.
B | Cannon taken from the Americans.
C | The City of Washington.
D | The American Flotilla destroyed.

THE CITY OF WASHINGTON THE CAPITAL OF THE UNITED STATES OF AMERICA WAS TAKEN BY THE BRITISH FORCES UNDER MAJOR GEN.ʳ ROSS

On Aug.ᵗ 24 1814 when we burnt and destroyed their Dock Yard with a Frigate and a Sloop of War Rope-walk Arsenal Senate House President's Palace War Office Treasury and the Great Bridge

With the Flotilla the public property destroyed amounted to thirty Million of Dollars. Published Oct 14. 1814 by G. Thompson N.º 43 Long Lane West Smithfield.

E | The Dock Yard and Arsenal burnt.
F | The Rope Walk. | G | The River Patowmack.
H | The Great bridge destroyd | I | The War Office
K | The President's Palace on fire.
L | The Senate House. | M | The Treasury

Below: An early nineteenth-century spyglass of the kind Dolley might have used to scan the burnished hills surrounding the White House.

Left: This 1814 wood engraving features a composite of the events encompassing the capture and occupation of the city, as seen from the Potomac River. The immolation of Barney's flying squadron at Pig Point is shown in the foreground; the Battle of Bladensburg in the top right; and the burning of the city and the Navy Yard in the top left.

In the wake of the imminent threat to Washington, Jones had rescinded his first orders to Rodgers and sent new ones rerouting him to Bladensburg "to preserve the national capital and its invaluable establishments from the ruthless hands of our vengeful foe." This message arrived too late, in the charred aftermath of Washington's fall, much to Jones' vexation. "Undoubtedly," he told Rodgers later, "you would have turned the scale." Nevertheless, Rodgers' presence, which eased the fearful, panic-stricken residents and invigorated their fallen spirits, was very much needed in Baltimore. "The people now begin to shew something like a patriotic spirit," Rodgers wrote to Jones. "They are Forti-fying the Town by all the means in their power." Some forty miles away in Havre de Grace, Minerva continued to fret over her husband's safety and comfort.

Minerva's personal seal.

Right: The letter that Minerva Rodgers wrote to her husband, the commodore, upon learning that he'd been ordered to Baltimore for the purpose of defending the city.

Below: John Rodgers' green sea trunk, perhaps the one that Minerva lovingly packed for his journey to Baltimore.

August 1814
My Dearest Husband,
I have this moment received the truly unpleasant intelligence that you are ordered to Baltimore. How unhappy I feel I need not say! But I trust ere long you will be returned to me in safety. Knowing that you were not provided with clothes for this separation I have sent a trunk containing some articles from which you can select such as you wish & leave the rest at N. Castle. I have also sent your great coat. God preserve you my love from every danger! I dare not say much.
Ever yours most tenderly, M.R.
Let me hear from you soon as possible. I shall be miserable till I hear from you.

Baltimore August 28, 1814
My beloved wife,
I have this instant received your letter. You have no serious cause of alarm for the evening hearing of the Force … I am more near the place from whence they embarked. I have now a Brigade under my command consisting of 1200 seamen & marines & expect in 48 hours to have double that number, & even in our present state I do not think the enemy dare attack us.
Yr own affectionate, J.R.

DEFENDING BALTIMORE

Rodgers' brief absence from Baltimore at the end of the month to quash a British squadron ransacking Alexandria had skittish Baltimoreans in an uproar. And it had Minerva worried again, too. She had just glimpsed a large mass of British ships heading up the bay. "There are now visible from the top of the house, about 25 or 30 sails," she scrawled. Knowing the ships would bear down on Rodgers and his "brave seamen," she was anxious but tried to remain strong. "I endeavor to be composed," she wrote. "I find all my fortitude is insufficient for the various calls upon it. Whenever you have a moment drop me a line! If I should hear a cannonading from Baltimore, Good Heavens!"

The sounds of artillery would indeed soon reach Havre de Grace, and Rodgers was itching to get back to Baltimore for its defense. "Would to God! it was in my power to return to Baltimore immediately as I am well assured that our seamen would be of more service there than they are likely to be here," he wrote to Major General Samuel Smith of the Maryland militia on September 1. Rodgers was preparing three "fire vessels" for raining fire on the enemy fleet.

> I can assure you that I feel a deep interest in the welfare of Baltm. & am Satisfied that I shall be with you with 7/8ths of my force should the Enemy attack you; & this is an object on which I have set my heart, as I feel confident from what I have already seen that they will be made to curse the hour they undertook the expedition—From what I have witnessed here I cease to be surprised at any thing the Enemy was permitted to do.

Once back in Baltimore a week later, Rodgers quickly set about creating defenses on the city's east side, facing the Patapsco River, the direction from which an attack would come. A mile of earthworks rose up. The center section on Hampstead Hill (now Patterson Park), known as "Rodgers' Bastion," was armed with sixteen artillery cannon, including 12-pounders borrowed from the sloop-of-war *Erie*.

Rodgers summoned naval forces from Philadelphia as well, and by September 9 he had "upwards of 15,000 Regulars and Militia exclusive of about 1,000 Seamen and Marines" bivouacked around the city. He ordered sailors to sink old hulks of ships in the river to block the British from the harbor. More than three hundred sailors manned a floating battery of barges in a row behind those sunken hulks, ready with cannons and carronades. Rodgers reported being heartened by the Baltimoreans' spirit and their intention "to defend the place to the last extremity." Still, many feared a devastating attack.

From Washington, the British had returned to the Chesapeake, eager to inflict punishment on Baltimore, the home port of the privateers who had burned or captured five hundred of their ships since the war began. With their troops, Cockburn and Ross met up with Admiral Cochrane's fleet on an island in the Chesapeake Bay and devised a strategy for their combined land and sea attack.

When they reached Baltimore, they found the harbor blocked by the vessels sunk there. Washington might have been safe from deep-water invasion, but the Patapsco permitted greater artillery bombardment. Five bomb ships, ominously named *Meteor*, *Devastation*, *Aetna*, *Volcano*, and *Terror*, opened fire on Fort McHenry near dawn on September 13. The bombshells filled with powder exploded above their targets and rained down shrapnel. Congreve rockets whistled overhead with their horrible hiss and set fires when they landed, though they were perhaps more terrifying than they were destructive. (Cockburn had groused to Cochrane about the overabundance of rocket boats to the exclusion of other ships. "They [the Sea Lords] persist in sending us Rockets & Rocket Vessels," he wrote, "which though of use in their way & tolerably good against a Column of Men are of no more [use] to throw against a Fort than a toasted Biscuit would be.") As the fireworks filled the sky, Ross' infantry landed at North Point and marched toward the Americans' line. As Ross rode back to secure reinforcements, however, he was killed by an American sharpshooter's bullet.

This charred chunk of timber, discovered during White House renovations in 1950, is believed to have survived the burning of the presidential mansion. Beneath the paint, soot stains still rim some of the White House's windows, and scorch marks can be seen on the sandstone blocks that form the original walls.

"NO HAIL COULD BE THICKER"

Congreve's Rockets

"The soul of artillery without the body" is how its inventor, Sir William Congreve, described the Congreve rocket, the rocket of "red glare" fame. Unlike conventional artillery, he was pointing out, rockets were light, maneuverable, and recoilless, meaning that they could be deployed just about anywhere. They packed a tremendous explosive punch, and unlike shells, their flight was of course visible, although their trajectories were sometimes completely unpredictable.

Congreve was naturally enthusiastic about his invention, which was spurred by a request from the British Bureau of Ordnance to develop a war rocket similar to those used against British forces in 1792 during the course of the Third Mysore War in India. "So pestered were we with the rocket boys that there was no moving without danger from the destructive missile," a young English officer remembered. "No hail could be thicker."

By 1804, the ingenious young lieutenant, whose father was the comptroller of the Royal Laboratory, had devised a 32-pounder rocket that could fit into a narrow, three-foot-long iron case. Equipped with a fifteen-foot-long stabilizing stick, it had a range exceeding three thousand yards. Although his rockets came in a variety of sizes, from ten-foot-tall 300-pounders to portable ones an infantryman could carry, the 32-pounder became the standard model.

Because they were recoilless, the rockets could be mounted on any warship, even those too small to carry an equivalent battery of heavy cannons. Two small sloops, *Erebus* and *Galguo*, were eventually outfitted as special rocket ships, complete with their own detachments of Royal Marine rocket men.

During the Napoleonic Wars, the British first used Congreve rockets, packed with incendiaries, on October 18, 1806, when eighteen Royal Navy warships fired some two hundred projectiles into the French coastal town of Boulogne, setting portions of it on fire. The following year, a British fleet launched 2,500 rockets into the Danish capital, Copenhagen, and the resulting conflagration nearly turned the city to ashes. On land, they were used with devastating effect at the tremendous Battle of Leipzig in October 1813.

Across the Atlantic, a barrage of Congreve rockets routed some green American units during the British attack on Bladensburg, Maryland, in August 1814. The most famous instance of their use, however, occurred a few weeks later, when on September 13 the rocket ship *Erebus* took her place among the other bomb vessels of the British fleet and together began a torrential, twenty-four-hour bombardment of Baltimore's Fort McHenry. Between 1,500 and 1,800 shells—the "bombs bursting in air"—were rained upon its star-shaped bulwarks. The rockets launched from *Erebus* that night may not have caused much damage, as the range was a bit too long, but thanks to Francis Scott Key, the red arc of their trajectory has never been forgotten.

PORTRAIT OF WILLIAM CONGREVE, ESQ.

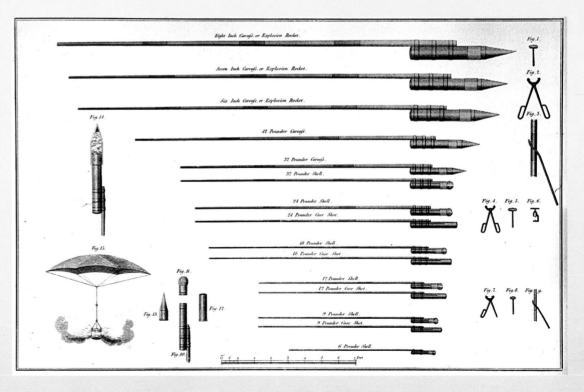

Fig. 1.

Plate 12

Fig. 3.

Fig. 4.

Fig. 2.

The original garrison flag that flew, triumphal, in the dawn sky over the ramparts of Fort McHenry following the day-long bombardment—a sight that so stirred young Washingtonian lawyer Francis Scott Key, aboard a truce ship on the Patapsco, that he took up his quill on the spot and penned "The Defence of Fort McHenry," a poem that would eventually become the national anthem. The flag, commissioned by Joshua Barney and his committee, was made out of wool bunting—the stars of cotton—and sewn by "maker of colours" Mary Pickersgill, a local widow, with the help of her mother and daughter. They spread the material out on the malthouse floor of Claggett's Brewery after it had closed for the evening and worked into the wee hours by candlelight for many a night. They charged a grand total of $405.90.

Opposite, left: Commodore John Rodgers sent this letter to Major General Smith accepting temporary command of Fort McHenry on September 17, 1814.

Opposite, right: The original manuscript of "The Star-Spangled Banner." Four crease marks remain from when Key folded it up and tucked it into his breast pocket.

Opposite, below: These three fragments were cut from the Star-Spangled Banner in 1880 by Eben Appleton, the grandson of the commander of Fort McHenry, who presented them to William Carter, a local historian, as souvenirs.

A BANNER UNDER SIEGE

While the British assumed their positions, a Washingtonian lawyer named Francis Scott Key was sent by Madison to negotiate the release of prisoners aboard a truce ship.

All day on September 13 and into the next, the bomb ships rained down an estimated 133 tons of shells onto Fort McHenry, roughly one shell every minute. The thundering warheads came with heavy rain and high winds. Despite the rain, the sky lit up with explosions, thunder mixing with the roar of the bombs.

By sunrise on September 14, the sky had cleared. The damage to several of the bomb ships and the failure of their infantry to advance forced the British to abandon the attack. Cochrane ordered the shelling to stop, and two hours later the ships were turning to leave when a British midshipman on one of the ships, Robert Barrett, noticed: "The Americans hoisted a most superb and splendid ensign on their battery, and fired at the same time a gun of defiance."

Key watched the morning brighten and in those moments of relief and excitement scrawled out three verses on the back of an envelope before a tender returned him to shore. Within weeks, his poem, renamed "The Star-Spangled Banner," was reprinted in newspapers throughout the states, sounding a note of hope that the young nation might still withstand the onslaught of the world's preeminent military.

Baltimore residents rejoiced. The city's defenders became heroes overnight. The joy was evident in Rodgers' report to Washington on Wednesday, September 14, 1814.

Sir
The enemy has been severely drubbed as well his Army as his Navy & is
now retiring down the river after expending many rons [rounds] of shot from
1800 to 2000 shells & at least 7 or 8 hundred rockets with great respect I
have the honor to be Sir yr obt. St
Jn Rodgers
I shall give you a more particular acct. as soon as I get a little rest. Genl Ross
of the B Army is said to be mortally wounded.

After serving at the Bladensburg fiasco, Charles Ball had proceeded to Baltimore and helped in the defense of that city. Once the British were repulsed, he later wrote, "I procured my discharge . . . and went to work in Baltimore . . . I worked in various places in Maryland as a free black man; sometimes in Baltimore, sometimes in Annapolis, and frequently in Washington." Barney, meanwhile, missed the bombardment of Fort McHenry. With a wound that would nettle him for the rest of his life, he recuperated at his farmhouse in Elkridge, his family by his side. "I fondly hope a few weeks will restore me

to health," he wrote in a letter to the secretary of the Navy, "and that an exchange will take place, that I may resume my command, or any other that you and the President may think proper to honour me with."

In the cataclysmic events of that autumn, the ability of both nations to endure the costs inflicted by war had been tested. In a state of the union address delivered by Madison to Congress on September 20, he cautiously raised hopes for peace. With minimal reference to the damage to Washington and its environs, he praised the Baltimore "militia and volunteers, aided by a small body of regulars and sea men" that forced a British retreat, as well the naval victories on the Great Lakes. As for privateers, he said, "In spite of the naval force of the enemy accumulated on our coasts, our private cruisers also have not ceased to annoy his commerce." In fact, Madison relied on mostly naval examples in his positive narrative of the war's progress, and cited again the acts of press gangs that helped to spark the conflict in the first place.

The U.S. Navy and its allies fought into that fall, even with a quixotic effort to turn the notion of a blockade against the British themselves.

CHAPTER FIVE

A print by T. Buttersworth depicting the January 1815 battle between *President* and *Endymion* that led to the capture of Commodore John Rodgers' cherished frigate.

Overleaf: This oil painting by Thomas L. Hornbrook (active between 1836 and 1844) depicts the Battle of Lake Borgne, which occurred on December 14, 1814.

"*WAR UNTIL PEACE SHALL BE SECURED*"

1814–1815

"[A]N UGLY ACCOUNT OF PEACE BEING SIGNED . . .
SEEMS TO PROMISE A SPEEDY DISMISSAL TO US FROM THIS COAST."

~ Admiral Sir George Cockburn

At the close of the year 1813, the new commandant of the Navy's small New Orleans Station, Daniel T. Patterson, had spent five years in the only posting that could be called exotic. A slice of France with a garnish of Spain, its streets a babble of tongues, its women the toast of the Southern gentry—New Orleans was still the most hated posting in the Navy.

For one thing, it was just too far away, and distance made things exasperating. Only a decade had passed since the United States purchased the French-speaking city and its immense hinterland, and it sometimes took weeks by sea and months by land to get there from the East Coast's naval stations. Officers were far away from family and friends. Supplies were invariably delayed, when they arrived at all. Money was scarce. The city moreover hung torpid with heat much of the year and was surrounded by impenetrable swamps—home to snakes, alligators, runaway slaves, smugglers, and the clouds of mosquitoes responsible for the most dreaded of tropical killers, yellow fever, widely if mistakenly blamed on the city's bad air.

Then there were the discouraging duties. The station's flotilla, consisting of about a dozen gunboats and two or three brigs, was responsible for patrolling an extensive tract of Gulf Coast shore, reaching from the Sabine River in the west to the Perdido River in the east, both of which bordered on Spanish territory. Florida in particular was contested country. Spain had claimed the entire coast from the Keys to the Mississippi River. The United States, meanwhile, had claimed as coming with the Louisiana Purchase that part of the coast from the Mississippi eastward to the Perdido, which flowed between the two finest harbors in the Gulf, Mobile and Pensacola, both thinly garrisoned by Spain.

This dispute had burst into flame with the outbreak of war in 1812. That's because the British had briefly owned West Florida before being ousted by the Spanish in 1783; they still had designs on Pensacola, which had been their capital. Furthermore, Spain was now their ally in the struggle against Napoleon, though she was officially neutral in their war with the United States.

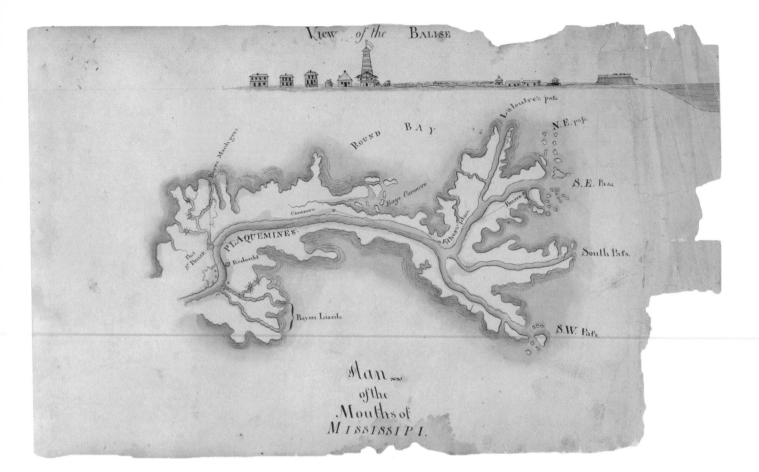

View of the Balise

Plan of the Mouths of MISSISSIPPI.

This 1814 ink and watercolor plan of the mouths of the Mississippi River shows fortifications, obstructions, and navigable passages. At the top is a view of the Balize's buildings and fort. The plan was drawn by Barthélémy Lafon, a high-standing city planner who eventually turned to smuggling and piracy, working in cahoots with the brothers Lafitte.

in the Battle of Burnt Corn. And when they attacked Fort Mims north of Mobile a month later, on August 30, 1813, and upward of five hundred people "were all destroyed by the Savages," as John Shaw, Daniel Patterson's predecessor as chief of the New Orleans Station, had put it—well, that only "bespeaks their design," their referring to the British, whose agents in Spanish Florida were widely assumed to have stirred up the trouble in the first place.

As a result, the United States was plunged into the Creek War, but with its army fighting the British along the Great Lakes front, local militias were being mustered to quell the Red Stick uprising. The Tennessee militia was already on the march south, led by its colonel, a hard-bitten planter named Andrew Jackson.

The Navy, however, was more concerned with matters to the southwest. One of its principal duties in the years before the war was the enforcement of the various embargos that the government had hoped might bring the warring European powers, dependent on New World trade, to heel. That meant hunting down smugglers, and the many-fingered delta of the Mississippi, with its innumerable miasmic swamps and bayous, had long been a smuggler's paradise.

Just to the west of the river's primary outlet, called the Balize, an entire community of smugglers had arisen—"a collection of pirates," as Shaw had called them—on the islands surrounding shallow Barataria Bay. These Baratarians, who had depots hidden throughout the labyrinth of swamps and mangroves, were headquartered on Grand Isle, where they had built nearly fifty buildings, and anchored in their protected harbor were all kinds of ships obtained in all manner of ways. Their leader was the dashing Jean Lafitte, who had long cut a figure in New Orleans society, a dark-eyed, smoldering man of mysterious origins who disdained the name "pirate" and preferred to be called a privateer. He did possess a letter of marque from the Caribbean city of Cartagena, chief port of the old Spanish Main, most of which, in the wake of Napoleon's subjugation of the mother country, had thrown off its colonial yoke and was fighting for independence. Yet pirates throughout the Caribbean and the Gulf of Mexico were cloaking their activities beneath similar letters of marque, preying principally on Spanish commerce but often taking any sail they encountered. Thus, there were many in New Orleans who preferred not to probe Lafitte too deeply.

Hoping to forestall the British from occupying the contested tract, in February Congress had met in secret session and approved the occupation of Mobile, which fell within the U.S. claim. Two months later, therefore, the New Orleans Station's gunboat flotilla had sailed into broad Mobile Bay, escorting the transports carrying General James Wilkinson's six hundred soldiers, who invested the city, leading the Spanish to soon surrender.

That would not be the end of the matter. The planters pushing into the forests of the Southeast from Georgia were encountering the Creek Indian Confederacy, and conflicts naturally arose. Americans accused the Spanish in Florida of supplying arms to the Indians, hoping that the Creeks might serve as a strong buffer between their crumbling presidios and the oncoming Americans. By 1813, inspired by the fiery words of Tecumseh, the Red Sticks, a radical faction of the Creeks, instigated a civil war with their more peaceful brethren. Then, in July, some American soldiers halted a party of Red Sticks and discovered that they had just received guns and ammunition from the Spanish governor at Pensacola. The Red Sticks eventually attacked the soldiers

But to Patterson, they were pirates pure and simple, and he was trying to secure permission to clean the nest of them out. Once the war began, however, British warships were regularly patrolling the mouths of the Mississippi and had nearly snatched up several of his sloops—those that hadn't been damaged by a hurricane, at least. Being a station that had trouble enough replacing its outmoded muskets and pistols, much less ships, it was fortunate that early in the war it had acquired a broad-beamed New York merchantman, *Remittance*, and was soon fitting her out as a 16-gun schooner, renamed *Louisiana*.

By late 1812, even the brigs were ordered elsewhere. When *Enterprise* was summoned to the Atlantic, her commander, Lieutenant Johnston Blakeley, couldn't have been more delighted. "Permit me to express to you," he had written Secretary of the Navy Paul Hamilton while anchored at the mouth of the

A swamp scene painted by Joseph Rusling Meeker (1827–1889), who sketched the brumous, cypress-filled bayous of Louisiana while traveling the length of the Mississippi River as a Union Navy paymaster.

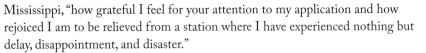

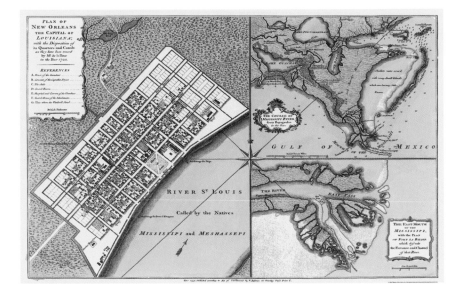

MASSACRE AT FORT MIMMS.

From an original Painting by Chappel in the possession of the Publishers.

Above, left: Captain John Dandridge Henley, who would go on to command the schooner *Carolina* in the Battle of New Orleans.

Above, middle: History's suavest pirate, the magnetic, law-flouting Frenchman Jean Lafitte.

Above, right: An 1858 lithograph after a painting by Alonzo Chappel depicting the massacre of American settlers at Fort Mims—the incident that kindled an open war between the United States and the "Red Sticks," a hostile faction of the Creek Nation.

Right: A 1759 plan of New Orleans.

Mississippi, "how grateful I feel for your attention to my application and how rejoiced I am to be relieved from a station where I have experienced nothing but delay, disappointment, and disaster."

Blakeley had been one of Commodore John Rodgers' three favorite midshipmen in the Mediterranean, the others being William Henry Allen, who would eventually captain *Argus*, and Robert Henley, then commanding gunboats in the Chesapeake but shortly to be transferred to Lake Champlain. It was Henley's older brother, John, who was in command of the New Orleans Station's other brig, *Viper*. December came before *Enterprise* and *Viper* could clear the river and together enter the Gulf. Although both were bound for destinations on the East Coast, only Blakeley sailed around Spanish Florida to arrive safely in Savannah. Henley turned back when *Viper* sprang a leak and, though he tried outrunning her, was picked up by HMS *Narcissus* in January.

The Henley brothers had grown up in Williamsburg, Virginia. Their aunt was Martha Dandridge, George Washington's wife. Another Virginian on the New Orleans Station was Patterson's gunboat commander, a plucky twenty-three-year-old named Thomas ap Catesby Jones. Wherever they were from, however, one and all—including Patterson, who had married a New Orleans girl—had applied at one time or another for a transfer. They wanted out of New Orleans so that they could get to the war.

The war was still found far to the southeast, off the great crescent of the Windward Islands and the Guiana coast of South America. The British still controlled these territories, and where the British were, so were merchantmen.

Only one commodore still had trouble finding the war he sought and still had to endure such toasts as the one the mayor of Baltimore honored him with in the spring of 1814: "Commodore Rodgers—hated and feared by the enemy, revered and beloved by his countrymen."

Rodgers had just returned from his fourth and final cruise of the war. Once again, he had made a daring escape from Newport, nimbly eluding the blockading squadrons and taking *President* across the blue Atlantic toward the Canary Islands. And once again the war had eluded him. As far south as the Cape Verdes, he hadn't picked up much of note. He ran down the fifteenth parallel toward Barbados. As he neared the Leeward Islands, his lookouts saw the sails of two warships—and they were frigates. Only they proved to be French frigates, *Méduse* and *Nymphe*, involved in some madcap scheme to retake nearby Guadeloupe from the English. For several days, he cruised to the windward of Barbados but only picked up a few small armed merchantmen, both of which he sank after liberating them of their valuable cargoes.

He had a daring run inshore along the southeastern coast, dodging British squadrons yet unable to lure single frigates into combat. On February 18, just as he approached Sandy Hook, the southern gate to New York Harbor, the commodore spied two of the blockaders. One he quickly determined was a schooner, but the other was considerably larger and seemed to be approaching him. Rodgers cleared for action and stood toward her. She seemed then to retreat, although she was certainly a frigate and perhaps something larger. He continued pressing toward her until overhauled by a speedy little revenue cutter, which hailed that she was indeed a 74. Though she turned out to be the frigate *Loire* instead, she was surely mousetrapping him, because yet a third sail soon appeared on the horizon. Bowing to the inevitable, Rodgers turned the helm, crossed the bar of Sandy Hook, and slipped home to New York.

Although the forty-two-year-old still had a lot of career left for him, he would always be disappointed that he never won a frigate duel. Though he had to watch his juniors and his protégés fight the war's spectacular sea duels, in point of fact he captured more merchantmen—twenty-five—than did any other U.S. Navy officer—more than David Porter did in *Essex*, more than Henry Allen did in *Argus*, and more than Lewis Warrington would do in *Peacock*. He had cost the Admiralty more trouble dispatching squadrons to chase him down than did any other American commander. And he brought that queen of frigates, the winged, hardwearing *President*, safely home every time; it would remain for another to lose her.

Meanwhile, as *President* had crept up the coast, out to sea *Constitution* was sailing south. After tiresome months either refitting or waiting for the opportunity to make her getaway, Lieutenant Charles Stewart had finally freed Old Ironsides from her Boston confinement. His had once been a promising career. Commissioned, like so many others, during the Quasi-War in 1798, Stewart had been assigned, alongside fellow Philadelphian Stephen Decatur, to the frigate *United States*. During the Barbary War, he was actually in overall command of the raid culminating in Decatur's burning of the captured frigate named for their city. After that, Decatur's star always seemed to burn the brighter, Stewart only switching from ship to ship until, in September 1812, he was given the storied *Constellation*. Unfortunately, she was blockaded in Norfolk and would never get to sea during the war. So, in May 1813, he was assigned to *Constitution* instead—only to see her, too, blockaded until December.

Thus, it was with some expectation that he embarked on a hunt in the West Indies. Yet the cruise proved as disappointing as had Rodgers'. Ten weeks out, on a course for Surinam, he had scooped up the armed merchant *Lovely Anne*. Then, several hours later, he also captured her escort, the 28-gun sloop *Pictou*, which he burned. He had chased several other British warships, but they had seen him coming and made good their escape. Stewart had carried enough stores for a six-month cruise, but he returned after barely three because *Constitution*'s mainmast had sprung. That forced a return to Boston—and an attempt to evade the patrolling frigates *Junon* and *Tenedos*. Overboard went all those carefully packed provisions as Stewart outran his pursuers, and facing the prospect of port or prison, so went all the spirits as well. Though practically becalmed before doing so, *Constitution* at last reached Marblehead, north of Salem, and two weeks later anchored in Boston—there to remain, blockaded, until December.

No other frigate would escape port that year. The war at sea would instead be carried on by, if anything, a more effective class of American warship—the sloop.

Commodore Charles Stewart, who took command of *Constitution* in 1813.

Two months after Congress had agreed to pass a landmark naval appropriations act in late 1812, funding the construction of more frigates and even 74-gun ships-of-the-line, Secretary of the Navy William Jones requested the addition of warships he was convinced would be even more versatile than frigates in the present conflict: "corvettes such as the *Hornet* or larger."

Corvette was originally a French term that came to be applied to a great many things but seems to have meant, at least in Jones' day, a small frigate, or at least the fastest, most powerful, most elusive warship short of the frigate class. What he had in mind, he wrote, was something like "*Argus* accurately extended," an enlarged version of the sloop that had proved to be the most effective commerce raider of 1813. Three "extended Arguses" would be raised on the stocks; none would see service in the war. Instead, what naval constructor William Doughty envisioned borrowed something from the Baltimore clippers he knew so well from the Chesapeake Bay and also something from Joshua Humphreys' tremendously strong frigates with their heavy scantlings. What resulted were three flush-decked sloops-of-war, each able to easily carry eighteen 32-pound carronades, each as tough as Old Ironsides, and each fast as the wind. They had no one best point of sailing; they were remarkable "off the wind" in any direction. Ranking high among the best-designed warships of their era, they were *Frolic*, *Peacock*, and *Wasp*.

Frolic was the first to put to sea, escaping Boston in February under Commander Joseph Bainbridge, younger brother of Commodore William Bainbridge, and an officer who had once been close friends with Stephen Decatur when both were midshipmen. He was even a member of Decatur's legendary raiding party that had slipped into Tripoli harbor and incinerated *Philadelphia*. But the younger Bainbridge had an intemperate streak in him that usually landed him in trouble. During the early months of the war, he grounded the brig *Siren* in the Gulf of Mexico, perhaps one reason why he was virtually kicked out of the New Orleans Station by John Shaw. With *Frolic*, though, he had a chance for a fresh start.

Things didn't go well from the start. His orders were to cruise in the West Indies before circuiting the Gulf of Mexico. But hardly had *Frolic* made sail out of Boston when the speedy *Junon* was on her. She outran the blockader but not before casting half of her stores into Cape Cod Bay. In a storm, she lost a foretopmast—and a good foretop man went overboard with it. In the Atlantic, she then "struck a dolphin."

At last, in the islands, she took several prizes and sank one of those privateer-turned-pirates out of Cartagena, drowning nearly one hundred of the crew. Before burning one merchantman, Bainbridge took the entire cargo of fresh sea turtles and smashed up her decks for firewood. At dawn on April 18, however, while *Frolic* was in the Florida Strait, he encountered two sails that unfortunately proved to be HMS *Orpheus*, a 22-gun frigate, and her 12-gun consort, HMS *Shelburne*. In a case of bad judgment, Bainbridge let his curiosity get the better of him until he realized too late that it was high time to run.

Though he had by far the speedier ship, he had allowed the chasers to gain on him, and though he ran for sixty miles for the shelter of Matanzas Bay in Cuba—casting overboard guns, anchors, and whatever supplies he had left, including the hapless turtles—they cornered him at last, and he struck. To seaman Benjamin Waine, the explanation was all too obvious: "Being under the frigate's guns, one broadside would have sent us to eternity." However, his surrender without even a fight appalled Bainbridge's naval colleagues. Even Royal Navy heads shook with the disgrace of it—when they weren't nodding in wonder at their prize, for *Frolic* was a "remarkably fine ship," as *Orpheus'* captain put it. Even with a new name, HMS *Florida*, she could beat any challenger when racing off the wind.

Her sister ship was just as impressive. *Peacock* had been built in New York, and when undergoing trials in New York's spacious harbor, her captain, Lewis Warrington, matched her against a privateer schooner. *Peacock* whipped her every time.

Warrington had grown up in Williamsburg, Virginia, with the Henley brothers. As a young officer he had spent nearly four years of unrelieved duty in the Mediterranean and had served with nearly every frigate in the fleet. He was first lieutenant aboard *Congress* when she roamed the fog-veiled seas, hunting for that elusive Jamaican convoy during Rodgers' first cruise in 1812. Now a master commandant, the thirty-one-year-old Warrington, at the helm of *Peacock*, had escaped New York in March 1813. A month later, having woven his way through the British blockaders to deliver stores to the St. Mary's station in Georgia, he was waiting off the Bahamas for *President* to run that cordon as well. The imperial frigate would not get away, but in the meantime Warrington lurked about the islands, lingering for another one of those rumored Jamaica convoys. At seven o'clock in the morning on April 28, just off Cape Canaveral in Spanish Florida, his lookouts spied sails to windward. They turned out to be a small convoy originating from Havana, and they were being escorted by a Royal Navy brig-sloop. She was the 18-gun *Epervier*, and her commander, Captain R. W. Wales, was the nephew of Admiral Sir John Borlase Warren, the former head of the North American Station.

As the *Peacock* made chase, the merchantmen made all sail and sped away. *Epervier*, however, came straight for the U.S. corvette. Soon after ten o'clock, with the wind in the south and both vessels approaching head on, *Peacock* began to shear off enough to bring her starboard battery to bear when Wales shoved down his helm, rounded to on *Peacock*'s bow, and loosened his starboard broadside first. Two shots slammed into the Americans' foreyard. Those would be the last shots to hit her. Firing his own broadside in return, Warrington had his men reload with bar shot and langrage, and as *Epervier* came about and bore down with her port guns run out, he let her have it. *Epervier*'s jibs and foresails were instantaneously ripped to shreds. As her bow came violently into the wind, her stern was then exposed to *Peacock*'s raking fire, and soon masts and spars were crashing down as well. From that point on, the Americans' guns fired relentlessly, shot after shot blasting into *Epervier*'s hull. As the crippled brig began to drift into the corvette, Wales called for boarders. His crew actually refused, flinching at the prospect. After forty-five minutes of battle, with eight men dead and fifteen wounded, he had no choice but to strike. Not a man in *Peacock* was killed, and only two were wounded. The shattered foreyard, "with a few topmast and topgallant backstays cut away, and a few shot through our sails," Warrington reported to Jones, "is the only injury the Peacock has sustained."

This medal was struck to commemorate Warrington's capture of *Epervier*. The obverse features a bust of Warrington, and the reverse shows a recreation of the battle scene, *Epervier* with her topmast shot away.

Not a round shot touched our hull, and our masts and spars are as sound as ever. When the enemy struck, he had five feet of water in his hold—his maintopmast was over the side—his mainboom shot away—his foremast cut nearly in two, and tottering—his fore-rigging and stays shot away—his bowsprit badly wounded, and forty-five shot holes in his hull, twenty of which were within a foot of his waterline, above and below.

That afternoon the prize crew worked just a little bit harder than usual to patch up the wrecked *Epervier* and make her seaworthy again, for *Epervier* was found to be carrying $118,000 in her hold.

It had been such a crushingly one-sided victory that Warrington would receive the customary Thanks of Congress and a gold-hilted sword from his native Virginia. But *Epervier*, it was subsequently determined, was not a well-run ship. Her crew was harshly disciplined but poorly trained in gunnery. Even her carronades, it was claimed, were dismounted by recoil alone, not by U.S. fire, so carelessly had they been maintained. The two British frigates, however, that menaced the Americans as they brought *Epervier* to Savannah were a different matter. *Peacock* toyed with them just long enough for the prize crew to successfully escape their attention before flying away herself, easily outrunning her pursuers.

And then there was *Wasp*, every bit the equal of her sisters in speed and grace. The Navy's first *Wasp*, a sloop, had been damaged by a gale off Delaware Bay in October 1812 when she happened upon a British convoy in similar straits and—notwithstanding the round of triumphal one-upmanship reflected in the

ship's names—closed for battle with its escort, HMS *Frolic*, a 22-gun sloop-of-war. Both vessels were only cut up the more by the fight, but it was bad luck for *Wasp*'s victorious captain, Jacob Jones, that *Poictiers*, a British 74, happened by. Jones' vessel was too damaged to flee and unquestionably facing the prospect of eternity, he could do little else but surrender.

Wasp redivivus was built in Newburyport, Massachusetts, and outfitted in nearby Portsmouth, New Hampshire. There she took on her captain, one of the most promising and admired up-and-coming officers in the service, Master Commandant Johnston Blakeley.

Born in Ireland but reared in North Carolina, Blakeley had studied law at the university in Chapel Hill before being appointed a midshipman by Secretary of the Navy Benjamin Stoddert in 1800. He was first assigned to *President*, where he fell under the considerable spell of Commodore Thomas Truxtun, before shipping on the little frigate *John Adams* with Rodgers. The small, compact young man with dark hair and a genuine, strikingly white-toothed grin won the regard of that increasingly respected officer, and Blakeley became perhaps Rodgers' favorite among the coterie of midshipmen he carried with him from frigate to frigate, from *Adams* to *President* to *Essex*. After being promoted to lieutenant, he served with *Hornet*, *Argus*, and a Norfolk gunboat flotilla before finally being assigned to *Enterprise* as commander. It was with *Enterprise* that he had been so miserable in New Orleans, and it was *Enterprise*, with his trained crew—William Burrows having been captain but a day or two—that defeated *Boxer* off the coast of Maine.

On May 1, 1814, Master Commandant Blakeley eased *Wasp* from her moorings in Portsmouth and embarked on the cruise that would make him famous. It proved to be a stormy passage to his assigned hunting grounds, the western approaches to the English Channel, but when not battened down the gun ports were open and the cannons were blazing, as the crew was drilled relentlessly in gunnery. On the rain-swept second day of June, *Wasp* took her first prize, the barque *Neptune*, with a trove of "sundries" and supplies that would help fit out her conqueror; most were removed before *Neptune* was burned. On June 13, in another driving gale, *Wasp* took her second trophy—and then they started coming thick and fast, three more in the next two weeks.

On June 28, in the last watch before dawn, another sail was discovered. Studying it in the gloom, Blakeley concluded that it was an approaching British warship. It turned out to be the 18-gun sloop *Reindeer*, patrolling for privateers. At sunrise, and all the morning after that, they eyed each other, both of them on a westward course, *Reindeer* to windward, the breeze then coming out of the northeast. Captain William Manners knew that he had the smaller, more fragile vessel; his plan was nevertheless to use the weather gauge to advantage, position his brig so as to rake the enemy, and then quickly seize her by boarding. With that in mind, he double-shotted his guns with ball and grape.

From Abel Bowen's *Naval Monument* (1816), this print depicts the June 1814 engagement between *Wasp* and *Reindeer*.

M. Corne, p.

A. Bowen, sc.

As the afternoon drew on and the wind backed into the north, Manners positioned *Reindeer* so as to gain *Wasp*'s stern and opened fire. She was about to attain the corvette's vulnerable starboard quarter when Blakeley put his helm hard alee and, sliding his ship in the sea, came round with his starboard cannons firing. "Luffing athwart our bows," recalled one British seaman, "he poured in a deadly broadside, which mowed down our people like grass." The deadly hail of "langrage, swan shot, and other unfair pieces of missile instruments" wounded Manners in the legs, but as *Wasp*'s bow swung into view, *Reindeer* shot ahead and crossed the U.S. ship's bows, delivering a merciless raking fire. Yet those bows "were made of solid oak," another English survivor related, "which proved impenetrable to the *Reindeer*'s shot."

As *Wasp* continued her swing, her port battery came into play, catching *Reindeer* at a vulnerable moment. Then there began a work of destruction so severe that the British sloop was literally being chopped to pieces. As the vessels had now collided, Manners called for boarders, but as he hung in the main shrouds, two musket balls smashed into his skull, and twelve more reportedly riddled his body before it hit the deck. His boarders nearly succeeded, however. Eventually, they were bloodily repelled, and Blakeley, sword in hand, called for his own men to carry *Reindeer*. The Americans had won the day.

Only nineteen minutes had elapsed, but "the carnage was dreadful." *Reindeer* had twenty-five men killed, including Manners, and forty-two others grievously wounded. Both vessels were wrecks, but *Wasp* was in the better shape of the two. *Reindeer* was unsalvageable, and after a night and day of making repairs, treating the wounded, and consigning Manners and more than sixty others to the deep, *Wasp* set course for the safety of L'Orient. Behind her she left the smoldering shell of a warship, and when several Royal Navy sloops came in search of her, all that they found were the bits and bobs left floating among the waves after *Reindeer* had exploded.

MEN-OF-WAR

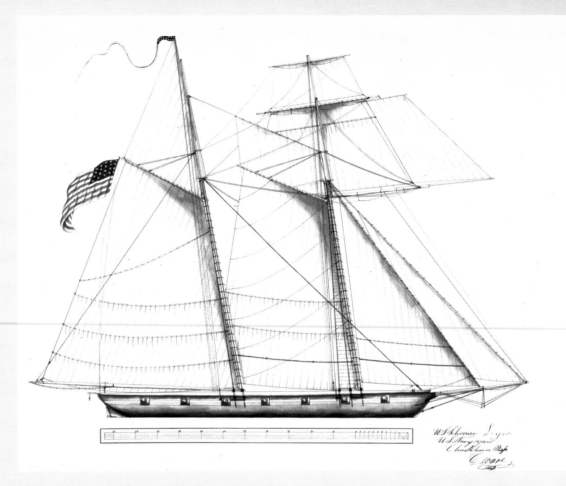

Early nineteenth-century sailmaker Charles Ware, who fashioned the sails for the ship-of-the-line *Independence* before she headed for the Mediterranean in 1815 under the command of Commodore William Bainbridge, created these drafts and drawings of various classes of U.S. warships.

Right: The schooner *Lynx.*

Opposite, top left: The spar plan of the sloop *Wasp.*

Opposite, top right: The brig *Spark.*

Opposite, bottom right: The sail plan of the frigate *Congress.*

Opposite, bottom left: The decks of the frigate *United States.*

The ships of the nascent U.S. Navy that won such renown in the War of 1812 belonged to several different classes widely recognized by the leading fleets of the era.

Having anywhere from two to four decks and mounting 64 to 120 guns, line-of-battle-ships, or "battleships," as a new abbreviation dubbed them, were the most formidable vessels afloat. These three-masted, square-rigged men-of-war were designed for fleet actions in which, lined bow to stern in single file, they might outgun by sheer weight of broadsides an opposing enemy line of battle. In 1812, when the mighty Royal Navy listed nearly two hundred ships rated at 74 guns or above, the small U.S. Navy possessed not a single one. In July 1814, however, the 74-gun *Independence*, the first of three such vessels authorized by Congress a year earlier, finally came off the stocks and slipped into the waters of Boston Harbor. Being the only ship of her kind in the American service, she had no line of battle to join and wasn't even officially commissioned until after the peace had been signed.

At sea, the War of 1812 was a conflict fought by cruisers, operating either singly or in small squadrons. The two-decked, three-masted, square-rigged frigates dominated this class of ships. Mounting between 38 and 60 guns, frigates were more powerful than anything afloat except for battleships, but they could easily outrun those cumbersome behemoths. With room to spare in their long hulls for six months' worth of stores, and with their admirable sailing qualities, these majestic and versatile vessels could range over the oceans, scouting or raiding as needed. The U.S. Navy may have been tiny, but it was strong in frigates, the 44-gun *Constitution* being only the most famous of the names that also included *United States, President, Congress, Constellation, Chesapeake,* and *Essex.*

Various smaller men-of-war, including brigs and sloops-of-war, were considered light cruisers. Though less imposing than frigates, they were more maneuverable in

tight quarters and inshore waters. Brigs featured only two square-rigged masts and were generally armed with between twelve and twenty short, powerful cannons of limited range called carronades. These graceful, all-purpose vessels included *Argus, Syren,* and *Lawrence.* Brigs were often classed as sloops-of-war, a name widely applied to any medium-sized vessel, whether square-rigged or fore-and-aft rigged, that carried all of its guns on a single deck. Smaller sloops might carry as few as ten cannons, while the famous *Hornet* carried eighteen. By 1813, American shipyards were building sloops-of-war large enough to carry at least twenty 32-pound carronades in addition to a pair of bow chasers. These ships, which included *Wasp, Frolic,* and *Peacock,* were powerful enough to defeat anything less than a small frigate.

Schooners were the primary warships on the Great Lakes. A distinctively American breed, schooners were fore-and-aft rigged on two masts, the mainmast being stepped almost amidships. Light and fast, they could sail into the wind and usually carried anywhere from three to eight guns. *Lady of the Lake, Growler,* and *Scorpion* won fame on these inland waters. Lurking in the remote reaches of rivers and estuaries were many of the 257 gunboats that Congress had mandated several years before the war began. Light of draft but able to mount at least one large gun, they could navigate shallows that no other warship dared to approach.

Finally, there were specialized bomb vessels or bomb ketches, their two masts stepped far aft so that mortars placed forward had clearance for their high, arcing trajectories. American bomb ketches included *Vengeance, Spitfire,* and—following the Royal Navy, which named their "bombards" after volcanoes—*Etna* and *Vesuvius.*

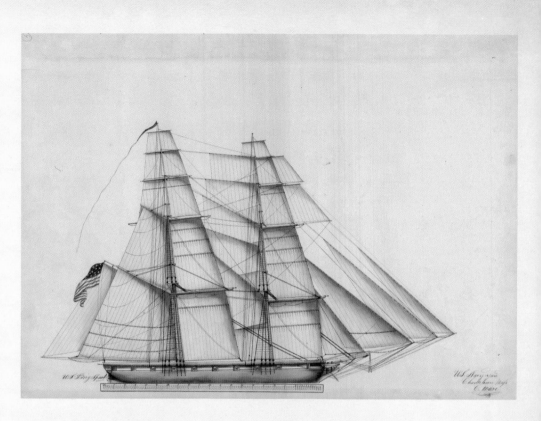

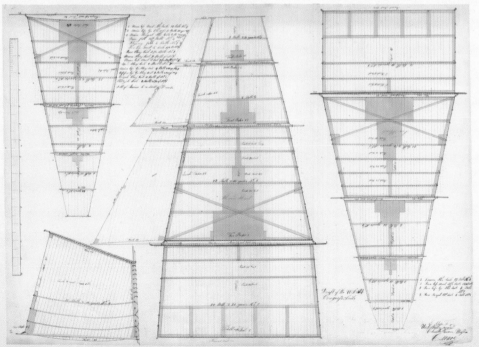

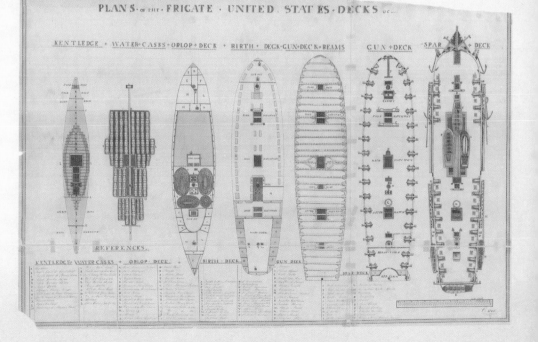

PLANS OF THE FRIGATE UNITED STATES DECKS &c.

KENTLEDGE WATER CASKS ORLOP DECK BIRTH DECK GUN DECK BEAMS GUN DECK SPAR DECK

REFERENCES.

KENTLEDGE & WATER CASKS ORLOP DECK BIRTH DECK GUN DECK SPAR DECK

An 1814 cartoon by William Charles lampooning Great Britain's feverish ship-building efforts in an attempt to recover after enduring crushing naval losses on the Great Lakes. In the center, King George III feeds a tray of miniature ships into a bread oven as two other men stand by with additional trays of ships and cannons. A Frenchman stands to the left holding a trough of "French Dough."

The dawn of a new year on Lake Ontario promised only more ice and snow for the thousands of soldiers along the front just trying to keep warm. Before the armies had ground to a halt, the British had retaken most of the territory that the Americans had won on the Niagara frontier. Only in Kingston and Sackets Harbor had there been no real change. In those places, the descent of winter had not slowed activities. On the contrary, the ice and snow were welcomed, as they meant easier transport of heavy guns and naval stores, which could be moved more quickly and efficiently by sleigh.

Otherwise, the chief activity in the two harbors was obsessively watching the other. Thanks to spies and deserters, hardly a spar was raised or a deck planked without the enemy knowing about it. Both Yeo and Chauncey realized, as did their superiors in London and Washington, that the first to build the most ships and get them out onto the lake would win the battle. The Americans were hammering away at several sloops and a 64-gun frigate, *Superior,* while the British had two frigates—*Princess Charlotte* (42 guns) and *Prince Regent* (56 guns)—and three large gunboats rolling out.

Each, of course, believed that the other was ahead—and had no compunction stressing, or exaggerating, that conviction in their reports. "[S]o short a time back as the 20th of January, not a keel was laid at Sackett's," wrote Yeo on March 5. "Now they have 400 Shipwrights, and two of their new Ships nearly ready for launching . . . The Roads from Albany, Boston, and New York are covered with Ordnance and Stores for these Vessels, which, when added to their old Squadron, will be far Superior to anything I can bring against them."

Three days later, Chauncey wrote, "They have two Ships caulked and decks laid—the materials for a third prepared, but not room to build her until one of those the most forward is launched." On whichever side of the St. Lawrence the reports were penned, the burden was always the same: send more men and materials.

On Lake Erie, meanwhile, American negligence had gone so far since the great victory of the previous September that when Master Commandant Arthur Sinclair arrived in April—Jesse Elliott having been transferred back to Ontario—he found the fifteen or so ships in bad shape: many of the hulls were still wrecked, pistols and cutlasses were lying in the bilges, 32-pound solid shots were scattered about the sand, and the damaged *Detroit* and *Queen Charlotte* were just lolling in Put-in-Bay.

The British, it seemed, were planning to reconquer Lake Erie by way of Lake Superior. By bateau and birchbark canoe and keelboat, they would work their way up the small lakes to the north and secure the lonely outpost on Mackinac Island. Then, on an even more remote wilderness river, they planned to build another fleet.

Lakes Ontario and Erie might have been, as Jones put it, the "great theatres of action" in 1813, but it would be the turn of Lake Champlain to hold that honor in 1814. While the snow and ice still gripped those waters, Thomas Macdonough was planning on rebuilding his fleet to counter the one being built by the British at Isle aux Noix in the Richelieu River. Jones warned him, though, that he would have to draw on the same Albany cache of guns, cables, anchors, and other supplies that Chauncey was exhausting for Lake Ontario. But in late February, Jones sent him Noah Brown, who promised to have five galleys ready by March 2 and then to shape the heap of timber lying on the frozen ground into a sloop. By April 11—remarkably just thirty-five days after her keel was laid—the 26-gun *Saratoga* was duly launched.

Meanwhile, Macdonough was considering converting a 125-foot hull intended for a steamboat into what would become the world's first steam-powered warship, able to maneuver independently of the wind. Concerned about a possible lack of spare parts, however, he decided to turn her into a 20-gun schooner instead. He was soon making real progress in building his wilderness fleet. By the end of April, he was rigging his flotilla, and the first guns and sails were finally arriving. His major concern, though, was manpower; he might need seven hundred men to man the ships—two hundred for *Saratoga* alone—and he had nothing even approaching that number by the time the ice began

disappearing from the lake. Meanwhile, the British had reportedly finished building their new brig but hadn't rigged it yet. "We are using every exertion to enter the Lake before him," Macdonough informed Jones.

Across the mountains, Sir James Lucas Yeo was the first to enter Lake Ontario. On May 5, his four ships, three brigs, and profusion of gunboats hove into view before the old fort overlooking Oswego, New York. At his side was the new military governor of Upper Canada, General Gordon Drummond, while arrayed against him was Master Commandant Melancthon Taylor Woolsey, a man used to facing long odds. Piled in depots beneath the fort's batteries were guns, cables, naval stores, and supplies bound for Sackets Harbor. Woolsey's rallying of the local militia and the fort's cannons had staved off destruction that day, but the following dawn the crumbling bastion, perched on a bluff above the lake, was no match for the 500 infantrymen and 350 Royal Marines who landed in boats, supported by naval guns and Congreve rockets, and stormed its ramparts. Besides munitions and naval stores, at least seven heavy guns were taken or destroyed. After torching the fort and parts of the town, the raiders departed, confident that they had just delayed the arming of the new frigate being built at Sackets Harbor—and ignorant of the more valuable stores secreted below the falls of the Oswego River.

Since Yeo could now blockade Sackets Harbor, Woolsey had to transport its guns and cables by night. Using small boats that could be hidden up narrow, foliage-cloaked creeks with the approach of dawn, he and a detachment of soldiers and Oneida Indians kept the vital supply line open. The British, of course, tried cutting it off. One night they did manage to capture one of his little convoy's boats, chasing the others up a stream called Sandy Creek, where the pursuers were promptly ambushed, the ten-minute gun battle resulting in the capture of six Royal Navy officers and nearly two hundred men. When *Superior* launched in early June, Yeo acknowledged that his blockade had failed and pulled his fleet back to the safety of Kingston. "[You] cannot act otherwise than cautiously on *the defensive*," Drummond had advised him. So while Chauncey in his new 64-gun flagship now ruled the lake, Yeo bent his energies to finishing one that should put him back on top, a proposed 80-gun ship-of-the-line.

The British were raiding on Lake Champlain, too. On May 14, fourteen galleys, three sloops, and the new brig *Linnet* sailed down the lake intent on destroying the American fleet fitting out in Otter Creek. When Macdonough heard that they were coming, he moved ten of his galleys down to the mouth of the creek, which he desperately needed to keep open so that *Saratoga* and the steamboat-turned-schooner *Ticonderoga* could escape when ready. So he managed to erect a makeshift shore battery on the point overlooking the creek's mouth. An artillery captain commanded the guns, which for an hour and a half kept the British fleet from approaching any closer than two and a half miles.

Soon, it disappeared back to the north, but not before Macdonough had a good look at that new brig, which struck him as being a "remarkably fine-looking vessel."

There had been raids and counter-raids but no decisive battle. Meanwhile, the costly work of shipbuilding never eased up—little wonder, then, that Jones, writing to President Madison on May 25, 1814, could kvetch that "one fourth of our naval force is employed for the defence of a wilderness, while our Atlantic frontier—our flourishing Cities, towns & villages, cultivated farms, rising manufactories, public works & edifices, are deprived of the services and protection of this valuable body of men, the loss of whom by any casualty would be to the nation a deep calamity." After all, on the Lakes the enemy could always choose his time and circumstances, but this was "[n]ot so in the ocean where twenty of his ships cannot check the depredations of one of our ships."

A contemporary print showing the storming of Fort Oswego on May 6, 1814.

THIS "IRKSOME CONTEST
OF SHIPBUILDING"

By summer, as the shadow of a pillaging British fleet moved remorselessly up the Chesapeake Bay, the war on the Lakes was proving only the more vexatious to Jones. A U.S. Army raid on Port Dover on the Canadian side of Lake Erie, for which Arthur Sinclair's Erie fleet provided transportation and support, degenerated from a mission to destroy stores and depots into a rampage that left behind burning houses and looted homes—actions for which the inevitable reactions would soon be visited upon Baltimore and Washington.

There had also been the exasperatingly on-again, off-again attack on the starving little garrison at Mackinac Island, the reduction of which was believed would banish the British from the Upper Great Lakes and finally sever their ties to the Native Americans. While the War Department dithered, two companies of Royal Newfoundlanders, with some seamen and artillery-men, climbed into thirty-four bateaux and crossed 360 cold, gale-swept miles to reinforce the garrison. By the time Sinclair's fleet, with its accompanying assault troops, landed there, resistance had stiffened, and every attempt to take the fort was defeated. The tiny island would remain with the British until the end of the war.

On the Niagara frontier, the armies just continued surging back and forth—the American tide flowing after the Battle of Chippawa on July 5, then ebbing after the bloody encounter at Lundy's Lane three weeks later. The blame for that reverse was pinned on Jones' most trusted officer, Commodore Isaac Chauncey, whose fleet never showed up to support the soldiers.

Chauncey had been ill with a fever, it turned out, but Jones was beginning to lose some faith in the commander of Sackets Harbor. He even had Stephen Decatur, still blockaded in New London, on standby to relieve him. Knowing the risks of failure, Chauncey—and Yeo, too—seemed less and less willing to risk his large and increasingly larger fleet. It was a "warfare of dockyards and arsenals," Jones grumbled, an "irksome contest of shipbuilding" that threat-ened to bankrupt the treasury. Chauncey had just launched *Superior*, an immense 64-gun warship that was larger than any of the Navy's storied seagoing frigates, but Yeo would soon complete HMS *St. Lawrence*, a 102-gun ship-of-the-line that would easily dominate the lake for the rest of the year. Chauncey wanted to counter with three ships-of-the-line. Jones refused, but Madison overruled him. Chauncey's quill was soon flying.

There will be required to build the Three Ships contemplated—600 Ship Carpenters—60 Ship Joiners—60 Pair or 120 Sawyers—75 Blacksmiths—25 Block and Pump Makers—10 Boatbuilders. 10 Spar Makers.—15 Carriage Makers.— 10 Armorers and 5 Tinmen—It will also be necessary to build 2 Blacksmiths Shops with Six fires each—1 Joiners Shop 1 Block Makers Shop 1 Boatbuilders Shed, 1 Armorer and Tinmen Shop—1 Powder Magazine—2 Wharves to launch over— 1 Rope-Walk with all the Machinery required to lay a Cable of 24 Inches.

The Quantity of Tools and Machinery required in the various Depart-ments would be better regulated by the Heads of the different branches that are to be employed here.

. . . I think it will be better to transport the Yarns and erect Rope-Walks here for the purpose of laying the Cables and Standing Rigging.

. . . It will be necessary to manufacture in the Atlantic Ports all the running Rigging Seizing Stuff—White Lines Marline Spun Yarn &c. &c. all Cogs and Pins for Blocks Anchors—Rudder Pintles and Braces, Iron Tillers Fids Hawse and Scupper Leads, Pump Chambers Galleys Bells, Cannon Locks, Powder Horns Match Rope, Magazine Signal and Battle Lanthorns, Rocketts Port-Fires Blue Lights &c. &c. Canvass Twine and Bolt Rope and whatever Shot and Kentledge cannot be furnished in this vicinity—bolt and bar Iron Spikes Nails and all the Tools which will be required in the various Departments.

Jones, daring to wonder if Lake Ontario would be worth it, only reminded the president again that, in contrast, "we have but three small vessels on the Ocean which to be sure are well employed and serve to enliven the spirit of the nation by the fame of their exploits."

THE FAVORITE OF FORTUNE

In March 1814, Admiral Sir Alexander Cochrane had put the finishing touches on the British blockade of the United States when he proclaimed that even New England, the only region of the country that had been thus far exempted, was now "in a state of strict and rigorous blockade."

Six months later, in early September, those who frequented Lloyd's maritime insurance exchange in London could peruse, posted there, a new proclamation, dated August 30. Scanning it quickly, they might have picked up certain key phrases.

> Whereas it has become customary with the Admirals of Great Britain commanding the small forces on the coast of the United States . . . to declare the coast of the United States in a state of strict and rigorous blockade, without possessing the power to justify such a declaration . . .
>
> I do, therefore, by virtue of the power and authority in me vested (possessing sufficient force) declare all the ports, harbours, bays, creeks, rivers, inlets, outlets, islands and sea coast of the United Kingdom of Great Britain and Ireland in a state of strict and rigorous blockade . . . I hereby require the respective officers . . . on the coast of England, Ireland and Scotland to pay strict attention to execution of this my Proclamation . . . Given under my hand on board the Chasseur . . .
> Thomas Boyle

The dreaded Boyle, the bane of British commerce, the privateer who in the first year and a half of the war had captured twenty-seven prizes with *Comet*, had been raiding in the English Channel with a vessel so sleek and fast that he easily evaded any squadron the Royal Navy sent after him. "She is, perhaps, the most beautiful vessel that ever floated on the ocean," as the clipper *Chasseur*, 16-gun "Pride of Baltimore," was once described. And with her, Boyle could show his heels to any frigate and feel confident and impudent enough to issue his mock blockade.

He and his one hundred crewmen, however, were not a single-handed operation. By this point in the war, the seas around the British Isles were not only teeming with American privateers but were also rarely without the presence of a U.S. Navy cruiser. Hardly had *Wasp* reached L'Orient in France for repairs and reprovisioning when Captain Lewis Warrington and *Peacock* arrived off the western coast of Ireland. After weeks of preying on commerce as far north as the Faroes, *Peacock* swung south for the Bay of Biscay, Barbados, and home, having taken fourteen prizes valued at nearly $1.5 million. By then, *Wasp* was ready to emerge again.

On August 27, she got the favorable wind that she needed and was soon back in the Channel, harrying every merchantman her lookouts could spy. In the first four days, the merchantmen all turned out to be neutrals, but things quickly changed. For those who survived it, September 1 proved to be a very long but exhilarating day.

The audacious proclamation issued by Thomas Boyle on August 30, 1814. Despite its outrageousness, British merchants didn't take it lightly.

brass cannons from Spain, all of which were soon emplaced at the bottom of the Channel, for *Mary* was set ablaze and burned to the waterline before she sank.

As evening drew on and *Wasp* continued to dodge *Armada*, several more sails were soon discerned. One apparently belonged to an American privateer that had been skulking in the region, while the others, it turned out, were two British sloops-of-war hoping to run that privateer down. *Castillian* and *Avon* were 18-gun sister ships—solid, oak-built vessels that for weeks had been scattering off the hordes of privateers infesting the British seas. Hoping to be the first to capture Thomas Boyle and *Chasseur*, they were chasing the unknown privateer to the southwest just as dusk began falling over the ocean.

Castillian was miles ahead of her sister when her captain saw, far astern against the duskiness of oncoming night, the rockets and blue lights that signified *Avon*'s distress call. They were soon followed by distant flashes and muffled thunder— the unmistakable signs of a sea fight.

There had still been some light in the sky when *Avon*'s captain, James Arbuthnot, first saw the unknown vessel that was then approaching him from the south. When she failed to answer his signals, he had beat to quarters and cleared for action. He had no way of knowing that the warship closing on him so fast was the same one that had nearly destroyed *Reindeer* only weeks before.

Shortly before nine o'clock, it had become too dark to see when *Wasp* pulled up nearly alongside the other ship, despite having had at least one shot fired at her while she approached.

"What ship is that?" hailed a voice from *Avon*.

"Heave-to and find out," Blakeley replied.

The only answer was another shot from the stern chaser. With that, Blakeley put up his helm and, surging up under *Avon*'s quarter, fired a raking bar-shotted broadside into his enemy's rigging, and the battle glimpsed from afar by *Castillian*'s captain began.

For nearly an hour, the flashing and pounding continued, both vessels crashing westward over the sea, sometimes yardarm to yardarm, sometimes

That morning, the horizon was crowded with sail, for a ten-ship convoy was passing several hundred miles to the south of Ireland. Blakeley didn't hesitate to wade into them, despite the presence of their escort, HMS *Armada*, a 74. Like the best of the privateers, he contrived to simply stay out of reach while still wreaking havoc among the merchantmen. One escaped him, but another, *Mary*, soon fell into his clutches. She was found to be carrying a veritable arsenal—

yawing to fire and to avoid being fired upon. The adroit British gunners—Arbuthnot had drilled them mercilessly—shot high, aiming to demolish their enemy's spars and rigging, while the Americans mostly aimed low, sending one 32-pound ball after another barreling into their adversary's hull. The dark of night and the heave of the swell, however, sent many a round shot plunging innocuously into the sea.

By ten o'clock, Arbuthnot was wounded, and a third of his men were dead or injured. His mainmast had gone by the side, and his wheel was shattered. His shrouds were in shreds and his bowlines all shot away. Yet when a voice from out of the darkness demanded his surrender, he still dared to send a few brash shots in reply. After *Avon* endured a few more broadsides, though, her crew hailed again, this time weakly. "What ship is that?"

"The *Wasp* to be sure!" Blakely bellowed in response. He had no time, however, to learn the identity of his defeated rival, for just then *Castillian* heaved out of the cloak of night, arriving too late to save her sister ship. With a parting broadside singing overhead, *Wasp* made good her escape, despite her tattered spars and rigging and the numerous 32-pound round shots lodged in her hull. *Castillian* could not follow. With water pouring through the holes in *Avon*'s hull, *Castillian*'s captain and crew didn't even have time to remove all of her men before she went under.

Whether *Wasp*'s captain and crew, busily splicing and knotting in the hours before dawn, were aware of it or not, between *Reindeer* and *Avon*, *Wasp* had just become the third ship in the history of the U.S. Navy—the others being *Constellation* (in the Quasi-War) and *Constitution*—to win more than one duel with an equivalently ranked opponent. She had also become the first American warship—and history would prove her to be the only one during the age of fighting sail—to accomplish that feat on a single cruise, making Blakeley the only naval captain in the War of 1812 to claim two such victories in the same vessel.

Two weeks later, off Madeira, *Wasp* took her thirteenth prize, the brig *Atalanta*, her holds filled with wine and brandy and fine linens. Blakeley sent her back to Savannah, but before the prize crew got underway, those men who could penned letters to loved ones. "The Wasp has been one of the most successful cruisers out of the United States," stated one such epistle, anonymously published in the *Savannah Republican*. "She has been the favorite of Fortune, and we offer thanksgiving to divine Providence for support and protection . . . The Wasp is a beautiful ship and the finest sea boat, I believe, in the world."

Before sending him away, Blakeley ordered the midshipman who would be prize master to avoid every sail he saw and then wished him luck, "as I firmly believe you will have a speedy and safe passage." It would prove to be the longest kind of goodbye.

THERE AND BACK AGAIN

Not every warship had the dash of a *Chasseur* or *Peacock* or *Wasp*. That same summer, the U.S. sloop *John Adams* was also roving in the neighborhood. A former frigate that had been cut down to mount 28 guns, *Adams* was under the command of Captain Charles Morris, who as the first lieutenant aboard *Constitution* had been severely wounded in the battle with *Guerrière*. Having escaped from the Chesapeake Bay on the night of January 18, 1814, *Adams* had been mostly at sea ever since, chasing convoys, eluding escorts, and taking and destroying prizes. By midsummer she, too, had arrived off the coast of Ireland, on July 4 chasing merchantmen into the broad estuary of the Shannon River. A few days later, however, just west of the Scilly Isles, she happened upon a British frigate, and another long chase, augmented by the appearance of several more frigates, ensued. Though he managed to escape them all, Morris had a worn-out ship and crew on his hands, so he made for home.

In the thick weather off the rocky coast of Maine, though, he ran aground on one of the offshore islands before struggling up the Penobscot River almost as far as Bangor. No sooner had Morris disembarked his crew, however, than he found himself fighting a land battle. On September 3, eight British warships and ten transports carrying some 3,500 troops sailed up the Penobscot to invade eastern Maine. So Morris removed his guns and set up a battery beside the local militia, but they broke and ran at the sight of an oncoming tide of bayonets. Thus, he was forced to abandon *Adams*, burning her as he left. Captain and crew then had to cut two hundred miles through spruce and fir forests to reach the safety of Portland.

Other cruisers, though, couldn't outrun their pursuers. On June 22, the U.S. brig *Rattlesnake*, exhausted after a long chase, had finally been captured off fog-bound Sable Island, south of Newfoundland, by the frigate HMS *Leander*. Three weeks later, and four thousand miles to the southeast, the U.S. brig *Syren* had also submitted—not to the leveled guns of a frigate but rather to those of a ship-of-the-line.

In February 1814, easing out of Salem to make her break for freedom, *Syren* had passed the fort guarding the harbor's approaches. "Brig ahoy!" the sentry had sang out. "Where are you bound to?" The first lieutenant had replied, "There and back again, on a man of war's cruise!"

That detail was remembered decades later by Samuel Leech, who only a year and a half earlier had been a powder monkey aboard HMS *Macedonian*. After Stephen Decatur had brought that defeated frigate into New York Harbor in triumph, the adaptable Leech had not only managed to escape imprisonment but also succeeded in enlisting in the U.S. Navy. By early 1814, his hair grown long and tied neatly in a queue, his dress and mannerisms carefully cultivated so as to blend in with those of any other American tar, he was a seaman aboard

A colored lithograph depicting the Battle of Lake Champlain. One shoreside spectator, a young lawyer by the name of Julius Hubbell, gave his account of the scene to a local newspaper: "The firing was terrific, fairly shaking the ground, and so rapid that it seemed to be one continuous roar, intermingled with spiteful flashing from the mouths of the guns, and dense clouds of smoke soon hung over the two fleets."

Courtesy of The Mariners' Museum, Newport News, Virginia

AMERICAN NAVAL SCENES

MACDONOUGH'S VICTORY ON LAKE CHAMPLAIN

Showing in the background the military action at Plattsburg, in which the British Army was defeated by Americans under General Macomb, September 11, 1814.

Syren, earnestly hoping that he wouldn't fall back into the hands of the Royal Navy.

Syren soon reached her appointed cruising grounds off Africa, though she lost her captain to disease during the voyage. With the first lieutenant now in command, she escaped one British frigate at night by casting off a raft of false lights and then racing off under the cover of darkness in a different direction. That had been a close call. Her next encounter, Leech recalled, was "not so formidable."

> She was an English vessel at anchor in the Senegal River. We approached her and hailed. Her officer returned an insolent reply, which so exasperated our captain that he passed the word to fire into her, but recalled it almost immediately. The countermand was too late, for in a moment, everything being ready for action, we poured a whole broadside into our unfortunate foe. The current carried us away from the stranger. We attempted to beat up again, but our guns had roused the garrison in a fort which commanded the river; they began to blaze away at us in so expressive a manner that we found it prudent to get a little beyond the reach of their shot and patiently wait for daylight.
>
> The next morning we saw our enemy hauled close in shore, under the protection of the fort, and filled with soldiers. At first, it was resolved to man the boats and cut her out; but this, after weighing the subject maturely, was pronounced to be too hazardous an experiment, and, notwithstanding our men begged to make the attempt, it was wisely abandoned. How many were killed by our hasty broadside, we never learned, but doubtless several poor fellows were hurried to a watery and unexpected grave, affording another illustration of the *beauty* of war. This affair our men humorously styled "the battle of Senegal."

The next encounter, however, was only too formidable. After running down to Angola, capturing along the way a few merchantmen—one ship crawling with a cargo of monkeys—*Syren* stood out to sea for the lonely volcanic peak of Ascension Island. That's where she met HMS *Medway*, a 74. "Of course, fighting was out of the question," Leech later wrote.

> It would be like the assault of a dog on an elephant, or a dolphin on a whale. We therefore crowded all possible sail, threw our guns, cables, anchors, hatches, &c, overboard, to increase her speed. But it soon became apparent that we could not escape. The wind blew quite fresh, which gave our opponent the advantage: she gained on us very fast. We shifted our course, in hopes to baffle her until night, when we felt pretty sure of getting out of her way. It was of no use, she still gained . . .
>
> The sound of a gun now came booming through the air. It was a signal for us to heave to, or to look out for consequences. What might have been, we learned afterwards, for a division of the crew of the seventy-four had orders to sink us if we made the least show of resistance. Finding it useless to prolong the chase, our commander reluctantly ordered the flag to be struck. We then hove to, and our foe came rolling down upon us, looking like a huge avalanche rushing down the mountainside to crush some poor peasant's dwelling.

Once again in the clutches of the Royal Navy, a terrified Leech saw among *Medway*'s crew old shipmates from *Macedonian*. Fortunately enough, he went unrecognized.

Finally, there was one special ship that never came back again. After November 4, when *Atalanta* slipped through the blockade into Savannah, all eyes expected to see *Wasp* soon follow. But she appeared neither outside Savannah nor outside Charleston or Wilmington, Johnston Blakeley's other preferred ports. Weeks, and then months, passed, but she never turned up anywhere at all. She had been sighted enough, though—or so rumor had it. From the Caribbean to the Cape Verdes, from the chops of the Channel to the "coast of the Brazils," came reports of a mysterious American corvette on the prowl, boarding vessels and burning prizes. They were followed by other accounts of naval battles in which an American warship was sunk. But no evidence ever surfaced—no broken masts or sailor's bodies were recorded as having washed up on some likely shore. *Wasp* seemed to have vanished into thin air.

The war ended without providing an answer to the mystery. Five years afterward, however, the log of a Swedish merchantman surfaced, containing what came to be accepted as the most reliable last sighting of Johnston Blakeley and his ship. On October 9, 1814, the master of *Avon* recorded being stopped by an American corvette whose captain was "Bleaky, or Blake." This was three hundred miles northwest of the Cape Verdes, though afterward the vessel was seen "making all sail in the direction of the line," meaning the equator, where a convoy might be found.

That final encounter was not far south of the area, stretching from Cape Finisterre in Spain down to the Canary Islands, where sightings of *Wasp* had been most numerous and most convincing—including tantalizing reports of an American warship sinking after a night battle with a British frigate off Tenerife. A battle-ravaged frigate was indeed said to have put into Cádiz, Spain, but an examination of available logbooks revealed that *storm*-ravaged frigates had put into the Spanish port that autumn.

And this, finally, suggests the most plausible answer, for despite tales of improbable ship battles in faraway seas or of warships wrecked on the African coast, with crewmen captured and sold into slavery, in all likelihood *Wasp* disappeared in a storm somewhere in the mid-Atlantic, where, caught during the height of hurricane season, blown over on her beam ends or toppled by a wave, she foundered, taking all hands down with her.

A WAR OF BROAD AXES

Back on Lake Champlain, summer had begun hopefully enough for Thomas Macdonough. By the end of May, his flotilla of gunboats was being squired across the lake's waters by two newly outfitted vessels: the 12-gun, schooner-rigged former steamship *Ticonderoga* and the handsome 26-gun sloop *Saratoga*. *Saratoga* especially had the potential to put him on top in the looming battle with the British for control of the lake.

Then the inevitable war clouds darkened his outlook. The British, he heard, were busily building another ship at Isle aux Noix, and this, it was rumored, was going to be a 32-gun frigate. They laid her keel in mid-June. More galleys were reportedly arriving from Québec, too.

That news presented him with a dilemma. Though by midsummer he had the run of the lake, having boxed his adversaries in the Richelieu River, the entrance to which his vessels were constantly patrolling, he would not be able to maintain that station every day. The lake's severe weather might blow him off, and he also had orders to cooperate with Major General George Izard's army, contemplating a move from its lines at Plattsburgh, New York. Whenever he did leave his station at the northern tip of the lake, the augmented British fleet would surely emerge.

His dilemma was whether or not to trap the enemy—if not in the river, then in the narrow confines of the northern lake, where the abundance of islands and peninsulas might be fortified and the extensive shallows and reefs might constrain his movements—or to build yet another ship—in a hurry.

He opted for a ship. Galleys might be less expensive and quicker to build, he told Jones, but they demanded huge crews—and skilled men were the greatest shortage of them all. A brig, on the other hand, might be easier to man. Macdonough began to implore the secretary for permission and resources, for rumors had it that the British vessel was progressing even more rapidly than expected. Jones had to give in, grousing, "I see no end to this war of Broad Axes."

But it was almost certainly too late. All of the carpenters had long since returned to New York, and even worse, the first of Wellington's Invincibles were sailing down the St. Lawrence. Sir George Prevost had decided to mount a major invasion of the United States, and he had chosen the Lake Champlain route for his advance. His legions would soon be on the move, and Izard was drawing a defensive line across the high south bank of the Saranac River, which flowed into Lake Champlain at Plattsburgh. A major battle was fast approaching, and there might be no time to build a brig.

Nevertheless, by mid-July Noah Brown and a crew of New York ship's carpenters had returned to Vergennes. What happened next was perhaps the most astonishing shipbuilding feat in a war filled with them: nineteen days after her keel was laid—while the British infantry was amassing at the border and the

caulkers were working on the British frigate—the brig *Eagle* was launched. Fourteen days after that—all of the sails, cables, cordage, anchors, guns, and shot having again been trundled across the wilderness—she was outfitted and ready for battle. At her helm was Lieutenant Robert Henley.

Confiance, as the British were calling their 37-gun frigate, was nearly—but not quite—finished.

On August 31, the first of nearly eleven thousand British soldiers crossed the border. Many regimental flags bore such proud names as Badajoz, Salamanca, Vittoria, La Corunna—the battles in which they had fought Napoleon's armies, first to a standstill and then to a victory. Rolling through the dust behind each brigade were the 6-pounder fieldpieces and five-inch howitzers of the Royal Artillery.

With one eye on that artillery, Macdonough assembled his fleet in the shelter of Plattsburgh Bay, where he would be better positioned to help the soldiers, now reduced to desperate New York militiamen frantically extending their trenches because Izard had been ordered to take most of the army across the mountains to Sackets Harbor. Word might already have reached them that their national capital had nearly been burned to the ground by another British invasion force. If they were to forestall that same fate being inflicted on New York, here was where they needed to make a stand, and both the U.S. Army and the U.S. Navy would have to work together.

By September 5, Sir George's vanguard was approaching Plattsburgh. There was still no sign of the British fleet, so Macdonough sent some of his gunboats to harass their line of march along the shore road. The soldiers simply unlimbered their small fieldpieces and drove the gunboats off.

What Macdonough could not know was that Commodore George Downie, now in charge of the fleet that had just emerged from Isle aux Noix into the lake, was being berated by a governor-general furious that his columns were halted because he had no ships to outflank the enemy positions on the Saranac. Because the Royal Navy wasn't ready, the army was delayed. Downie *must* do everything in his power to get his ships to battle.

Downie responded as any upstanding, long-serving Royal Navy officer would: he prepared to weigh anchor and hunt down the enemy wherever that enemy could be found. But he still faced pressing problems. He, too, had trouble finding enough sailors to man his fleet. Furthermore, *Confiance*, which should have been the most formidable vessel on the lake, was not quite completed.

So, as his flotilla sailed down the lake for its fateful rendezvous, past the unending lines of Wellington's battle-hardened veterans waiting beside stacked arms, carpenters were still working on *Confiance*'s decks, and because no proper gunlocks could be obtained, carronade locks had been clumsily fitted to her long guns, copper hoops used to bind them in place.

THE SIGNAL VICTORY

"Now, my lads, there are the American ships and batteries," Downie, having just returned from scouting Macdonough's fleet, told his officers on the lovely morning of September 11. "At the same moment we attack the ships our army are to storm the batteries. And, mind, don't let us be left behind."

The American ships were anchored in a line, tucked into Plattsburgh Bay behind the south-reaching point of Cumberland Head. From north to south *Eagle, Saratoga, Ticonderoga,* and *Preble* waited, starboard broadsides foremost. The gunboats were scattered in and among them. Macdonough was cool-headed, almost relaxed.

At about nine o'clock, Downie's squadron rounded the Head and, in the order *Chubb, Linnet, Confiance,* and *Finch,* came bows-on to the American line, its gunboats hanging back to the south.

Eagle fired first, the shot dropping short. *Linnet* responded with a broadside that did little damage. Then Macdonough personally aimed one of his long 24s directly at the oncoming *Confiance.* The solid shot smashed its way down the length of her deck, shattering her wheel. And then the battle erupted. For the next two brutal, bruising hours, each side hammered away at the other with increasing confusion. Initially, *Confiance,* though being punished by *Saratoga*'s guns, held her fire, and then Downie loosened a broadside that practically knocked the American flagship on her beam ends, felling scores of her crewmen. Moments later, however, a blast from *Saratoga* demolished one of *Confiance*'s guns, the dismounted barrel nose-diving straight into the British commodore, killing him instantly.

Meanwhile, *Finch* and the British gunboats battered the little *Preble* so badly that she could only cut her anchor and drift out of the action. *Ticonderoga* fought them off but was nearly boarded in the attempt. Then *Finch* grounded in the shallows around Crab Island, where an American military hospital was located, and the patients there turned their small 6-pounder on her. Helpless, she was forced to surrender. By that point, most of the British gunboats, manned by timorous Canadian militiamen, had fled the battle altogether. Its outcome, however, hinged on the four-way struggle between the larger warships. *Linnet* crossed *Eagle*'s bow, raking her as she went until, her anchor cables severed, *Eagle* slipped down the line until Henley could rig new ones. That

BATTLE OF LAKE CHAMPLAIN.—M'DONOVGH'S VICTORY.

opened *Saratoga* to *Linnet*'s raking, while *Eagle* saw an opportunity to fire at *Confiance.* Her steering compromised, she was also fighting at anchor, making the battle almost one between floating batteries. In the midst of this smoke and confusion, a falling spar momentarily stunned Macdonough. He was then knocked into the ship's scuppers by the impact of a severed head volleying into his midriff. But he recovered sufficiently to undertake a masterful maneuver.

A uniform coat worn by Macdonough.

Above, left: Naval battles have always been a favorite subject among scrimshanders. This whale's tooth, carved with a Battle of Lake Champlain scene copied from a Nathaniel Currier print, was brought home by the captain of the barque *Bramin,* which sailed from New Bedford in 1847. Scrimshaw gained in popularity after Captain David Porter's journal exposed the market and the source of the teeth. Sailing needles were the early scrimshander's tools, and his artistry was influenced by the movement of the ship. Improvised pigments were made out of soot, candle black, and tobacco juice.

Left: Sailing master Daniel Stellwagen, who took command of the third division of galleys under Macdonough on Lake Champlain, was awarded this blade for his gallant conduct.

Below: The state of Delaware, Macdonough's birthplace, presented him with this ceremonial sword and scabbard, made by William Rose and Sons and etched by John Meer of Philadelphia. The blade is decorated with the Delaware state seal.

MACDONOUGH

Macdonough received these gold-mounted flintlock pistols from the state of Connecticut in honor of his victory on Lake Champlain. A scene of the battle is engraved on the gold plate.

Right: A broadside celebrating Macdonough's victory. As Macdonough's friend, Commodore William Bainbridge, promised him, "Your victory on Champlain will be a bright ornament in our naval history."

A medal commemorating Macdonough and the Battle of Lake Champlain. A bust of the captain in uniform is shown on the reverse, and a general view of the action is presented on the obverse, accompanied by a Latin phrase, "Uno latere percusso alterum impavide vertit," or, "Hard hit on one side, undaunted he turns the other." The phrase refers to Macdonough's crafty rigging of anchors and cables to swing the undamaged side of his flagship around, giving him the edge in firepower.

Since most of *Saratoga*'s starboard guns had been put out of action, Macdonough cut his bow anchor and, hauling on his kedge anchors, which he had positioned in advance for this very purpose, now spun *Saratoga* around so that her undamaged port guns swung into action. Soon, she was shooting *Confiance* to splinters. When the British vessel's surviving lieutenant tried to pull the same move, however, he was unable to complete it, his kedge anchors having been fouled by shot. *Confiance* was left helpless, stern-first to the American guns, which raked her until she was forced to strike.

Hauling further on his kedge anchors, Macdonough spun his port broadside around until his guns bore on *Linnet*, pounding her so severely that she, too, was forced to strike.

The cannonading stopped. The smoke cleared. As Macdonough put it, "There was not a Mast in either squadron that could stand to make sail on."

Watching from the lakeshore, where an artillery duel had also been underway, Governor General Prevost saw the result and made an instant decision. He ordered that the buglers call the retreat. There might still be time, before the snows arrived, to get his army to Sackets Harbor and win a victory there. It was finished on this front. "Our hopes are now centered on the Ontario fleet," he wrote.

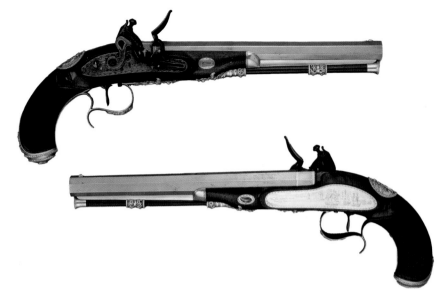

Ironically English-made, this blue Staffordshire china teapot commemorates Macdonough's victory.

The long lines of British infantrymen raised the siege and began trudging back up the road to Canada. They were so dispirited that many stragglers soon had to be picked up.

That afternoon, the devout Episcopalian Macdonough wrote a simple note to Jones.

Sir,
The Almighty had been pleased to Grant us a signal victory on Lake Champlain in the capture of one Frigate, one Brig and two sloops of war of the enemy.

By defeating a fleet, he had also, as the fading tramp of thousands of feet could attest, defeated a major army as well.

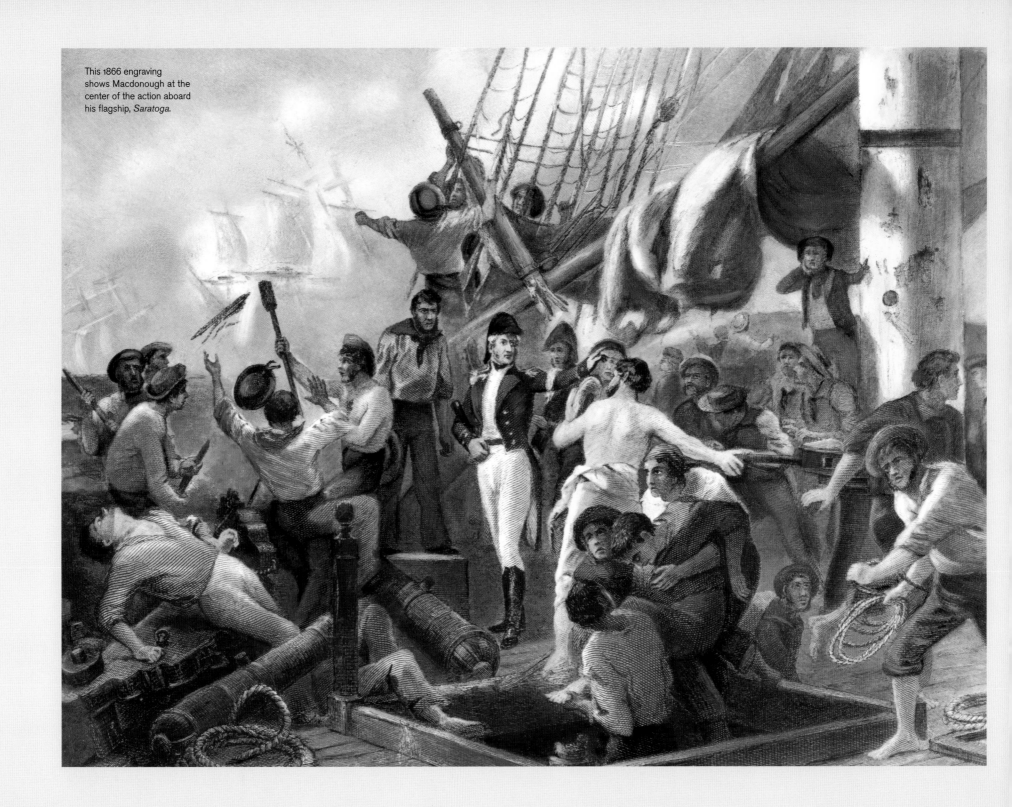

This 1866 engraving shows Macdonough at the center of the action aboard his flagship, *Saratoga*.

THE PROSPECT OF PEACE

Early in March 1814, attending a banquet in his honor at New York's Tammany Hall, a dutiful John Rodgers proposed a customary toast: "Peace; if it can be obtained without the sacrifice of national honor or the abandonment of maritime rights; otherwise, war until peace shall be secured without the sacrifice of either."

Could the commodore have known that six months later the battle for those maritime rights would be essentially abandoned, he might indeed have felt a little dishonored.

The war had hardly commenced in 1812 before the Madison administration, perhaps worried that matters had gotten out of hand, was putting out peace feelers. Only days before war had been declared—but unfortunately three thousand miles away—the British had suspended their odious Orders in Council, one of the two leading grievances that had led to the impasse. But the ships had put to sea by the time that news arrived in Washington, though along the northern frontier a cease-fire had soon prevailed, the British hoping that word of the repeal would change American minds. It didn't, because there had been no budging on the other chief grievance: impressment.

In early 1813, Tsar Alexander of Russia had offered to mediate a peace between Britain and the United States. President Madison quickly dispatched three commissioners—Albert Gallatin, James Bayard, and John Quincy Adams—to St. Petersburg, only to have them fritter away their time at diplomatic receptions because the British distrusted the Russians. London instead offered to hold direct negotiations, and Madison, accepting, appointed Adams to lead a contingent that also included Bayard, Jonathan Russell, and the young Henry Clay.

Meanwhile, a significant development had unfolded. Napoleon, crippled by his Russian disaster, had managed to fend off the forces of yet another coalition through most of 1813, but during the summer, one of his armies, which had been fighting the Duke of Wellington's redcoats in the Iberian Peninsula for five long years, fled back to France. And in the fall, his remaining army had been hamstrung at the colossal Battle of Leipzig in Germany. By March 1814, the Allies were marching on Paris, and a month later, on April 11, cornered at last in the palace of Fontainebleau, Napoleon abdicated.

Across the Atlantic, this news was received with considerable foreboding. It meant that Britain was at last free to turn its fleet and its soldiers against American shores. As the British indeed began laying the plans that would ripen into the invasions of the Chesapeake Bay, of Maine, and of New York, the Madison administration secretly dropped its insistence that the British curtail their practice of impressment.

While Rodgers and the Navy's other senior officers were awaiting their new commands—Rodgers was being given the 44-gun *Guerriere*, which had been

commissioned in June in Philadelphia; Captain Oliver Hazard Perry was slated for a sister ship, *Java*, still being constructed in Baltimore; Commodore William Bainbridge had been assigned to the nation's first 74-gun ship-of-the-line, *Independence*, which splashed into the water on July 20 in Boston; and David

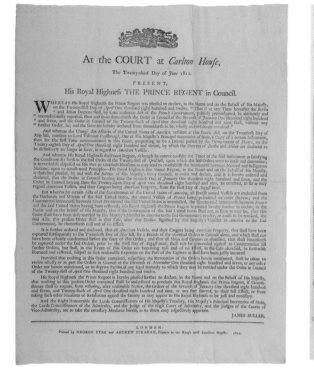

A broadside repealing the British Orders in Council, which helped to ignite the outbreak of war. Unfortunately, news of the repeal arrived too late—America declared war on June 18, and the messages missed one another in transit across the Atlantic.

A TRUE PICTURE OF A FIELD OF BATTLE.

An 1819 print by Londoner Edward Orme depicting the aftermath of the decisive Battle of Lepzeig, which drove Napoleon into exile.

Porter was soon to helm the revolutionary *Demologos*, the world's first steam-powered warship, being built at Noah and Adam Brown's shipyard—the American envoys prepared to fight the diplomatic battles, in August finally sitting down with their British counterparts in the old medieval town of Ghent, at that time still in the Netherlands because Belgium was not yet an independent state.

The British opened with a long list of demands, including the demilitarization of the Great Lakes, the cession of northern Maine, and the setting aside of most of the Old Northwest as a Native American reserve. On that last issue, the American envoys might have suspected their adversaries' motives, for the British had long harbored designs on the same territory. But despite the valiant stand of the little garrison on Mackinac Island, Perry's victory at Lake Erie had left the British effectively powerless on the Upper Great Lakes. They had no fleet left there, without which they could not hope to dictate the region's destiny. Eventually, therefore, the British delegates backed off of this demand, and the tribes were abandoned once again.

Behind the maneuvering were two countries heartily sick of war. The blockade had stifled the American economy, and the nation's financial system had been dangerously undermined. Internal rifts had widened to the point that Federalist-dominated New England, never keen on "Mr. Madison's War" in the first place, held a regional convention in Hartford to consider, it was rumored, the question of secession. Great Britain had been fighting France for more than two decades, and its leading diplomats were at the Congress of Vienna promoting the new "Concert of Europe." On the one hand, the news that Washington had fallen gave their representatives at Ghent additional impetus to push their agenda. The victories at Baltimore and Lake Champlain, on the other hand, heartened the Americans. As negotiations continued, the U.S. delegation adroitly staved off every British attempt to win territorial concessions or expand various rights, from fishing to navigation, vouchsafed in earlier treaties. Only on maritime issues did they give in.

Therefore, as the darkness of oncoming winter settled over Northern Europe, the diplomats' various gambits were gradually reduced to a single formula: *status quo ante bellum*, a return to the state of affairs existing before hostilities began. The banners proclaiming "Free Trade and Sailors' Rights" might as well have been furled.

Meanwhile, the war continued. By November, on the other side of the ocean, the third major British offensive of 1814 was getting underway. Nearly ten thousand troops, gathered from various parts of the empire, were being assembled in Jamaica. A fleet of transports was under sail. Their target was the Gulf Coast of North America, specifically that stretch from Pensacola to New Orleans.

PIRATES AND RAIDERS

On March 27, 1814, at the Battle of Horseshoe Bend in Alabama, Colonel Andrew Jackson of the Tennessee Militia so decisively defeated the militant Red Sticks that he brought an end to the Creek War and soon found himself a major general in the U.S. Army and commander of its southwestern theater. He was also not far north of the border with Spanish West Florida—Pensacola, where British warships arrived and departed at will, dangled like a prize just out of reach.

Jackson was quietly encouraged to march in and seize it. During the months he needed to reorganize and outfit an army, American officials privately worried whether the insult it would inflict on Spain would drive that country—neutral in the present conflict—only deeper into the arms of her ally Britain. Publicly, they chastised Spain for using Pensacola as a base for arming militant Native Americans in the United States. The Spanish merely retorted that the United States was offering a base for pirates who attacked Spanish commerce—meaning Jean Lafitte's Baratarian lair in Louisiana.

That was a good reason to sweep them out. In fact, Jones had already ordered Commodore Daniel Patterson of the Navy's small New Orleans Station to plan a raid on the Baratarians and had sent him the 14-gun schooner *Carolina* to help. Her captain was John Henley, returned from captivity, whose brother would helm *Eagle* in the Battle of Lake Champlain.

In the meantime, Jean Lafitte let the Americans know that he had been approached by the British. A certain Captain Nicholas Lockyer of the brig *Sophie* had landed at Barataria and talked with Lafitte, urging him to join the king's side. At first, he offered blandishments, but he soon followed them up with threats of force. In New Orleans, the question was whether or not this was for real. Would the Baratarians, with their ample fleet and their knowledge of the hidden approaches to the city, actually join the British? Was this instead a ruse to spring Jean's brother, Pierre Lafitte, from prison? Or to forestall a U.S. Navy attack? The station commandant merely continued his planning.

At dawn on September 15, Patterson's fleet of six gunboats and *Carolina* sailed out of the Mississippi and appeared before Grand Isle. Troops waded ashore, meeting little or no resistance and capturing but eighty of the hundreds of Baratarians usually present. Most had just faded into the swamp, including Lafitte, who had already secured the more valuable goods—mostly arms and ammunition—in case Lockyer returned to carry out his threat. Before melting away, however, the "pirates" had set fire to several of the ships in their mast-crowded harbor, and the smoke from those blazes mingled with that from the dozens of palmetto-thatched houses Patterson's men put to the torch. After confiscating everything of value left in the warehouses—some $500,000 worth of goods—they captured twenty-seven vessels—including seven schooners, a brig, and a felucca—whose ownership might never be traced, as well as twenty cannons. *Niles' Weekly Register* hailed the raid as a "major conquest for the United States."

Howsoever that might be, another conquest soon followed. In early November, Jackson marched four thousand troops across the border with Florida

and toward the small town with its mud-and-timber garrison on Pensacola Bay. The British force fell back, destroying one fort as it left, sails hoisted and heading for Mobile, but still managed to hang onto another. Were the British to invade New Orleans, however, their fleet would not be able to safely anchor there while their soldiers tramped dryshod through the pinewoods to the Mississippi.

Jackson had intended to move next to Mobile, to prevent the Royal Navy vessels flushed out of Pensacola from trying to land there. But he soon changed his mind and marched for Louisiana instead. Word had come from Lafitte, who had it from his agents in Havana, that a massive British fleet was on the way. On September 18, sixty warships had left England for the Caribbean. They were to be augmented by ships and troops from the smoldering Chesapeake Bay, as well as by some from the West Indies. They were heading for New Orleans, and for Patterson's little makeshift flotilla.

THE HURRICANE APPROACHES

Admiral Cochrane and his commanders decided that there was only one viable approach to New Orleans. Their ships couldn't cross the bar into the mouth of the river, much less fight its strong current and the guns of Fort St. Philip, and the failure to bribe the Baratarian pirates precluded a westerly approach through the swamps. Only from the east, through the shallows of Lake Borgne, might they draw close to the city.

But there was one obstacle: the line of five gunboats—Numbers 5, 23, 156, 162, and 163—that Lieutenant Thomas ap Catesby Jones had drawn up, anchored bow to stern, across the narrow entrance to the lake. With only twenty-three guns between them, Jones acknowledged that he would never stop the invasion. He only hoped, by cleverly withdrawing, to harry and slow it down. In the early light of dawn on December 14, he could spy through his telescope, far to the east, where the massive British fleet rested at anchor off Cat Island, the forty-five gunboats, loaded with nearly 1,200 Royal Marines and sailors, steadily approaching him, Captain Lockyer of *Sophie* in command.

Lockyer let them rest and have breakfast; then, at midmorning, he moved in for the attack.

Once they had come into range, Jones put those twenty-three guns through their paces, firing them as fast as his men could serve them. He got off five volleys, mostly grapeshot, sinking two of the oncoming boats and ripping through nearly a hundred British bodies before the boats closed in for boarding. Preventive netting failed to stop hundreds of men from scrambling aboard with pistols and cutlasses, many of them, including a wounded Lockyer, vaulting over the bulwarks into Jones' own No. 156. Shot in the shoulder, the American commander could not stop them from turning his guns on the rest of his squadron.

Mercifully, the hand-to-hand combat soon ended, with all the gunboats having been captured.

When word of the fight sifted back to Jackson, he struck the note by which the "insolent little flotilla" and the Battle of Lake Borgne would henceforth be remembered: "The conflict was dreadful, and in their fall they have nobly (from the report of the Spectators) sustained the American Character." Patterson, too, would chime in, predicting that the "action will be classed among the most brilliant of our Navy."

Despite claims to the contrary, Jones' doomed stand did not delay the British for a bit. Jackson, who had been expecting the attack to fall north of New Orleans, realized that the British were quickly approaching the city from the south instead. While he galloped sleeplessly about, ordering his scattered forces to converge, the British had established a kind of shallow-water depot, Isle aux Pois in Lake Borgne, and two of their more daring officers had discovered a route, winding from bayou to bayou, beneath gloomy cypress and towering gum trees, that opened eventually on a reedy canal crossing acres of sugarcane before finally spilling into the Mississippi. The officers might have simply strolled the nine miles up the river road running along the levee to reach the city.

The very next night, 1,800 men were moving up that same twenty-four-mile route through the bayous, led by Lieutenant Colonel William Thornton and accompanied by senior army officer Major General Thomas Keane. Thornton urged that they push on up and take New Orleans; an uncertain Keane ordered them to go into bivouac instead, awaiting reinforcements.

They might indeed have taken the city, for on December 20, Jackson's forces were only beginning to assemble. Nearly a thousand of General John Coffee's backwoods Tennesseans, having force-marched for 135 miles, were beginning to file through the city's iron-grilled streets, a picturesque sight in their ragged buckskins and fox-skin caps, their long rifles and their tomahawks. They went to join U.S. Army regulars in tall shakos and cross-straps, Louisiana militiamen, Creoles with inlaid fowling pieces, refugees from Santo Domingo, even some Choctaw warriors—all the citizen-soldiery, any man who was neither too young nor too old to fight, 2,100 altogether by the evening of December 23.

Most colorfully, and most importantly, were the Baratarian pirates. Old Hickory, who had once dismissed the idea of welcoming the "Banditti," was now in open alliance with Jean Lafitte—no doubt because Lafitte could supply cannons, powder, ammunition, and thousands of flints for small arms, none of which Jackson, the district commander, could obtain. He could also supply fighting men. Patterson, reduced to only two schooners, could now fully crew both of them, the Baratarians mixing with the tars who had been their foes only a few weeks prior. The entire U.S. Navy on the New Orleans Station was thus prepared to play a crucial role in the coming battle.

Opposite: Samuel Lovett Waldo (1783-1861) painted this portrait of Andrew Jackson in 1819. "Old Hickory" is wearing the uniform of a United States Infantry major general, circa 1814, with gold epaulettes and a red sash. Lanky and gaunt with arrow-straight posture, slate-blue eyes, and gunmetal-gray hair always swept back high above his forehead, he was a startling sight when he arrived in New Orleans on December 1, 1814, weak with dysentery and looking even more pinched than usual. Jackson had an irascible temper and was fond of expletives. "By the Eternal, they shall not sleep on our soil!" he reportedly cursed upon learning that the British army had landed and set up camp near New Orleans.

"INFERNAL MACHINES"
And Their Ingenious Deviser

On October 15, 1805, overlooking the Strait of Dover near Deal in England, a group of politicians and high-ranking Royal Navy officers watched as several boats placed a copper cylinder, filled with 180 pounds of gunpowder, against the hull of the condemned brig *Dorothea* just beneath her waterline. Fifteen minutes later, the clockwork gunlock fired, and *Dorothea* exploded, snapped in two, and promptly sank.

It was an impressive demonstration of what its American inventor, Robert Fulton, variously called a "torpedo," a "carcass," or a "bomb," but what history would know as an underwater mine. His idea was that the British might deploy a fleet of stealthy boats, approach the blockaded French fleet in its harbors, and send dozens of such weapons drifting in to destroy the enemy warships at random. Such weapons, he had persuaded himself, might even sweep the sea of conventional battle fleets. Prime Minister William Pitt, aghast, remarked that it indeed portended "the annihilation of all military marines." To this, Earl St. Vincent, a former First Lord of the Admiralty, later grumbled, "Pitt was the greatest fool that ever existed to encourage a mode of war which they who commanded the seas did not want, and which, if successful, would deprive them of it."

Fulton had every intention of making such a mode of warfare successful. A native Pennsylvanian who had lived for years in Revolutionary France (whose fleet he was proposing to destroy), he was a brilliant engineer and designer of canals who had grown obsessed with solving two technical problems: how to build a submarine and how to destroy a ship using underwater weapons. His torpedoes were one solution; his *Nautilus* was the other. The three-man, hand-cranked, screw-propelled *Nautilus* was the first submarine to successfully submerge, remain twenty-five feet in the murky depths, and reliably surface again. Fulton, some friends, and a lighted candle had proved it by spending many companionable hours together at the bottom of the River Seine.

Originally it was the French navy that showed interest in his devices, so Citizen Fulton had been granted an audience with a certain "Citizen Bounaparte." With *Nautilus* and some "torpedoes," the inventor believed, the French could not only destroy the Royal Navy blockade but also destabilize the British Empire. Napoleon, though, eventually spurned his offer. Fulton, an ardent republican, had anyway grown disenchanted with France's imperial turn. So he had crossed the Channel and promptly offered the British the same deal.

Six days after *Dorothea*'s demise came the Battle of Trafalgar, and with that overwhelming victory the British won full command of the seas and hence had no need for unconventional weapons. Crestfallen, Fulton returned to the United States, and there his fortunes turned around. First he improved the design of steam engines, making them more practical and efficient. Then he built the first passenger steamboat to ply the Hudson River between New York City and Albany. A young New Yorker named Samuel Holbrook remembered how Fulton "was looked upon as *certainly a crazy man*," but "when the wheels began to move, a tremendous shout went forth that made all ring again."

His country, though, would soon have every need for unconventional weapons. As tensions between Britain and the United States increased, Fulton, now a stalwart American patriot, arranged to demonstrate his "torpedoes" to naval officials in New York Harbor. It was only partially successful. Nevertheless, when war did break out two years later, the inventor wrote to Secretary of the Navy Paul Hamilton, proposing to pick up where he left off, and further suggesting that the government offer prize money for every British warship disabled or destroyed by weapons.

Two bills for *Demologos'* parts.

An 1852 lithograph depicting the ceremonious launch of the world's first steam-powered warship in New York on October 29, 1814.

Courtesy of The New York Public Library

AMERICAN NAVAL SCENES

STEAM FRIGATE, FULTON, the FIRST

Ceremonies attending the launching of an early American battleship at New York, October 29, 1814.

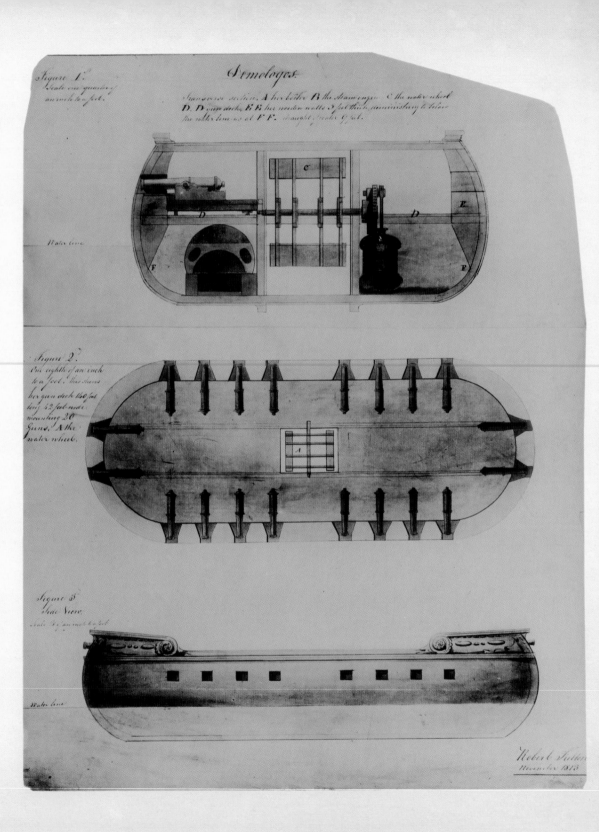

Above: A purchase order signed by Paul Revere for $6,972.70 worth of plate copper, which was used to make boilers.

Right: Dated November 1813, this drawing of *Demologos* by Robert Fulton shows her general arrangement.

"How can government get rid of 74 or 80 Gun Ships so Cheap as by this means?" he queried.

In March 1813, Congress did pass what was called the "Torpedo Act," providing a bounty equal to half the value of an enemy ship and cargo to anyone enterprising enough to blow one up. No one successfully did so, though any number of daring hopefuls attempted to. One was Elijah Mix—"an intrepid Zealous man," according to William Jones, who had succeeded Hamilton as secretary of the Navy. Mix, inspired by Fulton and with government assistance, planned to row out one night to an anchored British warship in the Chesapeake Bay, ease a torpedo in the water, and hope it drifted into its target. It took seven tries before he could approach one close enough—only the torpedo exploded prematurely.

The British were appalled that the Americans would stoop to the use of such "infernal machines." Admiral Sir George Cockburn, after his boats retrieved a bobbing mine, "commonly known by the name of Fulton's," sneered that his opponents clearly hoped to "dispose of us by wholesale Six Hundred at a time, without further trouble or risk." This was admittedly the whole point, though such randomly floating weapons, Cockburn emphasized, could just as easily destroy American or even neutral vessels as they could British ones. Fulton had once admitted it was indeed "barbarous to blow up a ship with all her crew …

but all wars are barbarous." Yet he also maintained that it was "barbarous to bombard Copenhagen, set fire to the city, and destroy innocent women and children"—referring to the British deployment of "Pyrotechnic arrows," better known as Congreve rockets, against the Danish capital.

As the war progressed, Fulton experimented with spar torpedoes, charges placed on the ends of long poles, that a boat could direct more precisely at a target. Though he himself had turned his back on submarines, a citizen of Norwich, Connecticut, tried building one so that he could attach a torpedo via spar to the hull of the hated HMS *Ramillies*, the 74-gun *bête noire* menacing New London, where the U.S. frigate *United States* lay blockaded. But the contraption didn't work. Fulton then experimented with "submarine batteries," managing to fire giant hundred-pounder columbiads, powerful cannons newly developed for coastal forts, while they were submerged underwater.

His next proposal, though still unconventional, was refreshingly above board: large, steam-powered frigates, able to operate on the high seas without regard to the wind. Though the Navy Department wasn't quite convinced that was yet feasible, in March 1814 Congress authorized the construction of a "steam battery," a mobile if mammoth gun platform that could maneuver at will to defend New York Harbor.

On June 20, her keel was laid at Adam and Noah Brown's Manhattan shipyard, and a few weeks later, when Samuel Holbrook arrived as a first carpenter's mate, her frame had been raised and she was nearly ready for planking. He found her to be a "novel and mighty" warship. Around 175 feet long, she had an enormous sixty-foot beam, for below decks she was actually a twin-hulled catamaran, the better to sandwich the central paddlewheel and its engine between thick protective oak walls. That design also allowed the "steam battery" to mount full broadsides— and what broadsides: "The guns, thirty in number, were to be columbiads," marveled Holbrook, "carrying a shot of 100 pounds: the carriage was to run on a slide, and they were the best constructed gun carriages I have ever seen."

So innovative was the vessel rising on the stocks that senior Navy officers couldn't resist pitching in with their ideas. To deter boarders, Commodore Stephen Decatur suggested ringing her decks with iron spikes. Captain David Porter, who took command of *Demologos*— "Voice of the People," as the still-unwaveringly Republican

Fulton was calling her—insisted that she also be outfitted with two ninety-foot, lateen-rigged masts as well. Day in and day out, though, Fulton was at the shipyard, and "it was very evident that he labored under a doubt about her coming up to his guaranty," Holbrook remembered. Nonetheless, "he was very agreeable and sociable with the workmen, and I thought him one of the finest men I had ever met."

Her launching on October 29, 1814, was a magnificent occasion. "It happened on one of our bright autumnal days, multitudes of spectators crowded the surrounding shores, and were seen upon the hills," Holbrook recalled. "The river and bay were filled with vessels of war, dressed in all their variety of colors . . . In the midst of these was the enormous floating mass, whose bulk and unwieldy form seemed to render her as unfit for motion as the land batteries which were saluting her. Through the fleet of vessels which occupied this part of the harbor were seen gliding in every direction several of the large steamboats of the burden of three and four hundred tons. These with bands of music and crowds of gay and joyous company were winding through passages . . . as if they were moving by enchantment."

As it turned out, *Demologos* was a trifle lumbering. The addition of masts and associated bulwarks and decking added greatly to her already substantial weight. The columbiads had not worked out, so she was launched with 32-pounders instead. And with a head of steam up, she could make just over five knots, not blistering speed but better than any sailing ship could do in a calm. She didn't finish her sea trials until 1816, long after the war had ended. By then she was no longer *Demologos* but rather *Fulton* (or *Fulton the First*, when further steam batteries were envisioned), named in honor of her inventor, who died at the age of 49 in February 1815.

She had but one day of glory in her fifteen-year existence, parading President James Monroe around New York Harbor one fine June afternoon in 1816. After that, she was either laid up in ordinary or used as a floating barracks for the Brooklyn Navy Yard. In 1829, she was

blown to smithereens by an accidental discharge in her powder magazine.

Nevertheless, she had been the first steam-powered warship, the first to be unshackled from the tyranny of the winds. "The advantages of steam over sail ships are beyond calculation," wrote Holbrook many years later, "and this was accomplished through the indubitable and persevering, yet unremunerated energy of Robert Fulton." The great inventor's predictions that such devices might change the nature of naval warfare would of course come true. A century after the War of 1812 ended, steam-powered battleships, underwater minefields, and above all (or below all), submarines were the dominant features of the First World War at sea.

An exquisitely detailed model of *Demologos*, part of the Naval Academy Museum's collections.

At dusk, *Carolina*, partially crewed by Baratarians, eased down the river. There was no wind. Soon the campfires of the enemy came into view. Soldiers had stacked arms and were cooking their evening meals in cauldrons liberated from nearby plantations. Astonishingly enough, they believed themselves to be still undiscovered. They even mistook *Carolina* for a merchantman or a British vessel that was slipping quietly into place. Only her masts were visible against the western sky as she anchored little more than a musket shot away. The moment was Patterson's to decide. Around 7:30 p.m., when full darkness had descended, he nodded to Henley, and *Carolina*'s gunners opened the Battle of New Orleans.

For ten minutes, she rained an unremitting fire into the bivouac, scattering men and guns and pots everywhere. "Flash, flash, flash, came from the river," one British officer remembered. "The roar of cannon followed, and the light of her own broadside displayed to us an enemy's vessel at anchor near the opposite bank, and pouring a perfect shower of grape and round shot, into the camp." In the meantime, Jackson's infantrymen crossed the thousand yards and pitched into their foe. The result was a bloody melee in the dark. Though the Americans pulled back before dawn, the British had been shaken.

Over the next few drizzly days, while both *Carolina* and *Louisiana* pitched a constant hail of shot into the enemy camp, Jackson's scratch army constructed a line of earthworks, reinforced with cotton bales and cypress logs, thirty yards behind the Rodriguez Canal, which cut arrow-straight across seven hundred yards of sugarcane field from a vast cypress swamp in the north to the Mississippi on the south. The city was only seven miles behind it.

On Christmas Day, the British received the gift of reinforcements, as up that twisting swamp path came Lieutenant General Sir Edward Pakenham, the Duke of Wellington's thirty-six-year-old brother-in-law and a highly decorated veteran of the Peninsular War. While Pakenham quickly assumed command on the field, the artillery commander he brought, Lieutenant Colonel Sir Alexander Dickson, wasted no time in targeting the nuisance that was *Carolina*. The next day, men were hauling heavy guns sixty miles through the bayous; they were emplaced under cover of darkness while a furnace to heat hot shot was erected. At daylight on December 27, these guns opened up on *Carolina*.

The lack of wind and the Mississippi's strong flow had prevented the two ships from sailing back upstream. Now that the British had brought up artillery, they were sitting ducks. Shrapnel quickly brought down *Carolina*'s spars and rigging, while hot shot seared into her hull and soon set her ablaze. Henley gave the order to abandon ship, and the men piled over the other side and quickly escaped by boat. Shortly after nine o'clock, *Carolina* exploded with a crackling roar, the flaming fragments raining down on friend and foe alike.

While the British were concentrating on *Carolina*'s fiery demise, the Baratarians manning *Louisiana* had set out in her boats and, before the enemy could switch its aim, were towing her to safety upstream, anchoring her anew in a position from which she could still enfilade any British assault on Jackson's line.

That line was now nearly a mile long and, on Lafitte's recommendation, stretched deep into the cypress swamp. Interspersed among the uniformed regulars and Louisiana militiamen, the "dirty shirt" Tennesseans and the Free Men of Color, the Kentucky riflemen and Choctaws and Baratarian pirates, were seven artillery batteries. Battery Number One, covering the river road, was manned by U.S. Army regulars; Battery Number Two, a little to the north, was served by gunners from *Carolina*; Battery Number Three belonged to the fearless Dominique You, Lafitte's half-brother and a former artillerist in the French army; at Battery Number Four were more *Carolina* men and Baratarians; and so on up the line, where even an ex-state legislator commanded one. All were armed with a motley assortment of 24- and 32-pound pieces.

On December 28, the British army advanced over the two miles of cane stubble as if on parade. It was the kind of grand assault that might have been launched at one of Napoleon's divisions. Both scarlet-coated officers and men regarded Americans with "the most sovereign contempt," as a young Scottish lieutenant, George Robert Gleig, put it. But that was before being caught in the devastating crossfire between the artillery batteries blasting away in front of them and the broadsides from *Louisiana* raking down their flank. The schooner fired no fewer than eight hundred rounds in seven hours, one solid shot reportedly plowing through fifteen men. Most of the British soldiers soon went humbly enough to ground; only with the fall of darkness were they able to retreat.

Because *Louisiana* remained vulnerable to the kind of attack that had destroyed *Carolina*, Patterson removed most of her guns and placed them in a fortified "marine battery" located directly across the river from Jackson's line. From there he could enfilade any further attack along that front.

Jean Lafitte's half-brother and partner in crime, Dominique You.

After that, Vice Admiral Sir Alexander Cochrane summoned his heavy naval guns. That meant his sailors had to row out to the anchored fleet off Cat Island, load the monsters, row them back through the bayous, and heave them into place on the last night of the year 1814. More than two dozen 18- and 24-pounders were mounted on logs in three immense emplacements. One battery was situated on the levee itself, where an enormous mortar was trained on Patterson and *Louisiana*.

Blinded by the darkness, neither the commandant nor anyone else in the American lines could see what was happening, but they could hear all the activity. Dawn on January 1, 1815, was then shattered by the crash of artillery. The sudden bombardment caught the Americans by surprise, but they soon enough recovered, manned their own guns, and began responding in kind. For the next three hours, a terrific din and roar, intermixed with the scream of Congreve rockets, rent the air. The delta literally quaked with the impact. While *Louisiana* stayed anchored out of range, Patterson's marine battery poured its fire upon those guns emplaced on the levee. Battery Number One soon joined in, and the British howitzers were soon put out of action.

Along the main line, Dominique You stood fully exposed on the rampart of Battery Number Two, directing a steady fire of round shot, chain shot, and canister; even the explosion of a nearby ammunition wagon didn't move him. At Battery Number Three, *Carolina*'s men gamely worked their piece. Along the rear, Old Hickory strode back and forth, visiting each battery in turn, doffing his hat and offering words of encouragement. "Too much praise cannot be bestowed on those who managed my artillery," he later wrote.

Gradually, the British fire slackened and died. Their hastily sited emplacements could not adequately protect their guns, which were soon dismounted. The thick American bulwarks, on the other hand, dense with packed earth and cypress logs, had withstood the punishment better. The British also couldn't maintain the kind of supply line through the bayous that Lafitte and his Baratarians, with their constant flow of powder and shot, could sustain with ease. The Americans had so many munitions on hand that they could continue firing all day, keeping English heads well down. Night again had to fall before the defeated Royal Artillerymen could retrieve their guns from the mud.

Over the next few chilly, sodden days, while Patterson and his naval detachment shivered alongside the soldiers in the trenches, another one of Wellington's favorites arrived on the scene. Major General John Lambert, accompanying the reinforcements, had been one of Wellington's stalwarts on the Peninsula. He had also been the older brother of HMS *Java*'s late captain, Henry Lambert, for whom a monument would soon be raised in London's St. Paul's Cathedral.

After nightfall on January 7, Patterson eased down the levee on his side of the river to a point across the way from the British camp. The noise of boats occasionally plashing into the water confirmed for him reports that the enemy was digging a canal across nearly a thousand yards of cane stubble to the riverbank. He was going to ferry soldiers across to the western side and then take Jackson's forces in flank. Yet after being apprised of this latest development, Old Hickory steadfastly maintained that the British were going to assault *his* front, not the ragtag elements positioned across the river.

But Pakenham's original plan was to cross the river, roll through the weak defenders stationed there, and head straight for Patterson's marine battery, which dominated the river road. Once Patterson was overrun, the British could turn his naval guns on the main American line, with potentially devastating results. Only there were not enough boats to ferry his 1,200 men across the river. Only 450 actually made it, and they got tied up and couldn't launch the attack on schedule.

An impatient Pakenham then decided to launch the main attack anyway. A Congreve rocket spun high in the sky as an opening signal. But, as Gleig recalled, it was not Sir Edward's day.

> Instead of perceiving everything in readiness for the assault, he saw his troops in battle array, indeed, but not a ladder or fascine upon the field. The Forty-fourth, which was appointed to carry them, had either misunderstood or neglected their orders and now headed the column of attack, without any means being provided for crossing the enemy's ditch or scaling his rampart . . . [O]ur troops were by this time visible to the enemy. A dreadful fire was accordingly opened upon them, and they were mowed down by hundreds, while they stood waiting for orders.

Every American battery seemed to erupt at once. "It was the most awful and grandest mixture of sounds to be conceived," Gleig remembered, an ear splitting roar that even seven miles away rolled like thunder through the streets of the city.

Right: Jackson's sword and scabbard.

Left: The uniform coat that Jackson wore in the Battle of New Orleans. Single-breasted and made of dark blue wool with four buttons placed lengthwise on the sleeves and skirts, it adheres to the 1813 uniform regulations. A gold star is embroidered on each turnback, and gold embroidery adorns the collar and cuffs. The epaulettes are made of bullion and gold lace.

Being British soldiers, they soon recovered their discipline, and a two-pronged scarlet wave began to advance through the smoke. The American fire only redoubled in intensity, riflemen standing four ranks deep firing volley after deadly volley. While *Carolina* and Baratarian gunners knocked out the British batteries, Patterson's salvos of grapeshot helped to ruin an attack up the river road. His 12-pounders then forced General Keane's brigade on the British left to edge obliquely toward the right, thus crossing the front of Batteries Two, Three, and Four, whose gunners only ran their pieces the more furiously.

Entire regiments were being chewed to pieces. General Samuel Gibbs fell mortally wounded, and those of his men who succeeded in mounting the breastworks were captured or killed. General Keane was hit and went down. Sir Edward himself galloped among men beginning to break under the withering fire, crying, "For shame, recollect that you are British soldiers!" An American volley felled his horse, and a bullet smashed his shoulder. Struggling to his feet, he seized another mount, but a few moments later he was again shot down. Dragged off and propped beneath an oak tree on the border of an American swamp, the Duke of Wellington's brother-in-law soon left this world.

General Lambert, left in command on the field, threw in the Scottish Highlanders, one of his reserves. Only Patterson's marine battery strewed the field with their ostrich feather bonnets. Then his guns fell silent. Thornton's 450 soldiers on the west bank had broken the few militiamen opposing them and were advancing on the double trot. Recognizing the threat, Patterson spiked his pieces, and with a heave, his men pushed them off the bank and into the river. Then they scrambled aboard *Louisiana* and floated out into the river.

Lambert called off the attack. Three generals, seven colonels, seventy-five officers, and nearly two thousand of his men lay dead, dying, crippled, maimed, or mutilated on those shot-torn fields.

Only thirteen Americans had been killed. And only half an hour had elapsed.

JANUARY 8, 1815. BRITISH (GEN. PAKENHAM) LOSS: GEN. PAK. & OVER 2000 Ke & Wd. AMERICAN (GEN. JACKSON) LOSS: 7 Kd & 6 Wd.

COPYRIGHTED 1890 BY KURZ & ALLISON-ART PUBLISHERS, 76 & 78 WABASH AVE., CHICAGO.

BATTLE OF NEW ORLEANS.

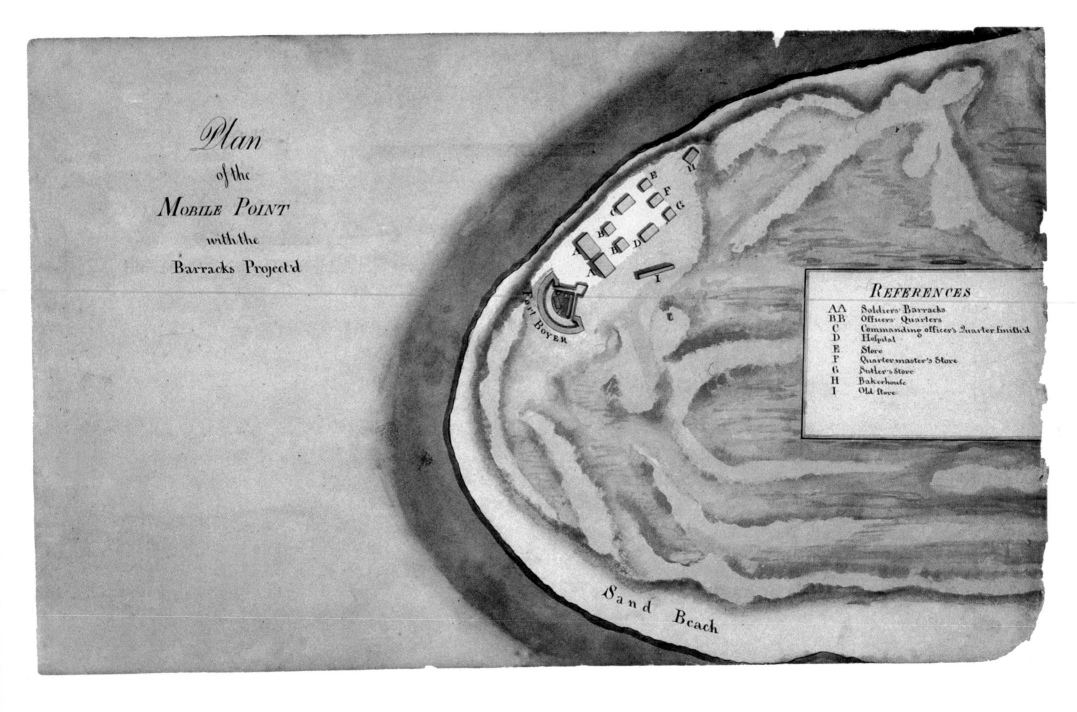

Plan

of the

MOBILE POINT

with the

Barracks Project'd

Fort Boyer

Sand Beach

REFERENCES

AA	Soldiers Barracks
BB	Officers' Quarters
C	Commanding officer's Quarter finish'd
D	Hospital
E	Store
F	Quartermaster's Store
G	Sutler's Store
H	Bakerhouse
I	Old Store

A SPEEDY DISMISSAL

Lambert waited ten days before quietly staging a retreat. Though his five thousand troops had all come up that twisting bayou path from Lake Borgne, they had arrived piecemeal. Now, though, with significantly diminished numbers, they needed to escape together. The boats would not be able to carry all of them through the miles of twisting channels, so bundles of reeds were cut and a kind of walkway laid across the swamp—which took nine of the ten days that Lambert waited.

Scarcely a month earlier, at the faraway Congress of Vienna, Lord Castlereagh had confidently predicted the imminent fall of most American seaports and the conquest of New Orleans. On the night of January 18, however, leaving straw-packed, scarlet-coated dummies behind on sentinel, the remnants of the British army were blindly slogging their uncertain way through a snake-infested, owl-haunted quagmire, crossing deep channels on cypress logs, following a dim path of reeds "resting upon a foundation so infirm, the treading of the first corps unavoidably beat it to pieces," Gleig recalled. "Those who followed were therefore compelled to flounder on in the best way they could."

> Not only were the reeds torn asunder and sunk by the pressure of those who had gone before . . . every step sunk us to the knees, and frequently higher . . . as the night was dark, there being no moon, it was difficult to select our steps, or even to follow those who called to us that they were safe on the opposite side. At one of these places I myself beheld an unfortunate wretch gradually sink until he totally disappeared. I saw him floundering, heard his cry for help, and ran forward with the intention of saving him, but I myself sunk at once as high as the breast . . . I was forced to beg assistance for myself; when a leathern canteen strap being thrown to me, I laid hold of it, and was dragged out just as my fellow sufferer became invisible.

Three weeks later, in an attempt to snatch some victory out of the jaws of defeat, General Lambert and Admiral Cochrane descended on Mobile, the first stop in a desperate campaign to ravage the southeastern coast in concert with Admiral Cockburn in Georgia. Fort Bowyer, which guarded Mobile Bay, fell to their combined forces on February 12, 1815. Meanwhile, Cockburn was writing to a captain in Lambert's army.

> I have learnt by a few hasty lines the unfortunate result of our first endeavors against New Orleans, yet excepting as far as relates to the poor generals and to the gross numbers you lost, I know no particulars, not even which of my many friends amongst you are dead or alive, or which have broken bones or whole skins.

SALEM GAZETTE OFFICE, Monday Morning

Treaty of Peace
signed & arrived !!

CENTINEL OFFICE, BOSTON,
February 13, 1815.

My dear Sir,

I have the pleasure of enclosing you a hand bill containing the happy news of the signing of PEACE, on which I most heartily congratulate you.

Your's truly,   GEO. CUSHING.

Mr. T. C. Cushing.

CENTINEL-OFFICE, Feb. 13, 8 o'clock in the morning.

WE have this instant received in Thirty-two hours from New-York, the following

GREAT AND HAPPY NEWS
FOR THE PUBLIC !!

To BENJAMIN RUSSELL. Esq. Centinel Office, Boston.

New-York, Feb 11, 1815—Saturday Evening 10 o'clock.

SIR—

I HASTEN to acquaint you, for the information of the Public, of the arrival here this afternoon of H. Br. M. sloop of war *Favorite*, in which has come passenger Mr. CARROLL, American Messenger, having in his possession

A TREATY OF PEACE

Between this Country and Great-Britain, signed on the 26th December last.

Mr. BAKER also is on board, as Agent for the British Government, the same who was formerly Charge des Affaires here.

Mr. CARROLL reached town at eight o'clock this evening. He shewed to a friend of mine, who is acquainted with him, the pacquet containing the *Treaty*, and a London news-paper of the last date of December, announcing the signing of the Treaty.

It depends, however, as my friend observed, upon the act of the President to suspend hostilities on this side.

I have undertaken to send you this by Express—the rider engaging to deliver it by Eight o'clock on Monday morning. The expense will be 225 dollars,—If you can collect so much to indemnify me I will thank you to do so.

I am with respect, Sir, your obedient servant,

JONATHAN GOODHUE.

☞ *We most heartily felicitate our Country on this auspicious news, which may be relied on as wholly true.*
CENTINEL.

And so do we——*Salem Gazette.*

Left: This broadside, announcing news of peace, was printed in the *Salem Gazette* on February 13, 1815.

Above: The American envoys' signatures, with individual wax seals affixed, on the last page of the Treaty of Ghent, which was handwritten on fine linen paper and signed on Christmas Eve of 1814. By the treaty articles, Great Britain gave up its claims to the Northwest Territory, and both sides pledged to work toward abolishing slavery. News of peace, however, spread slowly.

Opposite: Barthélémy Lafon drew this 1814 plan showing Fort Bowyer on Mobile Point. Included are soldiers' barracks and officers' quarters, as well as a hospital, store, quartermaster store, butler's store, bakehouse, and old store.

He added, however, that "an ugly account of peace being signed . . . seems to promise a speedy dismissal to us from this coast."

He was right. The day before Fort Bowyer fell, President Madison learned that the Treaty of Ghent had been signed.

ARMAMENT AND AMULETS

A broadside—the simultaneous discharge of all the guns ranged along one side of a warship—was the most devastating concentration of naval firepower in the age of sail. Once the considerable smoke cleared, however, the guns and ordnance behind it were remarkably similar from one navy to the next.

Arranged in rows along each side of a ship's gun deck were muzzle-loading smoothbore cannons mounted on wheeled wooden carriages. They usually stayed snugly braced and secured behind closed gun ports, but when the decks were cleared for action and battle loomed, the ports were thrown open and the guns were run out. These cannon came in many different sizes, being rated by the weight of the round iron solid shot stacked beside them: 6-, 8-, 9-, 12-, 18-, 24-, and 32-pound cannons accounting for most of the batteries. The heavier the gun, as a general rule, the larger the ship that carried it, but many of the guns could hurl their heavy shot several thousand yards. At closer range, shot was propelled so fast and hard that it ploughed through thick oak planks, dismounted enemy cannons, toppled masts and spars, and easily severed heads and limbs.

After each broadside's crashing discharge, the guns leaped back in recoil, straining against their rope braces.

The barrels were given a wet swab to extinguish any burning residue. Fresh powder, wadding, and shot were then rammed home. They were rolled back out, re-aimed, and again fired, the entire operation working against the heave and pitch of the sea. Well-trained gun crews could fire at least three shots every five minutes.

By the War of 1812, a dozen men might serve a single gun in the U.S. Navy, twice the number assigned in the Royal Navy. The Americans often displayed more accurate gunnery, due no doubt to drills involving live firing. The British, hampered by official restrictions on the use of powder, too often had to practice by merely running the guns in and out and hoping that would suffice when real action came. And the American frigates generally mounted 24-pounders, which had a much greater shattering effect than did the 18-pounders usually found on British ones. On the U.S. frigate *President*, each gun crew individually named its particular cannon, often in honor of a famous patriot, a practice probably observed on other vessels, too.

These "long guns," as they were sometimes called, were supplemented by squat, short-barreled ones called carronades. The War of 1812 might have been the heyday of these "smashers," both sides deploying them in large numbers. They took up less room, could be served by a smaller crew, and

since they were comparatively light, they could be placed on the topmost deck without making a vessel unwieldy. Yet they could still hurl a heavy 24-, 32-, or even 46-pound shot—but only so far. The carronade's chief drawback was its shorter range when compared to that of long guns, as Captain David Porter of the U.S. frigate *Essex* discovered to his dismay on March 28, 1814. *Essex* was one of the few American frigates to be armed almost exclusively with carronades. Having left her haven at Valparaíso, Chile, *Essex* was surrounded by British warships that stood conveniently out of range, pounding the American vessel with their longer reach until, having lost nearly half his crew, Porter was forced to surrender, having barely damaged his opponents.

A wood-and-iron model of a 32-pounder on a wooden, four-wheeled carriage. It is fitted with a lever and tracks on the rear of the carriage for lifting the rear truck from the deck to reduce the labor of traversing.

Simeon North Pistol, 1808. The Navy had been using the same make of pistol since its inception in 1797, and many different contractors were hired to make these pistols, generally in small batches. In 1808, the Navy sent a prototype of a new pistol to Simeon North, a farmer by birth who ran a small scythe-making shop out of an old mill. After suggesting some of his own changes and obtaining their approval, North signed a contract with the Navy for 2,000 pistols at $5.87½ per pistol. The gun has a belt hook, which was standard issue on this type of pistol, though many were removed. The cracks in the handle were common, as it was the weak point in this pistol's design. One of North's changes was adding reinforcement to the grip, and this is probably all that kept this gun from breaking entirely.

Grapeshot, which was often used in carronades and usually pre-packed, scattering as it left the gun muzzle. Each iron ball is larger than two inches around.

Left: This Bible, published in 1813 by Hudson & Goodwin of Hartford and distributed by the Nassau Hall Bible Society, was taken from USS *President* after her capture. British seaman William Clark was among those who boarded the defeated frigate, and he found this holy book tucked into the cheekpiece of the carriage of a gun named for General Richard Montgomery, who perished during the attack on Québec in December 1775. It has been said that "there are no Sundays off soundings," meaning that at sea, few sailors adhered to the strictures of religious teaching. The Reverend Edward Mangin, chaplain of HMS *Gloucester* in 1812, even wrote that "nothing can possibly be more unsuitably or more awkwardly situated than a clergyman in a ship of war; every object around him is at variance with the sensibilities of a rational and enlightened mind." This Bible would seem to be at odds with these sentiments. It's not hard to imagine the gun crew reading from it during the long, tense hours of the chase. Even if they never cracked the covers, which had been wrapped in linen duck, the Bible's presence on the engine of destruction turned the book into an amulet of sorts.

Below: Nathan Starr cutlass, 1808. Starr, of Connecticut, acquired the contract to make cutlasses for the Navy in 1808, and he was commissioned to produce 2,000 of them, very few of which still exist. Edged weapons and small arms, such as the Simeon North pistol, were crucial to close-range naval warfare.

Long gun or carronade, as fighting ships drew nearer, the cannons might be double- or even triple-shotted for maximum demolition. They might be charged with grapeshot—a package of nine iron balls, each greater than two inches in diameter, that when fired flew apart and scattered in a deadly hail that might tear enemy sailors or boarders to pieces. Or they might be loaded with chain shot or bar shot—packages of small iron balls united by short chains or solid bars that hurtled out like so many spinning blades to shred rigging and knock down spars. On January 15, 1815, as the U.S. brig *President*

desperately fought off the assaults of HMS *Endymion*, Captain Stephen Decatur charged his guns with what was called "dismantling shot," iron bars joined by rings at their ends, which stripped the British sails from their yards but failed to topple a single spar.

After darkness fell, *President* was finally cornered by HMS *Pomone* and, already battered by *Endymion*'s 24-pounders, was subjected to another point-blank broadside. With all three of his lieutenants and more than twenty other crewmen killed, Decatur, badly wounded by a splinter, surrendered. A member of the British boarding party

found on *President*'s shredded gun deck a Bible tucked into a gun carriage. Quite likely, each gun had been issued its own Bible; many had been dispatched throughout the fleet by religious organizations bent on improving sailors' notoriously lax morals. The sailors, however, knowing that they would eventually be on both the receiving and delivery ends of all this fearsome ordnance, their gun deck turned into a chaos of careening grape and solid shot and splinters, apparently put those Bibles to a more practical use. Not trusting the protection of their wooden walls alone, perhaps they hoped for some divine safekeeping as well.

A wood-and-brass model of a carronade. These short-range guns were introduced in 1778 and known in the Royal Navy as "smashers."

Swivel Howitzer, circa 1797. This three-inch bore gun was possibly cast by Paul Revere. Many first-hand accounts document guns like this one being used "for the ship's tops" on USS *Constitution* and other frigates. From this high perch, they would be fired down on the opposing crew. Some reports suggest that American frigates would also mount them on the front of their boats like carronades. While Howitzers could fire grenades, one of this size would have been used like a big shotgun, firing canister or grapeshot.

THE PRESIDENT AT LAST

Peace.

Stephen Decatur had not been to war—or to sea—since 1812. For two long years, he had paced the deck of *United States*, his frigate, securely bottled up in Connecticut's Thames River. Most of the guns and crew of *Macedonian* had been sent to Sackets Harbor; Decatur nearly had, too, when Isaac Chauncey had fallen ill. Since there was little prospect of ever freeing *United States*, Decatur and his crew had been transferred to *President*, Rodgers' old faithful ship. Though she was similarly blockaded in New York, she had a better chance of escaping.

By mid-December 1814, a formidable little squadron had gathered in New York Harbor. *President,* along with the powerful sloops *Peacock* and *Hornet*, was waiting for winter gales to blow the British blockaders off station. Only then could they escape and strike out for the South Atlantic. Nearly a month passed, however, before a suitable blizzard came roaring out of the northwest. That's when an increasingly impatient Decatur decided to make his break. On the night of January 13, 1815, her commodore having agreed to rendezvous with Warrington and Biddle at distant Tristan da Cunha, *President* weighed anchor and, gambling that the powerful razee HMS *Majestic* and the frigates *Endymion, Pomone,* and *Tenedos*, had been blown far to the southeast, Decatur made for the open sea.

He probably would have made it had not the harbor pilots failed to clearly mark the harbor's exit. With a sickening crunch, *President* grounded on the bar. There she remained for nearly two hours, pounded relentlessly by the sea, before her laboring crew was able to free her. But the damage had been done: some of her masts had sprung and her hull had hogged, the center of her keel having been bent upward. There was no turning again for port, however, as the same gale that blew the blockaders off station was pushing *President* to sea, too. The crippled frigate had to make a run for it, whether her legendary sailing qualities had been undermined or not.

Decatur chose to hold close to the south shore of Long Island. A clouded winter dawn was just lightening the Atlantic when, out on *President's* starboard quarter, the first British cruiser appeared.

The blockading ships had not been pushed that far off. They had quickly beat their way back, suspecting that American warships might have escaped on the wings of the storm. It was a bad moment for Decatur; his only chance lay in outrunning what turned out to be *Majestic*. He immediately hurled stores and boats overboard and started his water, but *President* had been fatally crippled, and she just could not make way. Soon, the speedy *Pomone* was gaining on her, but then she hauled off to investigate a strange sail to the south. As cloudy morning turned to dark afternoon and the wind continued dropping, *President* continued slowing, and now it was *Endymion,* the fastest frigate of them all, that overtook her.

They were soon exchanging shots, and by dusk *Endymion* began yawing, loosening broadsides into *President's* vulnerable starboard quarter, regaining her position, and then repeating the maneuver. As his ship shuddered and splintered from the impact of *Endymion's* 24-pounders, Decatur's options began to run out. In the darkness, the Long Island shore to the north was simply too close for him to maneuver in that direction. So after a third broadside smashed through his bulwarks and carried off his men, Decatur turned the helm to starboard and crossed *Endymion's* bows. The nimble British frigate merely matched his move, and the two ships headed south, flashing and thundering across the dark Atlantic as broadside was exchanged for broadside. Decatur had his surviving gunners charge their pieces with dismantling shot and fire it into *Endymion's* rigging, tearing up ropes and sails and sending spars spinning down to the deck.

That finally slowed *Endymion*, but even running with the wind *President* was simply too damaged to go much farther. Decatur had already acknowledged the inevitable when, two hours later, *Pomone* hove out of the blackness. Scarcely could he hail surrender before *Pomone* was firing two point-blank broadsides into his shattered hull. Only a lantern hauled down from the stern convinced the British crew that the legendary *President* had at last been taken.

It had been a costly gamble. Decatur himself had been wounded by a flying splinter. Three of his lieutenants had been among the twenty-four men killed, and another fifty-five were wounded or dying. The wrecked ship was taken to Bermuda, where the commodore and his surviving crewmen were slapped in prison. They were released soon enough when peace was ratified, but *President*, John Rodgers' favorite frigate, was taken into the Royal Navy—only to be broken up three years later.

A BRACE OF SLOOPS

Peace.

It was one of the ironies of war that the most remarkable instance of naval combat occurred after the war had officially ended.

Charles Stewart had heard about the signing of the Treaty of Ghent while detaining neutral merchantmen in the sea west of Portugal. It was early February, and cold, but in lieu of orders to the contrary, and with no certain knowledge that the rumored treaty had been ratified, he continued with his cruise.

Back in December, after nine months of watchful waiting, the winter gales had opened a hole in the British blockade, and *Constitution* once more escaped Boston Harbor. In the succeeding weeks, she had captured but two prizes, one of which—*Lord Nelson*—had stores ample enough to provide Stewart's crew with a Christmas dinner, for he had left so quickly that he was not able to stow enough supplies. The other, *Susanna*, had a cargo of animal skins and apparently two live jaguars as well.

By February 20, *Constitution* was off Madeira, running with a north wind but heading for the tropic sun when, off to the south, her lookouts spied a sail.

As was usual when an inviting target appeared, Stewart made chase, but he had lost a main royal mast, and that slowed *Constitution* somewhat. Before she could close the distance, her lookouts spied another sail. Both, it turned out, were British sloops-of-war—HMS *Cyane* and *Levant*, which had been escorting a pair of convoys from Gibraltar.

They had drawn close to each other, exchanging signals; their respective captains knew what they were up against, but they hoped that together they might cripple the big American frigate and escape into the oncoming night. *Constitution*, meanwhile, was still holding the weather gauge and swiftly narrowing the gap. The British sloops, *Levant* in front and *Cyane* lined up behind her, went to fighting sails. All three vessels were now on a westward course, the wind on their starboard beam. Evening was beginning to fall.

Then the broadsides began. Back and forth they rumbled over the sea. *Cyane* and *Levant* were both mainly armed with 32-pound carronades, while *Constitution* had 24-pound long guns. She had the advantage of longer range, and her captain would make the most of it. He first had to let the smoke of the initial exchanges dissipate in order to determine his position. He had pulled even with *Levant*, which meant that *Cyane* was preparing to luff up into the wind and cross *Constitution*'s stern, where she might level a devastating broadside.

Only the quickest-thinking of captains and most responsive of crews could pull off what happened next. Stewart fired his port broadside into *Levant*, immediately backed sail so that he fell back to *Cyane*, and fired a remarkably fast second port broadside at her. Then, as *Levant* turned to rake his bow, he wore ship to port, passed between his antagonists, raked *Levant*'s stern instead, and while still turning came under *Cyane*'s port quarter and stern and let her have it.

TIGERS.

THE Ladies and Gentlemen of *Worcester* and its vicinity,

are informed that

Two Royal Brazilian TIGERS,

Remarkably Elegant and Docile, taken by the U. S. frigate Constitution, out of the ship Susannah, will be Exhibited at *Capt Burleans Tavern* *on Friday oct gon the 56*

To gratify the curiosity of those who may desire to see the Monarchs of this Continent.

Admittance, 12 C

And let her have it until her captain struck.

Dusk was falling over the sea. *Levant* had drawn off to make emergency repairs, but no sooner had Stewart manned *Cyane* with a prize crew than she was returning on the attack. Stewart could only charge her in return. They passed within pistol shot of each other, broadsides flaming. Staggered, *Levant* turned into the darkness, attempting to flee, only to be raked from stern to forecastle. Somehow, she still kept going, for two more hours, until Old Ironsides ran her down.

And Old Ironsides she proved herself again to be: a dozen 32-pound solid shots were found lodged in her hull. She had not suffered much more damage than that. "The whole of this business," wrote Assheton Humphreys, one of her

Edward Savage, owner of the "New York Museum," part museum, part gallery, opened in Boston's Boylston Market, ran this advertisement in the *Columbian Centinel* announcing the exhibition of the two big cats corralled off *Susanna* and taken aboard *Constitution* in December 1814.

sailors, "occupied about three hours, only forty-five minutes of which were taken up in compelling both ships to yield to our superior gunnery. The *Cyane* when she struck had five feet of water in the hold and [was] otherwise very much cut up, her masts tottering and nothing but the smoothness of the sea preventing them from going over the side. The *Levant* [was] in a condition somewhat better, her spars having generally escaped, but her hull pretty well drilled and her deck a perfect slaughterhouse."

It was only weeks later, on April 2, 1815, when *Constitution* had put into Maranhão, Brazil, that Stewart finally learned the Treaty of Ghent had indeed been ratified and that it was time now to go home.

FINAL SHOTS AT THE BOTTOM OF THE WORLD

On January 23, 1815, nearly a month to the day after the "Peace of Christmas Eve" had been signed—but two weeks before that news had crossed the ocean—three more U.S. Navy vessels slipped out of New York Harbor and ran the blockade. Lewis Warrington with the corvette *Peacock* was accompanied by James Biddle with the sloop *Hornet* and by a tender, *Tom Bowline*, as well, for they were expecting a long cruise in the East Indies alongside Stephen Decatur and *President*. Their orders had been among the last official documents signed by the outgoing secretary, William Jones—who was returning to private life—before he had turned over the office to Benjamin Crowninshield in December.

As they stood out to sea, no officer aboard the three vessels had any idea that Decatur and *President* had been captured. They only knew that they were to rendezvous some seven thousand miles away, at distant Tristan da Cunha, one of the small volcanic islands rearing their crests above the vast and lonely South Atlantic.

During the weeks it took the ships to pass those windswept, wave-lashed rocks—Ascension and St. Helena—two bits of joyous news had engulfed their country. It had been mid-January before Washington had any inkling that a massive British invasion force was menacing New Orleans. For weeks, everyone was on tenterhooks awaiting news of developments. Surely, the British had taken that key to the Mississippi River and would soon be in control of the entire Mississippi Valley. It wasn't until February 4 that word reached the capital: Andrew Jackson had not only turned the British back but also destroyed their army, strewing the fields with redcoated dead. People were at first incredulous, disbelieving. Disbelief soon turned to elation and elation to euphoria. The tidings of victory spread like wildfire throughout the country. Mass celebrations spontaneously erupted, and Shakespeare's line from *Henry VI*—"Rescued is Orleans from the English wolves"—appeared over and over again in the nation's papers. When *Favorite* arrived in New York Harbor eleven days later on February 15, bringing the breathless news that a peace treaty had been signed, and that the country would lose none of its territory, and that the war was over, euphoria became rapture. Congress then ratified the agreement, and everywhere the joyous pealing of bells rang through cities and towns illuminated by torchlight parades.

By then, *Peacock* and *Hornet* were approaching their destination. *Hornet* was the first to arrive off Tristan da Cunha. She quickly had unwelcome company, for on March 23, as she was about to anchor there, her lookouts spied a sail approaching from the south. The closer that vessel came, the more Biddle was sure that she was a British warship. At around two o'clock in the afternoon, when she hoisted British colors and fired a shot, *Hornet*'s gunners were at the ready. They responded with a fatal broadside, and for the next twenty-two minutes,

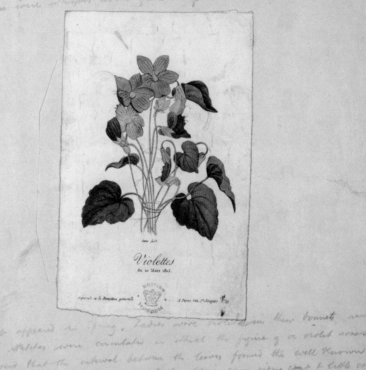

despite the considerable swell, kept up such a murderous fire that the oncoming British ship flew to pieces as she doggedly closed the distance. Before it all ended, her bowsprit sheared between *Hornet*'s main and mizzen rigging, but no boarders appeared. Instead, a voice cried out in the midst of the musketry that the ship was surrendering. Though the Americans duly paused, a British marine then shot Captain Biddle in the neck. Though only wounded, he had trouble restraining his now enraged crew from firing yet more volleys, as the enemy vessel, shorn of her foremast and bowsprit, had indeed surrendered.

She proved to be HMS *Penguin,* and her captain, James Dickinson, had just been killed, along with ten of his crew; another twenty-eight had been wounded. Remarkably, only two men aboard *Hornet* were dead, and except for damage to her spars and rigging, the ship was practically unmarked. Not a single round shot studded her hull. The few casualties were due almost entirely to Royal Marine musketry.

Thus ended the last naval engagement of the war, though not the last encounter. *Hornet* now joined *Constellation, Constitution,* and *Wasp* in having defeated at least two equivalently matched enemy warships in single-ship duels.

Soon, *Peacock,* the American namesake of her first conquest, hove into view, along with *Tom Bowline,* the tender. Given that *Penguin* was heavily damaged, and being so far away from a friendly port, Biddle had concluded that the only thing he could do was scuttle her. But the prisoners were loaded onto *Tom Bowline,* which would take them north to San Salvador.

Only two ships of the original squadron were now left, but the end of the war was approaching for *Hornet,* too.

Now knowing that *President* would never arrive, the two sloops-of-war departed the surging seas surrounding Tristan da Cunha and set out together to round the Cape of Good Hope. On April 25, a sail on the far horizon suggested a richly laden Indiaman but proved instead to be HMS *Cornwallis,* a 74-gun ship-of-the-line, and the Americans nearly paid the price for having edged too close out of curiosity. While *Peacock* escaped in one direction, *Hornet* ran in another, and *Cornwallis* followed *Hornet.* During the long and grueling chase that ensued, Biddle was forced to jettison everything of weight, including most of his guns, in order to lighten his ship. Although he managed at long last to shake off his pursuer, his days as a commerce raider were done. The merchantmen might be carrying more guns than he had now, so he turned north for the long voyage home.

Peacock plunged on alone into the Indian Ocean. By the time the Westerlies had carried him to the volcanic islands of St. Paul and Amsterdam, the next rendezvous point, it was the middle of May. Captain Warrington had long suspected that *Hornet* would never show. Unknown to him, however, a deadline of ninety days after the Peace of Ghent was ratified was about to elapse, and any prize he might take in the Southern Hemisphere after that would henceforth need to be restored.

Instead, he made for the Sunda Strait, the narrows between the islands of Java and Sumatra in the Dutch East Indies, through which funneled much of Europe's trade with the Spice Islands, Singapore, and China. Ships' holds had long been filled with such cargos as the peppers, opium, silk, and saffron that *Peacock*'s crew discovered aboard their first prize, and aboard an English East

Indiaman taken on June 13 just outside the Straits. For the better part of two weeks, Warrington prowled those sweltering waters, taking three prizes, two of which he burned and one of which also carried some $5,000 in gold.

On the morning of June 30, *Peacock,* flying British colors, sailed into the Straits, past the looming basaltic cone of Krakatoa, to the Dutch settlement at Anjier Point. That afternoon, as *Peacock* stood outside the roadstead, a brig left the harbor and began to approach her. At the same time, a small boat carrying some town officials was pulling alongside. What happened next would become a matter of some controversy over the succeeding years, but clearly Warrington hoisted American colors, and Lieutenant Charles Boyce of the British East India Company's armed brig *Nautilus* hailed that the war was over. If that was true, Warrington replied, than Boyce should haul down his colors. Boyce refused. One thing led to another, and before long both ships were pummeling each other with broadsides.

The skirmish lasted barely fifteen minutes, but the damage was done. *Nautilus* had sustained heavy damage, with fifteen casualties, including Boyce, who would lose his leg. Meanwhile, the town officials on board *Peacock* were corroborating the report that the war was indeed over. Finally persuaded that this was the case, on July 2 Warrington set sail for home, half a world away.

While *Peacock* had been in the East Indies, Napoleon, back from exile on Elba, was defeated once and for all in the Battle of Waterloo. (Escorting him on his final banishment to the far-off bleak island of St. Helena was none other than Admiral Sir George Cockburn, whom even Napoleon found "capricious, choleric, vain, and overbearing." The feeling was mutual. "It is clear he is still inclined to act the sovereign occasionally," the emperor's new jailer scribbled in his diary, "but I cannot allow it.")

As *Peacock* began her long, four-month voyage to the United States, Commodore Stephen Decatur was leading a squadron into the Mediterranean Sea. The names of some of his ships were redolent of the war just fought— the frigates *Guerriere* and *Macedonian* and the sloop *Epervier,* sailing alongside the legendary *Constellation,* finally released from her long imprisonment. Hardly had one war concluded when President James Madison persuaded Congress to declare another: Decatur's squadron was on a mission to subdue the Barbary pirates of North Africa, and he was soon joined in the Mediterranean by Commodore William Bainbridge's squadron, led by the impressive 74-gun ship-of-the-line *Independence* and including another new frigate, *Java.* It was quite a navy, powerful and proud, that gathered in those waters that summer.

It wasn't until October 30, 1815, that *Peacock* finally made it back to New York, the last vessel to return home from the old conflict, the conflict that had not only been engendered by contentious maritime issues but also concluded with one, for the controversial broadsides that *Peacock* and *Nautilus* exchanged in the Sunda Strait had been the final shots of the War of 1812.

EPILOGUE

THE LONG ECHO

"THE WAR HAS RENEWED AND REINSTATED THE NATIONAL FEELINGS
AND CHARACTER WHICH THE REVOLUTION HAD GIVEN, AND WHICH WERE DAILY LESSENED. THE PEOPLE . . .
ARE MORE AMERICAN; THEY FEEL AND ACT MORE AS A NATION; AND I HOPE THE PERMANENCY
OF THE UNION IS THEREBY BETTER SECURED."

~ Secretary of the Treasury Albert Gallatin, 1816

Overleaf: An 1878 lithograph depicting the much-hailed Battle of Lake Erie.

The war had left a mixed legacy. Patriotic fervor may have unified the country, and the repulse of the attacking redcoats buoyed the notion that the nation had just won its "Second War of Independence," but in other respects, the war had ended badly. The national capital had been burned to the ground. The British still clung to impressment. Gone was any chance of acquiring Canada, burned ruins up and down the Niagara and Thames River valleys having scorched away any pro-American sympathies. Sentiment for union would soon abate and sectional rifts re-emerge, deepening and widening. And though the war would propel two soldiers, Andrew Jackson and William Henry Harrison, into the rebuilt White House, the Army as a whole had performed unevenly.

But the Navy had never been so popular.

While its British counterpart was rapidly contracting—Napoleon having finally been defeated—forcing many of its officers ashore on half pay, the U.S. Congress was authorizing an annual investment of $1 million for the next eight years to bolster its own fleet with more frigates and ships-of-the-line. American commerce and American interests needed protecting on more far-flung stations. In the Mediterranean, the Barbary corsairs needed watching. In the West Indies, the Caribbean pirates had only grown more troublesome. Off West Africa, the slave trade needed suppressing. And in the Pacific, the British were encroaching on the Sandwich Islands (modern-day Hawaii) and the Northwest Coast.

Meanwhile, the Navy basked in glory. Like ancient Romans, the profiles of Hull, Decatur, Lawrence, Perry, Stewart, and Macdonough were engraved in newspapers, stamped on medallions, and even set on the china to which the heroes sat down at any of the numerous fêtes held to honor them. Songs were written to glorify their accomplishments. Streets and towns soon bore their names.

Some places chose to bear a more tangible witness: the courthouse bell in Erie, Pennsylvania, for instance, was a war trophy from HMS *Queen Charlotte*.

Fame, however, soon carried her favorites away. Three hundred miles up the Orinoco River and back proved for Oliver Hazard Perry a fruitless attempt to persuade Venezuela's government to restrain its privateers-turned-pirates. It also proved a fatal one, for the river's swarms of voracious mosquitoes soon had Perry writhing with yellow fever. On August 23, 1819, three days after his thirty-fourth birthday, his ship just outside Port-of-Spain, Trinidad, he died. Upon hearing the news, Stephen Decatur declared that the "American Navy has lost its brightest ornament."

Seven months later, on the chilly morning of March 3, 1820, Decatur himself lay in the dirt on the old dueling ground at Bladensburg. A bullet was in his gut and on his lips, it was said, a regret that his life was not sacrificed for his country but had rather been thrown foolishly away in answering an old enemy's challenge. Though Captain James Barron, lying wounded eight paces away, had been insulted by his adversary's criticisms of his courage and competence, he would recover. But the forty-one-year-old Decatur died that night in his Washington mansion. Ten thousand people watched the funeral procession, the pallbearers including John Rodgers, David Porter, Isaac Chauncey, and Thomas Macdonough.

Five years later, Macdonough captained *Constitution* across the Atlantic to join the Mediterranean Squadron. It was a cruise he would not finish. Tuberculosis had finally gotten the better of him, and he left Old Ironsides at Gibraltar and found a berth on a merchant ship returning to America. It was a stormy passage, but a peaceful quietus, for the devout forty-one-year-old Episcopalian. He died on November 10, 1825, just as the ship approached the Delaware Capes, not far from where he had been born.

All was black crape and muffled drums as his coffin was carried through the streets of New York. Everyone watching knew that Macdonough's momentous victory at Lake Champlain had quite possibly saved the city. It had certainly turned the tide in those dark days of 1814. Indeed, "[d]own to the time of the Civil War," Theodore Roosevelt would later assert, he was "the greatest figure in our naval history."

Although it went unnoticed, a few weeks earlier Thomas Boyle, the dashing privateer who had singlehandedly blockaded England, had also died at sea. Joshua Barney, a privateer in the Revolution, had been fifty-six when the second war with England had ended; he'd died in 1818 from complications related to the bullet he took at Bladensburg.

Most of the war's naval heroes, though, faced a return to years of peacetime routine. Bluff, good-natured Isaac Hull, who despised politics, wound up somehow caught in their snare. In 1815 he had been given command of the Charlestown Navy Yard in Boston, but that only won him

the ire of Commodore William Bainbridge, who returned from the Mediterranean expecting to repossess a position he considered his by right. Bainbridge ended his career contriving schemes against Hull, Charles Stewart, or anyone else he concluded was his enemy before breathing his last in 1833.

By the time he became commander of the Pacific Squadron, good, clean sea air had restored Hull's buoyancy. He next took charge of the Washington Navy Yard and was only released from that duty by undertaking two tours in the Mediterranean: one on a leave of absence so that his wife could regain her health and the other as commander of the Mediterranean Squadron, striding the quarterdeck of an American ship-of-the-line, *Ohio*. But two strokes heralded the end of both his career and his life, and he died in 1843.

In the decades following the end of the war, nearly every high-ranking officer served some time on the Board of Naval Commissioners, established in 1815 to inject more professionalism into such functions as the building and equipping of ships, the procuring of stores and provisions, the testing of ordnance, and the drafting of rules and regulations. But no one dominated the board's activities in these early years as did its first president, Commodore John Rodgers.

Though his two terms as president—1815-24 and 1827-37—would consume most of his energies and keep him largely confined to Washington, he did in the interim serve his turn as commander of the Mediterranean Squadron. Still a man of "Herculean form and martial figure," as one admirer put it, he worked with his fleet captain, Daniel Patterson, the naval hero of the Battle of New Orleans and the man who took the helm of *Constitution* from the ailing Macdonough. Together they did more than just show the flag in the Mediterranean's principal ports; Rodgers, for instance, also worked toward establishing diplomatic relations with the Ottoman Empire, or Turkey. And that would have an impact on the officer Rodgers considered a "man of far more than ordinary natural talents"—David Porter.

Porter had served with Rodgers as a naval commissioner, but he escaped back to sea in 1823, leading a squadron down to the West Indies to suppress the worsening piracy problem. But his tendency to follow the buccaneers wherever they fled soon landed him in trouble. After Spanish authorities in Fajardo, Puerto Rico, jailed one of his officers, the fiery-tempered Porter responded by practically invading the port. That led to his being court-martialed and, embittered and resentful, to his resignation.

In 1826, Porter accepted an offer to lead the Mexican navy. But the resulting three years of intrigue and faction only deepened his frustration, so he leaped at the chance to represent the United States, first as its chargé d'affaires and then as its full-fledged minister to Turkey. There, in a villa overlooking the domes and minarets so vividly evoked in his *Constantinople and Its Environs*, he lived out the rest of his days in relative contentment. Though estranged from his former service, he did have an eight-oared caique to carry him up and down the Bosporus, and he did welcome old friends who made their way to that colorful crossroads, including Commodore Daniel Patterson, whose daughter would wed Porter's son, the future Civil War hero David Dixon Porter.

In Washington, meanwhile, in the Rodgers' spacious house on Greenleaf Point, overlooking the Potomac River, Minerva's sister was married to Commodore John Henley, who had commanded the gunboat *Carolina* for Patterson during the Battle of New Orleans. The Navy's families remained tightly interlaced.

Yet Rodgers' health was beginning to fail. On May 1, 1837, he resigned from the Navy and sailed for England. In Plymouth, he enjoyed the hospitality of Admiral Sir James Hillyar, who had trapped Porter and *Essex* in Valparaíso a quarter century earlier. Among other erstwhile opponents, Sir James Yeo was long dead, having succumbed to malaria in 1818, while Captain James Dacres, absolved of blame for losing *Guerrière*, was on track to end his career as chief of the Cape of Good Hope station. Rear Admiral Sir Philip Bowes Vere Broke, former captain of *Shannon*, had won a baronetcy for capturing *Chesapeake*, but he would soon die of the wounds he received that day, having never returned to sea duty. Nor, with one brief exception, had Robert Heriot Barclay, though he, too, had been acquitted for losing his makeshift fleet in the Battle of Lake Erie. Most of his limbs had been shot away, however, and he had died while Rodgers was embarking for England.

It wasn't long after he returned to the United States that Rodgers' powers began rapidly to ebb, and on August 1, 1838, at the Philadelphia Naval Asylum, he slipped into the deep forever. Minerva arrived too late to be there at the end. The sixty-six-year-old hero died in the arms of his servant instead.

Minerva would not join him beneath their shared headstone in Washington's Congressional Cemetery for another thirty-nine years. By that time, the grass was deeply rooted over such nearby graves as those holding the remains of Daniel Patterson, whose death had followed Rodgers' by a year, and Isaac Chauncey, who died but a few months after that. At least three grandsons and five great-grandsons would bear the Rodgers name in naval service. One of them, buried across the river in Arlington National Cemetery, was John Rodgers the pioneering naval aviator, also the great-grandson of Matthew Calbraith Perry, the commodore's midshipman years earlier with *President*. He was Oliver Hazard Perry's younger brother, and the Perry who won fame by opening Japan in the 1850s.

Thomas ap Catesby Jones, a former commander of the Pacific Squadron, had hoped to lead that Japan-bound flotilla. His bravery in the Battle of Lake Borgne, which had left him with a crippled arm, had won him national renown and a ceremonial sword from his native Virginia. But his subsequent career was a checkered one. Though he would negotiate the first U.S. treaty with the King of Hawaii and forestall British designs on those islands, Jones turned out to be an overly impetuous commander whose blunders proved diplomatically embarrassing and whose perceived injustices to his junior officers led to a court-martial and suspension.

He moreover had the misfortune of inciting the enmity of Herman Melville, who had been dragged aboard Jones' flagship, *United States*, for having deserted a whaler in Nuku Hiva. The author not only pilloried the stuffy commodore in his scathing indictment of naval life, *White Jacket*, but also inserted him into *Moby Dick*, where as "Commodore J" he "peremptorily denied . . . that any whale could so smite his stout sloop-of-war as to cause her to leak so much as a thimbleful"—only to have one nearly stove it in, as had actually happened to Jones when a sperm whale hit *Peacock* in 1827.

No wonder some veterans chose to tell their own stories. Charles Ball, the freed African American who had fought with Barney before Washington in 1814, related his in *The Life and Adventures of Charles Ball* (1835), which should have caused many a reader to wince. By 1830, he was living happily near Baltimore as a small farmer. One day, he was seized while working in his fields, told he had been bought by the brother of his former owner, and sent south to Georgia. The road leading back to bondage passed, ironically enough, through Bladensburg. "It seemed as if it had been but yesterday that I had seen the British columns advancing across the bridge now before me, directing their fire against me, and my companions in arms," Ball remembered. "The thought now struck me that if I had deserted that day, and gone over to the enemies of the United States, how different would my situation at this moment have been. And this, thought I, is the reward of the part I bore in the dangers and fatigues of that disastrous battle."

While Ball eventually regained his freedom, fate had been altogether kinder to another exile, English-born Samuel Leech, who had received his baptism of fire as a powder boy aboard HMS *Macedonian* in 1812. But it wasn't the same ship that he visited one day many years later in New York. "Change, with an unsparing hand, had remodeled the decks and cabins, so that I felt somewhat lost where once every timber was familiar," he recounted in *Thirty Years from Home; Or, a Voice From the Main Deck* (1843). Nothing, in fact, was left of the old *Macedonian* except her keel, the former vessel having been broken up in 1828. Nevertheless, the prosperous Massachusetts shopkeeper "stood on the spot where I had fought in the din of battle; and with many a serious reflection recalled the horrors of that dreadful scene." Soon the "old tars gathered round me, eagerly listening to my tale of the battle . . ."

No survivor had bobbed right side up more often, or had more tales to tell, than had the old sailor who contacted James Fenimore Cooper one day in 1843. Ned Myers had been Cooper's shipmate in the years before the war; he had spent the following decades almost entirely under canvas, including one ship-of-the-line, two frigates, three sloops-of-war, and numerous merchantmen—not a few of them smugglers—which carried him wherever in the world the trade winds blew. Along the way he had survived four additional shipwrecks and founderings. Cooper was so enchanted with his old mate that he suspended work on his current books and instead produced *Ned Myers, a Life Before the Mast*.

As the years passed, the veterans kept dropping away. Melancthon Woolsey, after leaving Sackets Harbor, had commanded *Constellation* and eventually the Brazilian Station before he died in 1838. Daniel Dobbins, who had seen a fleet in the forest trees, spent a few fitful and unsatisfying years in the Navy and Revenue Cutter Service before returning to his beloved Erie for good, dying there in 1856. Lewis Warrington, cleared by a naval court of inquiry for firing on *Nautilus* in the Sunda Strait, relieved David Porter on the West Indies Station, and before his own death in 1851 had commanded the Norfolk Navy Yard, was chief of the Ordnance Bureau, and even served as a temporary secretary of the Navy after the confirmed one was killed when the "Peacemaker" cannon exploded during an 1844 demonstration.

By the time of the Civil War, only one of the great captains of 1812 was still alive. Charles Stewart, in the course of a seventy-one-year career, had distinguished himself both ashore and afloat, commanding the Mediterranean and Pacific Squadrons as well as the Philadelphia Navy Yard. He was the first officer in the U.S. Navy to achieve flag rank, a position created especially for him in 1859. He had even been urged to run for president back in 1840. But after his daughter married a wealthy Irishman, it would remain for his grandson and namesake, Charles Stewart Parnell, to hitch his wagon to a political star. As the champion of Irish Home Rule, Parnell would be reckoned the father of modern Ireland, though remembered as much for his meteoric career and tragic downfall, so familiar to readers of Yeats and Joyce.

Stewart's death in 1869 was followed within the year by that of one made famous by a different war. David Farragut, Porter's foster son and midshipman with *Essex*, had added to the Navy's fund of catchphrases when, leading his fleet past the Confederate forts guarding Mobile Bay, he reportedly barked, "Damn the torpedoes, full speed ahead!" The irascible Farragut was subsequently made the first full admiral in the history of the service.

"They are gone—all gone," mourned poet Edmund Clarence Stedman after Stewart was buried. There was, however, one durable survivor still afloat.

Many of the country's first frigates were gone by 1830. *Philadelphia*'s bones could be seen for years in the harbor at Tripoli. The captured *Chesapeake*, *Essex*, and *President* had all been broken up by the Royal Navy. And in that year, *Constitution* was deemed to need such a substantial overhaul, rumors began to swirl that, to save an expensive repair, she, too, might be broken up.

She was saved by public indignation. "Such a national object of interest, so endeared to our national pride as Old Ironsides is, should never by any act of our government cease to belong to the Navy, so long as our country is to

be found upon the map of nations," rebuked the Boston *Daily Intelligencer*. Don't let "the harpies of the shore," cried Oliver Wendell Holmes in a celebrated poem, "pluck the eagle of the sea." If she must be destroyed, give her instead, he urged, "to the god of storms, the lightning and the gale." Much nobler to let "her shattered hulk . . . sink beneath the wave." That would soon be the fate of *Peacock*, that splendid sloop whose war record in the summer of 1814 had been unsurpassed. Rebuilt to serve with the U.S. Exploring Expedition, it would be from her mastheads that the Antarctic continent would first be sighted. But in 1841 she would be trapped on a sandbar at the mouth of the Columbia River to be pulled and pounded to pieces by wave and tide.

Constitution, of course, was neither demolished nor given to the storm. When her refurbishing was completed, the first in a long line of dignitaries, eventually to include presidents, kings, queens, emperors, and even a pope, came ceremoniously aboard. Meanwhile, her sister frigate *Congress* would be broken up to little or no fanfare. In 1853, the dashing little *Constellation* was also broken up and entirely rebuilt. With the coming of the Civil War, *Constitution*, then merely a training ship, was evacuated from Annapolis and sent to safe harbor in New England. But *United States*, laid up at Norfolk, was allowed to fall into Confederate hands. Though scuttled and raised again from her muddy grave she, too, was finally broken up at war's end, though her timbers, which had proved so resistant to Confederate axes, had known the tread of Stephen Decatur.

Old Ironsides would always be exceptional, for she had become the emblem of the "Fighting Navy." Though subjected to innumerable indignities, first as a training vessel and then as a receiving one, she was never suffered to be demolished ashore or towed out to sea to be shot to pieces for target practice. The inevitable cry would always arise, "Don't give up the ship!" Although she was always discovered to be leaking, rotting, or falling apart, money was always found to repair her, even schoolchildren pitching in with their pennies. The ceaseless battle against deterioration has meant that nearly all of her original oak framing has been replaced, but a 25,000-acre oak grove has even been set aside to provide for her future needs.

In 1997, the bicentennial of her original commissioning, her sails once more filled with the breeze, and she put to sea after spending the past 116 of her 200 years at moorings. From keel to maintop, she had been painstakingly restored to the way she appeared during the War of 1812, a war that above all epitomized the struggle to secure the freedom of the seas. More particularly, she had been restored to the way she appeared during her finest moment, when on that blustery August afternoon, *Guerrière* reduced to a shambles, she emerged out of the battle smoke having broken the spell of invincibility that the world's mightiest fleet had cast over the sea—the moment, that is, when the United States Navy came of age.

AFTERWORD

The American Navy came of age during the War of 1812. This "Second War for Independence" tested the mettle of our fledgling U.S. Navy in combat and forged the professional culture of our sailors that endures to this day. Most remember the War of 1812 for its leaders, like Perry, Porter, Decatur, and Lawrence; for the engagement between USS *Constitution* and HMS *Guerrière* that gave America's Ship of State her moniker, "Old Ironsides;" and for the defense of Baltimore that inspired our national anthem, "The Star-Spangled Banner."

The War of 1812, however, offers broader lessons for our navy and our nation. The war demonstrated, foremost, that America is a maritime nation that relies on its navy to protect the free flow of commerce and the security of its people. It showed that the capability of the U.S. Fleet is essential to its dominance at sea and its ability to influence events on shore. It proved that motivated and well-trained sailors, under strong leadership, make the difference in a sea-fight. These lessons are the foundation of the professional, global navy we are today, and they continue to portend how our nation will rely upon its navy in the future.

Despite the two hundred years that separate the Navy of the War of 1812 and the Navy today, the need for a strong U.S. Navy endures. President Theodore Roosevelt observed of the Navy's role in the War of 1812: "We had a few ships—a very few ships—and they did so well as to show the utter folly of not having enough of them." After the war, the nation recognized the enduring need for a navy, and instead of reducing the size of the Navy as it had after earlier conflicts Congress enacted provisions for an increase in the size of the Navy. In 1812, the Navy consisted of only a dozen warships capable of sea-keeping and a couple hundred small gunboats suitable for inshore defense; today, the Navy consists of 288 ships, more than 3,700 aircraft, and more than 400,000 active duty and reserve sailors. Since 1812, we have evolved from a continental navy to a global navy with global reach and responsibility.

Our mission to provide for U.S. prosperity and security endures from 1812 to today, but our responsibilities have expanded with our national interests. The maritime domain is the domain of global commerce, communications, and resources. Today, ninety percent of commerce travels over the seas. Ninety-five percent of intercontinental communications and $3 trillion of Internet trade moves on undersea cables. Sixty-five percent of oil and thirty-five percent of natural gas reserves exist in the littoral regions of the world. Trends in demographics,

economics, competition for natural resources, climate change, and the proliferation of new technology and weapons among state and non-state actors are driving significant changes in the maritime and global security environments.

Our Maritime Strategy reflects these environments, and the degree to which our navy has matured since 1812, through the six strategic imperatives it establishes for our nation's sea power: limit regional conflict with forward-deployed, decisive maritime power; deter major power wars; win our nation's wars; contribute to homeland defense; foster and sustain cooperative relationships with more international partners; and prevent or contain local disruptions before they impact the global system. In meeting these imperatives, we remember the lesson from 1812 that superior capability matters in a fight, and it matters in the influence that can be brought to bear. In 1812, the U.S. was outnumbered at sea, but our 44-gun frigates had superior speed, maneuverability, and firepower over the British 38-gun frigates, which enabled the U.S. frigates to handily defeat less capable British ships. Today, our Navy is the world's dominant maritime power with unmatched capability and global reach.

Our aircraft carriers and attack aircraft project power far inshore. They are sovereign U.S. airfields off the coast, unencumbered by basing and overflight constraints. Our ballistic missile submarines are the most survivable leg of our nation's nuclear deterrent triad, and our nuclear attack submarines quietly patrol deep in the oceans and along shallow coasts. Our Aegis ballistic missile defense capability can track and intercept short- and intermediate-range ballistic missiles from sea, and, in the coming years, we will take this capability ashore. Our amphibious ships, landing craft, and our brothers and sisters in the U.S. Marine Corps give our nation unmatched power projection and contingency-response options from sea to shore. Our manned and unmanned aircraft provide persistent intelligence, surveillance, and reconnaissance that aid operational commanders and decision makers twenty-four hours a day, seven days a week. Our capabilities in space and cyberspace protect our networks, ensure the rapid flow of information to our operators, and enable effective command and control across many miles. These capabilities, and many others, are postured around the world to assure our allies and partners, deter aggression, respond to crises, and extend U.S. influence in critical areas overseas. We are cooperating extensively with allies; international partners; other U.S. agencies; and the other sea services, the U.S.

This gilt brass button is a variant of the officer's button authorized by the U.S. Navy uniform regulations of 1802. According to the regulations, the buttons were of "yellow metal with the foul anchor and American eagle, surrounded with fifteen stars." This button has sixteen stars, a common variant produced before Ohio was admitted as the seventeenth state in March 1803.

Marine Corps and the U.S. Coast Guard, to ensure security and stability in the global system today and in the future.

Essential to our success today, as in the War of 1812, are our people. The small but determined group of American sailors who served in the War of 1812 demonstrated that their motivation and preparation, coupled with strong leadership, could match any seagoing force afloat, including the battle-hardened Royal Navy. The war fostered an enhanced esprit de corps and generated a professional ethos that shaped the development of our Fleet well into the nineteenth century. The group of officers who led the Fleet in 1812 epitomized naval leadership, demonstrating the core values of honor, courage, and commitment to which the U.S. Navy adheres today. Our sailors, Navy civilians, and their families remain the Navy's strongest asset. The skill, innovation, and dedication of our sailors turn our ships, aircraft, weapons, and systems into global capabilities that prevent conflict, build partnerships, and, when necessary, project combat power to prevail in war. The Navy today is the highest quality we have seen, and our sailors continue to embody the professionalism and ethos forged in battle two centuries ago.

The Navy has come a long way from the defense of "Free Trade and Sailors' Rights" in 1812. Demand for the Navy today is high and will remain so as long as our nation's interests are vested in locations far from our shores. President George Washington recognized at the founding of our nation that for "an active external commerce, the protection of a naval force is indispensable." The War of 1812 reaffirmed the need for a strong navy capable of protecting our national security and prosperity. It also proved nations go to war with what they have. The small Fleet we had in 1812 was the direct result of deliberate investments of our Congress and the American people. When Congress passed the Naval Act of 1794, it did not know that America would enter into a second conflict with Great Britain. Yet, almost twenty years later, the small Navy the United States had built in fits and starts through 1812 sailed into battle and won victories against the world's greatest navy at the time. After the War of 1812, Congress affirmed its constitutional mandate to "provide and maintain" a navy and began to grow the American Fleet into the global force that has served our nation so proudly in peacetime and war.

Today, your global, ready, and capable Navy continues to provide the offshore options that make it the nation's best asset for applying military capability in support of a greater goal: protecting American security and the global system upon which the United States and its partners, friends, and allies depend.

~ADMIRAL GARY ROUGHEAD, USN
Chief of Naval Operations

SELECTED BIBLIOGRAPHY

Abell, Francis. *Prisoners of War in Britain, 1756-1815: A Record of Their Lives, Their Romance, and Their Suffering.* Oxford: Oxford University Press, 1914.

Adams, Henry. *History of the United States during the Administrations of James Madison.* New York: Library of America, 1986.

———. *History of the United States during the Administrations of Thomas Jefferson.* New York: Library of America, 1986.

Adkins, Roy and Leslie. *The War for All the Oceans: From Nelson at the Nile to Napoleon at Waterloo.* New York: Viking Penguin, 2007.

Albion, Robert C. "Brief History of Civilian Personnel in the U.S. Navy Department." The Navy Department Library. http://www.history.navy.mil/library/special/civilian_personnel.htm

Altoff, Gerard T. *Amongst My Best Men: African-Americans and the War of 1812.* Put-in-Bay, OH: Perry Group, 1996.

Auchinleck, Gilbert. *A History of the War between Great Britain and the United States of America.* Toronto: MacLear and Co., 1855.

Bacon, Lydia B. (Stetson). *Biography of Mrs. Lydia B. Bacon.* Boston: Massachusetts Sabbath School Society, 1856.

Ball, Charles. *Fifty Years in Chains.* New York: Dover Publications, 2003. First published 1837 by John S. Taylor.

Benn, Carl. *The War of 1812.* Botley, Oxfordshire: Osprey Publishing, 2002.

Berton, Pierre. *Flames Across the Border: The Canadian-American Tragedy, 1813-1814.* Boston: Little, Brown, 1981.

Berube, Claude G., and John A. Rodgaard. *A Call to the Sea: Captain Charles Stewart of the USS Constitution.* Washington, DC: Potomac Books, 2005.

Boot, Max. *The Savage Wars of Peace: Small Wars and the Rise of American Power.* New York: Basic Books, 2002.

Borneman, Walter R. *1812: The War That Forged a Nation.* New York: HarperCollins, 2004.

Brenton, Edward Pelham. *The Naval History of Great Britain.* London: Henry Colburn, 1837.

Brinkley, Douglas, ed. *Witness to America: A Documentary History of the United States from the Revolution to Today.* Updated ed. New York: Harper, 2010.

Broadside. "The Impress Service." Broadside. http://www.nelsonsnavy.co.uk/broadside7.html

Brodine, Charles E., Jr., et al. *Against All Odds: U.S. Sailors in the War of 1812.* Washington, DC: Naval Historical Center, 2004.

Brodine, Charles E., Jr., Michael J. Crawford, and Christine F. Hughes. *Ironsides!: The Ship, the Men and the Wars of the USS Constitution.* Tucson: Fireship Press, 2007.

Bunnell, David. *The Travels and Adventures of David C. Bunnell.* Palmyra, NY: J. H. Bortles, 1831.

Calkins, C.G. Captain. "Sea Stores and Refreshments: Experiments and Accidents in Naval Diet." *Proceedings of the United States Naval Institute* 33, no. 1 (1907).

Chambers, William and Robert. "Press-Gangs of the Last War." *Chambers's Journal of Popular Literature, Science, and Arts* 1, no. 36 (1854): 165.

———. "What is a Congreve Rocket?" *Harper's Magazine,* July 1854.

Chapelle, Howard. "Clipper Ships." Global Index. http://www.globalindex.com/clippers/museum/ms_clipp.htm

Chapman, Allan. "Health on the Ocean Waves: The Sea Doctor Afloat and in Port." Gresham College. http://www.gresham.ac.uk/event.asp?PageId=45&EventId=414

Choundas, George. "Pirate Medicine: Pestilence and Pain during the Golden Age of Piracy." Blindkat Publishers. http://blindkat.hegewisch.net/pirates/Pestilence_Pain.html

Clark, Thomas. *Sketches of the Naval History of the United States*. Philadelphia: M. Carey, 1813.

Coggeshall, George. *History of the American Privateers and Letters-of-Marque During Our War with England in the Years 1812, '13, and '14*. New York: George Coggeshall, 1856.

Congreve, William Sir. *A Treatise on the Congreve Rocket System*. London: Longman, Rees, Orme, Brown, and Green, 1827.

Cooke, A. P. *A Text-Book of Naval Ordnance and Gunnery*. New York: John Wiley & Sons, 1875.

Cooper, James Fenimore. *History of the Navy of the United States of America*. Second ed. Philadelphia: Lea and Blanchard, 1840.

———. *Ned Myers, Or a Life before the Mast*. Edited by William S. Dudley. Annapolis: Naval Institute Press, 1989.

Côté, Richard N. *Strength and Honor: The Life of Dolley Madison*. Mount Pleasant, SC: Corinthian Books, 2005.

Crawford, Michael J., Christine F. Hughes, Charles E. Brodine, Jr., and Carolyn M. Stallings, eds. *The Naval War of 1812: A Documentary History*. Vol. 3. Washington, DC: Naval Historical Center, 2002.

Daughan, George C. *If By Sea: The Forging of the American Navy—From the Revolution to the War of 1812*. New York: Basic Books, 2008.

Davis, Charles G. *American Sailing Ships: Their Plans and History*. New York: Dover Publications, 1984.

Davis, William C. *The Pirates Lafitte: The Treacherous World of the Corsairs of the Gulf*. New York: Harcourt Books, 2005.

Dobbins, W. W. *Battle of Lake Erie: Reminiscences of the Flagships "Lawrence" and "Niagara."* Second ed. Erie, PA: Ashby Printing Co., 1913.

Dodd, George. "Eyewitness to the *Chesapeake* Capture." *Connecticut Historical Society Bulletin*, July 1965, 81-87.

Drake, Frederick C. "Sir John Borlase Warren." Dictionary of Canadian Biography Online. http://www.biographi.ca/009004-119.01-e.php?&id_nbr=3189

Dudley, Wade G. *Splintering the Wooden Wall: The British Blockade of the United States*. Annapolis: Naval Institute Press, 2003.

Dudley, William S., and Michael J. Crawford. *The Early Republic and the Sea: Essays in the Naval and Maritime History of the Early United States*. Washington, DC: Brassey's Inc., 2001.

Dudley, William S., ed. *The Naval War of 1812: A Documentary History*. Vol. 1. Washington, DC: Naval Historical Center, 1985.

———. *The Naval War of 1812: A Documentary History*. Vol 2. Washington, DC: Naval Historical Center, 1992.

Duffy, Stephen W. H. *Captain Blakeley and the Wasp: The Cruise of 1814*. Annapolis: Naval Institute Press, 2001.

Dún Laoghaire Harbor Company. "The Essex Hulk: Is This the Essex Anchor?" Dún Laoghaire Harbour Company. http://www.dlharbour.ie/content/history/essex/

Dye, Ira. *The Fatal Cruise of the Argus: Two Captains in the War of 1812*. Annapolis: Naval Institute Press, 1994.

Eden, Lieutenant Colonel Steven. "Commodore Barney at the Bladensburg Races." *Naval History Magazine* 24, no. 5 (2010).

Ellis, James H. *A Ruinous and Unhappy War: New England and the War of 1812*. New York: Algora Publishing, 2009.

Evans, Amos A. "Journal kept on board the Frigate 'Constitution,' 1812." *The Pennsylvania Magazine of History and Biography* 19, no. 2 (1895): 152-169.

Forester, C. S. *The Age of Fighting Sail: The Story of the Naval War of 1812*. Garden City, NJ: Doubleday, 1956.

Fredriksen, John C., compiler. *War of 1812 Eyewitness Accounts: An Annotated Bibliography*. Westport, CT: Greenwood Press, 1997.

Fremont-Barnes, Gregory. *The Royal Navy: 1793-1815*. Botley, Oxfordshire: Osprey Publishing, 2007.

Fulton, Robert. *Torpedo War and Submarine Explosions*. 1810. Reprint, New York: William Abbatt, 1914.

———. *The Wars of the Barbary Pirates*. Botley, Oxfordshire: Osprey Publishing, 2006.

Gamble, John M. *The Memorial of Lieut. Colonel J. M. Gamble, United States Marine Corps, to Congress*. New York: Hopkins and Son, 1828.

George, Christopher T. *Terror on the Chesapeake: The War of 1812 on the Bay*. Shippensburg, PA: White Mane Books, 2000.

Gleaves, Albert. *James Lawrence: Captain, United States Navy*. New York: G. P. Putnam's Sons, 1904.

Graves, Dianne. *In the Midst of Alarms: The Untold Story of Women and the War of 1812*. Montreal: Robin Brass Studio, 2007.

Groom, Winston. *Patriotic Fire: Andrew Jackson and Jean Lafitte at the Battle of New Orleans*. New York: Random House, 2006.

Guttridge, Leonard F. *Mutiny: A History of Naval Insurrection*. Annapolis: Naval Institute Press, 1992.

Hall, Henry. *American Navigation: With Some Accounts of the Causes of Its Former Prosperity and Present Decline*. New York: D. Appleton and Co., 1878.

Harland, John. *Seamanship in the Age of Sail*. Annapolis: Naval Institute Press, 1985.

Healey, David. *1812: Rediscovering Chesapeake Bay's Forgotten War*. Rock Hill, SC: Bella Rosa Books, 2005.

Heidler, David S., and Jeanne T. Heidler, eds. *Encyclopedia of the War of 1812*. Annapolis: Naval Institute Press, 1997.

Hickey, Donald R. *Don't Give Up the Ship! Myths of the War of 1812*. Chicago: University of Illinois Press, 2006.

———. *The War of 1812: A Short History*. Urbana and Chicago: University of Illinois Press, 1995.

Hilliard, Mark. "Biscuits, Bugs, & Broadsides." *The Journal of the War of 1812* VIII, no. 2 (2004): 12-16.

Holbrook, Samuel F. *Threescore Years: An Autobiography*. Boston: J. French, 1857.

Hollis, Ira N. *The Frigate Constitution*. Boston and New York: Houghton Mifflin, 1900.

Hoxse, John. *The Yankee Tar: An Authentic Narrative of the Voyages and Hardships of John Hoxse*. Northampton, MA: J. Metcalf, 1840.

Hughes, Christine F. "Lewis Warrington and the USS *Peacock* in the Sunda Strait, June 1815." In *The Early Republic and the Sea*, edited by William S. Dudley and Michael J. Crawford, 117-118. Washington, DC: Brassey's, Inc., 2001.

Hughes, W. S. "A Famous Ship of the 'Old Navy.'" *Frank Leslie's Popular Monthly* 21 (1886).

Ilisevich, Robert D. *Daniel Dobbins: Frontier Mariner*. Erie, PA: Erie County Historical Society, 1993.

Key, Francis Scott. *Oration Delivered by Francis S. Key, Esq., in the Rotundo of the Capitol of the U. States, on the 4th of July, 1831*. Washington, DC, 1831.

Kimball, Horace. *The Naval Battles of the United States*. Boston: Higgins, Bradley, and Dayton, 1857.

King, Irving H. *The Coast Guard Under Sail: The U.S. Revenue Service, 1789-1865*. Annapolis: Naval Institute Press, 1989.

Knox, Thomas W. *The Life of Robert Fulton*. New York: G. P. Putnam's Sons, 1886.

Krafft, Herman F., and Walter B. Norris. *Sea Power in American History: The Influence of the Navy and the Merchant Marine upon American Development*. New York: The Century Co., 1920.

Langguth, A. J. *Union 1812: The Americans Who Fought the Second War of Independence*. New York: Simon & Schuster, 2006.

Lardas, Mark. *Constitution vs. Guerriere: Frigates During the War of 1812*. New York: Osprey, 2009.

Larson, Edward J. *Evolution's Workshop: God and Science on the Galápagos Islands*. New York: Basic Books, 2001.

La Violette, Paul Estronza. *Sink or Be Sunk!: The Naval Battle in the Mississippi Sound that Preceded the Battle of New Orleans*. Waveland, MS: Annabelle Books, 2002.

Leech, Samuel. *Thirty Years from Home*. Boston: Tappan & Dennet, 1843.

Little, George. *Life on the Ocean, or Twenty Years at Sea*. New York: Clark, Austin, and Smith, 1852.

Longmore, Sir Thomas. *Gunshot Injuries*. London: Longmans, Green, and Co., 1877.

Lossing, Benson John. *The Pictorial Field-Book of the War of 1812*. New York: Harper and Brothers, 1868.

Lowenherz, David H., ed. *The 50 Greatest Love Letters of All Time*. New York: Gramercy Books, 2002.

MacDonough, Rodney. *Life of Commodore Thomas Macdonough, U.S. Navy*. Boston: Fort Hill Press, 1909.

MacGregor, David R. *The Schooner: Its Design and Development from 1600 to the Present*. Annapolis: Naval Institute Press, 2001.

Malcomson, Robert. *Lords of the Lake: The Naval War on Lake Ontario, 1812-1814*. Toronto: Robin Brass Studio, 1998.

———. "Public Trophies, Private Plunder: The American Harvest after the Battle at York." *The Fife and Drum* 12, no. 3 (2008).

Marsh, Ruth, and Dorothy S. Truesdale. "War on Lake Ontario: 181-1814." *Rochester History* 4, no. 4 (1942).

Martin, Tyrone G., ed. *The USS Constitution's Finest Fight, 1815: Journal of Acting Chaplain Assheton Humphreys, U.S. Navy*. Mount Pleasant, SC: Nautical & Aviation Publishing Company of America, 2000.

Maclay, Edgar Stanton. *A History of American Privateers*. London: Sampson Low, Marston & Co., 1900.

———. "Early Victories of the American Navy." *The Century Illustrated Magazine* 41, no. 1 (1890).

Macquarie University. "Naval Officers and Crew." Lachlan and Elizabeth Macquarie Archive. http://www.lib.mq.edu.au/digital/lema/maritime/officers-and-crew.html

Mahan, Alfred Thayer. *Sea Power in Its Relation to the War of 1812*. Boston: Little, Brown, 1905.

Mahon, John K. *The War of 1812*. Gainesville: University of Florida Press, 1972.

Mayer, Nancy. "Naval Medicine in 1812." Nancy Mayer. http://www.susannaives.com/nancyregencyresearcher/pages/med3.html

McGuignon, Ron. "British Generals of the Napoleonic Wars: John Lambert." The Napoleonic Series. http://www.napoleon-series.org/research/biographies/BritishGenerals/c_Britishgenerals92.html

McKee, Christopher. *A Gentlemanly and Honorable Profession: The Creation of the U.S. Naval Officer Corps, 1794-1815*. Annapolis: Naval Institute Press, 1991.

Melville, Herman. *White-Jacket, or the World in a Man-of-War*. Boston: L. C. Page & Co., 1892.

Middlebrook, Louis F. "Old Navigation." *Proceedings of the United States Naval Institute* 48, (1922).

Miller, Nathan. *The U.S. Navy: An Illustrated History*. New York: American Heritage Publishing Co., 1982.

Mills, James Cook. *Oliver Hazard Perry and the Battle of Lake Erie*. Detroit: John Phelps, 1913.

Moore, John Hamilton. *The Practical Navigator*. Twentieth ed. London: William Clowes, 1828.

Mostert, Noel. *The Line Upon a Wind: The Great War at Sea 1793-1815*. New York: W. W. Norton, 2007.

Napier, Charles. *Narrative of the Operations in the Potomac by the Squadron under the Orders of Capt. Sir James A. Gordon, in 1814*. Library of Congress, Manuscripts Division.

Nelson, Daniel A. "Hamilton and Scourge: Ghost Ships of the War of 1812." *National Geographic Magazine*, March 1983.

Norie, J. W. *A New and Complete Epitome of Practical Navigation*. London: Navigation Warehouse, 1805.

Norton, Louis Arthur. *Joshua Barney: Hero of the Revolution and 1812*. Annapolis: Naval Institute Press, 2000.

O'Brien, Karen. "Urban Workers." In *British Colonial America: People and Perspectives*, edited by John A. Grigg. Santa Barbara: ABC-CLIO Inc., 2008.

Paine, Ralph D. *The Old Merchant Marine*. Ann Arbor: University of Michigan Press, 2009. First published 1919 by Yale University Press. Also available online at http://www.authorama.com/old-merchant-marine-6.html

Paltsits, Victor Hugo, ed. *Cruise of the U.S. Brig Argus in 1813: The Journal of Surgeon James Inderwick*. New York: New York Public Library, 1917.

Parsons, Usher. *The Battle of Lake Erie*. Providence: Benjamin Albro, 1854.

Parsons, William Barclay. *Robert Fulton and the Submarine*. New York: Columbia University Press, 1922.

Patton, Philip. *Observations of an Admiral on the State of the Navy, and More Particularly as it is Connected with the American War*. Fareham, Hampshire, UK: 1813. Library of Congress Rare Book and Special Collections Room.

Paullin, Charles Oscar. *Commodore John Rodgers: A Biography*. Cleveland: Arthur H. Clark Company, 1910.

———. "Dueling in the Old Navy." *United States Naval Institute Proceedings* 35, no. 4 (1909).

Perkins, Bradford, ed. *The Causes of the War of 1812: National Honor or National Interest*. Huntington, NY: Robert E. Krieger Publishing Co., 1976.

Pitch, Anthony S. *The Burning of Washington: The British Invasion of 1814*. Annapolis: Naval Institute Press, 1998.

Pleadwell, Frank Lester. "William Paul Crillon Barton, Surgeon United States Navy, Pioneer in American Naval Medicine." In *Annals of Medical History*, Vol. 2, edited by Francis R. Packard. New York: Paul B. Hoeber, 1920.

Porter, David. *Journal of a Cruise*. Edited by R. D. Madison and Karen Hamon. Annapolis: Naval Institute Press, 1986.

Poyer, David. "The Chesapeake-Leopard Affair." *Shipmate*, June-July 2007.

Ramsey, H. C. *Elementary Naval Ordnance and Gunnery*. Boston: Little, Brown, 1918.

Reilly, John. "Proud Beginnings: History of Warrant Officers in the U.S. Navy." Naval Historical Center. http://www.history.navy.mil/trivia/triv4-5n.html

Remini, Robert V. *The Battle of New Orleans: Andrew Jackson and America's First Military Victory*. New York: Viking Penguin, 1999.

Richmond, Helen. *Isaac Hull: A Forgotten American Hero*. Boston: USS Constitution Museum, 1983.

Riddle, John. *A Treatise on Navigation and Nautical Astronomy*. London: Edward Law, 1859.

Rodger, N. A. M. *The Command of the Ocean: A Naval History of Britain 1649-1815*. New York: W. W. Norton, 2004.

Rodgers, Minerva, and John Rodgers. Correspondence, 1805-1815. Library of Congress, Rodgers Family Collection.

Roosevelt, Franklin D. "Our First Frigates: Some Unpublished Facts About Their Construction." In *Transactions of the Society of Naval Architects and Marine Engineers*, Vol 22. New York: Society of Naval Architects and Marine Engineers, 1915.

Roosevelt, Theodore. *The Naval War of 1812*. New York: G. P. Putnam's Sons, 1882.

Rosenberg, Max. *The Building of Perry's Fleet on Lake Erie, 1812-1813*. Harrisburg: Pennsylvania Historical and Museum Commission, 1987.

Rowe, John Carlos. *Literary Culture and U.S. Imperialism: From the Revolution to World War II*. New York: Oxford University Press, 2000.

Rowen, Bob. "American Privateers in the War of 1812." A paper presented at the New York Military Affairs Symposium, New York. http://nymas.org/warof1812paper/paperrevised2006.html

Royal Navy Museum Library. "Impressment: The Press Gangs and Naval Recruitment." The Royal Naval Museum. http://www.royalnavalmuseum.org/info_sheet_impressment.htm

Rutter, Frank R. *The South American Trade of Baltimore*. Baltimore: The Johns Hopkins Press, 1897.

Semple, Ellen Churchill. *American History and Its Geographic Conditions*. Boston and New York: Houghton Mifflin Co., 1903.

Severance, Frank H., ed. "The Dobbins Papers." In *Publications of the Buffalo Historical Society*, vol. 8, edited by Frank H. Severance, 255-419. New York: Buffalo Historical Society, 1905.

Skaggs, David Curtis. *A Signal Victory: The Lake Erie Campaign, 1812-13*. Annapolis: Naval Institute Press, 1997.

———. *Oliver Hazard Perry.* Annapolis: Naval Institute Press, 2006.

Smith, Gene A. *Thomas ap Catesby Jones: Commodore of Manifest Destiny.* Annapolis: Naval Institute Press, 2000.

Smith, George, ed. *Physician and Friend: Alexander Grant, F. R.C .S.* London: John Murray, 1902.

Snider, Charles Henry Jeremiah. *In the Wake of the Eighteen-Twelvers.* London: John Lane, 1913.

———. *Under the Red Jack: Privateers of the Maritime Provinces of Canada in the War of 1812.* London: M. Hopkinson, 1928.

Spurr, John W. "Sir James Lucas Yeo." *Dictionary of Canadian Biography Online.* http://www.biographi.ca/

Tertius de Kay, James. *A Rage for Glory: The Life of Commodore Stephen Decatur, USN.* New York: Free Press, 2004.

Thorpe, Francis Newton. "The Building of the Fleet." *The Pennsylvania Magazine of History and Biography* 37, no. 3 (1913).

Toll, Ian W. *Six Frigates: The Epic History of the Founding of the U.S. Navy.* New York: W. W. Norton, 2006.

Turner, Gerard L'Estrange. *Nineteenth Century Scientific Instruments.* Berkeley: University of California Press, 1983.

Turner, Wesley B. *The War of 1812: The War that Both Sides Won.* Toronto: Dundurn Press, 2000.

Upton, Francis H. *The Law of Nations Affecting Commerce During War with a Review of the Jurisdiction, Practice, and Proceedings of Prize Courts.* New York: John S. Voorhies, 1861.

Urquhart, Thomas. *Letters on the Evils of Impressment.* London: J. Richardson, Cornhill, 1816.

Vallar, Cindy. "Medicine at Sea." *Pirates and Privateers: The History of Maritime Piracy.* http://www.cindyvallar.com/medicine.html

Valle, James E. "The Navy's Battle Doctrine in the War of 1812." *American Neptune* 44, no.3 (1984): 171-178.

———. *Rocks & Shoals: Naval Discipline in the Age of Fighting Sail.* Annapolis: Naval Institute Press, 1980.

Villiers, Alan. *Men, Ships, and the Sea.* Washington, DC: National Geographic Society, 1963.

Ward, James H. *Elementary Instruction in Naval Ordnance and Gunnery.* New York: D. Van Nostrand, 1861.

West, Lucy (Brewer). *The Female Marine.* Boston, 1817. Copy in Library of Congress, Rare Book and Special Collections Room.

Williams, Daniel E., and Christina Riley Brown. *Liberty's Captives: Narratives of Confinement in the Print Culture of the Early Republic.* Athens: University of Georgia Press, 2006

Wilson, Thomas. *The Biography of the Principal American Military and Naval Heroes.* New York: John Low, 1817.

Wood, Virginia S. *Live Oaking: Southern Timber for Tall Ships.* Boston: Northeastern University Press, 1981. Reprint, Annapolis: Naval Institute Press, 1995.

Wright, C. Milton. *Our Harford Heritage: A History of Harford County, Maryland.* Havre de Grace: Wright, 1967.

FURTHER EXPLORATION

Profiles of U.S. Navy warships can be found in the online *Dictionary of American Fighting Ships*, a component of the Naval History and Heritage Command's website: http://www.history.navy.mil/index.html

See also the following museums, collections, and historical sites:
USS Constitution Museum and Library:
http://www.ussconstitutionmuseum.org/index.htm
U.S. Naval Academy Museum: http://www.usna.edu/Museum/
Royal Naval Museum: http://www.royalnavalmuseum.org
Hamilton and Scourge National Historic Site:
http://www.hamilton-scourge.hamilton.ca/default.asp
Erie Maritime Museum: http://flagshipniagara.org/maritime_museum/

ILLUSTRATION CREDITS

For pages with multiple images, from top, left to right.

Pg. vi: Museum of Fine Arts, Boston, Massachusetts, USA/Ernest Wadsworth Longfellow Fund/ Emily L. Ainsley Fund/The Bridgeman Art Library International; Pg. x: Collection of the New York Historical Society, USA /The Bridgeman Art Library International; Pg. viii: Courtesy, USS Constitution Museum, Boston; Pg. 3: Courtesy, U.S. Naval Academy Museum; Pg. 4: Bibliotheque Nationale, Paris, France/Giraudon/The Bridgeman Art Library International

I Pp. 6-7: Courtesy of the Peabody Essex Museum, Salem, Massachusetts; Pg. 8: National Maritime Museum; Pg. 10: National Maritime Museum; Pg. 11: Mike Scott/The Mountain Club of South Africa; Pg. 12a: National Maritime Museum; Pg. 12b: David Bohl/Courtesy, USS Constitution Museum, Boston; Pg. 13a: AP Images; Pg. 13b: Division of Work & Industry, National Museum of American History, Smithsonian Institution; Pg. 13c: Library of Congress, American Memory Historical Collections; Pg. 14: Courtesy, U.S. Navy Art Collection; Pg. 15: Reprinted With the Permission of Suzy Barnard, All Rights Reserved; Pg 16: George Emery Collection Pg. 17a-b George Emery Collection; Pg. 18: David Bohl/Courtesy, Sion Hill ; Pg. 19: Courtesy, U.S. Navy Museum; Pg. 21: Library of Congress,

Prints and Photographs Division; Pg 22: David Bohl/Courtesy, Naval History & Heritage Command; Pg. 23a: David Bohl/Courtesy, U.S. Naval Academy Museum; Pg. 23b: David Bohl/Courtesy, USS Constitution Museum, Boston; Pg. 24a: David Bohl/Courtesy, USS Constitution Museum, Boston; Pg. 24b: David Bohl/Courtesy, USS Constitution Museum, Boston; Pg. 25: David Bohl/Courtesy, U.S. Naval Academy Museum; Pg. 26: David Bohl/Courtesy, U.S. Naval Academy Museum; Pg. 27: © Mystic Seaport Collection, Mystic, CT, #1962.23; Pg. 28a: Mariners' Museum; Pg. 28b: National Archives and Records Administration; Pg. 29: New York Public Library Picture Collection ; Pg. 30a: David Bohl/U.S. Navy Collection/Courtesy, USS Constitution Museum, Boston; Pg. 30b: David Bohl/Courtesy, USS Constitution Museum, Boston; Pg. 30c: David Bohl/Courtesy, USS Constitution Museum, Boston; Pg. 30d: David Bohl/Courtesy, U.S. Navy Museum; Pg. 30e: David Bohl/Courtesy, U.S. Navy Museum; Pg. 30f: David Bohl/Courtesy, USS Constitution Museum, Boston; Pg. 30g: David Bohl/Courtesy, USS Constitution Museum, Boston; Pg. 30h: David Bohl/Courtesy, USS Constitution Museum, Boston; Pg. 30i: David Bohl/ Courtesy, U.S. Navy Museum; Pg. 31a: North Wind Picture Archives; Pg. 31b: David Bohl/Courtesy, U.S. Navy Museum; Pg. 32a: David Bohl/Hull P. Fulweiler Collection/Courtesy, USS Constitution Museum, Boston; Pg. 32b: David Bohl/Hull P. Fulweiler Collection/Courtesy, USS Constitution Museum, Boston; Pg. 32c: David Bohl/Hull P. Fulweiler Collection/Courtesy, USS Constitution Museum, Boston ; Pg. 32d: David Bohl/Courtesy, USS Constitution Museum, Boston; Pg. 33a: David Bohl/Courtesy, USS Constitution Museum, Boston; Pg. 33b: David Bohl/Courtesy, USS Constitution Museum, Boston; Pg. 33c: David Bohl/ Hull P. Fulweiler Collection/Courtesy, USS Constitution Museum, Boston; Pg. 34: Courtesy, USS Constitution Museum, Boston; Pg. 35: Library of Congress, Manuscript Division; Pg. 36: David Bohl/Courtesy, USS Constitution Museum, Boston; Pg. 37a: David Bohl/Courtesy, USS Constitution Museum, Boston; Pg. 37b: Library of Congress, Manuscript Division; Pg. 38: Courtesy, USS Constitution Museum, Boston; Pg. 39: Courtesy, USS Constitution Museum, Boston; Pg. 40: Courtesy, USS Constitution Museum, Boston; Pg. 41: Courtesy, USS Constitution Museum, Boston; Pg. 42a: David Bohl/Courtesy, U.S. Naval Academy Museum; Pg. 42b: U.S. Navy Art Collection; Pg. 43: Smithsonian American Art Museum, Gift of Sheldon and Caroline Keck in Honor of Elizabeth Brown; Pg. 44: Roy Andersen; Pg. 45: David Bohl/Courtesy, USS Constitution Museum, Boston; Pg. 46a: David Bohl/Courtesy, U.S. Naval Academy Museum; Pg. 46b: David Bohl/New York Historical Society; Pg. 47: Library of Congress, Prints and Photographs Division; Pg. 48: David Bohl/Courtesy, USS Constitution

Museum, Boston; Pg. 49a: David Bohl/Courtesy, USS Constitution Museum, Boston; Pg. 49b: David Bohl/Courtesy, USS Constitution Museum, Boston; Pg. 50: National Maritime Museum; Pg. 51a: National Maritime Museum; Pg. 51b: David Bohl/Massachusetts Historical Society; Pg. 51c: David Bohl/Massachusetts Historical Society; Pg. 51d: David Bohl/Massachusetts Historical Society; Pg. 51e: David Bohl/Massachusetts Historical Society; Pg. 52a: David Bohl/Courtesy, USS Constitution Museum, Boston; Pg. 52b: David Bohl/Courtesy, USS Constitution Museum, Boston; Pg. 52c: David Bohl/Massachusetts Historical Society; Pg. 53: National Maritime Museum; Pg. 54a: David Bohl/U.S. Navy Collection/Courtesy, USS Constitution Museum, Boston; Pg. 54b: David Bohl/Courtesy, U.S. Naval Academy Museum; Pg. 54c: David Bohl/Courtesy, USS Constitution Museum, Boston; Pg. 55: David Bohl/Courtesy, USS Constitution Museum, Boston

2

Pp. 56-57: Dixson Galleries, State Library of New South Wales/The Bridgeman Art Library; Pg. 58: National Maritime Museum; Pg. 60a: Beverly Historical Society; Pg. 60b: David Bohl/Courtesy, U.S. Naval Academy Museum; Pg. 61: David Bohl/Courtesy, U.S. Navy Museum; Pg. 62: © Mystic Seaport Collection, Mystic, CT, #1940.324; Pg. 63: Memorial Art Library, University of Rochester; Pg. 64: © Mystic Seaport Collection, Mystic, CT, #1957.998; Pg. 65a-c: Courtesy of the Phillips Library at the Peabody Essex Museum, Salem, Massachusetts; Pg. 65d: David Bohl/Courtesy, U.S. Navy Department Library; Pg. 67: American Antiquarian Society, Worcester, Massachusetts/The Bridgeman Art Library; Pg. 68: Courtesy, U.S. Naval Academy Museum; Pg. 69a: Boston Publishing Company Collection; Pg. 69b: National Maritime Museum; Pg. 70: David Bohl/Courtesy, U.S. Navy Museum; Pg. 71a: David Bohl/Courtesy, U.S. Naval Academy Museum; Pg. 71b: David Bohl/Courtesy, U.S. Naval Academy Museum; Pg. 71c: David Bohl/Courtesy, U.S. Naval Academy Museum; Pg. 71d: David Bohl/Courtesy, U.S. Navy Department Library; Pg. 72a-c: David Bohl/Courtesy, USS Constitution Museum, Boston; Pg. 72d: David Bohl/Mariners' Museum; Pg. 73: David Bohl/Courtesy, USS Constitution Museum, Boston; Pg. 74a-c: David Bohl/Courtesy, USS Constitution Museum, Boston; Pg. 75: David Bohl/Courtesy, USS Constitution Museum, Boston; Pg. 77a: Courtesy, U.S. Naval Academy Museum; Pg. 77b: Courtesy, Naval History & Heritage Command; Pg. 78: Robin Brooks/

Private Collection/The Bridgeman Art Library; Pg. 79: David Bohl/Courtesy, Naval History and Heritage Command; Pg. 80: National Maritime Museum; Pg. 81: David Bohl/Courtesy, U.S. Naval Academy Museum; Pg. 82a: David Bohl/Courtesy, U.S. Naval Academy Museum; Pg. 82b: Courtesy of the Phillips Library at the Peabody Essex Museum, Salem, Massachusetts; Pg. 82c: Burlington Historical Society; Pg. 83a-b: Courtesy of the Phillips Library at the Peabody Essex Museum, Salem, Massachusetts; Pg. 84: © Mystic Seaport, Denison-Rodgers Collection, Mystic, CT; Pg. 85: National Maritime Museum; Pg. 86: Private Collection/The Stapleton Collection/ The Bridgeman Art Library; Pg. 87a-b: © Mystic Seaport, Denison-Rodgers Collection, Mystic, CT; Pg. 87c: Courtesy, Naval History and Heritage Command; Pg. 88: David Bohl/Courtesy, USS Constitution Museum, Boston; Pg. 89a: David Bohl/Courtesy, U.S. Navy Department Library; Pg. 89b: American Antiquarian Society, Worcester, Massachusetts; Pg. 91a-c: David Bohl/Courtesy, U.S. Naval Academy Museum; Pg. 91d: National Maritime Museum; Pg. 92: Courtesy of the Peabody Essex Museum, Salem, Massachusetts/The Bridgeman Art Library; Pg. 93a-b: National Maritime Museum; Pg. 93c: David Bohl/Courtesy, U.S. Navy Museum; Pg. 94: National Maritime Museum; Pg. 95a: Private Collection/The Bridgeman Art Library; Pg. 95b: Hulton Archive/Getty Images; Pg. 96a-b: David Bohl/Courtesy, USS Constitution Museum, Boston; Pg. 97a-b: National Maritime Museum; Pg. 98: National Maritime Museum; Pg. 99: American Antiquarian Society, Worcester, Massachusetts; Pg. 101: American Antiquarian Society, Worcester, Massachusetts/The Bridgeman Art Library; Pg. 102: © Mystic Seaport, Denison-Rodgers Collection, Mystic, CT; Pg. 103a-b: © Mystic Seaport, Denison-Rodgers Collection, Mystic, CT; Pg. 104a: The Trustees of the British Museum; Pg. 104b: British Museum Images; Pg. 105a: Private Collection/The Bridgeman Art Library; Pg. 105b: From *Journal of a Cruise* (David Porter); Pg. 105c: Courtesy, U.S. Navy Art Collection; Pg. 105d: Period Paper; Pg. 106a-b: David Bohl/Courtesy, Sion Hill; Pg. 107: Anne S. K. Brown Military Collection, Brown University Library; Pg. 108: David Bohl/Courtesy, U.S. Naval Academy Museum; Pg. 108b: David Bohl/Courtesy, U.S. Naval Academy Museum; Pg. 109: Courtesy of the Peabody Essex Museum, Salem, Massachusetts

3

Pp. 110-111: New York Historical Society; Pg. 112: Courtesy, U.S. Naval Academy Museum; Pg. 114a: National Maritime Museum; Pg. 114b: Mapping Specialists, Ltd.; Pg. 115: Private Collection/Peter Newark American Pictures/The Bridgeman Art Library; Pg. 116a: James Scherzi/Courtesy, Clayton Nans; Pg. 116b: Courtesy, Naval History & Heritage Command; Pg. 117: National Archives of Canada; Pg. 118: Mackinac State Historic Parks Collection; Pg. 119: The Buffalo & Erie County Historical Society; Pg. 120: Archives of Ontario; Pg. 121: Rare Book and Special Collections Division, Library of Congress; Pg. 122: National Maritime Museum; Pg. 123a-b: National Maritime Museum; Pg. 124a: Courtesy of the Phillips Library at the Peabody Essex Museum, Salem, Massachusetts; Pg. 124b: National Maritime Museum; Pg. 124c: Courtesy of the Phillips Library at the Peabody Essex Museum, Salem, Massachusetts; Pg. 125: American Antiquarian Society; Pg. 126a-b: David Bohl/Courtesy, Naval History & Heritage Command; Pg. 127: Image Reproduced Courtesy of Colonel Waterhouse and the Waterhouse Museum; Pg. 128: Metropolitan Toronto Reference Library; Pg. 129: Courtesy, Navy Art Collection; Pg. 131a-b: The Buffalo & Erie County Historical Society; Pg. 132a: John Baker/Erie Maritime Museum; Pg. 132b-c: David Bohl/Courtesy, U.S. Naval Academy Museum; Pg. 133a-f: John Baker/Erie Maritime Museum; Pg. 134: David Bohl/Courtesy, U.S. Naval Academy Museum; Pg. 135: New York Public Library Picture Collection; Pg. 136: American Antiquarian Society; Pg. 137: Library and Archives of Canada; Pg. 138a: New York Historical Society; Pg. 138b: David Bohl/Courtesy, U.S. Naval Academy Museum; Pg. 138c: David Bohl/U.S. Navy Department Library; Pg. 139a: John Baker/Erie County Historical Society; Pg. 139b: David Bohl/Courtesy, U.S. Naval Academy Museum; Pg. 139c: David Bohl/Courtesy, U.S. Navy Museum; Pg. 139d: John Baker/Erie Maritime Museum; Pg. 140: Anne S. K. Brown Military Collection, Brown University Library; Pg. 142a: George Emery Collection; Pg. 142b: Courtesy, U.S. Navy Art Collection; Pg. 143a-e: Courtesy, U.S. Navy Art Collection; Pg. 145: National Geographic Stock; Pg. 146a-c: National Geographic Stock; Pg. 147: National Geographic Stock; Pg. 148: John Baker/Erie Maritime Museum; Pg. 149a: David Bohl/Courtesy, U.S. Naval Academy Museum; Pg. 149b: John Baker/Erie County Historical Society; Pg. 150: Brown University Library; Pg. 151: U.S. Senate Collection; Pg. 152: David Bohl/Courtesy, U.S. Naval Academy Museum Pg. 153: Alamy Images; Pg. 154a-b: David Bohl/Courtesy, U.S. Naval Academy Museum ; Pg. 154c: David Bohl/Courtesy, U.S. Navy Department Library; Pg. 155: Western Reserve Historical Society; Pg. 156a: David Bohl/Courtesy, U.S. Naval Academy Museum; Pg. 156b: John Baker, Erie Maritime Museum; Pg. 157a-b: David Bohl/Courtesy, U.S. Naval Academy Museum

4

Pp. 158-159: Maryland Historical Society; Pg. 160: Bettmann/CORBIS; Pg. 162: Anne S. K. Brown Military Collection, Brown University Library; Pg. 163: Library of Congress; Pg. 165: National Maritime Museum; Pg. 166: National Maritime Museum; Pg. 168: David Rumsey Map Collection; Pg. 169a: Library of Congress; Pg. 169b: John Carter Brown Library, Brown University; Pg. 170a: National Archives and Records Administration; Pg. 170b: Courtesy, U.S. Navy Art Collection; Pg. 171a: David Bohl/Courtesy, U.S. Navy Department Library; Pg. 171b: David Bohl/Courtesy, U.S. Naval Academy Museum; Pg. 172: Tom Freeman/Christine Hughes; Pg. 173: National Archives and Records Administration; Pg. 174a-c: National Maritime Museum; Pg. 175: National Maritime Museum; Pg. 176: Collection of the New York Historical Society/ The Bridgeman Art Library; Pg. 178a-b: David Bohl/Courtesy, U.S. Navy Museum/Courtesy, Naval History & Heritage Command's Underwater Archaeology Branch; Pg. 179a-e: David Bohl/Courtesy, U.S. Navy Museum/Courtesy, Naval History & Heritage Command's Underwater Archaeology Branch; Pg. 180: Library of Congress, Prints and Photographs Division; Pg. 181: Courtesy, U.S. Navy Art Collection; Pg. 182: Brooklyn Museum of Art/The Bridgeman Art Library; Pg. 183: Boston Publishing Company Collection; Pg. 184: Archive Photos/Getty Images; Pg. 185a: New York Public Library Picture Collection; Pg. 185b: Division of Medicine & Science, National Museum of American History, Smithsonian Institution; Pg. 186a: Courtesy of the Denison Homestead, Mystic, Connecticut; Pg. 186b: Library of Congress; Pg. 186c: David Bohl/Courtesy, Sion Hill; Pg. 187: Division of Political History, National Museum of American History, Smithsonian Institution; Pg. 188a: Anne S. K. Brown Military Collection, Brown University Library; Pg. 188b: The Stonington Historical Society; Pg. 189: Anne S. K. Brown Military Collection, Brown University Library; Pg. 190: Smithsonian Institution/CORBIS; Pg. 191a: David Bohl/Courtesy, U.S. Naval Academy Museum; Pg. 191b: Maryland Historical Society; Pg. 191c-e: Division of Military History and Diplomacy, National Museum of American History, Smithsonian Institution

5 Pp. 192-193: David Bohl/Courtesy, Naval History & Heritage Command; Pg. 194: Courtesy, U.S. Navy Art Collection; Pg. 196: Historic New Orleans Collection; Pg. 197: Louisiana State Museum; Pg. 198a: Courtesy, U.S. Navy Art Collection; Pg. 198b: Historic New Orleans Collection; Pg. 198c: American Antiquarian Society; Pg. 198d: Historic Maps Restored; Pg. 199: Courtesy, U.S. Navy Art Collection; Pg. 200: Courtesy, U.S. Navy Art Collection; Pg. 201: David Bohl/Courtesy, U.S. Naval Academy Museum; Pg. 202: David Bohl/ Courtesy, U.S. Navy Museum; Pg. 203: Courtesy, Naval History & Heritage Command; Pg. 204: National Archives and Records Administration; Pg. 205a-d: National Archives and Records Administration; Pg. 206: Courtesy, Naval History and Heritage Command; Pg. 207: © Mystic Seaport Collection, Mystic, CT, #1946.188.8; Pg. 209: Maryland Historical Society; Pg. 210: Maryland Historical Society; Pg. 212: © Mystic Seaport Collection, Mystic, CT, #19946.188.10; Pg. 215a: David Bohl/Courtesy, U.S. Navy Department Library; Pg. 215b: Connecticut Historical Society; Pg. 215c: © Mystic Seaport Collection, Mystic, CT, #1946.188.10; Pg. 215d-f: David Bohl/Courtesy, U.S. Naval Academy Museum; Pg. 216a: Division of Military History and Diplomacy, National Museum of American History, Smithsonian Institution; Pg. 216b: Courtesy of the Phillips Library at the Peabody Essex Museum, Salem, Massachusetts; Pg. 216c: National Maritime Museum; Pg. 216d: © Mystic Seaport Collection, Mystic, CT, #50.86; Pg. 217: Bettmann/CORBIS; Pg. 218: Bibliotheque Nationale, Paris, France/Giraudon/The Bridgeman Art Library; Pg. 219a: David Bohl/Courtesy, USS Constitution Museum, Boston; Pg. 219b: British Museum Images; Pg. 220a: Historic New Orleans Collection; Pg. 220b: Historic New Orleans Collection; Pg. 222a-b: David Bohl/Courtesy, U.S. Naval Academy Museum; Pg. 223: © Mystic Seaport Collection, Mystic, CT, #1946.188.5; Pg. 224a: David Bohl/Courtesy, U.S. Naval Academy Museum; Pg. 225: David Bohl/Courtesy, U.S. Naval Academy Museum; Pg. 226: Historic New Orleans Collection; Pg. 227: Division of Military History and Diplomacy, National Museum of American History, Smithsonian Institution; Pg. 228a: Louisiana State Museum; Pg. 228b: Historic New Orleans Collection; Pg. 229: Library of Congress, Prints and Photographs Division; Pg. 230: Historic New Orleans Collection; Pg. 231a: Courtesy of the Phillips Library at the Peabody Essex Museum, Salem, Massachusetts; Pg. 231b: CORBIS; Pg. 232a: David Bohl/Courtesy, USS Constitution Museum, Boston; Pg. 232b-c: National Maritime Museum; Pg. 233a-c, e: David Bohl/Courtesy, USS Constitution Museum, Boston; Pg. 233d:

National Maritime Museum; Pg. 235: American Antiquarian Society; Pg. 236: David Bohl/Courtesy, USS Constitution Museum, Boston; Pg. 237: British Museum Images; Pg. 239: Private Collection/The Stapleton Collection/The Bridgeman Art Library

Pg. 240: Library of Congress; Pg. 245: Courtesy, USS Constitution Museum, Boston

ACKNOWLEDGMENTS

The writers and editors wish to thank the following institutions and individuals, without which and whom the creation of this book would not have been possible.

For oversight of the project, gratitude is owed to the entire Naval History & Heritage Command Commemorations Division. From the Naval History and Heritage Command, we would specifically like to thank Director RDML Jay A. DeLoach, USN (ret). From the Commemorations Office, we would specifically like to thank CAPT Patrick C. Burns, director; Mr. Dan Dayton; Ms. Meghan Cunningham; and the rest of the Commemorations team. For generously sharing their time, wealth of subject matter expertise, and more, we are indebted to the Naval History & Heritage Command's diligent historians, particularly Charles E. Brodine, Dr. Michael J. Crawford, and Christine F. Hughes. We'd also like to thank the various Navy staff members who went above and beyond in assisting us with our research efforts, granting us access to their vast collections, and facilitating photo shoots, including Jennifer Marland of the National Museum of the United States Navy; Glenn Helm and James Allen Knechtman of the Navy Department Library; Gale Munro of the Navy Art Collection; Robert Doane, James Cheevers, Dr. Scott Harmon, Don Leonard, Leo Mehalic, and Donald Preul of the U.S. Naval Academy Museum; Karen France and Robert Hanshew of the Naval History & Heritage Command's Photographic Section; and the Underwater Archaeology Branch. For editorial and design input, we thank Sandy Doyle and Wendy Sauvageot of the Naval History & Heritage Command. Further thanks are due to the knowledgeable and ever-patient staff of Boston's USS Constitution Museum, including Sarah Watkins, Matthew Brenckle, Rebecca Parmer, and Harrie Slootbeek, who permitted us to explore and photograph their fascinating collection—and stood by to assist and answer our myriad questions.

We'd also like to thank Diane and Jonathan Green of Sion Hill, along with their daughter, Libby. Descendants of the storied Rodgers family, they opened up their home and let us comb through a trove of family heirlooms, in addition to providing us with a detailed history of the family. We credit Peter Ianniello and the Mt. Felix Vineyard and Winery with helping us to locate the Greens.

The wonderful Louisa Watrous (a distant relative of Minerva Denison Rodgers) of the Mystic Seaport Museum also deserves a special thanks for graciously providing us with invaluable research assistance and making available artifacts from the Denison Homestead. Her colleagues at the Mystic Seaport Museum, including Maribeth Bielinski, Fred Calabretta (who gave us an exhaustive tour of the museum's collections), and Paul O'Pecko have our many thanks. Linda Bolla of the Erie Maritime Museum was extraordinarily helpful in our endeavor to locate artifacts and imagery pertaining to the Great Lakes region, as was Dr. Gary Gibson, whose encyclopedic knowledge led us to many little-known treasures.

Thanks go to Christine Bertoni and Eric Wolin of the Peabody Essex Museum; to Kathy Flynn of the Phillips Library at the Peabody Essex Museum; to Julie Cochrane of the National Maritime Museum; to the librarians at the American Antiquarian Society; and to the curatorial staff of the Smithsonian's National Museum of American History.

For giving us access to their private collections, we thank Suzy Barnard, George Emery, Clayton Nans, and Mike Scott.

Last but certainly not least, we'd like to thank the sublimely talented and accommodating David Bohl, who photographed most of the artifacts in the book, and John Baker, who photographed the artifacts from the Great Lakes region. For their photographic expertise, we also thank John Bashian, Michael Campbell, and Jim Scherzi. And, finally, for digging up long-buried archival imagery from the National Archives and the Library of Congress, thanks go to Kevin Morrow.

READER'S NOTE

For the sake of authenticity, historical accuracy, and character, we have attempted to faithfully reproduce firsthand accounts, including excerpts from letters, memos, diaries, and other manuscripts, as they were originally written, retaining grammatical errors, individual writing idiosyncrasies, and other particularities of the quill-and-ink age.

The War of 1812 and the Rise of the U.S. Navy
Mark Collins Jenkins and David A. Taylor

Developed and produced by Boston Publishing Company
in association with the United States Navy

The Navy Emblem is a trademark of the Department of the Navy
and is used with permission.

BOSTON PUBLISHING COMPANY
President: Robert J. George
Editor: Lauren K. Morgan
Managing Editor: Carolyn M. Medeiros
Photo Editors: Marcy Kagan and Lauren K. Morgan
Copy Editor: Karen Hwa
Indexer: Wanda A. Dietrich
www.bostonpublishing.com

BOOK DESIGN
Carrie Hamilton/KISMET

PUBLISHED BY THE
NATIONAL GEOGRAPHIC SOCIETY
John M. Fahey, Jr., Chairman of the Board
    and Chief Executive Officer
Timothy T. Kelly, President
Declan Moore, Executive Vice President;
    President, Publishing
Melina Gerosa Bellows, Executive Vice President;
    Chief Creative Officer, Books, Kids, and Family

PREPARED BY THE
NATIONAL GEOGRAPHIC SOCIETY'S BOOK DIVISION
Barbara Brownell Grogan, Vice President
    and Editor in Chief
Jonathan Halling, Design Director,
    Books and Children's Publishing
Marianne R. Koszorus, Design Director, Books
Lisa Thomas, Senior Editor
Carl Mehler, Director of Maps
R. Gary Colbert, Production Director
Jennifer A. Thornton, Managing Editor
Meredith C. Wilcox, Administrative Director, Illustrations
Garrett Brown, Project Manager

The National Geographic Society is one of the world's largest nonprofit
scientific and educational organizations. Founded in 1888 to "increase
and diffuse geographic knowledge," the Society's mission is to inspire people
to care about the planet. It reaches more than 400 million people worldwide each month through its official journal, *National Geographic*, and other
magazines; National Geographic Channel; television documentaries;
music; radio; films; books; DVDs; maps; exhibitions; live events; school
publishing programs; interactive media; and merchandise. National
Geographic has funded more than 9,600 scientific research, conservation
and exploration projects and supports an education program promoting
geographic literacy. For more information, visit www.nationalgeographic.com.

For more information, please call 1-800-NGS LINE (647-5463)
or write to the following address:

National Geographic Society
1145 17th Street N.W.
Washington, D.C. 20036-4688 U.S.A.

For information about special discounts for bulk purchases, please contact
National Geographic Books Special Sales: ngspecsales@ngs.org

For rights or permissions inquiries, please contact National Geographic
Books Subsidiary Rights: ngbookrights@ngs.org

ISBN 978-1-4262-0933-8

Printed in China
11/BP/1